WORKING CANADIANS

WORKING CANADIANS

Readings in the Sociology of Work and Industry

Graham S. Lowe and Harvey J. Krahn, editors
University of Alberta

 METHUEN

Toronto   New York   London   Sydney   Auckland

Canadian Cataloguing in Publication Data
Main entry under title:
Working Canadians

ISBN 0-458-97370-X

1. Industrial sociology — Canada — Addresses, essays, lectures. 2. Labour and labouring classes — Canada — Addresses, essays, lectures. 3. Industrial relations — Canada — Addresses, essays lectures. I. Lowe, Graham S. II. Krahn, Harvey J.

HD8106.5.W67 1984   331'.0971   C83-099310-X

Printed and bound in Canada
1 2 3 4   84   88 87 86 85

Contents

Preface

Growing specialization in sociology, as in other academic disciplines, has produced a variety of sub-areas of study. Industrial sociology became a distinctive field of inquiry several decades ago. Subsequently, its territory has been further divided as scholars focus more closely on the industrialization process, occupational change and mobility, labour-management relations, alienation and job (dis)satisfaction, unions, and industrial conflict — to mention only some of the more prominent topics. While such specialization may be necessary for the development of a discipline, it also undermines our ability to develop a broad understanding of the nature of work in society today. This can be especially confusing for the student who, upon encountering the subject for the first time, deals only with fragments of the larger reality. But it is essential that the links between industrialization, the organization of workplaces and the labour process, and workers' responses to their jobs be firmly established in the student's mind. Hence, this collection of writings about workers and workplaces in Canada includes discussions and debates on a wide variety of topics. We have expanded the scope of this reader in the sociology of work and industry in the interests of presenting a more complete view of work in Canada.

There are, however, several topics that we consider to be outside our purview. With the exception of several articles that contrast female labour-force participation with women's unpaid labour in the home, there is little discussion of domestic labour. This is not to deny the importance of housework. Rather, we distinguish between paid and unpaid labour, concentrating on the former because it encompasses the experiences of the majority of Canadians. We also do not include articles on work in agriculture, or on labour in a non-industrial mode of production such as hunting and trapping. These omissions are partly a function of the relative absence of suitable sociological materials. But perhaps more importantly, the few chapters we could devote to these subjects would not be adequate representations of them.

One further restriction limiting our choice of articles was a self-imposed Canadian content rule. All of the contributions focus on Canada, with the exception of several cross-cultural comparisons that were written by Canadians. The forty-seven chapters, many of them abridged from longer original works, were selected from an initial bibliography of several hundred books, government reports, and magazine and academic journal articles spanning the fields of industrial sociology, industrial relations, and business management. The range of high-quality material available clearly indicates that one can no longer claim that "little good Canadian work exists in this area."

We have attempted to balance reports of sophisticated social science research with more descriptive journalistic discussions. Some of the contributions are very careful theoretical statements, while others are more polemic in tone. Certainly the final choice of articles was influenced by our own "critical" or "political economy" perspective. Yet we have tried to include some contributions from a management orientation in order to familiarize students with both sides of certain key issues. Most of the chapters focus on contemporary Canadian society, but some historical analyses of the industrialization process and resulting changes in the organization of work are also included. As already noted, several discussions of workplace organization in other societies are included in order to place our discussion of major problems into a comparative framework. In short, this reader combines examples of research in several different traditions, discussions growing out of different ideological perspectives, as well as historical and comparative dimensions. We believe that the eclectic character of the volume will make it a useful supplementary text for university and community college courses in industrial sociology, labour studies, industrial relations, and the sociology of work and occupations.

The articles are organized into seven parts. Each part begins with an editors' introduction that attempts to highlight central themes and concepts, as well as the key questions addressed and conclusions drawn by the authors. Introductions also suggest further readings that interested students might examine for term papers or more in-depth study. In those instances where we have abridged chapters or articles, we urge students seeking more information to begin by going back to the original sources.

Part I considers work values and job satisfaction, examining workers' subjective experiences of their work. In Part II, students are introduced to historical accounts of changes in workplace organization and to contemporary research on various aspects of the labour process. Part III contains five chapters addressing the particular experiences and problems of women active in the paid labour force. Management strategies for controlling labour and increasing productivity are discussed in Part IV. Part V contains discussions of the origins, functions, and future of unions. In addition, recent developments in the areas of "quality of work life" and "industrial democracy" are considered. Four current issues — unemployment, the impact of microtechnology on employment, occupational health and safety, and leisure and retirement — are examined in Part VI. The volume concludes with five cross-cultural comparisons of workplace organization, labour legislation, and industrial relations, with particular emphasis on the Japanese and Swedish cases.

The production of this reader has been very much a collective effort. Laura C. Hargrave has done a masterful job of utilizing the latest computer techology to word process and typeset the text. Denise Joseph assisted with entry of text into the computer. Tim Trytten and Anastasia Avramides ably compiled an extensive bibliography from which the forty-seven selections were drawn. And without the encouragement of the staff of Methuen Publications, especially Peter Milroy, Jean Gordon, and Herb Hilderley, the project might never have left the ground.

GRAHAM S. LOWE
HARVEY J. KRAHN

Part I/Work Values and Job Satisfaction

Editors' Introduction

Have you ever contemplated what motivates people to work? Why, day after day, do we trudge off to perform tasks that, for many, are best described as "the daily grind"? Certainly there is the compulsion of economic necessity: without a job one risks destitution. But there are deeper motives, woven into the very fabric of society, that explain why the vast majority value an honest day's work for its own sake. These basic attitudes toward work, known as the "work ethic," form the subjective underpinnings of the capitalist economic system. Equally important, however, are the attitudes workers have toward the specific jobs they perform. This leads us into the topic of job satisfaction. Often it is the case that although individuals consider work a central part of their life, and a means of achieving personal goals, the jobs available to them offer little in the way of basic satisfactions. These subjective dimensions of work are the basic themes in the first section of readings.

Worker laziness has long been exposed in the media and decried by politicians and management as the source of lagging Canadian productivity. As the baby-boom generation with its non-traditional values began flooding into the workforce in the late 1960s and early 1970s, the pressing question became: "Is the work ethic dead?" It was against this background that the federal government commissioned a national survey of Canadians' attitudes toward work, with a survey of their job satisfaction to follow, in 1973-74. As M. Burstein and his colleagues document in Chapter 1, the survey gave the work ethic a very clean bill of health. Canadians are highly committed to work in general, and next to their families, it is the most important thing in their lives.

The focus of the chapter then shifts to Canadians' job satisfaction. It may come as a surprise that about 90 per cent of those surveyed in 1973-74 claimed to derive some level of satisfaction from their job. What we want most in a job, according to the survey results, are interesting tasks, adequate information and authority to get the job done, and a chance to develop our special abilities. In short, money is no longer enough — if it ever was — to provide happiness. Of course, many jobs do not live up to this ideal. Nor, for that matter, do all workers have similar expectations and evaluations of their work. Two very important sources of variation in work-related attitudes are age and gender. Younger workers report less job satisfaction than do older workers, perhaps because they expect more. And women, because of their socialization into the "wife-mother" role, often expect different things out of a job than do men. A final issue concerns how job satisfaction is measured. One clear finding to emerge from the huge research literature on the topic is that questions of a global nature ("Generally, how satisfied are you with your job?") elicit more positive responses than do more focussed questions asking about specific aspects such as pay, promotions, or supervision.

Case studies of particular industries or occupations are a good way of examining the factors underlying job satisfaction. J.D. House's research on the Calgary oil industry involved the use of survey questionnaires (as in the two national surveys discussed in Chapter 1), as well as more in-depth interviews. The latter, the subject of Chapter 2, offer rich descriptions of why oil industry professionals and managers find their work so challenging and rewarding. The work satisfaction of the oil men (there are very few women) can largely be accounted for by the organizational structure of the industry. The oil business operates as a tightly integrated community. This facilitates career shifts between companies of varying size and type, making it much easier for an individual to find the right "niche." Furthermore, oil men feel they have abundant opportunity to be involved in, and to complete, challenging and interesting projects.

The working conditions House documents are undoubtedly more the exception than the rule. For many lower-level white-collar and semi- and unskilled blue-collar employees, the reality of their working lives is one of drudgery. In Chapter 3, James Rinehart takes a critical look at some of the basic assumptions previous researchers have made about job satisfaction among blue-collar workers. His primary concern is with the disparity between the job-related attitudes of this group of workers and their behaviours. On one hand, manual workers' attitudes seem to indicate job satisfaction or, at least, passive indifference. Yet on the other hand, their behaviour in the form of strikes, sabotage, turnover, absenteeism, and active resistance to managerial authority signals a deep dissatisfaction with work.

The thrust of Rinehart's argument is that historical changes in work organization and the labour process have fragmented and deskilled manual work. Industrial progress, it would appear, has been achieved at a high cost to the traditional working class. Scientific management, popularized in the early part of the century by F.W. Taylor, best exemplifies this managerial assault on worker control of production. Given that manual jobs are now largely devoid of "intrinsic" rewards — such as the challenge, autonomy, and variety that House found in the oil industry — workers adjust their expectations accordingly. Often this entails an "instrumental" approach to work in which high pay becomes the definition of a good job. This does not mean, however, that such workers prefer meaningless jobs. Rather, their evaluations of good, and bad, jobs must be interpreted in the context of the few alternatives available to them. Their apparent job satisfaction is therefore relative, and discontent may well be brewing just below the surface. The paradox, which has captured the attention of social analysts since the time of Karl Marx, is that this discontent does not fuel working-class collective action aimed at transforming the economic system. In Rinehart's words, the behaviour of blue-collar workers remains "a curious blend of acquiescence and defiance."

Suggested Readings

P.D. Anthony, *The Ideology of Work* (London: Tavistock, 1977).

Arne Kalleberg, "Work values and job rewards: a theory of job satisfaction," *American Sociological Review* 42(1) 1977: 124-43.

Melvin L. Kohn, "Occupational structure and alienation," *American Journal of Sociology* 82(1) 1976: 111-130.

Edwin Locke, "The nature and causes of job satisfaction," in M. Dunnette, ed., *Handbook of Industrial and Organizational Psychology* (Chicago: Rand McNally, 1976), pp. 1297-1349.

Joseph Smucker, *Industrialization in Canada* (Scarborough: Prentice-Hall, 1980).

1/Canadian Work Values*

M. Burstein, N. Tienhaara, P. Hewson, and B. Warrander

This chapter sets current work attitudes in an historical context. A definition of the "work ethic" is derived which centres not on industriousness but on the desire to work. This distinction between the personal desire to work and industriousness is stressed, and present concerns with the demise of the work ethic are related to fears of a decline in this desire. . . .

The Meaning of Work Historically

Beginning with the Greek Era through to the rise of Calvinism, gradual but repeated modifications in work attitudes can be documented; the work ethic was just one.

To the ancient Greeks, work was a curse — a burden. Their name for work was *ponos*, which has the same root as the Latin *poena*, meaning sorrow. According to Homer, the gods hated mankind and out of spite condemned men to toil. Romans shared the same harsh definition of work, while to the Hebrews, toil, "wresting bread from a thorny earth," was a means of expiating the sins of Adam and Eve. "If man," says the Talmud, "does not find his food like animals and birds but must earn it, that is due to sin."

Early Christianity followed the Hebrew tradition in regarding work as a divine punishment for man's original sin, but also introduced other reasons for working. St. Augustine decreed that work was obligatory for monks because:

. . . it supplies the needs of the monastery; it fosters brotherly love; (and it) purges body and soul of evil pleasures.

---

* Abridged from M. Burstein, N. Tienhaara, P. Hewson, and B. Warrender, *Canadian Work Values: Findings of a Work Ethic Survey and a Job Satisfaction Survey* (Ottawa: Information Canada, 1975), pp. 10-12, 14-15, 60-62. Reproduced by permission of the Minister of Supply and Services Canada.

However, the shift in the approach to work was only slight. For St. Augustine and other leading figures in the early Christian Church, only work which provided the basic needs for subsistence was acceptable. For the many religious sects which blossomed in Europe between the eleventh and fourteenth centuries, work continued to be exalted as a scourge for the pride of the flesh. St. Francis of Assisi obliged his Friars Minor to live by their own work, namely heavy manual labour, with the sole purpose of earning their daily bread plus a few coppers to be given as alms.

As the centuries passed, the Catholic Church's evaluation of work began to merge more closely with worldly standards of the time. This evolution perhaps began with St. Thomas Aquinas, a thirteenth-century monk who ranked all the professions and trades according to their value to society, with agriculture at the top of the hierarchy, then handcrafts, and commerce at the bottom. Money lending was not included in the hierarchy, and centuries were to pass before such economic practices were to become acceptable to the Church. However, with St. Thomas Aquinas' doctrine of labour commenced the important concept of work as a natural right and duty, the sole legitimate foundation for property and profit; but, work was still not a social obligation for man. As in the Hebrew tradition, "He who did not need to work to maintain himself should better contemplate God."

Increasingly, economic practices made inroads on the Catholic Church's conception of work. Both St. Antoninus of Florence and Bernardino of Siena, while clinging to many earlier ideas of work, made an important change from previous doctrines in that they allowed capitalistic profits on investments (with the provision that the investor take some part in the conduct of the enterprise). Wealth was also allowed and even preferred, unlike in earlier eras. But work was always subordinate to concern for the life hereafter.

Not so for the Protestant sects that had been developing during the Renaissance. To Martin Luther work was a form of serving God. In fact, to Luther, "There is just one best way to serve God — to do most perfectly the work of one's profession." Yet Luther still clung to the medieval notion that work should provide only sustenance, not profit; also, he firmly believed that it was against God's laws to use work as a means of passing from one class or profession to another, thereby rising in the social hierarchy.

The Development of the Work Ethic

Both convictions of Luther were rejected by John Calvin and the religious creeds of Calvinism. Profit was deemed acceptable and was actually viewed as the certain indication of a man's success in pleasing God in his chosen profession. Also, Calvinism maintained it was man's religious duty not to remain in one station for life but to seek actively a profession that would bring to him, and hence to society, the greatest return, even if it meant leaving one's inherited position.

It is this Calvinist innovation that is the *essence* of the work ethic; for the first time, a desire to work was included with other suitable attitudes to work that had existed for centuries. This concept of the work ethic that emerged in the Western world with Calvinism has been described by Max Weber as being a personal desire to work on the part of members of a society. Weber's definition of the work ethic was that a man should work well in his gainful occupation, not merely because he had to but because he wanted to; it was a sign of his virtue and a source of personal satisfaction. To Weber, this personal desire to work was of such importance that he saw it as being *embedded* in the social values of the Calvinist society. The desire to work became, therefore, not only a personal matter but also a social obligation. However, many references to the Protestant work ethic of that period lump together not only the desire to work but also the manner in which the work should be done. Consider, for example, the following modern-day interpretation of what was involved in the work ethic:

The principal aspects of (the) Protestant Ethic. . . are individualism, asceticism, and industriousness. The emphasis placed on a man's industriousness probably represents the most critical aspect of (the) Protestant Ethic.[1]

Industriousness, however, is an example of a work trait that seems to have been universally extolled, and its opposite — laziness or idleness — had been condemned in numerous societies long before Calvinism and the first references to a work ethic. Hesiod told the Greeks that "No toil can shame thee; idleness is shame." St. Jerome wrote in Latin: "Find some work for your hands to do so that the devil may never find you idle." And St. Benedict, the sixth-century abbot who is considered the founder of Western monasticism, expressed the opinion that "Idleness is the enemy of the soul." To most societies, if not all, industriousness has been an essential attribute for workers. However, although a work-related virtue such as industriousness is important, a prior concern is the desire of persons to work — a concept that emerged with the Calvinists.

The first flowering of such a "work ethic" among Calvinists was not the end-point in the development of the Western world's work values. Instead, the position of work continued to be elevated through subsequent centuries. Leon Battista Alberti warned about the perils of idleness and unemployment and exulted in labouriousness "which fills so well the slow passage of the hours." Voltaire's *Candide* closed with the agreement of the three heroes that work is the best practical solution to the enigma of life. The economic typology of Adam Smith envisioned the productive classes as composed of workers of every sort, with only those members living in idleness called sterile.

As the centuries passed, so did the popular conception of work as an end in itself: "The nineteenth century was the Golden Age for the idea of work," according to one historian.[2] Leading philosophers attributed to work all human progress — material, intellectual, and spiritual. For the socialist thinkers at the end of the nineteenth century people liked to work, and in the socialist-ideal state everyone would work.

It is this legacy that the twentieth century has inherited. The sentiments expressed by Theodore Roosevelt at a Labour Day meeting in Syracuse, New York, in 1903 still apply in Western societies:

Far and away the best prize that life offers is the chance to work hard at work worth doing.

The "work ethic," this desire to work, is not, however, unique to Western societies, which have inherited their work attitudes from many diverse traditions. Work attitudes esteemed by Western civilizations — industriousness, for example — are also found elsewhere.

Eastern nations have developed concepts of work similar to our own, although their beliefs have evolved along a different path. An old Chinese proverb "Never was good work done without much trouble"[3] suggests the emphasis placed on work in that society. Similarly, Japan, "unquestionably an achieving nation," possesses a set of values which in many aspects resembles those of the Calvinists; the transmission of these values has, naturally, been different, but diligence, thrift, and achievement are certainly Japanese ideals. Ninomiya Sontuba, the Peasant Saint, exhorted the populace to "work much, earn much, (and) spend little." He espoused the virtues of practical self-help, piety, and loyalty — virtues found in the Confucian set of ethics which were incorporated in some teachings of Buddhism and Shintoism.

Almost identical work attitudes have been found among small cultural groups usually labelled primitive by modern industrial standards. The anthropologist Firth has pointed out that "work for its own sake is a constant characteristic of Maori industry."[4] In fact, "To put one's labour at the command of another is a social service, not merely an economic service."[5] Similarly, "The Andaman islanders regard laziness as anti-social behaviour,"[6] and Thurnwald in his *Economics in Primitive Communities* emphasizes that "work is never limited to the unavoidable minimum but exceeds the necessary amount, owing to a naturally acquired functional urge to activity."[7]

Concerns about the Health of the Work Ethic

Obviously, a work ethic that dictates a strong personal motivation to work has had much broader appeal than only to the Calvinist sect of the seventeenth century, which Western societies generally consider the model for desirable work attitudes. Furthermore, just as the work ethic is not specific to any particular culture, reports of its imminent death are not bound to any particular phase of its existence.

The 1970s are certainly not unique in the extent to which fears have been expressed that the work ethic is declining. The following quotation from a work historian could easily be expressing current-day sentiments:

...It is certainly a serious matter that in the country which until yesterday was the veritable Holy Land of this new faith, in the United States of America, the religion of work should seem paradoxically but inevitably to be producing a religion its exact opposite, the religion of recreation, pleasure, and amusement.... As far as that goes, the phenomenon is universal. Every country resounds to the lament that the work-fever does not burn in the younger generation, the post-war generation....[8]

This statement was uttered not in the 1970s but in the late 1920s, and refers to the post-World War I, not post-World War II, generation of young people. And references to a failure of the work ethic can be found going back even further. Abraham Lincoln, in a sarcastic note to Major Ramsey in 1861, wrote:

The lady bearer of this says she has two sons who want to work. Set them at it if possible. Wanting to work is so rare a want that it should be encouraged.

There are several reasons for the recurrence of fears about the decline of the work ethic. Perhaps foremost among these reasons is the myth that at some time in the past, the work ethic characterized every member of society. Earlier references to the theme of industriousness versus laziness and idleness throughout history suggest that there have always been individuals who refuse to toe society's line on matters of work, and societies characterized by a work ethic are no different. Previous generations of North Americans were not uniform in their zeal for work; as Reisman has pointed out:

... Americans in earlier periods were not uniformly work-minded. In Horace Greeley's accounts of his famous trip West in 1859... he commented with disgust on the many squatters on Kansas homesteads who, in contrast to the industrious Mormons, sat around improvidently, building decent shelter neither for themselves nor for their stock.... Similarly, the correspondence of railroad managers in the last century... is full of complaints about the lack of labour discipline; this is one reason that the Chinese were brought in to work on the transcontinental roads. There were, it is evident, many backsliders in the earlier era from the all-pervading gospel of work, and the frontier, like many city slums, harbored a number of drifters.[9]

Consequently, fears of a declining work ethic today can be attributed partly to the existence of groups in society that are not work oriented — groups that have always existed.

Current fears about the state of the work ethic may also be the natural side-effect of the continual process of change in any society's attitudes, values, and opinions. Attitudes do not stand still. Throughout Western history, as has been shown, attitudes to work have undergone repeated modifications, one of them, but certainly not the last, being the birth of the work ethic. Consequently, it is to be expected that some of our attitudes towards work are now undergoing change. The uncertainty of exactly what these changes are means that there is difficulty estimating their magnitude or their importance. It is therefore easy, but not necessarily correct, to assume that these changes include the destruction of the work ethic. Part of the problem is the confusion over what actually constitutes the work ethic. If the definition is sufficiently broad to take in all the work attitudes of Calvinism or of some other doctrine, then it is considerably more likely that the work ethic will be dead, by definition, as soon as even one of its minor components changes.

Today's concern centres on the apparently easier access of Canadians to public assistance, and since the social security schemes most often faulted are of fairly recent origin in Canada, it is possible that the work ethic has indeed been eroded by such programs. Perhaps a major shift in attitudes towards work *has* taken place, and Canadians no longer feel either inspired by a personal desire to work or constrained by society's insistence that they should feel such a desire. In this context, the Work Ethic Survey was undertaken as an attempt to characterize Canadian attitudes towards work. . . .

The Job Satisfaction Survey

In this section, the distinction between work and jobs is first discussed. The focus then shifts to jobs and job satisfaction, and to the characteristics of job satisfaction. . . .

Jobs and Job Satisfaction

In examining the subject of work, it is easy to overlook the significance of a term that has, in popular usage, become nearly synonymous with work, i.e., "job."

"Job," defined as "piece of work, especially one done for hire or profit," appears to originate from the Middle English *jobbe* meaning a piece or lump. The use of the word "job" to mean employment is so recent that some dictionaries still consider it colloquial.

Despite the apparent interchangeability of "job" and "work," it is important to differentiate between them. The works of various economic anthropologists, in particular Karl Polanyi, explain the origin of this distinction.

Throughout preindustrial history, work was completely enmeshed in the social life of a person. As Polanyi described it, "Under the guild system, as under every other economic system in previous history, the motives and circumstances of productive activities were embedded in the general organization of society. The relations of master, journeyman, and apprentice; the terms of the craft; the number of apprentices; the wages of workers were all regulated by the custom and rule of the guild and the town."[10]

A critical element of what Polanyi called the "great transformation" wrought by the Industrial Revolution was the development of a free market in which labour became a commodity which could be bought and sold:

Man under the name of labour, nature under the name of land, were made available for sale; the use of labour power could be universally bought and sold at a price called wages, and the use of land could be negotiated for a price called rent. There was a market in labour as well as in land, and supply and demand in either was regulated by the height of wages and rents respectively; . . .[11]

One could now distinguish between specific tasks and the more general notion of work; hence the origin of job — "a piece of work. . . done for hire. . . ."

But the Industrial Revolution, by elevating the role of the free market, created a need for protective institutions. Working conditions in the early stages of capitalism were often abysmal and resulted in widespread dissatisfaction with the physical hardships imposed by the work. Child labour laws and health and safety legislation were the first responses to the excesses of early industrialism and a tangible expression of job dissatisfaction.

Attitudes towards jobs, including the presence or absence of job satisfaction, have in one form or another influenced thinking and behaviour since the earliest days of the Industrial Revolution. Recently coined terms such as "job enrichment" and "job restructuring" appear daily in the media and give the impression that job satisfaction is a product of the space age; this is obviously erroneous.

As society developed means of coping with the divisive effects of an unregulated market economy and as our productive capacity and wealth grew, considerable improvement was effected in the physical conditions of work.

Concern with the physical aspects of work is, however, only one domain of job-related attitudes. In some occupations progress has been made towards higher level needs as suggested by Maslow's work in the area. He developed a "need" pyramid which arranges human needs with respect to work on a hierarchical basis.[12] The lowest stratum shows exclusive concern with the physical aspects of work, while the apex signifies a desire for creativity and self-fulfilment; needs at each level must be satisfied before the next stratum can be reached. Quite obviously, in many occupations today, the apex has not been reached. Recent studies both in America and Europe have again raised the spectre of a dissatisfied, alienated work force.[13] Furthermore, it is claimed that this dissatisfaction has manifested itself in terms of increased absenteeism and lateness, falling productivity, and even heightened industrial violence and sabotage.

The explanation of these phenomena depends heavily on the perspective of the analysts describing the situation. For our purposes, two polar positions can be utilized. On the one hand, the nature of work must alter to accommodate the inherent needs of the workers; on the other hand, the workers' values must change to conform to the current dictates of economic organization.

Humanists say that job satisfaction is unequivocally an individual psychological experience, with specific consequences for the worker's physical and mental health. They point out that modern workers, if they are unable to obtain a sense of fulfilment or self-esteem from their jobs, react by reducing their goals, distorting reality, or becoming aggressive or alienated. These reactions are costly. They result in a heightened incidence of chronic illnesses such as heart trouble, ulcers, alcoholism, etc.; in fact the best predictor of an individual's longevity would appear to be satisfaction on the job.[14] Therefore, humanists say the nature of work must change. Tasks must be enriched, reorganized, or eliminated in accordance with the social and psychological needs of workers.

In opposition to this point of view, there are analysts who, while accepting the need for decent working conditions, feel that efficiency should dictate economic organization, and deviations would be extremely costly. To adherents of this view absenteeism, lateness, and falling productivity are the prime elements in discussions of job satisfaction. Rather than uselessly devoting resources to redesigning jobs, it is felt that instead, attempts should be made to shore up declining work values, or to tighten what are identified as overly liberal welfare schemes. Job satisfaction is fine so long as it does not interfere with production.

From this, one can distil two important dimensions in the debate over job satisfaction: firstly, individual assessment of the work situation (the degree of job satisfaction) and secondly, the labour market behaviour induced by this assessment. Assessing this state of job satisfaction is a necessary step in determining the welfare, values, and aspirations of Canadians.

Although government can simultaneously pursue humanitarian and efficiency objectives, there may be trade-offs in this pursuit. Increasing job satisfaction, for example, may not be consistent with increases in productivity.

But public policy does attempt to reduce the trade-off between job satisfaction and efficiency by stimulating and testing innovative schemes to alter the manner in which human beings and machines combine to perform jobs and by promoting the full and effective utilization of human resources.

Paradoxically, by providing individuals with an opportunity for challenge and growth, not only job satisfaction but also productivity can perhaps be stimulated. Because of its overwhelming importance in our lives, work and its specific expression "job" must be of fundamental concern to both the public and private sectors.
. . .

Conclusions

The centrality of work in our lives was repeatedly affirmed by both the Work Ethic Survey and the Job Satisfaction Survey. Clearly, Canadians are committed to work. Work was named by more respondents to the Work Ethic Survey than any other option, including family and friends, as a way to achieving one's goals. Canadians see themselves as industrious people to whom work contributes a feeling of success and, for a large proportion, of personal fulfilment. It is not surprising, therefore, that the vast majority of respondents to the Work Ethic Survey expected to get satisfaction from their work, and satisfaction, or more precisely, the behaviour that it engenders, has social consequences. Unhappy workers change jobs more frequently, their absenteeism rate is often higher, and their general level of life satisfaction lower. Thus, high turnover and sagging productivity may be a reflection of worker unhappiness.

Canadians are selective about the type of jobs they will take, and are more prone to change employment because of financial remuneration, working conditions, and personal job relations, than for other reasons.

At face value, both studies in this report indicate that Canadians are generally content with their work. However, a more exact picture emerges from the Job Satisfaction Survey through an examination of what Canadians seek in an ideal job and how they evaluate their actual job situation.

While the survey results do not dispute the significance of income as a motivating force underlying labour market behaviour, they do call into question the assumption of salary as a universal panacea. Whereas trade-offs between various aspects of jobs can and indeed are made, they cannot offset completely the desire for ideal working situations.

In describing ideal jobs, the most important characteristics stressed by workers are that the work be interesting, that they have enough information and authority to do the job, and that they be given the opportunity to develop special abilities. Of lesser importance are job security, promotional considerations, pay, hours of work, and fringe benefits.

When aspects of jobs are ranked according to the satisfaction they provide in current employment, having enough authority and information, friendliness of co-workers and supervisors, having interesting tasks, and seeing the results of one's work emerge as the most satisfying characteristics. Less satisfaction is derived from job security, hours of work, quality of supervision, pay, fringe benefits, and promotional opportunities.

Matching up what Canadians desire in an ideal or abstract situation with the satisfaction they report for characteristics of their actual jobs provides a measure of unmet aspirations. In particular, the largest discrepancy was found with promotional opportunities in terms of actual versus ideal conditions. This was followed by the discrepancy between the ideal and actual situation as it pertains to financial considerations, including security and fringe benefits; the quality of supervision; and, finally, human resources that enter into, and support, job performance. With respect to personal relations on the job and the comfort and convenience afforded by work, Canadian aspirations seem to be relatively well satisfied.

Discussing aspirations at the national level, however, tends to compress the differences that exist across our population. These differences should not obscure the considerable agreement of Canadians in their view of work, but instead they should facilitate an appreciation of the diverse social and personal factors that affect the perception of features in the work environment. Specifically, therefore, the role of age and sex as they relate to job attitudes is brought out in the report.

The surveys and the group interviews confirm the difficulties faced by youth in their search for jobs, and indicate the relatively high level of job turnover among youth. The Work Ethic Survey indicates that many young respondents are unclear about the relationship between school and their subsequent experience in the job market. Indeed, the problems most frequently cited by youthful respondents as those they encounter in seeking employment centre on their relative inexperience, lack of specific skills, lack of training, and insufficient education.

The Work Ethic Survey also reveals that although most Canadians express commitment to work, the commitment of young people is slightly less strong than that of older groups. Young persons are equally inclined, however, to feel that they have to have a job, and are particularly desirous of a "career." Naturally, however, fewer young persons have found work that suits them. The proportion of respondents considering their present job a "career" rises from less than one-fifth for those under 20 years of age to over one-half for persons above 20. Younger persons are less inclined to feel that they are right for their jobs; less inclined to view work as interesting; more inclined to feel overqualified; and more inclined to opt for another job while feeling that their current employment does not measure up to expectations. In terms of collecting unemployment insurance, attitudes were quite similar across all age groups.

These findings are generally confirmed by the Job Satisfaction Survey, which makes further distinctions by age in how Canadians evaluate their current jobs and the importance they attach to particular job features in an idealized setting.

In terms of their actual jobs, it appears that respondents between the ages of 25 and 34 are the least satisfied over-all with the intrinsic aspects of their work, including the availability of supportive resources and promotional opportunities. Younger Canadians between the ages of 15 and 24, on the other hand, experience relatively greater dissatisfaction with the challenging nature of their work and with financial considerations. Satisfaction with financial considerations increases with age.

Abstracting from the actual job situation gives a slightly different picture of work aspirations by age group and shows the relative extent to which these aspirations are not met. In describing their ideal job, young workers emphasized the importance of supportive resources, whereas 25 to 34-year-olds emphasized challenge. Generally speaking, financial considerations are equally important to all age groups, although salary, specifically, is most important to 25 to 34-year-olds and least important to 15 to 24-year-olds. Personal relations, and comfort and convenience, are more important characteristics of ideal jobs to persons under 24, and are de-emphasized by workers between 25 and 34 years old. Over-all, it appears that the importance of intrinsic relative to extrinsic job aspects increases with age.

In assessing the match between actual jobs and workers' aspirations, it becomes clear that for all age groups, particularly 25 to 34-year-olds, promotional opportunities present the greatest difficulty. Actual jobs also fall short of the desires of 25 to 34-year-olds and to a somewhat lesser extent of 20 to 24-year-olds on most other intrinsic aspects. On the other hand, 15 to 19-year-olds felt that their aspirations with respect to personal relations and comfort aspects of jobs were relatively poorly met.

Financial aspirations in turn manifest the largest discrepancy for workers under 24 years of age. This is due not so much to the importance they attach to pay in describing an ideal job, but rather to their relatively greater dissatisfaction with their actual salaries.

Just as desires and aspirations are not entirely congruent across age groups, differences exist by sex as well. More women than men feel women should contribute to household income, although a substantial proportion among both sexes still feel that a woman's place is in the home. Significantly, this attitude is less pronounced among younger persons and those with higher education.

Also reported by the Work Ethic Survey is the lesser tendency of women to identify working with basic economic needs. Whereas men more frequently cite factors associated with the provision of income, a larger proportion of women cite recreational reasons, *extra* money, keeping busy, and the status and prestige attached to salaried employment.

The somewhat greater reluctance of women to make long-term commitments to work is revealed in several ways. Women are less inclined than men to rely on work for success, personal fulfilment, or a way of obtaining their most important goals in life. Furthermore, they are not as likely to feel "they had to have a job" but instead emphasize the family.

These differences in the importance of work to men and women also manifest themselves in the greater selectivity of women in choosing jobs, and the importance that women attach to various aspects of the work environment.

Both the Job Satisfaction and the Work Ethic Surveys indicate that women are more concerned than men with the amenities offered by their jobs and with having good hours and convenient travel facilities. Women are also less concerned than men with good pay and promotional opportunities, although they place almost equal importance on interesting or challenging work. On the other hand, they attach greater importance to the supervisory dimension of their jobs.

Results concerning satisfaction, in general, parallel those concerning the importance which women and men attach to various aspects of their work environment. Women seem to be more content with the supervisory features of their jobs and equally satisfied with the challenging nature of their work and with their salaries. Yet they express less contentment than men with promotional opportunities and fringe benefits.

In general then, it appears that for most women in paid employment, work is as important in their lives as it is to men. It is also clear, however, that the traditionally stronger ties of women to their families are much in evidence.

The importance of work in our lives goes well beyond economic survival or the provision of discretionary income. Work allows us to meet people and make friends, and is a major determinant of our social status. Moreover, work contributes to our self-esteem, and by providing us with socially useful and challenging tasks, it fosters a sense of self-fulfilment.

Given this expanded understanding of work, it becomes clear that our focus should be on increasing the scope for utilizing human capabilities in the broadest sense — not in a purely economic context. Work satisfaction, too, must be tempered by an understanding of the social, ethical, and political milieu from which it emerges, and must be embedded in a more general vision of the quality of working life. Specifically, work and its meaning to Canadians, must be examined against a backdrop of increasing affluence, rising levels of education and income, and changing aspirations. Briefly, this is what the studies set out to investigate: the attitudes of Canadians towards work in general and their own jobs in particular.

Notes

1. Page 331 in Wollack, Stephen, James G. Goodale, Jan P. Wijting and Patricia Cain Smith, "Development of the Survey of Work Values," *Journal of Applied Psychology*, Vol. 55, No. 4, 1971, pp. 331-338.

2. Page 90 in Tilgher, Adriano, *Homo Faber; Work Through the Ages*. Fisher, Dorothy C., tr. orig. Title: *Work: What it Has Meant to Man*, (Chicago: Regnery, Henry Co., 1964).

3. Pages 149-150 in Armstrong, William Cornell, *Just Before the Dawn, The Life and Works of Ninomiya Sontoku*. Reference found in Edward Norbeck's *Religion and Society in Modern Japan*. Reference to Armstrong's Work, p. 232 and to Ninomiya Sontoku p. 229 (New York: The MacMillan Co., 1912).

4. Page 17 in Firth, Raymond, "Some Features of Primitive Industry," *Economic History Series No. 1, The Economic Journal Supplement January 1926* — Quarterly Journal of the Royal Economic Society, pp. 13-22.

5. Page 16 in Firth, Raymond, *Primitive Polynesian Economy* (London: Routledge, 1939).

6. See Radcliffe-Brown, Alfred Reginald, *Andaman Islanders* (New York: Free Press, 1964).

7. Page 209 in Thurnwald, Richard, *Economics in Primitive Communities*. (New York: Humanities Press Inc., 1965).

8. See Tilgher, pp. 141-143.

9. Page 177 in Reisman, David, *Abundance for What? and Other Essays*. (Garden City, N.Y.: Doubleday, 1965).

10. Page 70 in Karl Polanyi, *The Great Transformation*, (Boston: Beacon Press, 1963).

11. See Polanyi, p. 131.

12. Maslow, Abraham H., *Toward a Psychology of Being*, 2nd ed., (New York: Van Nostrand Reinhold Co., Div. Litton Education Publishing Inc., 1968).

13. *Work in America*. Report of a special task force, U.S. Dept. of Health Education and Welfare (Chairman, James O'Toole). (Cambridge, Mass: The MIT Press, Massachusetts Institute of Technology, 1974). See also, Wilson, N.A.B., *On the Quality of Working Life*, Manpower Papers No. 7 (Great Britain Department of Employment, HMSO, London 1973); and Organization for Economic Cooperation and Development, "The Emerging Attitudes and Motivations of Workers," Report of Management Experts Meeting, Paris, 24-26th May 1971, (Organization for Economic Cooperation and Development Manpower and Social Affairs Directorate, Paris, 1972).

14. "A measure of work satisfaction was the strongest predictor of longevity." See page 5 in House, James D., "Occupational stress and physical health," *Manpower*, October, 1973 (U.S. Department of Labor), pp. 3-9.

2/The Structuring of Job Satisfaction in the Calgary Oil Industry*

J.D. House

The Varieties of Job Satisfaction

Interviewees were asked conversational, open-ended questions about job satisfaction, such as: "How do you enjoy your work?" "What do you like about it?"[1] "What do you dislike about it?" Their responses confirmed both impressions gained from the survey; most oilmen expressed high job satisfaction, and most cited the interesting nature of the work itself and their freedom to decide how to perform their own tasks as the main reasons for that satisfaction. The following comments, the first by an engineer and the second by a geologist, illustrate this finding:

I find it really challenging and satisfying to have the freedom to go ahead and organize this thing. The problems involved are really fundamental. So here's an example of a sort of task, a self-created job you might say. So there's great satisfaction in that.

I'm certainly getting job satisfaction. It's not the money; I could live quite comfortably on quite a lot less than I'm getting. I feel I have enough autonomy. It's not making decisions really, but we make recommendations to management. The more I'm getting into the job, the more autonomy I'm getting. It's not a rigid thing; there's no line that says "thou shalt not make a decision." We're just making more and more decisions, bigger and bigger recommendations, so there's no real constraint. If you feel that you need something, it doesn't matter what it is, or if you have to talk to somebody or visit somebody or get some engineering work done, the co-operation is there.

The interview data also give another insight into the reasons for job satisfaction within the industry that the quantitative study did not reveal. This is the great variety of sources of satisfaction that different individuals find in different jobs. They run the whole gamut of positions within the industry.

Production Engineer. I think I've been more fortunate than most in the respect that I haven't had to do much psyching of myself. I've always been involved in jobs that I think, from an objective point of view, would be considered relevant and challenging. Oh, there've been some lulls, I guess there are lulls in everybody's career, but by and large I've been very happy in my work.

Research Engineer. It's interesting work, challenging. I think what makes it even more exciting is that you're on the very forefront of technology.

---

* Abridged from J.D. House, *The Last of the Free Enterprisers: The Oil Men of Calgary* (Toronto: Macmillan of Canada, 1980), chapter 6, "The Structuring of Job Satisfaction." Reprinted with permission of the publisher and the author.

Geologist. There's never a dull moment. One of the nice things is that it's not as much routine as you'd think, 'cause every morning something else will happen. And one of the interesting things is you're on top of our current activity, knowing exactly what's happening in your part of the world.

Geophysicist. I think the over-all interest in drilling wells, well, it's like canoeing down a river; you don't know what's around the next bend. It's quite a thrill being part of an organization that can find a 500-million-barrel oil field or a major gas field.

Junior Manager. There's no question, I couldn't do some of the technical jobs. But a lot of our input is seeing the economic climate, seeing where the opportunities are going to lie, and making sure we have people that are already working on the problem at the right time. That's the real challenge because that's the innovative challenge. It's fascinating, fascinating. You've got all these experts, so from the mental point of view it's enormously stimulating.

Senior Manager. I don't have any frustration whatsoever; I feel that I haven't been inhibited from making decisions that I thought were important simply because I had to go through some prearranged formal ritual. I think it's one of the best jobs in the country; it's involved in a business that's critical. I feel myself part of the team responsible for one of the most important industries in Canada.

Staff position. For the last five or six years my work has been just fantastic. I've become involved in almost entirely environmental work in an advisory position, and it's taken me all over the continent. And I've been invited to speak on transportation at the Arctic summer school; it's been very satisfying.

Manager, Small Company. The thing I like about working for a small or independent company is that you're part of the decision-making and anything that happens you know about. It's part of your life, and everything that happens directly affects you. I find that really is the best part of working in the business.

Manager, Drilling Company. The satisfaction is that you can build it up. . . . It's a very competitive business; you feel that you can do something, drill a better well or a faster well or you can make more money or whatever it is.

Manager, Service Company. Every morning even now, I'm happy to come to work; I look forward to it. I think it's because this business is, well, you never know when you come here in the morning what's going to be asked of you. It could be different every day; generally it is.

Consultant. Well, personally, I really can't say anything nasty about the oil industry. It has been exceptionally good to me; I've enjoyed every minute of it; I enjoy the people who are in it; I would never leave it.

Underlying this high level of job satisfaction is the breadth of career choice that oilmen enjoy. They assess alternative career routes in the light of their own interests and, to a large extent, can choose the path that gives greatest satisfaction. For some people, however, there are structurally imposed limits upon career choice and job satisfaction.

The Sources of Job Dissatisfaction
Most oilmen, even the highly satisfied, do find certain aspects of their work and careers boring and unfulfilling. Within the large companies, in particular, a fair amount of paper work is required of professional workers and managers — filling in forms, completing reports on oneself and others, writing letters, answering

memos. Most find this work dull and frustrating, particularly the junior- and middle-level managers who do the greatest share of it.

Oilmen at all levels and within all types of companies also feel unhappy about the industry's poor public image. They believe in the value of their work and in their contribution to the Canadian economy and society, but feel that this contribution is unappreciated and misunderstood by governments and the public.

The main dissatisfaction for me is the poor public image we have. We give people good jobs, we work on the environment, we contribute a lot to this country — we work hard for it. But we just don't have that image. It makes me mad sometimes. Just compare us to the civil servants, try getting something out of them on a weekend. Well, we can't get away with that, we just have to get our work done.

Another much cited source of dissatisfaction, particularly in the big companies, is the communications problem, and the conflict arising from it, that seems to plague line-staff relations.[2] The source of this problem is usually structural and occurs when employees who lack authority over other employees are dependent upon them for certain tasks and services which may not be provided when needed. The frustration is particularly galling for those in staff positions who feel left out of the industry's main activities.

There's lots of frustrations to a staff assignment. I was always one that liked to be doing things, getting things done, working that old drilling schedule up. I don't get involved in that anymore; I have to force myself to stay out of somebody else's responsibility. Often you see things done less efficiently than you used to do them, but they don't like you bitching about other people's work. I'm used on a consulting basis, and this frustrates me because I'm getting bits and pieces. I'm not lining up how things should be done, really, because people are not working for me.

. . . . All of the above sources of dissatisfaction are found among people who, for the most part, enjoy their jobs. But there are two groups of oilmen, within the majors at least, who find their work more generally dissatisfying. The first are those whose careers have peaked and who find themselves suffering from the agonies caused by a career reversal and its attendant loss of status. The following comment is by a man who was demoted from the managerial to the technical career ladder.

I think, in supervisory work, it can get to be a real gut breaker; you've got to come to grips with having to fire a guy, so it makes more demands in certain respects. But I enjoyed it; it was probably the height of my working career with the company. When I came back to technical work, it was a letdown. It's frustrating because I came from supervisory operations into gas. My main occupation now is compressors — I'd never even seen one! It's a pretty traumatic experience. You go out and you know nothing. What the hell should you be doing? To me this is really poor handling of a guy's career. I don't know what else you can do. Maybe just quit. But you don't quit unless you're really unhappy. I'm not saying I'm unhappy, just let down.

Even though one may still have technically challenging work, the relative deprivation after demotion does cause dissatisfaction.

The second type of basic dissatisfaction is more serious, because it has to do with the nature of the work itself. Some exploration and engineering tasks are inherently boring and routine, particularly after a person has been doing them for some time. To an extent, the company deals with this problem by allocating such tasks to beginners, and reduces the monotony by circulating people among the tasks. But this strategy can only work to a limited extent. The other type of solution is to leave professional workers who are not considered to have great promise in such work for long periods. These people constitute the most alienated and dissatisfied of oilmen. . . .

Conclusion

. . .(O)ur quantitative survey data have established that most Calgary oilmen are, indeed, very satisfied with their work; and this satisfaction is highly correlated with work-related variables, particularly opportunities for achievement in one's immediate tasks. The more complex interview data illustrate and confirm both these findings. More broadly, they suggest that job satisfaction is essentially a function of finding work that is interesting and challenging. The oil industry in Calgary provides a great variety of such jobs to professionally trained people. From this perspective, careers are the processes whereby people sort themselves out into those jobs best suited to their interests, talents, and aspirations. Not all jobs, however, are satisfying, and not all careers are successful. Career failure, either in the initial stage or later after one's career has peaked and declined, is associated with job dissatisfaction and a feeling of alienation. Alienation, in this personal, qualitative sense, is not so much a product of a particular organizational form as it is the subjective concomitant of being stuck with the duller jobs within an exciting industry. On the whole, the internal organization of the capitalist oil industry in Alberta is striking for the high level of job satisfaction it provides for most of its professional employees.

Notes

1. For ease of expression, we will use "job satisfaction" as a general term to subsume low subjective alienation as well, except where otherwise specified. The two are closely related ($r = $ -0.47 for the over-all scales), and it is far from clear that they are distinct measures of distinctly separate variables.

2. See Melville Dalton, *Men Who Manage* (New York: John Wiley, 1959).

3/Contradictions of Work-Related Attitudes and Behaviour: An Interpretation*

James W. Rinehart

Are manual workers discontented with their jobs, or is the idea of alienated labour merely a creation of embittered intellectuals? Years of discussion and research have yielded no unequivocal answers to this question, and the nature of the relationship between workers and their jobs remains a contentious issue. One basis of the controversy can be located in the two distinct methods employed to generate data on the working class. The sanguine view of the world of work is derived mainly from attitude surveys, which depict jobs as tolerable and wage-earners as contented. In contrast, behavioural analysis is more likely to furnish evidence of industrial conflict and disenchantment with work. In this paper I shall evaluate these two approaches to the study of work and provide a conceptual framework to interpret and reconcile their divergent images.

The Happy Worker Thesis
In the 1950s, Harvey Swados (1957) assailed, fatally it seemed, the "myth of the happy worker." Two decades later, the myth is still alive, albeit somewhat shaken and perhaps a little more mature, for it has had to survive a frontal assault from the "discovery" of what has come to be known as the "blue collar blues." The "myth" continues to receive life-sustaining infusions from survey analyses which use forced-choice questions to elicit workers' evaluations of their jobs. What these surveys show is that although there are various degrees of satisfaction expressed by diverse occupational groups in industrial societies, substantial proportions of all groups state they are satisfied with their jobs (Blauner, 1960; Burstein et al., 1975; Form, 1973; Kahn, 1972; Loubser and Fullan, 1969).

There is a more sophisticated version of this thesis. It views work not as an attractive and fulfilling activity, but one that is treated indifferently by workers, who exchange gratification in work for satisfactions off the job. An early survey of manual workers undertaken by Dubin (1956), for example, revealed that work is not a central life interest. What happens on the job is much less important to wage-earners than what occurs outside of work.

Faunce (1968) interprets survey evidence as demonstrating that both blue collar and low-level white collar workers are "alienated" from work in the sense that their

* Abridged from James W. Rinehart, "Contradictions of Work-Related Attitudes and Behaviour: An Interpretation." Reprinted from *The Canadian Review of Sociology and Anthropology*, 15:1, 1978, pp. 1-15 by permission of the author and the publisher.

low status in work organizations prohibits the maintenance of a positive level of self-esteem, resulting in an absence of personal commitment to work and work organizations. Having defined alienation in terms of status and self-esteem, which Faunce assumes are of paramount importance to people, he then argues that individuals can insulate themselves from the demeaning impact of low-status jobs by seeking out other spheres of life in which to maintain a favourable self-image.

A roughly similar view of work attitudes has been advanced in the influential three-volume study by Goldthorpe and his associates (1969). These authors maintain that workers are instrumentally oriented to work. Wage-earners are interested solely in the amount of income they receive from the job; they are indifferent to the nature of work itself — some kind of skill and initiative it involves, the amount of responsibility and control it affords, and so on.

The authors find support for their position in responses to questionnaire items and in the fact that workers of the sample once held jobs which they regarded as more intrinsically satisfying than their present jobs; yet, they sacrificed the gratifying work for better pay. A concern for consumption standards "constituted the motivation for these men to take, and to retain, work of a particularly unrewarding and stressful kind which offered high pay in compensation for its inherent deprivations"[1] (Goldthorpe et al., 1969: 182). The authors (1969: 64) claim that the dilemma of the working class is one of "having to choose between work that offers variety, scope for initiative and relative autonomy, and work which, for any skill level, affords the highest going rate of economic return."

The Transformation of Work

What is at issue is not the *fact* that workers state they are satisfied with their jobs or that they are willing to sacrifice "enjoyment" in work for higher wages, but the interpretation of these data. To evaluate the meaning of these results, several points must be considered: the content of the work process, the degree of variation in the intrinsic characteristics of jobs, and the substance of workplace authority relations. The explanatory relevance of these properties of industrial organizations becomes clear only through an examination of a series of developments in the labour process which preceded the current organization of work. By locating work patterns in an historical perspective, one can discern a continual debasement of labour, which involves the progressive dilution of labour skills and the erosion of workers' control over the labour process. In this section I shall attempt to explain why labour degradation is integral to capitalist production and then go on to show in broad strokes how this process actually unfolded in Canadian society....

There are three basic ways of raising labour productivity: intensification of work (speed-up); application of progressively advanced machinery; rationalization of the *social* organization of the work process. The application of these techniques of surplus-value expansion underlies the massive changes in the labour process which have taken place over the last 130 years.

In the middle of the nineteenth century Canada was undergoing a transformation from a *petit bourgeois* society of small, independent producers to an industrial society in which growing numbers of people were dispossessed of the instruments of production and brought as wage-earners under the domination of capital. The capitalist production unit most characteristic of the initial phase of industrialization was the manufactory — a workshop where previously independent craftsmen were brought together and their activities coordinated by an employer.

In the manufactory several techniques of increasing labour productivity were introduced. First, the division of labour was extended. While the technical basis of manufactories was handicraft labour, the work of artisans, who once bore the responsibility for the production of an entire commodity, began to be subdivided and the job fragments were permanently assigned to individual workmen.[2] Although fewer and fewer manufactory workmen were capable of performing multiple production functions, the handicraft foundation of this transitional mode of production set limits on the extension of the division of labour. Consequently, skilled labour continued to predominate.

A second vehicle for expanding output revolved around control over the labour process. The work patterns of independent producers (artisans and farmers) typically were casual and sporadic (cf. Thompson, 1967; Rinehart, 1975: 25-9). By gathering together under one roof workers dependent on wages and subjecting their activities to supervision, employers were able to regularize and intensify the pace of toil. Nevertheless, the predominance of craftsmen in manufactories restricted employers' control over work routines. Because artisans monopolized craft knowledge, they, not employers, were responsible for the quality of the articles that were produced. Craftsmen also regulated the recruitment and training of apprentices, thus ensuring that skilled workmen would not be easily replaced. Such craft practices prevented employers from unilaterally determining the methods and pace of work.

The emergence of the factory system in the 1870s accelerated the dilution of labour skills and the reduction of workers' control. The introduction of new power sources (first steam and then electricity) and machinery created a stratum of semi-skilled machine tenders and eventually destroyed handicraft production. Machinery had multiple advantages for the capitalist. It decreased production time per unit and the value or price of commodities. As compared with handicraft technology, machines required less skilled, more easily replaceable, and cheaper labour. Finally, machines, particularly those that could be paced and controlled by employers, eroded workers' capacity to govern the labour process. . . .

Around 1890, capital started to concentrate and centralize, and Canada's economy began to change from entrepreneurial to corporate capitalism.[3] Corporate capitalism stimulated the mechanization, specialization, and rationalization of the work process, thereby causing a rapid multiplication of semi-skilled wage earners. In the first quarter of the twentieth century, the socio-technical innovations utilized in manufactories and early factories to increase the productiveness of labour and to facilitate the accumulation of capital were supplemented by scientific management and mass-production techniques.

Based on the writings of Frederick Taylor (1919), scientific management extended the division of labour horizontally by fragmenting work and vertically by transferring craft knowledge from the shop floor to the front office. Taylorists observed, recorded, and timed work practices. This enabled management[4] to subdivide the multiple tasks involved in a complex job and to reconstitute each operation as a single, repetitive job. At the same time, time and methods study placed at the disposal of management the knowledge of production held by skilled workman. Managers were now able to effect a sharp distinction between those who planned and those who executed work. Detailed plans specifying the task to be performed, the time to be taken, and the methods to be used were formulated by management rather than workers. While such practices were especially destructive of the prerogatives of skilled workmen, they also allowed management to impose more standardized and rigorous work routines on all grades of labour....

Despite its rather obscure origins and history in Canada, we can confidently assume that scientific management has exerted a profound and lasting influence on the organization of work in this country. The legacy of the new "science" is evident in a permanent thrust for efficiency, one form of which continues to be the standardizing, compartmentalizing, and timing of jobs. As Braverman (1974: 87) has pointed out, Taylorism has become the "bedrock of all work design" in advanced capitalist societies.

Mass production techniques, particularly the assembly line, were the twentieth century's mechanical counterpart of scientific management. Like the latter, they left a permanent imprint on the organization of work. Mass production is based on machines that put out standardized and interchangeable parts. It involves the principles of economy, accuracy, continuity, speed, and repetition. As Chinoy (1964: 56) has noted, "elimination of any substantial degree of skill from routine tasks is made possible by the pre-determination of tools and techniques by engineers and technicians. Each operation is precisely defined, tools are placed exactly where they are needed, and the amount of time allowed for a particular task is set by . . . time and motion study specialists."

The introduction of automation in the 1950s was hailed by some observers as portending a reversal of the long-term trend towards alienated labour. Blauner (1964) in particular argued that automated technology provided more complex, responsible jobs and allowed for greater control by workers over the labour process. This sanguine description of the organization of work (which was based on observations of a single chemical plant and interviews with twenty-one chemical workers) has received little research support.

Today, most workers are locked into jobs that require little knowledge and skill and that are defined and controlled from the upper echelons of complex organizations. The gratifications of craft work are denied to all but a few, and jobs which are officially designated as skilled usually bear little resemblance to the tasks performed by traditional craftsmen. Moreover, "the training requirements and the demands of the (semi-skilled operative) job upon the abilities of the workers are now so low that one can hardly imagine jobs that are significantly below them on any scale of skill" (Braverman, 1974: 430).

The impact of the development of industrial capitalism on the organization of work has been to degrade labour by extending the division of labour and creating a labour force of life-long detail workers and by progressively eliminating the control functions of workers. *This trend, when taken in conjunction with the precipitous decline of self-employment in the twentieth century (see Johnson, 1972), has virtually eliminated meaningful job alternatives for the majority of the Canadian labour force.*

The Meaning of Instrumentalism and Job Satisfaction
It is because variations in the intrinsic characteristics of most blue collar jobs are not large and because such differences as do exist are situated in authority relationships in which the process and purposes of production are not governed by workers that we are justified in raising questions about the meaning of "satisfied" and "instrumental" reactions to work. To argue, as Goldthorpe and his associates (1969) have, that the dilemma of the working class is a choice between high wages and gratifying work is to suggest a degree of variation in job complexity and control which simply does not exist. As Fox (1974: 161) remarks, "men who have never experienced intrinsically satisfying work can hardly be said to have 'chosen' intrinsically unsatisfying work." Consider the following statement of an "instrumental worker": "You don't achieve anything here. A robot could do it. The line here is made for morons. It doesn't need any thought. They tell you that. 'We don't pay you for thinking,' they say. Everyone comes to realize that they're not doing a worthwhile job. They're just on the line. For the money. Nobody likes to think that they're a little cog. You just look at your pay packet — you look at what it does for your wife and kids. That's the only answer." (Beynon, 1973: 114)

Instrumental orientations should be understood as rational adaptations to jobs that are characterized by extreme specialization, subordination, and inequalities of prestige and treatment. If jobs are selected on the basis of economic criteria, this only reveals the flatness of the world of blue collar work and not an absence of (abstract) desires for gratifying jobs. *Workers opt for jobs with relatively high wages in exchange for what can only be minor losses in intrinsic work satisfaction.*

Instrumentalism is shaped by objective realities. So too are "satisfied" responses to work, which should not be construed as statements of preference. They are no more than pragmatic judgments of one's position *vis-à-vis* the narrow range of available jobs. Also relevant to understanding the significance of job satisfaction is the permanent existence of the reserve army of the unemployed and the constant threat of redundancies, lay-offs, and plant shutdowns, all of which are responsible for pervasive feelings of insecurity among the working class. The "choice" that is presented to most workers is that between work which is intrinsically unsatisfying and no work. A job, any job, is preferable to none at all, and this necessarily affects evaluations of work. . . .

Among working-class youth the adjustment process initially entails eliminating the possibility of obtaining white-collar jobs; some time later expectations of blue-collar work are lowered. As early as age thirteen, Canadian working-class boys (70 per cent of whom are destined for blue-collar jobs) "select" a school curriculum that is "preparatory" for manual work (Breton, 1972). If aspirations for high status occupations initially survive such streaming, the objectives of the school program eventually are realized. A large percentage of the sons of manual workers who maintain some hope for white-collar work upon entering high school "will have changed this aspiration or recognized its futility within three or four years. . ." (Tepperman, 1975: 198).

As working-class youth enter the labour market, there remains (at least for some individuals) a residue of optimism about the possibilities of blue-collar work. Such hopes fade with time and job experience and are replaced by more realistic appraisals of the world of work and one's place in it. Research has shown that older workers and those with more work experience express greater job satisfaction than their younger and less experienced counterparts (Berg, 1970; Kornhauser, 1965; Sheppard and Herrick, 1972). When individuals "see their hopes still unrealized as they grow older, they begin to rationalize,[5] to reduce the pain of the discrepancy between their expectations and their achievements" (Berg, 1970: 131). It is this alignment of aspirations with the objective characteristics of blue collar work that is largely responsible for workers' pronouncements of job satisfaction. . .

The prevalence of abstract yearnings for decent work is also shown by a tendency of manual wage-earners who report job satisfaction to state they would select a line of work different from their own if they could start their lives over again. A national survey of Canadians found that 85 per cent of blue-collar workers were satisfied with their jobs. When these same persons were asked what type of work they would seek if they were to re-enter the labour market, 52 per cent of the skilled and 64 per cent of the unskilled chose an occupation different from the one in which they were then employed (Canada Department of Manpower and Immigration, 1974).[6] Coburn's (1973) study of Victoria residents revealed an equally large disparity in manual workers' expressions of job satisfaction and the jobs they would choose in hypothetical circumstances.[7]

It is not conceptions of *ideal* work that serve as the basis of job orientations, expectations, and choices. Rather, it is logical to conclude from the evidence that *the comparative frame of reference used by workers to select and evaluate their jobs is mainly a negative one.*

Working Class Activity: Conflict and Alienation

The argument I am advancing is that workers' attachments to jobs are in fact limited, pragmatic, and instrumental. But in contrast to the position taken by most observers — even the majority of those who view instrumentalism and job satisfaction as rational responses to limited job choice — my thesis is that such job orientations neither imply nor factually entail indifference to or acceptance of the nature of work.

High wages cannot neutralize the impact of what wage earners are obliged to do for over one-third of their waking hours, year in and year out. To argue that workers select jobs on economic grounds is not tantamount to saying that non-economic working conditions are a matter of indifference. It is unrealistic to believe that even the most calculating workers can effectively ignore and insulate themselves from daily workplace experiences. The validity of this argument is not shown by workers' attitudes, especially as they are expressed in survey analyses. Rather, it is most forcibly revealed by workers' actions.

Class conflict is endemic to capitalist societies. The outlines of Canada's turbulent history of industrial relations have been drawn by Jamieson (1971). Strikes are a persistent feature of the industrial system, and they periodically erupt to involve massive numbers of workers. This country has experienced five major strike waves in the twentieth century, the latest one occurring in 1974-5, when there was an all-time high in the number of man-days lost from strikes and lockouts. While many observers claim that this record is proof of workers' overriding concern with wages, the reality of work stoppages is more complex.

Without denying the salience of pecuniary interests, it is important to realize that strikes are a complex phenomenon. Work stoppages ordinarily arise out of a multiplicity of contentious issues, and during the course of a strike it is not unusual to find shifts in the importance workers attribute to the issues (cf. Hyman, 1972; Knowles, 1952). Even if we assume (along with government agencies) that the major causes of a strike can be classified and ranked in terms of salience, it is clear that a substantial number of work stoppages (now as in the past) are not rooted in economics per se, but are the result of grievances arising from working conditions broadly defined — job allocation and transfer, forced overtime, work loads and work speeds, safety and health problems, disciplinary measures and dismissals, etc. . . .

Strikes are only the most obvious expressions of working-class discontent, the tip of the iceberg as it were. Less visible workplace struggles are continuously waged over working conditions and managerial prerogatives. While organized labour has fought for economic gains, struggles over the organization and control of the workplace have been waged primarily by rank and file workers on the shop floor, independent (and sometimes in defiance) of the union.

Class relations are sharply etched in the daily encounter between bosses and workers, resulting in antagonisms which take various forms — slow downs and sit ins, restriction of output, wildcat strikes, working to rule, absenteeism and tardiness, personnel turnover, insubordination, and sabotage. In this constant "war of the workplace" workers not only resist managerial authority but at times collectively act to take over some part of management's role. What must be stressed is the routine character of factory conflicts. While ordinarily hidden to all but insiders, they are not an episodic phenomenon but a permanent feature of social relationships within capitalist enterprise (cf. Faber, 1976; Glaberman, 1975; Johnson, 1975; Rinehart, 1975; Roy, 1967; 1969; Watson, 1972).

Attitude-Behaviour Inconsistencies

If workers were really satisfied with or indifferent to their jobs, conflict and struggle would not be such a prominent feature of the world of work. But the disparity between job attitudes and on-the-job behaviour is only partly resolved by a re-interpretation of the meaning of attitudes. We are still left with an irreducible residue of uncertainty about such interpretations. How are we to treat the fact that workers do say they are satisfied with work, however minimal and qualified these assessments may be? There is no complete answer to this question. In fact, it would be surprising if attitude-behaviour discrepancies could be neatly reconciled, because what astute observations of the working class reveal is that such contradictions are not at all unusual. Consider the following examples of the striking inconsistency of values and behaviour.

Goldthorpe and his associates (1969) found that workers held privatized values; they were oriented to their immediate families and were not deeply involved with other workers or working class institutions. Moreover, these workers tended to view their relationship to the company as a cooperative one rather than one of opposition and conflict. Yet, it is now well known that shortly after the publication of the final volume of the study these same cooperative, privatized workers engaged in a militant strike that included threatening the life of the company director, running up the red flag, and singing the "Internationale."

A similar phenomenon has been described by Glaberman (1976) in his study of World War II no-strike pledges among the United Auto Workers. Prior to being presented with a secret ballot on the no-strike issue, workers were beseiged by patriotic proclamations of the media as well as their own union leaders. The message was clear — uninterrupted production was necessary for the effective pursuit of the war effort. The UAW membership voted two-to-one in favour of banning strikes. Nevertheless, "before the vote, during the vote, and after the vote, a majority of auto workers were on strike" (Glaberman, 1976: 29).

The disparity between consciousness and action is also emphasized in Mann's (1973: 51) discussion of a study of the turbulent 1960-61 general strike in Belgium. Workers interviewed just prior to the strike were described as "apathetic trade unionists, hostile to political strikes and completely ignorant of radical reform programs." Mann reported that the author of the study was surprised to learn that these same "apathetic" workers had assumed active, leading roles in the general strike.

The above cases are dramatic illustrations of an ordinary phenomenon. It is not unusual to find lip service being paid by workers to hegemonic values, with a corresponding behaviourial denial of them. Wage-earners generally adhere to the notion that improvements in one's socio-economic position are dependent on individual efforts. In practice, however, they rely on their union — a collective means — for such advancement. Workers have been known to condemn organized labour for holding too much power and yet evince fierce loyalty to their own union. They may oppose strikes in general and actively support a work stoppage at their own plant. Workers can endorse private enterprise one day and the next day occupy a factory and demand that it be taken over by workers, the community, or the government. And workers usually express some degree of job satisfaction at the same times as they are struggling against the way in which work is organized. . . .

Conclusions

Industrial conflict is a manifestation of antagonisms deriving from the unequal distribution of power. Because the purposes of production are determined by employers and their managerial minions, the needs and interests of workers are secondary to and often interfere with the central capitalist need of profitability. However, the immediate problem as perceived by workers is not capitalism or capitalist authority relations. Rather, their daily dilemma is how to exist within this system with the greatest amount of ease, security, and autonomy. To make life on (and off) the job more tolerable workers are forced to resist capitalist authority, to defend customary prerogatives, and to extend their own control over work routines.

This is not to imply that working-class struggles ordinarily are the result of a well-formulated philosophy of workers' control and socialism. In fact, resistance occurs despite workers' adherence (however inconsistent and superficial) to dominant values which justify and legitimize integral elements of capitalist production. But when workers react to specific irritants as they arise on the shop floor, the underlying cause of these conditions generally remains unchallenged.[8] The fundamental issue is not time clocks, wage rates, autocratic foremen, or repetitive jobs, but power, and each specific workplace deprivation is merely a manifestation of prevailing authority relations.

In the final analysis, struggles of instrumental and "satisfied" workers can only be described as a curious blend of acquiescence and defiance — an accommodation to the structure of capitalist authority and resistance to the actual exercise of this authority whenever it adversely affects working people. It is in the melange of tensions and contradictions arising from capitalist domination and the subordinate position of workers that one finds the dynamic of progressive social change.

Notes

1. Instrumental orientations to work are organically linked with "privatized" interests. The workers of this study were described as devoted homebodies, deeply involved with their immediate families, with whom they spent the major portion of their time away from work and around whom their strong consumer desires revolved.

2. The principle underlying this development and all subsequent extensions of the division of labour was first expounded in 1832 by Babbage, who demonstrated that labour power for a given task is "performed more cheaply as dissociated elements than as a capacity integrated into a single worker" (Braverman, 1974: 81). In addition, the division of labour was extended in order to solidify capitalists' control over the work process. Specialization allows employers to "divide and conquer." It also reduces workers' knowledge of the overall process of production, thereby increasing their dependency on employers. For a provocative discussion of the relationship between capitalist power and the division of labour, see Marglin (1974). The division of labour, then, was intentionally extended for capitalists' purposes. Because of this and because of the reciprocal relationship of capitalist authority and the division of labour, it is impossible to meaningfully assess their *independent* effects on industrial conflict and alienated labour.

3. The terms "entrepreneurial" and "corporate" capitalism are borrowed from Clement (1975). These terms are descriptive of a transformation in the size and ownership patterns of industrial firms. For example, in 1890, there was an average of five employees in the 70,000 Canadian manufacturing units. By 1920 there were only 22,000 manufacturing enterprises in Canada, but the mean number of employees per unit had grown to 26. Throughout this period production increased steadily (Urquhart and Buckley, 1965; Bertram, 1967). According to Acheson (1973), the *leading* manufacturing enterprises of the 1880s employed at most several hundred workers and were wholly owned by either a single family or by partners. Forty years later the joint-stock company dominated the Canadian industrial scene.

4. In the joint-stock company, managers assumed the daily operational functions once performed by the entrepreneur. Because the main goal of managers is the same as that of employers — to generate corporate growth and profitability — I treat the two interchangeably in this paper.

5. For some workers expressions of job satisfaction may be a rationalization devised because they feel they *ought* to be contented with work. To admit otherwise is to define oneself as a failure. Apparently such rationalizations are ineffective, for depth interviews have shown that many working class people are afflicted by feelings of self-degradation stemming from the nature and status of their jobs. The strength of such sentiments is revealed by working-class parents' efforts to ensure that their children grow up to be *unlike* the parents (Sennett and Cobb, 1973).

6. Data from the Department of Manpower and Immigration's "Work Ethic Survey" as re-analyzed by Peter Archibald, John Gartrell, and Owen Adams.

7. Such large response differences are not typical of groups such as professionals, managers, and proprietors. For example, Coburn (1973) found that 82.9 per cent of professionals were satisfied with their jobs, and 73.8 per cent would choose the same occupation if they could start again.

8. It is important to emphasize that "in trying to solve the problems of their daily lives, people sometimes find they must act in ways which also challenge the whole organization of society" (Brecher, 1972: ix). Canadian workers have periodically threatened constituted authority, most notably in the Winnipeg general strike and in the more recent general strike in Quebec. Outside Canada the most clearcut challenges to bourgeois authority have arisen recently in Italy through the formation of democratic worker committees and factory occupations and in the French events of 1968, where factories were occupied and "General Assemblies" of workers raised demands for workers' control of industry.

References

Acheson, T.W.
1973   "Changing social origins of the Canadian industrial elite, 1880-1910." In *Enterprise and National Development*, eds., G. Porter and R. Cuff, pp. 51-79. Toronto: Hakkert.

Berg, Ivar
1970   *Education and Jobs: The Great Training Robbery.* New York: Praeger.

Bertram, G.W.
1967   "Economic growth in Canadian industry, 1870-1915: the staple model." In *Approaches to Canadian Economic History*, eds., W.T. Easterbrook and M.H. Watkins. Toronto: McClelland and Stewart.

Beynon, Huw
1973   *Working for Ford.* London: Penguin.

Blauner, Robert
1960   "Work satisfaction and industrial trends in modern society." In *Labor and Trade Unionism*, eds., W. Galenson and S.M. Lipset, pp. 339-60. New York: Wiley.
1964   *Alienation and Freedom.* Chicago: University of Chicago Press.

Braverman, Harry
1974   *Labor and Monopoly Capital: The Degradation of Work in the Twentieth Century.* New York: Monthly Review Press.

Brecher, Jeremy
1972   *Strike!* San Francisco: Straight Arrow Books.

Breton, Raymond
1972   *Social and Academic Factors in Career Decisions of Canadian Youth.* Ottawa: Department of Manpower and Immigration, Queen's Printer.

Burstein, M., N. Tienhaara, P. Hewson, B. Warrander
1975   *Canadian Work Values: Findings of a Work Ethic Survey and a Job Satisfaction Survey.* Ottawa: Information Canada.

Canada Department of Manpower and Immigration
1974   "Work Ethic Survey." Ottawa.

Chinoy, Ely
1964   "Manning the machines — the assembly-line worker." In *The Human Shape of Work*, ed., P. Berger, pp. 51-81. New York: MacMillan.

Clement, Wallace
1975   *The Canadian Corporate Elite: An Analysis of Economic Power.* Toronto: McClelland and Stewart.

Coburn, David
1973   *Work and Society: The Social Correlates of Job Control and Job Complexity.* Ph.D. Dissertation. University of Toronto.

Dubin, Robert
1956   "Industrial workers' worlds: a study of the 'central life interests' of industrial workers." *Social Problems* 8: 131-42.

Faber, Seymour
1976   "Working class organization." *Our Generation* 11: 13-26.

Faunce, William A.
1968   *Problems of an Industrial Society.* New York: McGraw-Hill.

Form, William H.
1973   "Auto workers and their machines: a study of work, factory, and job satisfaction in four countries." *Social Forces* 52: 1-15.

Fox, Alan
1974   *Man Mismanagement.* London: Hutchinson.

Glaberman, Martin
  1975   *The Working Class and Social Change.* Toronto: New Hogtown Press.
Goldthorpe, J.H., D. Lockwood, F. Bechhofer, J. Platt
  1969   *The Affluent Worker in the Class Structure.* Cambridge: Cambridge University Press.
Hyman, Richard
  1972   *Strikes.* London: Fontana/Collins.
Jamieson, Stuart M.
  1971   *Times of Trouble: Labour Unrest and Industrial Conflict in Canada, 1900-66.* Ottawa: Information Canada.
Johnson, Leo A.
  1972   "The development of class in Canada in the twentieth century." In *Capitalism and the National Question in Canada,* ed., G. Teeple, pp. 141-83. Toronto: University of Toronto Press.
Johnson, Walter
  1975   *Working in Canada.* Montreal: Black Rose Books.
Kahn, Robert L.
  1972   "The meaning of work: interpretation and proposals for measurement." In *The Human Meaning of Social Change,* eds., A. Campbell and P.E. Converse. pp. 159-203. New York: Russell Sage Foundation.
Knowles, K.G.J.
  1952   *Strikes: A Study of Industrial Conflict.* Oxford: Blackwell.
Kornhauser, Arthur
  1965   *Mental Health of the Industrial Worker.* New York: Wiley.
Loubser, Jan J. and Michael Fullan
  1969   *Industrial Conversion and Workers' Attitudes to Change in Different Industries.* Ottawa: Information Canada.
Mann, Michael
  1973   *Consciousness and Action Among the Western Working Class.* London: Macmillan.
Marglin, Stephen A.
  1974   "What do bosses do? The origins and functions of hierarchy in capitalist production." *The Review of Radical Political Economics* 6: 60-112.
Rinehart, James W.
  1975   *The Tyranny of Work.* Don Mills: Longman Canada.
Roy, Donald
  1967   "Quota restriction and goldbricking in a machine shop." In *Readings in Industrial Sociology,* ed., W. Faunce, pp. 311-34. New York: Appleton-Century-Crofts.
  1969   "Making-out: a counter-system of workers' control of work situation and relationships." In *Industrial Man,* ed., T. Burns, pp. 359-79. Harmondsworth: Penguin.
Sennett, Richard and Jonathan Cobb
  1973   *The Hidden Injuries of Class.* New York: Alfred A, Knopf.
Sheppard, Harold L. and Neal Q. Herrick
  1972   *Where Have all the Robots Gone? Worker Dissatisfaction in the 70s.* New York: Free Press.
Swados, Harvey
  1957   "The myth of the happy worker." *The Nation* 185 (August): 65-9.
Taylor, Frederick W.
  1919   *The Principles of Scientific Management.* New York: Harper and Brothers.
Tepperman, Lorne
  1975   *Social Mobility in Canada.* Toronto: McGraw-Hill Ryerson.
Thompson, E.P.
  1967   "Time, work-discipline, and industrial capitalism." *Past and Present* (December): 56-97.
Urquhart, M.C. and K.A.H. Buckley
  1965   *Historical Statistics of Canada.* Toronto: Macmillan.
Watson, Bill
  1972   *Counterplanning on the Shop Floor.* Boston: New England Free Press.

Part II/Work Organization and the Labour Process

Editors' Introduction

The "labour process" is a broad concept describing the manner in which human labour and technology (itself a product of human labour) combine to provide socially useful services, or to transform raw materials into useful products. In contemporary capitalist society, where most workers exchange their labour for pay, the term encompasses the efforts of those hiring workers to control and direct their labour. In addition, workers' responses to these managerial initiatives, whether these responses are compliant, defiant, or simply passive, are part of the labour process. Rinehart's paper, which concluded the first part of this book, introduced the thesis that the labour process has changed dramatically as industrial capitalism has matured. Central to his argument are the propositions that, compared to an earlier era, many workers today have little control over their work and only few chances to develop work-related skills. Given such changes in the organization of work, Rinehart attempted to explain the behavioural and attitudinal responses of contemporary industrial workers. These, and other related themes, are explored further in the following readings on the labour process.

In Chapter 4, Craig Heron describes the power struggle between Hamilton's skilled metal workers in the early part of this century. The city's foundry owners were able to gain much greater control over production, at the expense of the artisans, through the introduction of new technology that made obsolete many previously hard-to-learn skills. The adoption of "modern" management techniques that systematized and routinized work also aided these industrial capitalists in their struggle with the craft unions. Wallace Clement's analysis in Chapter 5 of the "subordination of labour" in the Canadian mining industry includes both an historical and a contemporary look at changes in the labour process. He organizes his discussion around the concepts of formal subordination and real subordination of labour, arguing that the former occurred almost a century ago when large mining companies began to operate in the Canadian West. Independent miners working for them controlled their own labour but not the product of it, since the company owning the claim received half of its output. Over the years, underground miners continued to maintain considerable control over their work. But real subordination of labour has begun to occur with the mechanization and automation of mines operated by Canadian-based multinational corporations such as Inco. Again, we are shown how new technology has been used to gain more control over production.

Patricia Marchak makes the same point in Chapter 6. She describes how the mechanization of the west coast logging industry and the automation of pulp mills have reduced the need for skilled workers. Her detailed examination of changes in the labour process is presented within a broader discussion of the consequences of reliance on a single resource industry dominated by non-resident corporations. Large profits are removed while the local and regional economies fail to diversify, seasonal unemployment remains a problem for workers in the timber industry, and economic disparities between them and the more advantaged workers in the pulp and paper industry increase.

The work experiences of women employed in another primary industry, the east coast fisheries, are discussed in Chapter 7. Joan McFarland re-introduces the question asked earlier by James Rinehart: Why do workers who appear to derive few intrinsic satisfactions from their work continue to tolerate such a situation? McFarland argues that because these women live in a company town, their employer has an unusual amount of control over them. In addition, the piecework manner in which they are paid influences their response to their work. The same question is asked in Chapter 8, with respect to female sales clerks in a department store. These women express considerable discontent with the unrewarding nature of their work, yet they continue to accept the status quo. In her detailed look at this female job ghetto, Pamela Sugiman argues that the manner in which their work is organized and supervised severely limits the response options of these women. Instead, they make adjustments to the situation that allow them to ignore and forget, at least temporarily, the monotony and meaninglessness of their work.

A huge and impersonal, but sometimes very efficient, workplace is described in Chapter 9, where David MacFarlane recounts his impressions of the South Central postal terminal in Toronto — Canada's largest. Although his emphasis is not on the relationship between technology and worker control, he vividly portrays the alienating effects of an unbridled application of technology. Most of these postal employees are reasonably well paid and have secure jobs, yet they clearly are happiest when away from work. The same does not appear to be true of the Calgary oil men interviewed by J.D. House. Some of the sources of their job satisfaction were discussed in Chapter 2. In Chapter 10, House goes on to examine the typical career patterns of these professional workers. The variety of career options, all of which offer chances for stimulating and self-directed work, stand in sharp contrast to those available to the miners, loggers, fish packers, sales clerks, and postal employees encountered in earlier chapters.

We often make such comparisons between "good jobs" and "bad jobs" when considering our own occupational futures and those of others around us. However, a much more systematic way to analyze differences among jobs is found in the labour market segmentation literature. Donald Clairmont and his colleagues introduce this perspective on capitalist industrial society in Chapter 11. Using data collected in their research in the Maritimes, these writers describe the origins and characteristics of the central and marginal work worlds. According to this theoretical model, work rewards, job security, and career opportunities are much more extensive in the central work world. By contrast, poor working conditions, low pay, arbitrary supervision, and under-employment are common in the marginal work world. Minority ethnic and racial groups, women, recent immigrants, and the less educated are often trapped within this peripheral economic sector. As Clairmont *et al.* demonstrate, the labour market segmentation approach is a useful tool for integrating a wide variety of work-related topics.

Peter Li, in the last chapter of this part, uses a segmentation approach to describe and interpret the work experiences of Chinese immigrants in the prairie provinces earlier in this century. The case histories he presents clearly demonstrate how these Canadians were forced to work in a third economic sector — the ethnic business enclave. Formal and informal barriers to equal participation in more advantaged employment arenas severely restricted their occupational mobility opportunities.

Finally, it may be apparent that with the exception of Clement's comments on an earlier era of petty commodity production in the mining industry, these readings focus on workers within a capitalist mode of production. The working Canadians encountered in this volume are typically employed by someone else (an individual, corporation, or government) who owns the productive apparatus and consequently expects to have some control over what is produced and to reap the profit. While the majority of working Canadians exchange their labour for pay in such an arrangement, some Canadians continue to work for themselves. The two most prominent of such groups are those individuals operating their own farms and Native Canadians continuing to work within a hunting and gathering mode of production. We have chosen not to include readings focusing on these groups since a token representation would not do justice to the variety of work experiences within these distinct parallel modes of production.

Suggested Readings

Harry Braverman, *Labor and the Monopoly Capital: The Degradation of Work in the Twentieth Century* (New York: Monthly Review Press, 1974).

Wallace Clement, *Hardrock Mining: Industrial Relations and Technological Changes at Inco* (Toronto: McClelland and Stewart, 1981).

Richard Edwards, *Contested Terrain: The Transformation of the Workplace in the Twentieth Century* (New York: Basic Books, 1979).

Andrew L. Friedman, *Industry and Labour: Class Struggle at Work and Monopoly Capitalism* (London: Macmillan, 1977).

Gregory S. Kealey, *Toronto Workers Respond to Industrial Capitalism, 1867-1892* (Toronto: University of Toronto Press, 1980).

Patricia Marchak, *Green Gold: The Forestry Industry in British Columbia* (Vancouver: University of British Columbia Press, 1983).

Bryan Palmer, *A Culture in Conflict: Skilled Workers and Industrial Capitalism in Hamilton, Ontario, 1860-1914* (Montreal: McGill-Queen's University Press, 1979).

Claire H. Pentland, *Labour and Capital in Canada, 1650-1860* (Toronto: James Lorimer, 1981).

4/The Crisis of the Craftsman: Hamilton's Metal Workers in the Early Twentieth Century*

Craig Heron

I

"When you speak of 'skill,' do you mean 'ability'? What you term 'skill' or 'ability' might in reality be only dexterity." It was spring of 1916, and a panel of royal commissioners was seated in Hamilton's court house to hear evidence on unrest in the city's munitions industry. An unidentified machinist in the audience had just disrupted the proceedings by requesting permission to question his employer, who was on the witness stand. "Let us presume," the worker went on, "that a man comes into your employ who soon becomes proficient in operating a machine, from the fact that he is very bright, and becomes a piece worker, earning even more than your skilled men, such as toolmakers, would you call him a 'skilled' man?" Without waiting for a reply, the angry machinist turned to address the whole court room:

I have seen men right in this shop who, by reason of doing the one thing day after day and week after week, the operation has become a part and parcel of their lives. . . . I have seen these piece workers move with the automatic precision and perform a certain operation with unerring facility. Yet you term these men 'skilled.' They are not skilled, . . . they have become automatons. Their work requires no brain power, whereas the toolmaker requires both brain and brawn. He must have constructive ability. And you, sir (he continued with a wave of his arms towards the witness), know nothing about that.

The worker sat down to loud applause from "many tool-hardened hands." The voice of Hamilton's beleaguered craftsmen had been heard.[1]

In recent years labour historians have been increasingly fascinated with the lively history of the skilled stratum of the nineteenth-century working class, the artisans. Often colourful, articulate, tough-minded men, these craftsmen were not only leading actors in the emergence of a working class in the early years of the century; when they gave up their self-employed status and entered the "manufactory" to practise their craft under one employer's roof, they brought with them the accumulated traditions, values, and institutions of the pre-industrial era. A vibrant artisanal culture therefore continued to thrive in late nineteenth-century industry, where the skills of these men were indispensable to many sectors of production.

Artisanal culture had much broader dimensions than life in the workshops where the craftsmen toiled. They were confident of the social worth their skills bestowed upon them and expected to lead dignified, respectable lives. Central to

* Abridged from Craig Heron, "The Crisis of the Craftsmen: Hamilton's Metal Workers in the Early Twentieth Century." *Labour/Le Travailleur* 6 (Autumn) 1980, pp. 7-48. Reprinted by permission of the Committee on Canadian Labour History and the author.

their outlook on the world was a gritty spirit of independence and determination to resist subordination. In the workshops, and in society generally, they demanded for all men and women the maximum of personal liberty and freedom from coercion and patronage, and politically they became the staunchest proponents of egalitarian democracy. From employers they expected no interference with their traditional craft practices, which controlled the form and pace of production. Their "manhood," they insisted, demanded such treatment. The principal institutions of collective self-help which promoted and defended this artisanal life were, of course, their craft unions.

All of these social and ideological phenomena, however, rested on the craftsmen's continuing shop-floor power, and by the end of the nineteenth century that power was being challenged by employers who saw these men and their mode of work as serious obstacles to larger corporate strategies. . . .

II

Metal-working shops, especially foundries, machine shops, and agricultural implement works, had predominated in Hamilton's industrial structure since the mid-nineteenth century. According to one study, 50 metal-working firms employed 2,634 workers, or 38 per cent of the city's workforce, in 1891.[2] Particularly important were the stove-manufacturing shops, whose size and production made the city a national leader in the industry. The leading stove foundry, the Gurney-Tilden Company, was described in 1892 as "the largest industry of their kind in the Dominion."[3] It was in this industrial setting that Hamilton's artisans worked the metal into the wide range of products that won for Hamilton the epithet "The Birmingham of Canada."

Of the two most prominent groups of craftsmen in the city, the moulders could lay claim to the deepest roots in pre-industrial society. In fact, moulders liked to trace their ancient traditions to the biblical figure Tubal Cain. From their skilled hands came metal castings as diverse as stoves, machinery casings, and ornamental iron and brass work. Technological change had almost completely bypassed the foundry, which remained down to the end of the nineteenth century a classic "manufactory" of highly skilled craftsmen working in one employer's shop. A turn-of-the-century article in *Iron Age* emphasized that the craft "is learned almost entirely by the sense of feeling, a sense that cannot be transferred to paper. It is something that must be acquired by actual practice. A sense of touch plays such an important part in the construction of a mold that without it it is impossible to construct a mold with any reasonable expectation of success."[4] This sense was what craftsmen liked to call the "mystery" of their trade. With a few tools and the knowledge under his cap, the moulder prepared the moulds to receive the molten iron or brass. A mould began with a "pattern," usually wooden, in the shape of the finished casting, which was embedded in sand. Preparing and "ramming" the sand (that is, pounding it firmly with iron-shod poles) required great care and precision so that when the pattern was drawn out a perfect mould remained to hold the molten metal. If a cast product was to have a hollow space, the moulder inserted a "core," a lump of specially prepared sand that had been carefully shaped and baked hard at the coremaker's bench (originally moulders made their own cores, but gradually a division of labour emerged). Once cool, the casting was shaken out of the sand and cleaned, to be ready for any finishing processes. The size of the objects to the cast ranged so widely that the moulder might work on a bench or prepare his moulds in great stretches of sand on the foundry floor.[5] "The jobs he undertook," recalled one observer of Canadian foundries, "were varied in the extreme, a single job sometimes entailing days of careful labor, and the work being given a finish in which the maker took pride."[6]

That pride also fed on the physical demands of the work, which was notoriously heavy, dirty, and unhealthy. One Hamilton moulder described the city's foundries as "the darkest and rottenest places in Hamilton, and so stuffy that you can hardly breathe." He claimed the shop he was working in was so dark "that he had had to use a torch to see what he was doing." Ontario's factory inspectors repeatedly criticized foundry working conditions for the thick, smoky air, the extremes of heat and cold, and the heavy, dangerous tasks required. An American study also found abnormally high rates of death by respiratory diseases among foundry workers.[7] . . .

III

The 1890s marked a turning point in the work world of moulders and machinists. Over the next 30 years a transformation within metal-working factories swept away the artisanal culture of these workers which had flourished in the preceding decades. Technological and managerial innovations undermined and ultimately destroyed a work environment in which skilled craftsmen with indispensible expertise had presided over the pace and organization of the labour process.

The driving force behind this process of change sprang from the new shape of economic life in Canada. By the 1890s Hamilton's industrial life was being integrated into national and international markets which involved stiffer competition for the city's firms and the rise of increasingly large corporate enterprises. Hamilton not only participated in the Canadian merger movement in the pre-war decade, with the creation of such firms as the Steel Company of Canada and the Canadian Iron Corporation; it also opened its floodgates to branch plants of American giants like International Harvester and Canadian Westinghouse. These developments certainly increased both the scale of the average workplace in the city and the economic clout of employers and, perhaps more important, generated a sharpened concern about protecting profits against more powerful competition. Some of the city's oldest metal shops, especially the stove foundries, were particularly hard pressed in this new environment.

With their eyes fixed on profit margins, corporate managers in Hamilton attacked labour costs on two fronts. The first, aggressive anti-unionism, was ultimately the prerequisite for the second, the restructuring of the work process. The shop-floor power of craftsmen that was consolidated in their unions was a constant threat to corporate planning of production. Before 1900 individual employers, and occasionally groups of them, challenged unions in the city with varying degrees of success, but after the turn of the century anti-unionism became a cornerstone of labour relations for the largest Hamilton firms. The city's two largest employers of skilled metalworkers, in particular, had well-established reputations as union-busters before their arrival in Hamilton. International Harvester's predecessor companies had such an anti-labour record, dating from the 1880s, that the Hamilton labour movement mounted a vigorous and ultimately successful campaign to prevent the city fathers from granting the Deering company a bonus to locate in Hamilton.[8] Similarly in 1903 George Westinghouse, president of both the Canadian and American companies, engaged in a much publicized exchange with the American Federation of Labor President Samuel Gompers over the question of unionizing his staff; he made it quite clear that this was one corporation which would tolerate no workers' organizations in its plants.[9] The Westinghouse management in Hamilton never departed from that position.

The strikes in Hamilton's metalworking plants over the three decades from the 1890s to the 1920s fell into a pattern of union resurgence and employers' counterattack, in three periods of peak prosperity: 1899 to 1906, 1911 to 1913, and 1916 to 1919; and in most cases employers sought to use a strike as an occasion to drive out the union. Hamilton industrialists also participated in schemes to weaken the negotiating power of unions, like legislative restraints and promotion of immigration;[10] but probably more energy was directed to weakening the appeal of trade unionism through company-sponsored welfare programmes, which not only weaned workers away from reliance on the benefit schemes of the unions but also promoted loyalty to the corporation. Profit-sharing, benefit and pension schemes, and recreation programmes were introduced at the Steel Company of Canada, International Harvester, Canadian Westinghouse, Sawyer-Massey, and other large firms in the city before World War I and with new enthusiasm immediately after the war. In 1912 International Harvester and Canadian Westinghouse even undertook to pre-empt the social functions of trade unions and to promote craft pride within the confines of the company by inaugurating banquets of their most skilled machinists, the toolmakers. Seven years later International Harvester went so far as to launch an industrial council as an alternative form of "industrial democracy" to trade unionism. These corporations evidently saw themselves locked in a battle for the allegiance of their workers.[11] . . .

IV

Employers were not simply attempting to eliminate unions in order to push their workers harder; they were equally concerned about having the flexibility to re-organize the work process in order to rid themselves of their reliance on testy, independent-minded craftsmen whose union regulations kept the supply of new men and the pace of work strictly under control. After 1900 Hamilton employers' strategies fit into an emerging consensus about factory management in Canada. During the decade before World War I Canadian companies succumbed to the North American mania for more "system" in industrial organization.[12] At first the emphasis was on precise cost accounting as a means of determining the actual production cost of an item and of isolating areas in the entire manufacturing operation where costs needed to be reduced. "Broadly speaking," wrote accountant H.L.C. Hall in *Industrial Canada*, organ of the Canadian Manufacturers' Association, "factory economy means the production of your output for less money. . . ." He suggested a two-fold purpose for a costing system: "First to induce economy by elimination of waste and second to induce economy by intensifying production." The manager could expect the "system" to tell him "the efficiency of every man and every machine per labour hour and machine hour," as well as informing him of "all delays and the reasons for the failure to arrive at the maximum." Often tied to these new cost-accounting plans were special wage-incentive schemes which encouraged each worker to attempt to increase his output in return for a bonus or premium in addition to his regular wages.[13]

The fascination with "systematic" management began to reach full flower in Canada after 1911, when American writers, notably Frederick W. Taylor and his school of "scientific management," were catching great public attention. These new management specialists advocated complex procedures for establishing "scientific" norms for the speed of work based on stop-watch measurement, along with incentive wage payment systems that both rewarded the fast worker and punished the laggard. A key tenet of the Taylor system was the centralization of all control over the production process in the hands of the managers through planning, routing, scheduling, and standardization.[14] The Canadian business press generally applauded these new plans. *Canadian Machinery*, metal-trades journal of the Maclean publishing empire, declared that, "The principles are general in their application and where applied, valuable results will be obtained," and *Industrial Canada* concluded in 1914: "The experience of manufacturers seems to be that scientific management decreases a staff while it increases its efficiency. . . . Reports from firms on this continent show that scientific management has become practical."[15] Clearly new ideas were in the air about how to run a factory.

Managers in Hamilton's metalworking industries used three related tactics to pursue their goals of tightening their grip on the labour process, speeding up production, and reducing labour costs. Wherever possible the chief elements in a re-organization of production in the city's foundries and machine shops became narrowing the work of the skilled, upgrading labourers to become "handymen" who specialized in only one fragment of the process, and introducing new machinery. "If skilled labour is necessary," argued one foundry expert, "means must be used to apply the skill only to those operations in which it is needed, subdivision of labour and the use of mechanical appliances and power being applied wherever this can be profitably done."[16] As the subdivision of labour and co-ordination of production progressed, primitive notions of assembly-line production began to appear. A Hamilton *Herald* reporter spotted this trend on a tour through the new Westinghouse plant in 1905:

The thing that strikes the notice of the observer before all else is the manner in which everything is planned out so that everything that is being made makes a direct progression through the works. Economy is seen everywhere. The raw materials are delivered to the spot where they will be used. . . . And the machines are situated so that each piece passes right down the line to where the parts are assembled and put together ready for testing and shipping. Nothing is handled twice. . . . Everything works like clock-work, and all are truly "parts of one stupendous whole."[17]

. . . . Moulding machines were introduced into Canada relatively slowly. Canadian trade journals were passionate promoters of the new equipment and criticized Canadian foundrymen for their backwardness. The editor of the *Canadian Engineer* argued in 1906 that

the moulding machine is destined to revolutionize the foundry business, for when. . . a simple power machine, operated by one laborer, another shovelling sand, and one to carry out the flask, can turn out one mould per minute; or on a union rule of seven hours moulding, pouring 140 moulds per man; being twice as much as a union moulder can do by hand, then no enlightened owner of a foundry will submit to the primitive hand moulding methods of making duplicate castings, which we find in so many foundries in Canada today.[18]

In April 1908 *Canadian Machinery* was able to announce that "during the last one or two years Canadian foundrymen have been realizing the value of molding machines and several installations have been made, which are doing good work;" and in June it published a detailed analysis of moulding machine practice in an unidentified Canadian machinery foundry, where the installation of the machines and the use of handymen had cut production costs considerably. The same month, at the American Foundrymen's Association's first convention in Toronto, the new machinery was exhibited and discussed extensively, Canadian membership in the association immediately leaped from 17 to 57.[19]

Hamilton's foundries were not slow to adapt. The two biggest, International Harvester and Canadian Westinghouse, were, in fact, pioneers in the field. Henry Pridmore, a leading manufacturer of moulding machines, had begun his experiments in 1886 in the McCormick Harvester works in Chicago where the company introduced the new machinery in a successful attempt to drive out the local moulders' union. A company executive later boasted: "Their great foundries and their novel molding machinery were the admiration of the iron world." Not surprisingly then, a visitor to the new Hamilton Harvester plant's foundry in 1904 discovered moulding machinery in each moulder's stall.[20] The Canadian Westinghouse plant was similarly in the vanguard of managerial innovation. The superintendent of its foundry was David Reid, "one of the most prominent foundrymen of America." His extensive American experience had included managing a foundry where he had been responsible for some major restructuring of the work process: "By introducing modern methods here, such as molding machines, and dividing labor, whereby the molder practised the art of molding and nothing else, the melt was increased for 12 or 15 tons daily to between 50 and 60 tons."[21] Reid's influence, however, was not restricted to the Westinghouse foundry; in 1905 he became the president of the Associated Foundry Foremen of America, a scion of the American Foundrymen's Association, and launched a Hamilton branch. The purpose of the organization was "education" for better foremanship, and its meetings were devoted to discussions of more efficient foundry practice.[22]

Mechanization in other machinery foundries in Hamilton seems to have proceeded quickly. Gartshore-Thompson and the Berlin Machine works had them as early as 1908, Bowes-Jamieson by 1911, and Brown-Boggs, Dominion Steel Castings, and the Hamilton Malleable Iron Company by 1913.[23] The stove foundries showed some interest in the new machinery as well. Although this was not an arena where the moulding machine had been expected to make much impact,[24] the committee of the American Stove Founders' Defense Association which investigated the new technology in 1908 concluded that "All stove patterns can be molded with some form of machine or device now in use."[25] These discussions coincided with the assault of the Dominion Iron Founders' Defense Association on the moulders' union in Ontario and the foundrymen's desire to root out all obstacles to increased production at lower costs. As the Hamilton dispute reached the boiling point, the *Spectator* reported that stove manufacturers wanted to determine the value of the moulding machines and that "if they cannot secure the co-operation of the molders in trying them out, they will have to use other labor." Within a few weeks the strike-bound Gurney-Tilden Company introduced its first mechanical devices — a compressed air moulding machine and several squeezers — along with Italian labourers, and by May precipitated a strike of their scab moulders, who promptly joined the union.[26]

Mechanization did not sweep relentlessly over the whole industry; in 1916, for example, the NFA's committee on foundry methods found that not more than 25 per cent of its North American membership had taken advantage of the available mechanical appliances. But it was in the larger foundries, such as those that dominated the industrial landscape in Hamilton, that innovation was most advanced. By the 1920s most of the city's foundries had introduced a full range of mechanical devices. The machinery at the Hamilton Stove and Heater Company so impressed a foundry trade journalist in 1920 that he burbled, "Verily, the molding machine only requires to be taught to talk, when it will be perfect." By 1928 the *Canadian Foundryman* could gloat over the sweeping changes since the pre-war years:

Twenty years ago an unskilled man in the foundry would not have been permitted to handle even a slick, being only allowed to assist in the ramming of big jobs perhaps, lifting or similar work. Now unskilled labour can step into an up-to-date foundry and within a few days perform a task equal to that of the skilled molder, due to present day equipment.[27]

. . . . By the 1920s, therefore, the role of the artisan in the foundry had been re-duced to only those few tasks which could not be turned over to machines and handymen. Skilled workers had certainly not been banished from the industry, and their union survived down to the end of World War I on the basis of their continuing importance in the production process, however much that may have been eroded and confined. But they no longer wielded their artisanal control mechanisms for setting the pace of production as they had 30 years before. As early as 1909, Josiah Beare, a young union moulder in Hamilton, told a workmate: "Jim, I have worked too hard in my time; the pace is set too fast for the average man to keep up, and I am a nervous wreck;" he died six weeks later of "heart trouble." Half a century later Joe Davidson, future leader of Canada's postal workers, arrived in Hamilton as an experienced Scottish moulder and discovered "the more intense style of working" at Canada Iron Foundries; in nearby Dundas, he found, "The motto was 'produce or else' and every day was a mad race, the men working like beasts."[28]

V

Twenty years ago a molder was at home with his slick and trowel, but place the good mechanic of those years in the modern foundry and he would feel like a "fish out of water."[29]

In 1928 most observers would have agreed with this Canadian business journalist that the heyday of the craft worker in Canada's metalworking industries had passed. A new, rationalized, more highly mechanized mode of work had emerged to confine the skilled metal worker to small, unspecialized shops on the periphery of modern industry or to a sharply limited role in the process of mass production. On the one hand, in the case of both the moulders and the machinists, the crafts-men found large areas of their traditional work mechanized and divided up among less skilled labourers. On the other, a few "well-rounded mechanics" survived in-side large-scale industry, but these craftsmen found their work narrowed, circum-scribed, and intensified. In this new role in production there was increased pressure on the skilled men to apply themselves strictly to work that required their technical know-how. The old artisanal sense of working a product through all or most of its stages of production to completion was lost. And the pace of work, formerly so carefully regulated by custom and entrenched in union regulations was now set by corporate administrators.[30] The skilled metal workers who hung on in the context of mass production became simply a part of a complex continuum of industrial workers under the detailed supervision of efficiency-conscious managers. The arti-san of the 1890s gave way to the skilled production worker whose overall status in the workplace had undoubtedly declined.

If some craftsmen survived in the workplace, artisanal *culture* did not. The mode of work in the foundries and machine shops of the late nineteenth century had involved a commanding role for the artisans in determining the rhythms of the total production process. These men had nurtured an intense craft pride that fed on their indispensability to industry. Structurally the craftsmen's trade unions had been the repositories of both the mechanisms of job control and the ideology of craft superiority. Thirty years of conflict with employers who saw the manifestation of this culture in their factories as an obstacle to their larger corporate strategies, however, resulted in final defeat for the craft unions and all they represented by the early 1920s. . . .

Artisanal culture was thus highly ambivalent. It was often a reservoir of creative criticism of modernizing industrial practices, but its structure was still fundamentally a defence of craft privilege — "the clinging dross of exclusivism," to use James Hinton's apt phrase.[31] Yet, at the same time, it would be too easy to embrace a theory of an aristocracy of labour in the Hamilton working class. An examination of workplace behavior alone would be insufficient to confirm such a theory; for as the most sensitive British studies have emphasized,[32] we would need a fuller portrait of artisanal culture that took into account social and political associations outside the workplace. It was many of these same men, for example, who were prominent in the leadership of the city's working class political organization, the Independent Labor Party, which promoted class unity at the polls. The evidence presented here, in any case, should certainly raise doubts about any suggestion that these skilled workers were enjoying any special favours from capital; they were, in fact, being persistently harrassed by belligerent employers.

Notes

1. *Herald* (Hamilton), 4 May 1916. The literature on craftsmen has become voluminous. A few of the more insightful works which have influenced the ensuing discussion include the following: on Canada, Gregory S. Kealey, "'The Honest Workingman' and Workers' Control: The Experience of Toronto Skilled Workers, 1860-1892," *Labour/Le Travailleur*, 1 (1976): 32-68; Ian McKay, "Capital and Labour in the Halifax Baking and Confectionary Industry During the Last Half of the Nineteenth Century," *ibid.*, (1978): 63-108; Bryan D. Palmer, "Most Uncommon Common Men: Craft and Culture in Historical Perspective," *ibid.*, 1(1976): 5-31; Wayne Roberts, "The Last Artisans: Toronto Printers, 1896-1914," in Gregory S. Kealey and Peter Warrian, eds., *Essays in Canadian Working Class History* (Toronto 1976): 125-42; on Britain, Geoffrey Crossick, "The Labour Aristocracy and Its Values: A Study of Mid-Victorian Kentish London," *Victorian Studies*, 19 (1976), 301-28; R.Q. Gray, "Styles of Life, the 'Labour Aristocracy,' and Class Relations in Later Nineteenth Century Edinburgh," *International Review of Social History*, 17 (1973), 428-52; James Hinton, *The First Shop Stewards' Movement* (London 1973), 56-100; E.P. Thompson, *The Making of the English Working Class* (Harmondsworth 1968), 259-96; on the United States, Paul Faler, "Cultural Aspects of the Industrial Revolution: Lynn, Massachusetts, Shoemakers and Industrial Morality, 1826-1860," *Labor History*, 15 (1974), 367-94; Herbert Gutman, *Work, Culture and Society in Industrializing America* (New York 1976), 32-54; Bruce Laurie, "'Nothing on Compulsion': Life Styles of Philadelphia Artisans, 1820-1850," *Labor History*, (1974), 337-66; David Montgomery, "Workers' Control of Machine Production in the Nineteenth Century," *ibid.*, 17 (1976), 485-509.

2. R.D. Roberts, "The Changing Patterns in Distribution and Composition of Manufacturing Activity in Hamilton Between 1861 and 1921," MA thesis, McMaster University, 1964, 78.

3. *Hamilton: The Birmingham of Canada* (Hamilton 1892), n.p. The E.C. Gurney Company became Gurney-Tilden during the 1890s when John H. Tilden moved into control. The Toronto branch of

the firm became independent and retained the Gurney name. Stoves were Canada's most important foundry products at the turn of the century; in 1902 there were 297 stove foundries in Canada out of a total of 527. Clyde A. Saunders and Dudley C. Gould, *History Cast in Metal: The Founders of North America* (n.p. 1976), 15. On the growth of industry in Hamilton see, in particular, Marjorie Freeman Campbell, *A Mountain and a City: The Story of Hamilton* (Toronto 1966); C.M. Johnston, *The Head of the Lake: A History of Wentworth County* (rev. ed., Hamilton 1967); Bryan Douglas Palmer, "Most Uncommon Common Men: Craft, Culture and Conflict in a Canadian Community, 1860-1914," Ph.D. thesis, State University of New York at Binghampton, 1977; Roberts, "Manufacturing Activity"; Robert H. Storey, "Industrialization in Canada: The Emergence of the Hamilton Working Class, 1850-1970s," MA thesis, Dalhousie University, 1975.

4. John Sadlier, "The Problem of the Molder," *Iron Age* 6 June 1901, 26b.

5. Benjamin Brooks, "The Molders," reprinted from *Scribner's* in *Iron Molders' Journal* (hereafter *IMJ*), XLII, no. 11 (November 1906), 801-8; Margaret Loomis Stecker, "The Founders, the Molders, and the Molding Machine," in J.R. Commons, ed., *Trade Unionism and Labor Problems* (2nd ed., Boston 1921), 343-45.

6. *Canadian Foundryman* (hereafter *CF*), XIX, no. 5 (May 1928), 39.

7. *Herald*, 8 October 1910; Ontario, Factory Inspectors, *Report, 1908* (Toronto 1909), 34; *IMJ*, XLV, no. 5 (May 1909), 302-4.

8. Hamilton Public Library, Hamilton Collection, International Harvester Scrapbook, 1.

9. *Pittsburgh Dispatch*, 3 May 1903 (clipping in Westinghouse Canada Archives, P.J. Myler Scrapbook).

10. See Craig Heron and Bryan D. Palmer, "Through the Prism of the Strike: Industrial Conflict in Southern Ontario, 1901-14," *Canadian Historical Review*, 58 (1977), 446-56.

11. Public Archives of Ontario, RG 7, XV-4, v. 3; *Labour Gazette* (hereafter *LG*) IX, no. 4 (October 1908), 378; no. 7 (January 1909), 744-45; XIV, no. 2 (August 1913), 117; *Herald*, 30 January, 22 November 1912, 10 February 1913; *Canadian Machinery* (hereafter *CM*), IX, no. 7 (6 March 1913), 239; XI, no. 5 (29 January 1914), 76.

12. On the growing interest in "systematic" business management in the late nineteenth century, see Joseph A. Litterer, "Systematic Management: The Search for Order and Integration," *Business History Review*, 35 (1961), 461-76; Daniel Nelson, *Managers and Workers: Origins of the New Factory System in the United States 1880-1920* (Madison, Wisc. 1975), 48-54. Canadian business journals directed their readers' attention to various management theories and experiments in North America. In 1905 the *Canadian Engineer* began a two-year series of articles by one A.J. Lavoie on system in business operation. The outpouring from other publications included: G.C. Keith, "The General Scheme of Cost Keeping," *CM*, I, no. 4 (April 1905), 131-32; "Systematic Works Management," *ibid.*, I, no. 10 (October 1905), 403; G.C. Keith, "Is Piecework a Necessity?" *ibid.*, III, no. 4 (April 1907), 122-23; D.B. Swinton, "Day Work vs. Piecework," *ibid.*, II, no. 12 (December 1906), 453; "The Art of Handling Men, " *ibid.*, III, no. 9 (September 1907), 27-29; "Machine Shop Time and Cost System," *ibid.*, 32-34. Also H.C.L. Hall, "Economy in Manufacturing," *Industrial Canada* (hereafter *IC*), VI, no. 7 (February 1906), 430-31; no. 11 (June 1906), 732-35; VII, no. 2 (September 1906), 103-5; "The Model Factory," *ibid.*, VII, no. 7 (February 1907), 586-88; no. 9 (April 1907), 723-35; C.R. Stevenson, "System Applied to Factories," *ibid.*, no. 5 (December 1907), 420; L.E. Bowerman, "What a Cost System Will Accomplish," *ibid.*, VIII, no. 10 (May 1908), 774-75; Kenneth Falconer, "Cost Finding in the Factory," *ibid.*, VIII, no. 8 (March 1908), 639-40.

13. Hall, "Economy in Manufacturing," 420, 430, 732-33. The increasing use of time-clocks in Canadian factories facilitated the computation of precise labour-time. See my "Punching the Clock," *Canadian Dimension*, 14 (December 1979), 26-29.

14. Harry Braverman, *Labor and Monopoly Capital: The Degradation of Work in the Twentieth Century* (New York 1974), 85-138; Bryan Palmer, "Class, Conception and Conflict: The Thrust for Efficiency, Managerial Views of Labor and the Working Class Rebellion, 1903-22," *Review of Radical Political Economics*, 7 (1975), 31-49; Nelson, *Managers and Workers*, 55-78; Samuel Haber, *Efficiency and Uplift: Scientific Management in the Progressive Era, 1890-1920* (Chicago 1964), 52-55; Heron and Palmer, "Through the Prism of the Strike," 430-34; Graham S. Lowe, "The Rise of Modern Management in Canada" *Canadian Dimension*, 14 (December 1979), 32-38.

15. *CM*, VII, no. 2 (February 1911), 58; *IC*, XIV, no. 4 (November 1913), 423.

16. Arthur Smith, "Methods of Solving the Problem of Foundry Help," *CF*, V, no. 5 (May 1914), 85.

17. *Herald*, 14 October 1905 (clipping in Westinghouse Canada Archives, P.J. Myler Scrapbook).

18. "The Coming of the Molding Machine," *Canadian Engineering* (hereafter *CE*), XIII, no. 7 (July 1906), 265. The journal urged foundrymen to attend the annual convention of the American Foundrymen's Association to learn more about the new machinery. Among the few Canadians who did attend were Hamiltonians David Reid of Canadian Westinghouse and A.H. Tallman of Tallman Brass, *CM*, III, no. 6 (June, 1907), 36-37.

19. "Molding Machines: Principles Involved in their Operation," *CM*, IV, no. 4 (April 1908), 53-56; "Molding Machine Practice in a Canadian Machine Foundry," *ibid.*, IV, no. 6 (June 1908), 65-66; no. 7 (July 1908), 46-48, 52; *IC*, VIII, (July 1908), 1108. *Canadian Machinery* carried numerous descriptive articles and advertisements for the machinery, as did the *Canadian Foundrymen* when it was launched in 1910.

20. "Stripping Plate Machine: Inception and Development," *CF*, IX, no. 6 (June 1918), 123; Robert Ozanne, *A Century of Labor-Management Relations at McCormick and International Harvester* (Madison 1967), 20-28; Cyrus McCormick, *The Century of the Reaper: An Account of Cyrus Hall McCormick, the Inventor of the Reaper: of the McCormick Harvesting Machine Company, the Business He Created; and of the International Harvester Company, his Heir and chief Memorial* (Boston 1931), 131-250; *Iron Age*, 1 September 1904, 3. *This must have been one of the first installations of moulding equipment in Canada.*

21. *CM*, II, no. 4 (April 1906), 145-46.

22. *Ibid.*, 145-46; *LG*, V, no. 9 (April 1905), 1047; *CE*, XIII, no. 8 (August 1906), 303. The foundry foremen's association became the subject of considerable controversy in 1906, since the moulders' journal was convinced the new organization was yet another union-crushing apparatus of the foundrymen. David Reid vigorously denied the charge, but in some North American cities it did conform to the union's expectations. See National Founders' Association, *Review*, February 1906, 17-18; *IMJ*, XL, no. 8 (August 1904), 608-9; XLII, no. 2 (February 1906), 98; no. 3 (March 1906), 181-84; no. 5 (May 1906), 358-60; no. 7 (July 1906), 505-6; no. 9 (September 1906), 670.

23. *CM*, IV, no. 2 (February 1908), 58; no. 12 (December 1908), 32; IX, no. 1 (2 January 1913), 23, 52, 59; X, no. 2 (10 July 1913), 41; *CF*, II, no. 9 (September 1911), 18.

24. Abraham C. Mott, "Molding Machines for Stove Plates," *IMJ*, XXXV, no. 9 (September 1899), 456-58; Frey and Commons, "Conciliation in the Stove Industry," 129-30.

25. "Foundry Machinery — Molding Machines, Flasks, Mills, Etc.," *CM*, V, no. 1 (January 1909), 63-64; no. 2 (February 1909), 59-60. The cities which the committee visited in its investigations included Toronto.

26. *Spectator*, 23 February 1909; PAC, RG 27, v. 296, f. 3148.

27. Stecker, "Founders, Molders, and Molding Machines," 435; *CF*, X, no. 3 (March 1919), 58-59; XI, no. 4 (April 1920), 115, XIV, no. 10 (October 1923), 30; XVIII, no. 5 (May 1927), 6-9; no. 7 (July 1927), 6; no. 10 (October 1927), 8-10; XIX, no. 5 (May 1928), 17-18, 39.

28. *IMJ*, XLV, no. 9 (September 1909), 647; Joe Davidson and John Deverell, *Joe Davidson* (Toronto, 1978), 39-40.

29. *CF*, XIX, no. 5 (May 1928), 39.

30. Of course, while formal trade union controls disappeared, we should not ignore informal techniques that workers used to regulate the pace of work in North American industry for years to come. See Stanley B. Mathewson, *Restriction of Output Among Unorganized Workers* (New York 1931); Donald Roy, "Quota Restriction and Goldbricking in a Machine Shop," *American Journal of Sociology* 57 (March 1952), 427-42; Bill Watson, "Counter-Planning on the Shop Floor," *Radical America*, 5 (May-June 1971), 77-85.

31. Hinton, *First Shop Stewards' Movement*, 337. The evidence presented in this paper, therefore, suggests that a wholesale application of David Montgomery's influential conceptualization of American working class history in this period would be unwise, at least in the southern Ontario context. While his emphasis on struggles for control in the workplace is crucial for an understanding of craftsmen's activity, his suggestion that the workplace struggles of the skilled and unskilled tended to fuse during and after World War I is not sustained by the behaviour of Hamilton workers during these years. See David Montgomery, "The 'New Unionism' and the Transformation of Workers' Consciousness in America, 1902-22," *Journal of Social History*, VII, (1973), 519-20.

32. Gray, "Styles of Life"; Crossick, "Labour Aristocracy." For a discussion of the usefulness of a labour-aristocracy theory in a Canadian context, see Ian McKay, "Capital and Labour in the Halifax Baking and Confectionery Industry."

5/The Subordination of Labour in Canadian Mining*

Wallace Clement

The past century has witnessed two fundamental changes in Canadian mining's class relations. Around the turn of the century there was the transformation from petty commodity to capitalist relations of production representing the formal subordination of labour. More recently there has been the real subordination of labour accomplished by transformations within the capitalist mode of production. Both resulted in radical reorganizations of the social relations of production and were carried out with the infusion of large amounts of capital and technology. The first change, from owner-operated mining to capitalist control, was accomplished by capitalist ownership of mining sites. The second change is characterized by mechanization of underground operations and automation of surface plants, reducing the amount of direct labour required and the autonomy of the remaining mine workers, thus increasing the direct control of capital over the labour process.

* Abridged from Wallace Clement, "The Subordination of Labour in Canadian Mining." *Labour/Le Travilleur* 5(Spring) 1980, pp. 133-148. Reprinted by permission of the Committee on Canadian Labour History and the author.

This paper will analyze the impact of technology on the nature of work in mining, focusing on the implications for the number of workers required and their skill levels. In the analysis of the first change from petty commodity to capitalist production, we will briefly examine mining historically, while in the second change we will concentrate on recent transformations in the underground and surface operations of Inco Limited, Canada's largest mining company.[1]

I. Introduction

Property relations involve a series of rights which determine control over various aspects of production.[2] Independent commodity producers control, for example, access to the means of production, their own labour power, the products of their labour, and the way they organize the labour process. With the subordination of petty commodity production by capitalist relations these rights are eroded. A transformation results under capitalist relations, as Guglielmo Carchedi has argued, from the formal subordination of labour to real subordination. Formal subordination of labour means that only the products of labour are appropriated by capital while the prior technological conditions of production remain intact; that is to say, "At first, capital subordinates labour on the basis of the technical conditions in which it historically finds it."[3] Real subordination means the labourer is stripped of control over the products of his labour but also of control over the way his labour power is utilized in the social organization of work. Workers are transformed into "collective labourers" and subjected to a detailed division of labour.[4] This process is accomplished, Marx argued, by the "decomposition of handicrafts, by specialization of the instruments of labour, by the formation of detail labourers, and by grouping and combining the latter into a single mechanism."[5] Thus workers are stripped of the rights of property associated with petty commodity production only partially eroded with the formal subordination of labour and are left with only detailed labour to perform. Capital appropriates all the rights of property and uses technology to subject the labour process to minute units devoid of previously acquired skills.

In Canadian mining the formal subordination of labour occurred very rapidly, cutting short the independent commodity producer's premier place within the industry.[6] Formal subordination was accomplished primarily by capitalists gaining control over access to mining property by having the state transform mining areas from common property available to anyone to private property which the capitalists could appropriate.[7] The real subordination of labour in mining has, however, been a longer process. Control over the labour process within the mines has been accomplished primarily by the introduction of capital-intensive technology and training methods which dramatically reduce workers' autonomy and bring them directly under the control and supervision of capital. While mechanization has been the principal expression of capitalization underground, in surface operations the change has been toward greater automation; that is, interdependent control systems which involve both electronic machines directing other machines to perform pre-determined tasks, thus minimizing workers' intervention, and the centralization of reporting control information. Mechanization and automation have altered the skill levels of mining workers and made possible their loss of control over the production process. In both settings capitalization has decreased the amount of "bull-work" or heavy labour performed but it has also decreased the requirement for craftsmen and tradesmen within the mining industry. The mechanization of mines and automation of surface plants has been an important dimension of management's strategy to contain labour in what has always been a militant fraction of the working class. Additional strategies not to be discussed in detail here have included internalization of mine production centres and diversification of profit centres. . . .

II. Petty Commodity to Capitalist Relations

In Canada the historical moment of petty commodity production in mining was relatively brief. Part of the reason for its rapid demise was the existence elsewhere of capitalist mining which rapidly penetrated this activity in Canada, sometimes directly through branch plants and sometimes mediated by indigenous capitalists expanding their activities. The relationship between capital and technology is at the heart of the transition from petty commodity production and the realization of capital's success was made possible by favourable state policies. It is important to establish the relationship between capital and technology. Large amounts of capital are required to develop and, more importantly, to implement sophisticated technology in large-scale capitalist production. Since only the largest capitalists have access to such large capital pools, either internally generated or from outside financial sources, large capital tends to monopolize the benefits of technological advance. This advance tends at the same time to undercut the relative productivity of earlier forms of production. Further prerequisites to capitalism are control over the factors of production (in this case, mine sites) and the availability of labour unable to seek out its own means of production. Both of these conditions were met by the destruction of petty commodity mining and aided by state policies.

The gold rushes on the west coast between 1863 and 1898 were the heyday of petty commodity production in Canadian mining. Land for mining was readily available and only rudimentary technology was required for production, primarily in the form of "hand-picking." Miners typically worked in pairs. Once they located a pay-streak in a creek bed they would remove gravel along the shore and dig a shaft to the source of the gold-bearing ore. Drifts (parallel shafts underground) would then be made along the vein of ore by using picks and shovels. The ore would then be hoisted to the surface by hand. It was placed into sluice boxes to wash out the gold. Sluicing required access to large quantities of water and provided the first area for capitalist penetration, since capitalists were often able to gain control over water supplies.

The major toe-hold of capitalist penetration occurred, however, through the development of a speculative market in mine stakes and the emergence of a mining exchange to auction claims. This market made it possible for capitalists to concentrate many claims under their ownership. The high cost and scarcity of labour in the area, however, prevented the widespread use of wage labourers. Instead, a "lay system" was created. It was a transitional form of production between petty commodity relations and capitalist relations of production. Formal subordination occurred in the sense that capitalists owned the claims but let them out to miners who worked the claims using the same techniques as before. The miners covered all the costs of production while the owner paid the royalties and received half the gross output of the mines, the other half going to the miners. During the height of the gold boom of 1897-98 in the Klondike region, the lay system accounted for three-quarters of all claims.[8] . . .

These systems combined elements of both petty commodity and capitalist production but the direction of the relations of production was clear. The capitalists owned the mines and their products; the workers worked "for themselves," yet did not own the means of production. Today many remnants of these earlier systems persist in mining. There is still a bonus system distinct from hourly wages, as well as a "loose" supervisory system, and miners still control the organization and pace of their work. Recent developments, to be discussed shortly, are beginning to strip away these remnants and complete the real subordination of labour in mining. . . .

III. Transformations within Capitalist Relations

There has always been a formal subordination of labour in Canada's nickel mines but the real subordination of labour has involved a fairly lengthy process. This section will examine the way capital has penetrated the organization of work in nickel mines and undercut the relative autonomy of miners. These are processes still under way and by analyzing mines and surface operations at different stages of capitalization it is possible to understand the direction of the forces at work.

Until the late 1960s there were few changes in the labour process or the level of technology in Inco's mines. Miners worked in small crews performing an entire cycle of work: drilling, blasting, removing the ore, timbering, etc. There was a minimal amount of supervision: most miners saw a shift boss (or supervisor) only once a shift for a few minutes. Prior to large-scale mechanization the only significant technological innovations were the development of pneumatic drills to replace hand hammering or screw-drills and slushers to replace shovellers to move ore within the work place. Slushers reduced the amount of "bull-work" and were simple mechanical blade-like devices, operated by a member of the mining team, which scraped ore along the stope into an ore pass. Neither the pneumatic drills nor slushers seriously re-organized the social relations of production.

Since 1965 Inco has introduced over 500 pieces of trackless diesel equipment into its Canadian mines.[9] There are now four basic types of mines: traditional hand mines, captured-equipment mines, ramp mines, and open-pit mines. Traditional hand mines continue with essentially the same level of technology and organization of work that has been in place since the turn of the century. Captured-equipment mines have introduced scooptrams (diesel-powered, front-end loaders) into traditional stopes (or work areas). The effect has been to enlarge these work areas somewhat, but the basic organization of production is retained. In captured stopes the scooptrams are disassembled on the surface and taken into the work areas where they are reassembled and maintained. They replace slushers in traditional mines and increase the miner's capacity to move ore. They are integrated into the traditional mining cycle and a scooptram operator (in captured-equipment stopes) is also responsible for other phases of mining together with the driller and stope leader. Ramp mines have revolutionized the organization of work underground. In them, there is a ramp built from the surface so heavy diesel equipment can be driven throughout the mine. Ramp mines are of two types: either blast-hole mines (like Creighton No. 3) where huge slices of ore are blasted at one time after months of long-hole drilling or enlarged stope mines (like Levack West) where different phases of the mining cycle are performed by specialized crews rotating through the giant stopes. In both types the number of work areas in a mine is dramatically reduced and the scale of the work place enlarged. Rather than being responsible for an entire cycle of work, each miner is essentially a machine operator and continuously performs one aspect of the work process (drilling, blasting, removing ore, bolting and screening, or sand-fill). The final type of mine, and the one which has induced much of the mechanization underground, is the open-pit mine. Here heavy diesel equipment is used in a surface mine and each person has a specialized task involving the operation of a particular piece of equipment. The major limitation of open-pit mining is the depth below surface it can practically go before true underground procedures must be used (only about 11 per cent of ore removed from nickel mines in Canada is from open pits). . . .

In Inco's Sudbury mines, the cost of labour as a proportion of the overall production cost varies from less than 40 per cent in the most mechanized mines to over 70 per cent in the least mechanized. Increasing mechanization is being introduced into the mines, requiring less labour and less skilled miners to operate the equipment. The output of ore in the metal mining industry as a whole increased by 114 per cent between 1964 and 1973 and its value increased by 158 per cent, while the labour force grew by only 15 per cent. Obviously fewer workers using more equipment can produce more ore than they could using traditional methods.

The major types of trackless mining equipment introduced include diesel ore-moving machines such as scooptrams and load-haul-dumps (or ore carriers). A scooptram can move fifteen times the amount of ore per man shift as a slusher. Multi-boom jumbo drills, in which a driller stands on a platform and uses levers to control three drills are more common, together with another new form of drill, adopted from the petroleum industry, the in-the-hole drill which drills 6 1/2-inch holes two hundred feet in preparation for large-scale blast-hole mining (such as the Creighton No. 3 ramp mine). Compared to conventional drilling, in-the-hole drills reduce the drilling cost per ton from 55 to 24 cents. Raise borers have also been introduced. These machines make eight-foot diameter raises between levels underground; these raises are used for service passages, ore passes and ventilation. Traditionally this task has been performed by the most skilled miners, driving openings between the 200 foot levels. Raise borers drill 6 1/2-inch holes from one level until they break through below and then draw up huge bits 8 feet in diameter to carve out an opening. In 1968 there were only 10 raise borers in the world; by 1975 there were 200 (but only 25 in North America). In 1977 Inco had 14 of these machines and they had drilled 37 *miles* of raises in the Sudbury area alone. Each of the tasks now performed by these types of equipment was once done by skilled miners. Indeed, drilling, slushing, and driving raises were the three most skilled tasks underground. These same activities are now performed by machine operators who can be trained in a few weeks to perform tasks skilled miners took years to perfect.

The more equipment used underground, the more likely a miner will perform only one aspect of the mining cycle, the quicker he can be trained to perform his appointed task, and the greater the scale of the work area. From management's perspective, more mechanization means less reliance on the skills or individual initiative of the miner. Traditionally miners have trained one another in a *de facto* apprenticeship system. As a new miner was introduced into a mining crew he acquired the knowledge of the necessary skills from those he worked alongside. After a period of about two years as a driller working with a stope leader, the miner would move into another work area as a stope leader and train another driller. Both of these miners would be responsible for the entire cycle of work as outlined earlier. With the introduction of mechanized mining, management has appropriated the training process and designed it around each piece of equipment. This training will be discussed shortly.

Supervision in the mines is ambiguous in a number of respects. On the one hand, it has traditionally been very tough. Supervisors have exercised very arbitrary and at times ruthless power over workers in the past. On the other hand, miners have enjoyed a great deal of autonomy and seldom see their supervisors. They organized and paced their own work. In addition to this basic ambiguity, the nature of supervision has been changing in response to mechanization and to larger work areas. The transformation of the mines from many small production stopes, numbering upwards of 100 in traditional mines, into a few large areas means that supervisors can keep a closer watch over workers and that workers themselves have less discretion in organizing or pacing their own work, since they are confined in the operation of one machine and one task.

Supervisors (or shift bosses as they are called by the miners) are themselves in an ambiguous position in the hierarchy of the mines. They are directly on the firing line between workers and management. In all of the shaft mines they are expected to cover a very large area with many distinct work places — all on foot; in ramp mines supervisors have access to vehicles that can move quickly from one area to another and the workers themselves are concentrated into a few work sites. In the shaft mines the supervisor is pressured by management to insure production but cannot directly oversee the men's work. Moreover, a greater differentiation takes place among the miners themselves as a result of centralized production. Not only do they become specialized in one task, but the stope leader who used to work alongside his driller in a partnership now becomes a stope boss who gives direction to several machine operators rather than performing the tasks himself.

In place of close supervision, mines have traditionally used a system of production "incentives" or a bonus system. During the formative period and through the years, the bonus became an institution integral to mining. It came to be called an "invisible supervisor" by the workers which induced miners to maximize production. This bonus is outside the wage structure negotiated by the union and is controlled by management. In theory the bonus is a simple incentive or inducement to reward miners for producing more ore or doing more development work quickly. In practice it is much more complex. It is a source of pride for many miners since it sets them apart from most workers in other industries and among miners it is a measure of skill and dedication to their trade; it is also a justification for taking the risk of working underground. To the unions it is a source of danger, luring miners to work unsafely and taking jobs away from other miners. To the companies it is a means of social control, the carrot that reduces the amount of supervision needed. In the minds of many, it is "what makes the miners go."

About one-half of all those working underground are on bonus. Underground the miner still commands a great deal of control and the company relies on the miner's ability, not just his hard work. Tradition in the mines has had it that anyone who can affect the rate of production is on bonus. This system is still evident in all underground operations of Inco, but there are important variations as a result of mechanization. The most notable is Levack West, mentioned earlier as a ramp mine, where the entire mine is on a single contract rather than a bonus geared to a crew of miners in a single work area. Other mines have had the bonus system adjusted with mechanization as the rates of production needed to attain bonus have been revised upwards, mainly because the machine operator has less control over the rate of production and is deemed not to require as much inducement simply to keep his machine operating. When the machine sets the pace and supervision is direct, the bonus loses its original "invisible" control purpose.

Given the great distance between work crews and management, the bonus system is used to fill the gap. As tasks are subdivided and the co-ordinating role of management takes on greater importance as a result of mechanization, there is a trend away from this system. Supervisors have greater mobility and workers less control over their rate of production, leading some managers to conclude that the bonus is no longer necessary. The relationship between the bonus and the skill of the traditional miner is very close. There is not simply a correspondence between hard work and more money; technique has a lot to do with whether or not the miner will end up the month with no bonus or 500 dollars. This has at least been true in traditional mining. What is currently in dispute within Inco is whether or not the bonus is anachronistic in mechanized mines; that is, now that the real subordination of labour has been accomplished. Levack West may well be indicating the direction for the future: the open-pit mines, the most mechanized form of mining, have already abandoned the bonus.

The way technology has been introduced and the interests it serves have been controlled by capital, not by labour. Work has been re-organized *for* the miners, not *by* them. To be sure, it has reduced the amount of "bull-work" within the mines but at the expense of miners' jobs, not to create better ones. With the increase in mechanization it has been possible for management to penetrate — to a greater extent than in the past — the miner's control over the pace of his work and the skills he brings to bear. Management's strategy in introducing technology has been to decrease its reliance on the skills of the miners and to minimize the number and quality of workers needed, thus increasing their control over the work process and maximizing their profits from the benefits of technology. The miners have lost in many ways — in their ability to demand a bonus as a result of their control over the pace of work, in their knowledge of mining practices, in their numbers and, all too often, in their health and safety.[10] Technology is not neutral in the struggle between capital and labour because it has been employed from the outset to meet the needs of capital, not those of labour. It has been used to accomplish the real subordination of labour and to embellish the command of capital. Technological development does, however, offer the potential to humanize the labour process but only if it is adapted in a way most beneficial to those most directly affected — the miners. . . .

IV. Implications of Mechanization and Automation for Skills and Training

Changes in the use of equipment in mining have been accompanied by another form of technology — "people technology" as Inco managers refer to it — a form of training intended to meet the changed skill requirements brought about by greater capitalization and designed to give management even greater control over the labour process. The first major application of the MTS program (modular training) was at the highly automated Copper Cliff Nickel Refinery in 1972. As a result of operators being required to do maintenance work (at operator's rates), there were over 1000 grievances filed in the first year. Arbitration ruled for an expansion of operators' tasks without an increase in pay. Modular training gives management the tools for pushing operators into more maintenance work, and for an expansion of tasks contained in each job. The tasks themselves are simplified and regularized with the minute division of labour and standardization inherent in modular training. Since March 1977 Inco has pursued a policy of extending modular training across its entire Ontario division, both underground and on the surface.

Modular training means that each operation is broken down into its part and these parts become interchangeable and can be arranged in a variety of ways. At the same time performance rates and standards allow management to control precisely the performance of workers. Every process and piece of equipment is documented in a systematic way and inventoried. Production is rationalized and each task subdivided into minute parts, whether it is an operating or maintenance task. A training manual is produced for each piece of equipment and is administered largely by self-learning.

The system is not yet entirely in place but according to the MTS report outlining the program for Inco, "many operators will learn (or be asked to learn) to do things that do not fall within their present duties."[11] Maintenance workers will have more manuals than production workers but production workers will be trained on more than one manual. The unit is the equipment, not the person. In a trade there is a common core of skills. Principles and techniques are learned and these are then adapted to the situation. The training is broad. In modular training, however, the situation is determined by specific equipment: training is more immediate and "practical" (from the company's, not the worker's, perspective). The result for the worker is a limit on the marketability of their skills with modular training, hence reducing their mobility between companies and industries, unlike the wide applicability of skills learned by tradesmen.

MTS is a reaction to technology and is only applicable to highly mechanized and automated tasks. It gives management leverage in utilizing and policing the time it takes workers to perform pre-determined and measured tasks. A person can be trained for a number of tasks and these tasks are then codes attached to him. Inco is moving ahead rapidly in the area of "people technology" just as it has in other forms of technology.

While management has been attempting to narrow the jobs its employees perform in the mining industry, workers have been attempting to broaden their skills. This is expressed in a program known as "miner-as-a-trade." The intent is to certify miners as in trades such as plumbers and mechanics that require "tickets" to practice. Miners have been certified in several European countries since 1951 but the first program in North America began in January 1975 in Manitoba. The apprenticeship is over a three-year period and requires eight weeks of school a year with the rest of the time spent working in specified areas. The mining companies were reluctant to become involved but the program was implemented by the New Democratic government because of union pressure. "Grandfather" tickets were issued to about 300 experienced miners with four or more years of mining in 1975 but the program was not made compulsory, denying the essential exclusive quality of traditional apprenticeship practices. Miners in Ontario have not yet been successful in having the program implemented.

"Miner-as-a-trade" in its present form is not going to revolutionize the industry. At present it is a mere drop in the bucket. In 1977 the first graduates completed the course; there were only six of them. There are only about 20 people currently enrolled in the apprenticeship program in Inco's Thompson operation. As long as it is not a prerequisite to being a miner, there is little possibility that "miner-as-a-trade" will counteract the tendencies of fragmented labour inherent in mechanization and MTS as Inco is implementing them.

Contrary to the popular opinion that increased technology leads to greater skill requirements, the overall effects of automation and mechanization in combination with modular training have been the opposite. In part this is attributable to workers having less control over the functioning of machinery but it is also the result of simultaneous changes in the organization of work and the way workers are trained. In a classic study, James Bright of the Harvard School of Business identified this trend in 1958, arguing that "we tend to confuse the maintenance and design problems or exceptional operator jobs with the most common situation: namely that *growing automaticity tends to simplify operator duties*."[12] Capitalization clearly results in de-skilling within mining if, following Bright, we define skill as a "blending of several things — manual dexterity, knowledge of the art, knowledge of the theory, and comprehension and decision-making ability based upon experience."[13] While there has not been an increase in skill for production work, there has been in designing equipment and, in some cases, maintenance. In Canadian mining most of the equipment design takes place outside the country, thus reducing many of the potential benefits for the skilled component of the Canadian labour force in manufacturing.[14] . . .

For the most part, management has been successful in implementing changes in the techniques of production and training. They serve the twin goals of increasing the ability of capital to accumulate and of management to control the workers. These strategies have been costly; tremendous amounts of money have been invested in capital equipment and training programs. But in the long term management feels these investments will increase their power at the expense of workers. There is every reason to believe they are right, particularly since unions, at least at Inco, have been unsuccessful in resisting these developments.

V. Conclusion

Two aspects of class transformation have briefly been explored in the case of Canadian mining. The first was the transformation from petty commodity to capitalist production. It was argued that the autonomous organization of work, craft skills, and bonus system meant that all the characteristics of this form were not completely destroyed with the formal subordination of labour. These remnants are, however, disappearing with the real subordination of labour. The most obvious change in the property relations of mining occurred with the destruction of the petty commodity form, but there have also been significant changes within capitalism itself. As a result of mechanization, the autonomous organization of work and the bonus system are threatened. . . .

As a consequence of capitalization, management strategies toward workers have changed. Underground there has been a strong tendency to move away from the traditional "responsible autonomy" of mining crews towards greater direct control. On the surface direct control has always been more prevalent but with automation, new strategies have been devised. Automated plants like Clarabelle Mill and the Copper Cliff Nickel Refinery have different labour requirements than do labour-intensive operations. Workers are required more for patrol and maintenance than for detailed labour. As a result, there is at least the appearance and ideology of a "responsible autonomy" strategy on the part of management. In fact, workers and first-line supervisors find that what they are responsible for is accountability, not decision-making. They have virtually no control over the actual work process, this having been programmed into the equipment.

The effect of capitalization is to decrease dramatically the need for both skilled and unskilled labour. They are replaced by "semi-skilled" labour. Both heavy manual labour and craft skill give way to machine tenders and those patrolling equipment programmed to perform pre-designed tasks. This is not an automatic process — labour resists management strategies because many jobs are lost and the strongest faction of the working class, the tradesmen, are directly threatened. The consequence of the overall trend is towards a homogenization of the working class in mining. The net effect may well be a stronger, more unified class in a political and ideological sense since the impact of these processes tends to decrease traditional divisions within the working class between operations and maintenance, labourers and craft workers, and even surface and underground workers.

Class struggle focuses on control over the production process and the distribution of the expanding surplus which technology makes possible. Having broken the power of the craftsmen and eliminated most labourers, capital can afford to increase the wages of the remaining workers and still appropriate the lion's share of the surplus. Struggles for control rather than those for wages are much more threatening to capital. The forces outlined may well open the possibility for broad-based action by workers to appropriate the means of production.

It is not the introduction of technology *per se* or the technical division of labour that have caused the negative effects of technology, but the social relations of production and the way technology is used as a strategy by management to minimize control by workers. As Marx observed for the initial industrial revolution, "It took both time and experience before the workpeople learned to distinguish between machinery and its employment by capital, and to direct their attacks, not against the material instruments of production, but against the mode in which they are used."[15] It is no longer possible (or even desirable) to return to petty commodity production in mining. The forces of production have become "socialized" by giant multinational corporations. The only progressive direction would be to socialize the relations of production; that is, create a system of property relations whereby the means of production become the common property of those working them and providing rights and claims to the consumers of the products. It may first be necessary to nationalize the mines and processing facilities by turning them into state property, but this would have little bearing on the relations of production. If there are to be equitable and just relations of production and a guarantee of the safest working conditions, it will be necessary for those most directly affected to control the conditions and organization of their work.

Notes

1. This paper draws upon a thread of argument contained within my larger study, *Hardrock Mining: Industrial Relations and Technological Change at Inco* (Toronto 1980), which documents changes in the technology of mining and the labour process only touched upon here.The purpose of this paper is not to provide a history of mining, or even a survey of the labour process in that industry. Rather, it is to make a specific argument about changes in the labour requirements within the industry as it progresses through various relations of production.

2. For a discussion of this point, see Wallace Clement, "Class and Property Relations: A Preliminary Exploration of the Rights of Property and the Obligations of Labour," a paper presented to the International Structural Analysis Colloquium on "The State and the Economy," University of Toronto, 6-9 December 1979.

3. Karl Marx, *Capital*, I (New York 1967), 310.

4. See Guglielmo Carchedi, "Reproduction of Social Classes at the Level of Production Relations," *Economy and Society*, 4 (1975), 14-16, and his *On the Economic Identification of Social Classes* (London 1977), 53-55.

5. Marx, *Capital*, I, 364.

6. See Wallace Clement, "Class Transformations in Mining: A Critique of H.A. Innis," in Mel Watkins, ed., *The Legacy of Harold Innis* (Toronto 1980).

7. See Harold A. Innis's documentation of the development of mining exchanges and state regulations providing long-term leases on large mining areas requiring heavy capitalization in the Yukon at the turn of the century in *Settlement and the Mining Frontier* (Toronto 1936), 226-227.

8. *Ibid.*, 207.

9. All information in this section on Inco's operations comes from the management of its surface operations and mines, union officials, mining workers, or trade journals. For a thorough overview, see Clement, *Hardrock Mining*.

10. For an analysis of the relationship between health and safety and mechanization, see Clement, *Hardrock Mining*, ch. 7.

11. Management Training Systems, *Inco Consolidated Report*. Ontario Division (April 1976), 10.

12. James Bright, *Automation and Management* (Boston 1958), 183, emphasis in original.

13. *Ibid.*, 187.

14. See John N.H. Britton and James M. Gilmour, *The Weakest Link: A Technological Perspective on Canadian Industrial Underdevelopment.* Science Council of Canada Background Study, No. 43 (Ottawa 1978), 94.

15. Marx, *Capital*, I, 429.

6/Labour in a Staples Economy[*]

Patricia Marchak

Defences for overcutting the forest on which the British Columbia economy depends are most frequently phrased in terms of protecting employment. They sound a paradoxical overhead noise against technological change that is designed in no small part to reduce employers' dependence on labour, while not in any way reducing the economy's dependence on the export of lumber, pulp, and newsprint to the United States. The effects of a concentrated, integrated staples industry include highly unstable employment conditions, the development of regional pools of labour which are used in several industrial sectors but for which no employer has long-term responsibility, uneven development of regions, and community instability. This paper is concerned with the political economy of the B.C. forestry industry and some of its effects on labour as revealed in a study of three communities during 1977-1978.[1]

Organization of the Industry

The forestry industry in B.C. developed at the coast from about the 1880s, following the demise of the fur trade. Newsprint production sharply increased during the first war and afterward, in large part as a consequence of exemption for newsprint by U.S. tariffs.[2] Small lumber mills proliferated in the interior, serving a prairie and local as well as U.S. market, but the pulpmills were concentrated at the coast until the 1950s. The coastal timber is of exceptionally high quality, in high demand on world markets, and has low transportation costs via waterways. . . .

By 1974, ten companies controlled between 80 and 93 per cent of the forestry resource in each of the seven forestry districts, (via different licensing systems known as public sustained yield units and tree farm licenses) and owned about 35 per cent of the lumber facilities, 90 per cent of the pulp facilities, 100 per cent of the paper facilities, and 74 per cent of the plywood and veneer facilities. Five of these companies were foreign-owned, and seven altogether were owned outside

---

[*] Abridged from Patricia Marchak, "Labour in a Staples Economy," *Studies in Political Economy* 2 (Autumn) 1979, pp. 7-35. Reprinted with permission of the publisher and the author.

B.C.[3] Thirteen of the top twenty are foreign owned. Since 1974, and especially since the downturn of the markets after 1980, concentration levels have increased. Most of the take-overs have involved Canadian-owned companies.

Forestry is, without a doubt, a staples industry in that it involves the extraction of a raw material, is shipped out to export markets in a relatively unprocessed state, and it dominates the regional economies throughout most of the province. It has not spawned either forward or backward linkages, and there is not a significant manufacturing industry connected either with wood products or with machinery and chemicals for the production of wood and paper. There is not even a substantial quality-paper products industry, by far the larger part of the resource being utilized for dimensional lumber, pulp, and newsprint.

Although the industry produces neither technically sophisticated products, nor a range of manufactured items, it does produce its simple materials through a highly sophisticated imported technology. Logging has become increasingly mechanized. Sawmills were mechanized throughout the 1950s and 1960s, and newer mills are now partially automated. Pulpmills have been automated for most of the post-war period, each few years allowing for extension of that process. . . .

Overall Employment

About 9 per cent of all workers in B.C. are directly employed in the forestry industries.[4] Estimates of the total direct and indirect employment related to the industry have been calculated at 30 per cent.[5] The latter figure however does not tell much about the overall dependence on forests, because it includes the two major metropolitan areas which contain 56 per cent of the provincial population. Outside the lower mainland, almost every town and valley is dependent on forestry. In the towns where we conducted interviews between 30 and 70 per cent of all adult men earned their incomes in forestry industries varying with the presence of other resource industries and government employment in the region. The remainder of the population, adult women and other men, are, of necessity, indirectly dependent on the viability of the industry. Shares of forestry employment by sector for production workers are approximately 18 per cent in logging (22 per cent including salaried workers); 27 per cent in lumber manufacture (32 per cent total); and 13 per cent in pulp and paper manufacture (18 per cent total).[6]

While the industry has expanded regionally and production rates have greatly increased in the past two decades, there are relatively small increases in employment of production workers. Production worker increases are 11 per cent to 67 per cent in logging; and between 1961 and 1976, 22 to 90 per cent in sawmills; 24 to 80 per cent in plywood and veneer; and 85 to 167 and 105 per cent respectively in wood pulp and paper. The larger increase in pulp-mill employment is connected to the rise in the number of mills between 1964 and 1973. There have been larger additions in the number of salaried workers, especially in pulpmills, though even where these are included the production rates per worker have all increased substantially. The increases, then, reflect investments in capital rather than increases in labour for production. It may be noted that 1976 was a "good" year for forestry, and employment was at record levels.[7] . . .

Unemployment rates in B.C. have generally exceeded the national average. Seasonal unemployment is a normal phenomenon for wood-cutters, but a persistent and growing segment of the labour force encounters long periods of unemployment not attributable to the seasonality of logging. One study has provided evidence to the effect that unemployment in the forestry industries is particularly unstable, fluctuating directly with prices for wood products, and that unemployment in towns is greater, the greater the degree of dependence on the single staples production.[8] This underlines the weak position of labour in a non-diversified economy, especially in single-industry towns and regions. Since the surplus from the industry is not being reinvested in manufacturing facilities within the province (other than in expansion of the industry), this situation cannot be regarded as temporary. . . .

Figures for unemployment become ambiguous in a region dependent on a single resource, where seasonal and other lay-offs are part of "the normal package." . . .

Unemployment in forestry is somewhat masked by the interchangeability of unskilled workers and machine operators between forestry, mining, construction, and transportation. All of these sectors provide a substantial number of temporary jobs, and all are subject to considerable fluctuation in employment rates. Workers in one sector will move to other sectors between "preferred" jobs, so that unemployment rates for a region may not reflect the complete impact of a lay-off or strike in the dominant industry.

The division of the labour force by sex which occurs throughout the economy is sharpened in resource regions, especially in company or otherwise single-industry towns. Women are rarely employed in logging or mills. Since there are few clerical positions available at mill sites, and they are not considered for managerial positions controlled by head offices (and normally subject to geographical mobility requirements), they are restricted to service and clerical jobs in the non-forestry private sector and government offices or service sectors. Many of these jobs are temporary and/or part-time, and almost all provide incomes close to the minimum wage levels. Nonetheless these jobs are integral to service, retail, and industrial operations: labour is required in restaurants, hotels, banks, stores, schools, and hospitals. The wives of millworkers provide this labour, interspersing their periods of employment with periods of "homemaking, full time." Although their official unemployment rates have steadily increased throughout the 1970s, even these greatly under-represent their situation. For example, in the company town Mackenzie, there were a reported 115 applicants for a single post-office clerical position, 88 applicants for four cashiering jobs at a supermarket, and 77 applicants for six clerical positions in a mill.[9] In that same town, 15 out of 872 employees in the central mill during 1976 were women.[10] The number of positions available to women increases when the town has government offices, tourist facilities, or a regional shopping centre, as is the case in Campbell River. Nonetheless, the range of occupations remains limited mainly to services and clerical work. There are especially few openings for single women, and the wages are insufficient for their survival; thus daughters and estranged wives move out of resource towns.

Loggers

The logging sector of the industry has undergone substantial mechanization throughout the past decade. In one large camp where we conducted studies in 1977, 150 men were producing 24,000 cunits per day where it took 280 men to produce the same amount in 1967.[11] The cutback is attributable to a number of harvesting machines, especially useful on the flat terrain of the interior and the relatively small diameter trees there which permit machine operators to perform a range of tasks formerly requiring fallers, buckers, loaders, and numerous other specialized woodsmen. One faller and a skidder, together with a shearer or snipper machine, can now cut, delimb, and land 500 trees in a single day.

The composition of the remaining labour force has undergone a parallel change. A hierarchy associated with knowledge of the woods, experience, agility, and talent has been replaced with one dependent entirely on seniority. Recruits are required to have general machine operation skills, and these are, for the most part, interchangeable with the skills required in construction.

The organization of the labour force has also undergone changes. Loggers can no longer obtain their own supplies and small independent companies have virtually disappeared. However, about half of all logging is contracted out to small firms, known in the industry as "stump-to-dump" contractors. These, in turn, sub-contract about half of the work to "owner-operators." The stump-to-dump contractors are allotted a territory by the large corporation, and are responsible for logging it at a set piece or total rate. They employ maintenance workers on an hourly basis, and that part of the machinery which is too expensive for single owner-operators. The owner-operators do most of the actual logging and trucking, using their own skidders, trucks and other equipment, on a piece-rate basis. They have strong incentives to work at high speeds for long days and to complete the job as quickly as possible. The large company thereby obtains its labour and machinery and high productivity rates without incurring long-term liabilities. The risks are all shouldered by contractors and owner-operators under these arrangements. . . .

Milling

Sawmills and pulpmills are in different phases of development. Sawmills are mechanized, becoming automated; pulpmills are well into an automated stage. In addition, there are still some non-integrated and medium-sized sawmills in existence and a few speciality-cut mills. The selling market is fairly competitive — though increasingly oligopsonistic on supplies. Pulpmills operate in an oligopolistic international market. [Ed. note: oligopsony describes a market situation in which a few buyers control the demand from a large number of sellers, whereas oligopoly refers to a few sellers and many buyers.]

Both mechanization and automation lead to decreases in the labour component of production, but the decrease creates a higher ratio of capital to labour in automation, whereas mechanized industries are still labour intensive. Mechanization leads to a demand for unskilled workers; automation leads to a demand for skilled workers, and the ratio of skilled to unskilled is the reverse of mechanized industries. Because unskilled workers are in greater supply (and the definition of unskilled keeps being upgraded so that this proportion does not substantially change over time), mechanized industries can obtain a labour supply without providing long-term job security.

In addition, capital-intensive industries are extremely costly to operate at less than continuous and full production. The more capital invested in machinery, and the more reliant the industry on skilled workers, the more incentive there is to employers to create a permanent and secure labour force. Less expensive investments create fewer cost penalties for labour turnover.

These differences are evident in the working conditions, wage differentials, and employment practices of sawmills and pulpmills even where the two are owned by the same company and agglomerated at the same location. Sawmills, with a very high proportion of all workers doing unskilled and machine operation jobs under supervision, have high turnover rates. The employers' problems with transience, although much modified by the sharp increase in overall unemployment in B.C. since 1975, are the workers' responses to sawmill conditions. The work is repetitive, monotonous, individuated (assembly-style), and performed in extremely noisy and dusty conditions. Furthermore, the wage-scale is lower than in pulpmills, although wages for the same skill-levels — especially in integrated mills, where the comparison is accessible — would be the same. Jobs allow for little personal discretion, choice of pace or variability of quantity or content in the work, less than is the case for many workers in logging (not yet fully mechanized) or pulping (automated). Tradesmen are the only workers exempt from the general description. A small contingent of tradesmen is required for servicing machinery, and these operate on a sellers' market and so have both higher wages and more discretion. . . .

In order to obtain a stable core of workers, large mills have employed immigrants whose background is non-industrial and whose alternative employment opportunities are limited. At the present time many of these are from Portugal and India. These workers are extremely stable and unwilling to support strikes or other labour resistance actions. Their reasoning is that their first priority is to obtain steady incomes for their families, and their orientation is toward kin groups rather than work.[12] In this respect they resemble many earlier immigrant groups. The consequence is that these workers accumulate seniority though few become supervisors or tradesmen because of language barriers. This creates resentment amongst other workers, and these immigrants become the object of derision and hostility which is frequently expressed outside the mills in the streets, beer parlours, and town life. The racism cuts across the working class, divides it and weakens its bargaining capacity.

Pulpmills require fewer workers whose market value consists of physical strength, but also few craftsmen whose particular knowledge of the industry is necessary. Papermaking, for example, is now a computerized procedure ensuring high quality consistency. Thus engineering degrees take the place of apprenticeships in the art of papermaking. The skills demanded in automated mills are basic literacy, sometimes arithmetic literacy, ability to read computer printouts, and ability to learn how to operate automated control panels. A high proportion of workers in pulpmills is on salary, since the operation requires continuous production and the skills are consistent with traditional perceptions of technical and clerical rather than manual labour. This is symbolized by job titles, where machine-tenders rather than machine-operators predominate. Formal education levels are higher than for sawmills, and higher for the younger age groups than for the same groups in logging and sawmilling. It is only in the pulping sector of the industry that any perceptible difference in occupational levels and salary is connected with differences in education, though in all of the sectors the educational levels have steadily increased. An increasing number of younger workers have university degrees. . . .

As a consequence of the differences in working conditions, job security and wages, there is an increasing distance between the material standards, educational and skill levels, marketability, and lifestyles of pulpmill workers and saw and logging workers. The latter form the regional labour pool, mobile between jobs and available for various industrial employments throughout a region. The former become the stable core of industrial towns. The differences appear to be transferred in terms of opportunities to the next generation, but this must be stated tentatively because our sample is not large enough to provide compelling evidence, there are no secondary sources to test this, and the pulpmill industry of the interior is still too new to provide much inter-generational evidence. In our sample, the young recruits in a coastal pulp mill included more children of fathers in that sector than of fathers in sawmilling and logging, and altogether included a high portion of children whose fathers were owners, managers, or skilled tradesmen. In the youngest age group (18-24), several workers were regularly employed during summers by the pulp mill, and were undergoing university educations in engineering during the winters; their fathers were pulp-mill workers. Altogether there were very few immigrants in this work force except amongst tradesmen, and these were from industrial countries (a practice which allows employers to subsidize very little on-the-job apprenticeship training). . . .

Conclusions

There exists a body of theory for the industrial and social development of Canadian resource regions on which government and industrial policies are ostensibly based.[13] With minor variations, the theory posits an incremental growth in population size, employment, affluence, diversity of economic base, and stability and self-sufficiency of communities, around an initial staples base. Growth takes a sequential form by which the staples generate sufficient surplus to reinvest in further production facilities for new products out of the same staple (the forward linkages), and the machinery itself to produce both the original and new products (the backward linkages). These increments to the economic base will then demand a larger population of workers, and these in turn require ever more service and goods producing industries; an original resource community becomes a larger, more self-sufficient, and more stable town. . . .

The forestry industry has had a century to generate "spin-off" industrial growth in resource regions. Large companies have had highly favourable conditions for developing local economies, creating stability and self sufficiency of communities in which they have plants, and providing increasing levels of steady employment. They have had incentives in the form of long-term leases on their resource supplies and cooperative governments ready to supply infra-structure and helpful legislation. They have also had a labour force which is disciplined, schooled, and trained for an industrial society, a culture conducive to industrial development, and a physical environment suitable for a wide range of industries.

The evidence presented in this paper suggests, however, that the conventional theory cannot be sustained.

The alternative theory for the fate of a staples economy within monopoly capitalism rests on the assumption that industrial development will take place at the pace, in the form, and with the labour supplies and conditions which are most profitable to capital, and that stability will be determined by such factors as the relative profit incentives in various regions and the amortization costs of capital investments. It proceeds with no necessary expectations about the development of secondary industry, local utilization of surplus, or community growth and self sufficiency. These are all functions of cost-accounting decisions, and the accounting is done by large companies in their own interests and the class and metropolitan regions which most benefit from the extraction of resources from chronically under-developed regions. . . .

The long-term developments of this staples economy include widespread unemployment; steady decreases in labour control over pace and other working conditions even where the owner-operator form persists; skill debasement or machine-attendance as a substitute for skill; and disparities in rewards for participation. I would argue that these are not exclusively problems of capitalist economies, since precisely the same complex of conditions with the single exception of unemployment (which becomes under-employment instead) occurs within state monopoly industrial economies. Public ownership does not automatically lead to workers' control, community control, or self-sufficient regions. Both forms of monopoly have an imperative to destroy non-industrial cultures where these compete for the resource or the territory containing the resource. In Northern B.C. this especially affects native peoples who had managed to retain a hunting economy prior to the growth of forestry industries in the interior.[14]

Alternative strategies could be genuine alternatives only if power were dispersed, decentralized, and inaccessible to any single group of directors. With respect to the forestry industry, decentralization is entirely possible, without a loss in industrial capacity and with a potential net increase in productivity, a potential net decrease in destruction of the resource. Logging and sawmills are both recognized to be more efficient on smaller scales, and speciality products based on selective logging would increase the diversity of the economic base. The cost advantages of integrated facilities are not social advantages; they are merely advantages to capital and means of maintaining power over the industry. There is no reason to discard technological advantages of harvesting machines and efficient saws if these are, as they can easily be, situated in more and smaller locations under local control. Pulpmills are less easily dismantled. There is a stronger argument in favour of large units, but there is an even stronger argument in favour of less reliance on pulp and newsprint production in the overall economy. At the present time the technology rather than the needs of the workers, communities, or markets, determines the production rates.

One community group has analyzed the concentrated foreign-owned forestry industry in the central Kootenays, and detailed an alternative. This would involve a number of small mills each locally owned (type of ownership not specified), small logging companies engaged in selective logging, and both logging and manufacturing being directed toward specialized products rather than mass producton. These activities would be coordinated, together with resource utilization policies and reinvestment decisions, by a locally-based management committee. If both the resource and markets were accessible, this alternative would be feasible and it would significantly reduce the ecological damage presently occurring in local forest areas. There would be both a greater number of jobs and a greater range of occupational possibilities.[15]

The flaw in this plan, of course, is that neither the resource nor the market is accessible. Even if a provincial government were to radically alter resource policies in favour of small entrepreneurs, community-owned companies, or worker-controlled companies, these producers would require market access until their surplus could be reinvested in local communities and a more diverse range of industries. Protection of access would require cooperation at least at a national level; development would require financial support; and transportation of supplies as well as products would require a national-level government which is unable to ignore local needs and interests. In short, a small community cannot become independent or self-sufficient on its own, even where it has the resources and skills to produce a range of products. Without a restructuring of the larger economy, as long as the staple has market value or is depleted, a staples region will continue to produce staples. All that changes over time is labour, variable in more senses than one.

Notes

1. Exploratory research was conducted in the south-east region between 1974 and 1976. The major part of the study was conducted in Mackenzie (north-east), Terrace (north-west) and Campbell River (south coast) in 1977-1978. This consisted of interviews with all adult residents of 385 households, and questionnaire data for all residents over 12 years of age in 319 households. There were altogether 1418 respondents, 748 of these were interviewed. In addition, employers were interviewed, and data were gathered on regional economies and the industry. The research is still in progress, and analysis of interview and questionnaire data is not yet complete.

2. The exemption was brought about when the Hearst newspapers applied pressure on U.S. legislators. The suppliers in that country were claimed to be monopolistic in their pricing practices. For general histories of the industry see O.W. Taylor, *Timber, History of the Forest Industry in B.C.*, Vancouver: J.J. Douglas, 1975; Ed Gould, *Logging*, Saanichton: Hancock, 1975; and The B.C. Forest Industries *1965-66 Yearbook*, Section A, Vancouver: Mitchell, 1965.

3. MacMillan Bloedel is counted as a B.C. firm in this summary statement because the majority of its stockholders are in B.C., the head-offices and most of the production facilities are in the province. Nonetheless, the single largest stockholder is Canadian Pacific Investments, with 13.5 per cent.

4. Peter H. Pearse, Commissioner, Report of the Royal Commission on Forest Resources, *Timber Rights and Forest Policy in British Columbia*, Victoria: Queen's Printer, 1976, vol. I, Table 4.1, p. 36.

5. F.L.C. Reed and Associates Ltd., *The British Columbia Forest Industry, Its Direct and Indirect Impact on the Economy*, Report prepared for the B.C. Government, Department of Lands, Forests, and Water Resources, 1973, Table 7, p. 63.

6. Pearse, vol. 1, Table 4.1, p. 36.

7. All employment figures cited in this section are from special runs provided by Mr. Tony Laanemae, Forestry Advisor, Statistics Canada, Vancouver Office, and Statistics Canada Annual publications on Logging, Sawmills, and Pulpmills. Figures for 1961 employment in logging are not available in comparable form to subsequent years. It is the practice in the industry to base projections and summaries on good years. In the Reed publication cited above, for example, data for 1970 were the most recent data available, but data for 1969 were given as well because, in the opinion of the consultants, "1969 is a more representative year." F.L.C. Reed, op. cit., p. 9.

8. Ronald N. Byron, *Community Stability and Regional Economic Development*, unpublished Ph.D. thesis, University of British Columbia, 1976, pp. 90-137.

9. Joan Kotarski, "Mackenzie Report," in *Northern B.C. Women's Task Force on Single Industry Resource Communities*, 1977, p. 90. The mill figure was given to us by that company.

10. B.C. Forest Products, *Annual Report*, 1976, cited in Kotarski, op. cit., p. 90-94.

11. B.C. Forest Products camp, data provided by the company.

12. Interview data obtained with the aide of translators. The kin-group orientation has also been noted by Annama Joy in studies of immigrant workers in the Okanagan currently in progress, and I am grateful to her for sharing her information.

13. The theory is implicit throughout both federal and provincial regional reports and "social impact" studies conducted for new development proposals. At the level of theory, expansion around a staples base was discussed by W.A. Mackintosh, "Economic Factors in Canadian History," *The Canadian Historical Review*, vol. IV, No. 1, March 1923, pp. 12-25, and by the neo-classical economists who followed him; and in B.C. the theory is expressed most eloquently in P.A. Shearer, (ed.), *Exploiting our Economic Potential: Public Policy and the British Columbia Economy.*

14. The destruction of Indian communities by large-scale logging over hunting and trapping grounds is dealt with in other papers, and has recently been discussed by Douglas Hudson in "Bush and Bulldozer: A Clash of Staples in Northern British Columbia," *mimeo* paper presented to Science and Technology Studies Colloquium, University of British Columbia, October 19-20, 1978.

15. Slocan Valley Community Forest Management Project, *Report*, 1974.

7/Changing Modes of Social Control in a New Brunswick Fish Packing Town*

Joan McFarland

Along with the constantly diminishing number of the magnates of capital, who usurp and monopolise all advantages of this process of transformation, grows the mass of misery, oppression, slavery, degradation, exploitation; but with this too grows the *revolt* of the working class, a class always increasing in numbers, and disciplined, united, organized by the very mechanism of the process of capitalist production itself. (*Capital*, Vol. I, p. 715, italics mine)

Marx and Marxist writers in discussing worker revolt have been primarily concerned with the question of revolt against capitalism as a system. More recently, a literature has developed which looks at worker resistance which does not threaten the system.[1] A major aim of this paper is to explain the lack of revolt in the former sense by a group of women packers in a New Brunswick fish-packing town. A subsidiary aim is to examine worker resistance in the latter sense.

Of course, worker's failure to *revolt* in Marx's general sense of the term has been observed in different degrees throughout the western world, and has been the subject of much analysis. On the one hand, various factors external to the workplace have been invoked. Such institutions as the school and mass media are seen as playing major roles in this: the school system in preparing children ideologically to be workers and the mass media in persuading workers that satisfaction from higher levels of consumption can substitute for meaningful work. In addition, analysis of the family suggests that the woman's position of dependence there causes her to put conservative pressures on the worker both directly and indirectly.

---

* Abridged from Joan McFarland, "Changing Modes of Social Control in a New Brunswick Fish Packing Town," *Studies in Political Economy* 4 (Autumn) 1980, pp. 99-113. Reprinted with permission of the publisher and the author.

On the other hand, factors internal to the workplace have been examined. At the workplace itself, it is argued, the process of homogenization of labour characteristic of earlier stages of capitalist production (i.e. Marx's "modern industry") has been replaced by a process of labour market segmentation and stratification in monopoly capitalism. Workers thus develop a status consciousness which submerges class consciousness. And lastly, at the level of the labour process, certain forces have appeared which atomize rather than collectivize workers. Production does take place in the "large socialized workplaces" which Marx predicted would produce the "gravediggers of capitalism" but it is often organized serially so that workers are in fact physically separated from each other. In addition, noise and certain disciplinary factors severely limit worker interaction.[2]

Thus, at all levels, impediments to the emergence of workers' revolutionary consciousness have been identified. Of course, few of these impediments are accidental. Most have been created by capitalists as instruments of control over the workplace. Different instruments seem important in different situations. In the case of the fish packers, two particular instruments seem crucial — one external to the work situation, one internal. The first is the fact that the factory is located in a company town, and the second is the system of payment by piecework. From both of these there are spinoffs involving practically all of the other above mentioned elements.

But stating that the fish packers at the plant do not revolt is not to suggest that the packers always act in the interests of capital. Rather, they act in ways that they perceive to be in their own self-interest, regardless of the repercussions for capital. In the recent writings on worker resistance, it is argued that forms of worker resistance which do not directly challenge capitalist relations of production also require study since they have an effect on capitalist development; that is, capital undergoes changes in the course of accommodating and co-opting such resistance. Certain actions of the packers can be interpreted as worker resistance in the above sense, and there has been a response by capital to at least one of them. . . .

The Company Town
The town I studied has a population of sixteen hundred of whom about 80 per cent are of English-speaking origin, and 20 per cent French speaking. Many of the workers are third and fourth generation residents. People from other parts of the province have migrated there in search of work over the years, particularly during the Depression.

The Company is one of the biggest fish companies in New Brunswick. Figures from 1976 list it as having 2,000 employees, sales of $35 millions and profits of over one million dollars. It has had three owners. It was begun by a local family in 1883. In 1923, it was bought out by a prominent New Brunswick family which is primarily responsible for having built up the company and the town. This family sold out to one of the biggest Canadian conglomerates in 1966. However, in 1979 the son of the former owner was still the local boss. Thus much of the day to day routine remains unchanged. Also, there are few new faces on the plant floor, although this is not the case behind the scenes in upper management. One of the consequences of this situation is that some of the workers are either not aware, or only vaguely aware of the changed ownership. However, despite its deliberately low profile, the conglomerate has substantially changed the direction, policies and approach of the company including the handling of the workers.

The workers at the plant are presently not unionized and never have been. There has been only one attempt at unionization, in the early seventies. However, although the required number of workers were signed up — at the company town plant and two others — the company fought hard and was able to have the application for certification rejected on the basis that everyone in town was really a company employee, not just the plant workers.[3] The company's strong resistance might in part be explained by its experiences with a much larger British Columbia fish company under its control, organized by a very militant union. . . .

The Company Town as an Instrument of Social Control

The way this company town is set up allows it to act as a blunt but effective instrument of social control. First, it creates a situation of complete dependence by the employees on the company. Second, it enables the company to control the supply of labour by determining who may or may not live in the town. Specifically, it allows the company to get rid of actual and potential troublemakers. And finally, it gives the company ideological power by being the only public voice heard in the town, directly controlling such public institutions as the theatre and press, and indirectly controlling the school and churches.

Up until 1972 when the town was incorporated, the company owned all the property in it. Stories from the pre-1950s period include accounts of a stop-post on the main road into town where one was asked the nature of one's business before being allowed to proceed. The company still owns most of the houses in the town, many of them built during the war and heavily subsidized by the government. (A 1977 survey showed 83 houses occupier-owned, 1174 rented. The largest proportion of those owning would be management and retired people, while virtually all of those renting would be workers.) Company houses have always been rented out to employees at below market rents. The company owns the theatre, rink, restaurant, hotel, grocery and general store. Prior to 1972, they even had their own police force and firefighters.

The dependency of the employees on the company has resulted in a combination of feelings of fear and gratitude. The fear is a result of the company's authoritarianism and very harsh treatment of employees who do not tow the line. Firings are swift and arbitrary. The contract allows "dismissals for just cause," which is then left undefined. A worker is quietly drawn aside at the end of the day and told not to come back. If the individual is a member of a long-employed company family, the family pleads for a second chance. This is usually granted upon certain conditions — i.e. that the family take over responsibility for the individual's work conduct. However, if the individual is an outsider, that is the end of it.

The treatment of the employees who became involved in the union organizing of 1970-71 was particularly harsh. A committee of 45 to 50 people had been established to undertake the task which had to be carried out in complete secrecy. Following the decision by the Industrial Relations Board not to grant certification, the company fired all of the members of the secret committee and evicted them from the town. This incident seems to have left an indelible impression on the remaining employees.

As a last example, the company does not allow welfare recipients or unauthorized unemployment insurance recipients to live in the town. There was a widow with several young children whose husband, a plant employee, had died of cancer. She was on welfare, having refused to work in the plant because she attributed her husband's death to his work there. The company would not tolerate this. She was evicted from a company house and thus from the town. Similarly, if an individual tries to collect unemployment insurance benefits, the Unemployment Insurance Commission office calls up the personnel manager who will give assurances that work is available at the plant and the person's benefits are cut off. Through these policies, the message is effectively conveyed that every able-bodied person must work.

The gratitude arises from the fact that the company has provided employment and thus a livelihood for these families over the years, especially during the Depression when others in the province had gone hungry. Gratitude in the past was also a result of the personality of the previous owner. Evidently, he was the kind of boss who could be found every day on the plant floor and knew each employee and every member of his or her family by name. He was also the kind of man that any employee felt they could ask for a personal favour — e.g., a loan of $100 until next payday, or a better rental. He also "looked after" the poorer families by giving Christmas baskets with turkeys and all the trimmings once a year....

Another company strategy allowed by the company town is that of a news blackout. Previously, the company had its own paper. Now there is none and none of the newspapers in the surrounding area covers village news of any other than a birth, death, or reunion nature. The result is a total lack of perspective by the company workers regarding their own situation. They know very little about the company. For example, they can give only the vaguest accounts of the 1966 conglomerate take-over or the 1971 union certification failure. The company is particularly paranoid about the dangers of media stories, having been nearly burned by an article in a now defunct regional left magazine and subsequent CBC coverage. The company confiscated all copies of the magazine in town and dealt harshly with the CBC interviewee.[4] . . .

In conclusion, then, there is no way that this company could have had the kind of workforce it has employed over the past some fifty years were it not for its creation of a company town. The dependence, fear, gratitude, stability, and non-militance of the workers are all directly and indirectly bound up in this control by the company of their lives, as well as their labour-power.

Piecework as an Instrument of Social Control

If the company town maintains an obedient and stable workforce for the company, the system of piecework used for a particular group of workers, the fish packers, results not only in a maximum amount of output but also in very positive work attitudes, independently of either fear or gratitude. This does not mean there is no worker resistance of any description. Forms of worker resistance practised by these women which do not put them in opposition to capital, but which nevertheless are against the interests of capital, will be examined. Finally, it will be shown that piecework in this case also has the important side effect of dividing the workers, not by creating antagonisms between them but by creating in them different attitudes to their work and the company.

The packers' work consists of cutting the heads and tails off raw fish (herring) and placing the fish in cans. It is something anyone with at least some manual dexterity could do if they were able to take their time. But these women do it at a tremendous pace — and they have to in order to keep their jobs. With the fastest packers, you can't even see their hands when they are packing, they are moving so fast. They also develop unique body motions and rhythms to enable them to keep up their pace. In other words, although the operation itself is a fairly simple one, to do it at the pace that they keep up is a skilled job — a skill that takes from several years to a lifetime to develop.

Payment is by piecework. The packers get paid according to the number of cases of fish they pack. The rates vary according to the size of fish packed and the size of the cans. Until the end of the sixties, there was no base rate for packers. In the words of a packer, "what we packed was what we got." Now there is a base rate but it is the lowest hourly rate in the plant. Further, if a packer consistently does not pack the equivalent of a base rate, she is let go from the job. In the earliest Employee Committee contract, 1973-74, there were lower piece-rates and a bonus system based on annual piece-rates, presumably for the incentive effect.

The packers like their work — some of them even talk about loving it — and they work very hard at it. They also like the piecework system. The packers work hard because they believe that it is to their advantage to do so. The principal reason they give for working hard is the pay. Certainly, with the newer contracts, pay is much better than it used to be. And because the pay is by piecework, the harder they work, the more they get paid. A second reason why they work hard is because being a fast packer is a source of respect and recognition in the plant and community. The company fosters this aspect by sponsoring an annual packing contest where the fastest packers from each of the plants compete. Thirdly, they work hard because the faster they pack, the less boring the job is. Most of them race against the clock which makes the day go by much faster. By contrast, for the packers hourwork is deadly dull and almost without exception they hate it. Finally, the job involves self-discipline rather than discipline by management. As long as a packer "makes her hour," that is, packs at least the equivalent of the base rate, at piece-rates, then she is left pretty much alone. For example, she may talk but it slows down her packing and also it is hard to hear above the noise in the plant. Management's only apparent concern, beyond the packer making her hour, is that she arrive on time and stay at her table during the work period.

All of this is very advantageous to the company. It results in maximum productivity and workers with positive job attitudes. And this is in spite of very difficult working conditions. The new plant is a windowless structure where the packers work standing on a concrete floor. It is very cold and dank because of the freezing facilities and the fact that the outside door is often left open for receiving fish. Many of the packers suffer from rheumatism of the spine from the combination of standing on a concrete floor and from handling fish which haven't been sufficiently thawed. Soft fish also give many of the packers rashes on their arms. Packing is also dangerous work. Packers periodically cut their fingers or are stabbed by a tablemate when both grab for the same fish at the same time. However, all of this is accepted by the packers. They dismiss it all as being in the nature of the job.

Another of the packers' responses which is advantageous to the company is that they are not involved in "soldiering." Marx predicted that piece-workers would resist that system of payment when they realized that the faster they worked the lower the rates would be set.[5] There is evidence that piece-workers do indeed resist and that the most common form that this resistance takes is that of systematic soldiering — that is, a collective holding back of production to avoid the cutting of piece-rates.[6] There are several possible explanations for these packers' lack of systematic soldiering. First, there are over 120 packers at this plant to organize. Furthermore, all of the other company plants are under the same contract and this on the same piece-rates. It would be difficult to organize all of these workers. Secondly, the packers are under the impression that piece-rates have never been cut, only raised in the past. In fact, from my study of the rates in the contracts, it is true that piece-rates on the old products have only been raised. The effect of these rates on the workers' daily pay is substantial. However, the rates on a new type of fish which is already pre-cut by machine before it gets to the packers has been set extremely low. Thirdly, as mentioned already, much of the satisfaction in the job is from being able to pack fast — a kind of satisfaction which couldn't be derived from soldiering.

A final response of the packers, which plays into the company's hands, is that they are not in favour of unions and are glad that there is no union at the plant. They haven't forgotten the group of workers who were fired when the attempt at unionizing was tried, although they probably only vaguely know what actually occurred. However, in addition, they hate the idea of strikes since when there is a strike an employee cannot work even if she wants to. With the packer's interest in hard work for good money, the whole idea holds little appeal.

All this is evidence of the packers' lack of revolt in the Marxian sense of the term, revolt against the system itself. They do not see themselves as being in opposition to capital. Not only do they work incredibly hard but they do not collectively soldier and they are not in favour of unions and strikes. Their reason for the latter two responses is basically the first, that both systematic soldiering and unions would interfere with their opportunity to work as hard as possible. And they have their reasons for wanting to work hard: to make money, to earn respect in the plant and community, to make the day go by faster and for the autonomy involved in self-discipline.

But it is important to avoid oversimplifying the packers' responses. The basic explanation of their behaviour is that they act in ways that they believe will individually benefit themselves. And this is whether or not this benefits the company. Certain of their responses, indeed, are not to the advantage of the company. For example, the packers only "go all out" when they think that they can earn a lot of money by doing so. On the pre-cut fish, they don't "go all out" because they know that no matter how hard they work, they will only make the base rate. Also, when they are going all out, they waste a lot of fish by not packing all of the fish in the bucket. As they get towards the bottom of the bucket, where the pickings become slim, they throw the rest out for the production of piecemeal — a lower value product. Finally and apparently as a result of the perceived good wages, a group of packers only turns up three or four days a week for work. In other words, there is a "backward-bending" supply curve of labour. Management is aware of this situation but because of the shortage of packers — all of the available women in town are already employed — it chooses to close its eyes to this practice in the short-run. This has, however, stimulated the company to step up its automation plans — the pre-cut fish being a first step in this direction.

Finally, although the packers are not in favour of strikes and unions, there have been some walk-outs by the packers on a spontaneous basis. For example, several years ago, a group of packers walked out when they felt that compulsory overtime was becoming excessive. Originally, the company threatened to fire them all, then agreed to take them back if they came back within two days. Some went back within that time, others stayed out longer. Those that came back within the agreed time period lost their pay for those days while the ones who stayed longer lost all of their seniority with the company. A more recent incident involved a threatened walk-out over the parking facilities for packers at the new plant. In this case, the company did back down. It is also not uncommon for an individual packer to walk out if she becomes fed up enough. She is usually allowed back with the appropriate penalty — often the loss of all seniority.

These walk-outs would seem in contradiction to the packers' attitudes towards strikes. However, they are not really out of character. They are all voluntary. No one is telling the packers what to do. No collective organization seems to take place before or after the event. It is just that in these cases the packers involved all respond in the same way to the same aggravations.

Although the company has probably kept the piecework system over the years because of its effect on output and attitudes, it also had important side effects in dividing the workers. The division does not appear to be between male and female workers because quite a number of female workers are also in the plant doing assembly-line jobs. Rather, the division appears to be between piece-workers (the packers) and the rest — roughly a fifty-fifty split in terms of numbers at the plant. This division is not an antagonism — just as the English-French ethnic division is not an antagonism — but it creates different attitudes toward their own work and the others' work. The packers love packing, work as hard as possible and like the system of piecework. They hate the very idea of hourwork which they consider unbearably boring. The other workers are more or less indifferent to their jobs and only work as hard as they have to. They are very glad they are not packing, which they consider to be dirty and dangerous. In addition, they dislike the idea of a piecework system of payment which they believe forces one to work too hard. So although there are no apparent antagonisms between workers at the plant — they all identify with each other as workers — the division in attitudes has an effect on the general level of militancy and any potential collective action at the plant.

Notes

1. Of particular note here are the writings of Andrew L. Friedman. See his *Industry and Labour: Class Struggle at Work and Monopoly Capitalism* (London: Macmillan, 1977), especially the discussion in Ch. 4. Also suggesting this general approach is the article "Uncovering the Hidden History of the American Workplace" by the Work Relations Group in *The Review of Radical Political Economics*, Vol. 10, No. 4, Winter 1978.

2. Examples of this literature would include: re the schools, Samuel Bowles and Herbert Gintis, *Schooling in Capitalist America* (New York: Basic Books, 1976); re the mass media, Herbert Marcuse, *One Dimensional Man* (Boston: Beacon Press, 1964); re the family, Dorothy Smith, "Women, the Family and Corporate Capitalism" in *Women in Canada*, ed. Marylee Stephenson (Toronto: New Press, 1973); re labour market segmentation and stratification, Howard M. Wachtel, "Class Consciousness and Stratification in the Labour Process" in *Labour Market Segmentation*, ed. Richard C. Edwards, Michael Reich, and David M. Gordon (Lexington, Mass.: D.C. Heath, 1975); and re the labour process, John and Barbara Ehrenreich, "Work and Consciousness" in *Technology, the Labor Process and the Working Class* (New York: Monthly Review Press, 1976).

3. This information was obtained from the union which tried to organize the plant, and the Industrial Relations Board of New Brunswick.

4. A condition of my employment also was that I would not release my results to the media. Writing an article for an academic journal, however, did not seem to pose any problems for them.

5. *Capital* (Moscow: Progress Publishers), Vol. I, p. 523.

6. See, for example, the work of Donald F. Roy on this: "Quota Restriction and Goldbricking in a Machine Shop," *The American Journal of Sociology*, Vol. 57, No. 5, 1951-52; "Work Satisfaction and Social Reward in Quota Achievement: An Analysis of Piecework Incentive," *American Sociological Review*, Vol. 18, No. 5, 1953; and "Efficiency and 'The Fix': Informal Intergroup Relations in a Piecework Machine Shop," *The American Journal of Sociology*, Vol. 60, No. 3, 1954.

8/The Sales Clerks: Worker Discontent and Obstacles to its Collective Expression[*]

Pamela H. Sugiman

Research Problem

The current literature is overflowing with studies which focus on the quality of working life in advanced capitalist societies. One of the problems with this literature, however, is that most of the studies have looked solely at the male "blue-collar" industrial worker.[1] Although this worker remains a significant force in the Canadian economy,[2] there is another force which has acquired an equally important role — the female service worker. During the past few decades, Canadians have witnessed a dramatic expansion of the tertiary sector and a subsequent increase in the number of females entering the paid labour market.[3] As the women who enter this field possess a set of life experiences and problems which are quite different from those of men, one would assume that they would also have distinct work experiences.

The first part of this paper focuses on department store clerks as an example of women who participate in low-level service jobs. Here it is demonstrated that the work of store clerks is stress-inducing, boring and degrading and that the women perceive their jobs with much dissatisfaction and discontent. The second section of this paper examines the sale clerks' responses to this work situation. Generally, worker responses to negatively perceived working conditions fall into two categories: overt and covert. Overt responses include such actions as unionization, collective bargaining, strikes, worker sit-downs, wild-cat strikes and the like. Covert responses involve such behaviours as absenteeism, day-dreaming, and gameplaying. The latter are largely individual reactions while the former are collective. Industrial workers have tended to exhibit both types of behaviour.[4] Although they engage in the hidden behaviours, they have also been fairly organized, active, and somewhat militant in expressing their demands and discontents in the

* Abridged from Pamela H. Sugiman, "The Sales Clerks: Worker Discontent and Obstacles to its Collective Expression." *Atlantis* 8 (1) 1982, pp. 13-33. Reprinted with the permission of the publisher and the author.

workplace. The problem is that, although they are similarly discontented, retail clerks have tended to reveal this discontent mainly in covert and individual ways. The collective and open expression of discontent in the form of unionization, insurrection, and even unofficial on-the-job confrontation with employers, is exceedingly rare among this group of workers.[5] How can this tendency be explained?

There are several intervening variables to be considered. These may be divided into two major categories: worker adjustments and social structural conditions. Worker adjustments include such behaviours as daydreaming, consumerism, and social interaction. Adjustive behaviour is ironically both an indicator of discontent and a barrier against meaningful social change on a societal scale, and even on a company or industry-wide scale. The second set of obstacles is social structural. One asks questions such as: have sales clerks remained passive because of the social organization, content, or process of their work? Are sales clerks and service workers, as a whole, becoming increasingly "proletarianized," as scholars such as C. Wright Mills[6] and Braverman[7] have argued? Are sales clerks unorganized because there is a large reserve army of labour in this occupation? Is this occupation's overrepresentation of women a significant variable? And can the sales clerks' inaction be attributed to their size and lack of resources in terms of skill, time, and concentration? This study provides empirical evidence which allows these questions to be addressed more explicitly and fully than previously.

Methods

A combination of participant observation and informal interviewing was used in this study. The field work involved my part-time employment as a sales clerk in the book department of a large, urban, department store in Toronto. Observation was most appropriate for the study's objectives, as the research was largely descriptive. Furthermore, interviewing alone would have been insufficient to study actual working conditions and worker responses because of the problems of recall, selective perception, and reality versus the respondent's perception of reality. It was therefore preferable to observe behaviour, rather than to simply ask individuals about their behaviour. My employment permitted me to develop contacts for later interviews. The size of the interview sample remained small — nineteen sales clerks — because the interviews were very thorough and only supplemented the field work. . . .

The Pecking Order

For this company, a multi-national whose origins date back to pre-Confederation days, retailing is only one of its many functions. The retailing division itself is split into numerous regions. The region in which I worked is, in turn, divided into one central urban store and numerous suburban and small town branches. The store where I was employed is divided into divisions which, in turn, are split into departments.

The hierarchy or chain of command begins with the sales clerks who are divided into auxiliary, regular part-time, and full-time staff. These sales clerks report to their supervisor or department head. Their supervisor, in turn, reports to the assistant department manager who reports to her boss, the department manager. The department manager is responsible to the divisional manager who is responsible to the general manager who reports to the president. Parenthetically, the majority of sales clerks and supervisors are female, whereas most of the positions above that of assistant manager are held by males. Most large organizations have such divisions and hierarchical levels, but they are most striking in this store because lines of communication seldom if ever skip one level. As a divisional manager walks through your department and, for example, does not like the way a particular book is displayed, he does not tell you. He goes back to his office and sends a memo to your department manager. But your manager does not tell you either. Instead, he relays the message to your assistant manager who either informs your supervisor or approaches you directly. The entire process of communication seems ludicrous to the sales clerks. Because of this filtering process, only one out of all the clerks with whom I worked knew who her real bosses were, beyond her department manager. We encountered them everyday, but we certainly could not identify them.

Another important staff department is security. Many of the clerks are unaware of precisely who is and who is not with security. Security consists of people who wander about the department, lingering behind the shelves. Their authority is clearly above that of the clerks, for the job of catching shoplifters, in their view, is far more serious than processing customers' purchases. One often wonders, though, if they are more concerned with catching the sales staff than anyone else. Security demands that the clerks enter and exit by a specified door, and that they not shop during their breaks and lunch hours. Furthermore, these security officers inspect the clerk's store-bought parcels as well as her personal belongings. If the sales clerks fail to put these items in a specified room while they are working, security takes their names as they leave at night. Finally, a department manager must inspect their personal belongings and list the contents, with detailed descriptions, on a parcel slip. If a sales clerk is not able to produce such a parcel slip, security confiscates her belongings. The women whom I interviewed found all of these security measures insulting, not only to themselves, but also to the customers.

Authority
Apart from the staff specialists, authority is clearly defined and recognizable. In simple terms, there are those with coloured badges and those without. People with these badges must authorize all cheques, price changes, refunds, exchanges, and voids. People without them must run around the store chasing after those with them. This regulation produces desperation amongst some of the women, as they frequently have to go down to the next floor to find a "signature." This often means leaving the department unattended and facing an angry, impatient customer

upon return. It is degrading to the sales clerk to have to chase after one of these "signatures" for permission to give a refund of $3.95 or to accept a cheque for $10.00. But it is even more humiliating when many of these so-called "signatures" regard you as a pest and attempt to brush you off because they are busily on their way home or off to lunch. In the meantime, the clerk must show the utmost in deference and courteousness, both to the impertinent, condescending "signature" and to the impatient customer.

The sales clerk has no authority within the organization. The message is clear. She is constantly reminded of her position within the hierarchy. As one respondent states, "It's bad enough that they constantly enforce your lowly position through their rules and regulations, but it's colour-coded as well so that everyone can see your badge is one colour, theirs is another. To them, we're nothing but a big expense."

Rules

Rules about cheque authorization and security practices are only a few out of many. There are also rules concerning the women's telephone behaviour, their physical appearance and overall demeanor. The women are told to answer the telephone in a standardized way. Instead of simply saying "hello," they must say "good morning," state the company's name, their particular department, their own name, and politely ask, "May I help you?" All of this must be uttered in a pleasant, deferent tone. One woman describes how angry her manager became when she departed slightly from the mandatory script:

One afternoon, two weeks after I started, the phone rang. I answered it as I was told. But when the man on the other end asked for a clerk who was out, I responded, "I'm sorry, she's out to lunch." This man, who then identified himself as the manager, furiously told me never to say that again. He hysterically told me that customers don't like to hear that clerks are gone for lunch. According to him, I could have lost them a sale. I was supposed to ask for his phone number, so that she could call him back.

The company also issues a dress code. Women are told to wear "sensible" clothes. If pants are worn, they must be part of a pantsuit, and stockings are essential. Jeans, except for those who work in departments which sell jeans, are strictly forbidden. All of these dress regulations are instituted to keep up the company's image. In doing so, however, the employer dictates behaviour which is not related to the clerk's actual work performance.

Rules about time are also numerous. Upon arrival, the clerk is required to sign her name on the time sheets. If she fails to do this, she will not be paid. And although some managers are more lenient than others, punctuality is generally stressed. One manager hides the time schedule if a clerk is due at 9:15 and his watch reads 9:18. As a result, she cannot sign in. Respondents from one store also note that if they are three minutes late their pay is deducted for fifteen minutes. Yet, in the same store, the clerks are only paid until 9:00 even though they must stay and close the department until about twenty minutes past 9:00. . . .

Another illogical rule concerns pretending to look busy. Even if there are no customers in the department, the clerk must appear as though she is working steadfastly. Furthermore, she is prohibited from sitting down, reading a magazine (reading is a sin for which one woman was fired), and even standing still and staring into space. Partly because of the location of the department, and partly because of the presence of "spies," one must always try to look busy. This demand usually leads to pacing the department and straightening up the shelves — tasks which soon result in incredible fatigue.

The women adhere to all these rules and take them seriously because they have a lingering fear that someone is watching them. And to a large degree, their fears are well-founded. Initially, I thought they were acting in a somewhat paranoid fashion. I soon learned otherwise. "Spies" are the women's term for what the store calls "shoppers." These are people who inspect the clerks while posing as regular customers. The nastiness of this practice is obvious, but it is intensified as these inspectors are sent out during the busiest times of the year, times when the clerks are most likely to be irritable. In the words of one woman, "They test your tolerance level."

The clerk is graded according to her appearance, grooming, mannerisms, speech, pleasantness, salesmanship, and the like. She receives extra points if she says: "Will this be on your _____account?" rather than a simple "thank-you." A perfect score is one hundred. The report is never seen by the clerk, but is immediately transferred to her manager and eventually ends up in personnel files. In fact, most clerks are not even aware of having been inspected. . . .

A Typical Day

Most of the clerks and especially the younger women, arrive at work in a negative frame of mind. "Are you ready for another boring day?," "I'm so tired," "I don't feel like working today," and "I feel so sick," are phrases which both I and other sales clerks uttered with clock-like regularity about ten minutes after our arrival at the store. I doubt if we were even conscious of our dismal whining. Although we were aware of the time schedule one week in advance, when the time to work finally arrived we frequently tried to get out of it. For example, after about one hour's work, one young woman would evaluate her current financial status. "Do I need much money this week?" If the answer was no, she would try to get out of working her six hour shift by asking others if they would work for her. Rarely would anyone consent, but she made this attempt regularly. It is not that these women are dismal, pessimistic creatures by nature, they do not have bleak outlooks on life in general. However, when faced with the much dreaded prospect of spending another day at the store, a shroud seems to fall over them. Thus, while emotionally and mentally withdrawn, we physically carry out our patterned tasks and engage in a verbal exchange of negative rhetoric.

Content of the Work

What does a sales clerk do? The answer may seem obvious since this is a job which is performed in the public eye. But as with any occupation, a cursory look tells little about what is actually going on. One must, therefore, examine all aspects of the work from its content, the work process, and on-the-job interaction to its social organization.

Today a sales clerk actually does little selling. The main function of the clerk is to "process" the customers' purchases. The secondary functions are related to the maintenance of stock and similar duties. In the sense that the customer asks the clerk for directions or the price of an item, there is a certain amount of customer-clerk interaction, but the traditional sense of selling by way of promoting and discussing the merchandise is notably absent. Perhaps it has not disappeared as dramatically in the smaller, more personal retail outlets, but in large, bureaucratic department stores such as this one, it has become obsolete. Currently, the sales clerk is given so many other functions that, ironically, the customer is regarded as a nuisance.

Another striking aspect of the work is the similarity it bears to so-called "blue-collar work." As Rinehart says, technological and structural changes in the retailing industry have been pushing them closer and closer to this kind of work.[8] "White-collar" jobs have traditionally been viewed by many as an escape from factory work. But they now bear a strong resemblance to blue-collar work.

Just as the factory system eroded craft skills and centralized decision-making, so bureaucracies have simplified, mechanized, and rationalized jobs, placing the vast majority of white-collar employees in positions where their work is defined and controlled from above.[9]

With these two themes in mind, this is what happens during a typical day. Upon arrival, you head for the cash office where you state your terminal number, are handed a set of keys and pick up some forms. You then proceed to your department where you "open" the terminal. This consists of inserting the appropriate keys in the appropriate key holes and pressing numbers and codes in the proper sequence. The machine does all the work, recording, multiplying, and totalling the figures you enter. All of these steps require a minimum of concentration and effort. And, furthermore, these instructions are carefully written out under the titles, "opening procedures" and "closing procedures" in a manual which is affixed to the terminal. Anyone who can read can perform these operations. . . .

The meaninglessness and monotony of these repeated tasks help explain the clerks' detachment from their work. The bosses give them isolated tasks in the form of lists or abrupt, verbal instructions, offering little explanation about the purpose of the task or its relevance within a wider framework. Furthermore, the bosses dictate exactly how the job is to be done, when it is to be done and who is to do it. If they feel that Beth can tidy up most efficiently and Louise can count books more accurately, then Beth must tidy and Louise must count. There is little concern for the worker's individual choice in the matter. Similarly, the women are rarely, if ever, told about an upcoming sale or autograph session in their own department. They eventually learn about these events through customers. Few of us were even aware that the store was accepting a certain charge card until the customers handed them to us.

The Terminal

Aside from the above mentioned tasks, the central job of the clerk is to process the customers' purchases. A customer approaches the counter with a book. Sometimes the clerk says "hello," and asks how the merchandise will be paid for, slips the bill into the terminal, presses the codes, categories, and prices, places a pen and bill in front of the customer and asks him/her to sign. She then places the merchandise in a bag and utters a prefunctory "thank you." The most striking aspect of this process is its resemblance to assembly line work with its standardization of physical movements. This analogy becomes increasingly apparent during the Christmas season when customers are lined up in front of the counter like bottles waiting to be capped. They keep coming at you, you ring them through. The aim is to get through them as fast as possible. However, this is difficult since most of the sales clerks are far from adept at operating the machine. They continually make errors by pressing the wrong code or entering numbers in the wrong sequence. Consequently, they can often be seen simply standing in front of the terminal frantically pressing all the keys in the hope of at least retrieving the sales slip.
...

Discipline and Subordination

In light of the low opinion and lack of respect workers have toward their bosses, one wonders how discipline is enforced. The answer lies primarily in the employer's ultimate power to fire and, to a lesser extent, upon the supervisor's sole authority in assigning the women their weekly hours. This also helps explain the good surface relations between workers and management.

The supervisor not only dictates the pace, allocation, and performance of one's work, but also one's demeanor. The clerks fail to openly express their hostility towards management because a great deal rests on the latter's personal view of them, not as workers, but as individual people. Thus, to use a colloquial expression, much "ass-kissing" goes on. Friendship with management definitely helps the clerk on the job. A wage increase above the standard amount is given to the clerk only upon the boss's special request. The women, therefore, feel that it is wise to "get in good" with the supervisor. Also, as the supervisor makes up the weekly time schedule, being in her favour leads to the assignment of more hours. All this, of course, has an adverse effect on worker solidarity, as it causes the women to "pass the buck" when a job is improperly performed.

The supervisor's authority in making up the time schedule is indeed used as a threat to the clerks. Several times during the week our supervisor would call me up and ask me to come in to work on the very afternoon because she needed extra help. When I declined she became extremely agitated. Another day, before she called another woman for the same purpose, she remarked to me, "Well, if she doesn't want the hours now, she'll just see how many she gets next week." Often the supervisor reduces a clerk to three or zero hours a week, in order to "smarten her up." The women fear and obey management and its rules because they are clearly aware of the latter's power to fire them. Since the clerks are not unionized they are often fired arbitrarily.

Low-level management frequently uses this power as a disciplinary tactic. During my field work our supervisor told us we were not performing satisfactorily. She explained to me that, despite her absence, she knew when a clerk was busy by taking a sales reading from the terminal before leaving, and then taking another one upon her return. A few days later this supervisor fired a clerk, claiming that she was never available to work when asked. This was a flimsy excuse, as I later learned that the woman had previously informed the personnel department that she would only be available during specified days of the week and personnel consented to this arrangement. I also learned that, although this woman's name was taken off our department time schedule, she was not formally fired. Management told her that she was put on a waiting list for work in other departments, since the book department had no hours to give her. In the meantime, however, the book department hired another woman. After two months this woman was still on the waiting list, but she was never called. And she never received any separation pay.
. . .

Adjustments

In addition to all of the above, the continuous humming of the terminal and the dim lighting are a further source of aggravation. You go through the day looking at your watch. Your neck becomes stiff. Your legs and feet are sore. Fatigue and tension overcome your body and mind. Of course, in comparison with factory and other workers of the past and present, these conditions seem close to luxury, yet I think it is the combination of the monotony, ambiguity, fragmentation, and meaninglessness of the sales clerk's work, along with the rigidity of the rules, the humiliation, degradation, and tension, induced by both management and the public, that makes this work, in its own way, just as unbearable.

On an especially bad day, as we proceed to leave, the women in my department utter such statements as, "I think I'll quit," "I can't take this any longer," and "I must be a real masochist." But the next morning they are at work in the store again. I wondered why. One possible reason is the adjustments made by the women. Rinehart discusses the "activities that ordinarily elude public recognition. . .the largely unrecorded behaviours which involve, in part, the *ad hoc* devices workers employ to resist on a day-to-day basis the organization of work."[10] He interprets these not only as "angry reactions to work but also as attempts to humanize work and to establish control over the production."[11] Thus, says Rinehart,

"Work is never completely devoid of all meaning and gratifications, if only because working people fall back on their own imaginative and ingenious means. "[12]

Similarly, Donald Roy discovered the worker's ability to combat the "beast of monotony" and meaninglessness in work by making a game out of work and by informal social interaction with co-workers.[13] Walker and Guest in *The Man on the Assembly Line*, and Henri de Man in *The Psychology of Socialism*, note similar findings as well. De Man discussed the factory operative's struggle to cling to the remnants of joy in work. He says that it is psychologically impossible to deprive any kind of work of all its positive emotional elements as the worker will find some meaning in any type of work she/he is given.[14]

Like these factory operatives, the retail clerks I worked with create their own work when there is none. During particularly boring times, the women gather a pile of filed invoices, scatter them and refile them. Similarly, they take books off the shelves; one clerk erases all the prices and the other rewrites them in. Also on this premise, they take all the books off the shelves and put them back in alphabetical order. I think this particular behaviour, aside from being an attempt at some activity, represents an attempt to assert some control over their work. Because many of the women are fed up with the confusing and haphazard arrangement of stock, they try to rectify the situation. However, they often get in trouble with their supervisor for taking this initiative. Another tactic involves scattering books around the department and then tidying them up. When we were especially bored one woman would say, "Shall I go around the department and knock some books over so you can pick them up?" Initially, I thought she was being sarcastic, but eventually all of us found ourselves resorting to such methods in order to look busy, alleviate the boredom — and perhaps exert some kind of creative control over our work. . . .

The content of conversations between sales clerks is also worth noting. They range from complaints, to gossip, to mockery, to vivid and animated, often silly, routines, to moral issues and the discussion of "things." The complaint sessions usually involve a maximum of three workers. The women expel all their discontents, frustrations, and resentments. They freely relate to one another their ups and downs with management and customers. Management, of course, never hears these complaints.

Another type of social interaction which the sales clerks practise is "insulting the customer." As the customer approaches the counter, the women make "cracks" about him/her. Of course, these remarks are uttered under their breath, before the customer is within hearing range and after he/she leaves the area. Such remarks are usually directed only at those with airs of superiority and artificiality, for it is universally acknowledged that you do not ridicule someone who seems to have real problems. The clerks also laugh at the type of books people select. Such facetiousness is clearly an effort to make up for the degradation and subordination imposed upon the clerks by both management and the customers. Perhaps the most popular social interactions for the sales clerks were the "routines." They were made possible by the presence of Laura, an imaginative, aspiring actress. Most memorable are her re-enactments from "I Love Lucy" and other old television situation comedies. Although serious discussions also took place between the women, most interactions were marked by levity.

Elinor Langer, in her study of the women who worked for the New York Telephone company, notes how the women used consumerism to adjust to their work.[15] She vividly describes their discussions and pursuits of shopping, their fixation with brand names, packaging and wigs. Langer concludes that the clothes and wigs are:

a kind of tax, a tribute exacted by the social pressures of the work-place. For the preservation of their own egos against each other and against the system, they had to feel confident of their appearance on each and every day.[16] The women define themselves by their consumerism far more than by their work, "as if they were compensating for their exploitations as workers by a desperate attempt to express their individuality as consumers."[17]

Like the women in the telephone company, the sales clerks discuss objects with a passion. The talk of fashion is endless. This is supplemented by frequent trips to the magazine section of the store to leaf through *Vogue*, *Glamour*, and *Bazaar*. Perfumes, furniture, recent "loves" and other such topics also dominate the conversations. The women also speak to one another quite frequently about vacations outside Canada and future aspirations. The older women talk incessantly about their children and grandchildren. Robert Blauner calls such dreams and aspirations "safety-valves" against meaningful social unrest. Because the conversations between the sales clerks generally focussed on topics external to their work, they obviously helped these women cope with their degrading working conditions. It is interesting to note that these conversations were shared by only a core of the workers. This core consisted of the four women who had been working in the department the longest. The development of a distinct subculture was inhibited by the high turnover of workers in this department as in the store and industry as a whole. In any case, this informal interaction made the hours go by much more quickly than otherwise. The women referred to their conversations as "therapeutic." As one woman said, "It sounds strange, but there's some kind of gravitational force in this place. It draws you toward the other clerk. We just can't seem to stop talking. Otherwise it's so dreary here."

These adjustments, however, changed with the concrete realities we faced. About halfway through my field work, social interaction diminished for two reasons. The bosses decided that there was too much interaction among workers. And secondly, they reduced the department's financial expenditures on staff. Consequently, new shifts were implemented. Instead of having one person working all day and two people coming in from ten until five, one woman would work from 9:45 to 1:15, another from 12:00 to 3:00, and another from 2:45 to 6:15. In addition, people who were least likely to talk to each other were given the overlapping hours.

As a result, workers, for the most part, adjusted through apathy. They did their work, but morale was lowered. Many of these women also retaliated in even more individual and private ways. For example, when taking inventory of the books, instead of trying to find titles, the women just filled in any number they could think of. They made personal, lengthy phone calls when no one was around and refused to do any work (when the supervisor was absent) in the last half hour of their shifts. Accompanying this was an increase in absenteeism. But regardless of such covert indications of discontent, the women continued to work under the same conditions as before.

Summary and Conclusions

The sales clerks' job is a continual source of frustration, pressure, and tension. Conflicting demands, bureaucratic rules, and the rigidity with which they are enforced, standardization over human ingenuity, the elaborate division of labour, isolated and meaningless tasks, the routine, repetition, and boredom, combined with the necessity of looking busy, the fragmentation of work by continual interruptions by customers and the priority of profit maximization over all else, all contribute to this detrimental effect.

The women have almost no autonomy. Their supervisor allocates the work and determines exactly how and when certain tasks should be completed. In addition, supervision is of the "watch dog" type. When tasks are not performed according to instructions, the women are scolded and threatened. And arbitrary firing is frequent. Supervisors use the women's awareness of this power as a further disciplinary threat. Confronted with this inflexible structure, the sales clerks understandably suffer considerable stress. It is also important to note that the women feel a sense of superiority over their bosses and the customers. There is a lingering feeling amongst the clerks that the latter two groups are somewhat "dim-witted." Likewise, the customers display a condescending attitude towards the clerks. And although management attempts to maintain a surface "buddiness" with the women, both they and the customers, on the whole, treat the clerks as subordinates.

The women clerks lack any type of identification with either the company or the products which it carries. It is also evident that the women feel a sense of detachment toward each other. Within departments, they compete for raises, hours, and the favour of the supervisor. Between individual departments, the workers and managers alike, compete for budget increases. And the clerks in one department tend to adopt a condescending attitude to those in another department, as a result of this institutionalized rivalry. In short, work, in the opinion of the female sales clerks, has a purely instrumental meaning. If not for economic necessity, they would clearly avoid it. Going to work is, in fact, dreaded. One of the reasons for this is that the work does not permit self-expression. The women give as little of themselves as possible to their work.

This paper rests on the assumption that power relations are really behind the work conditions of the sales clerks. Because power is in the hands of a small capitalist class, the worker is compelled to sell her labour power in exchange for a wage. Thus work serves the needs of profit and capital, and not the individual worker. The data further demonstrate that service work, performed predominantly by women, is becoming increasingly like industrial work traditionally performed by men. For this reason, collar distinctions of any kind are useless indicators.

Many theorists have assumed that because a group of people remain passive and conservative in action, they have no desire for change. The assumption is based on the premise that such people are contented and favour the existing order of things. The data show that this is hardly the case. The sales clerks certainly are passive and have a strikingly low level of politicization. However, they are also very cynical about their work and clearly discontented. The problem is that these women express their resentment, anger, and discontent in subtle and individual ways. As a result, no change is implemented on their behalf. They fail to collectively and forcefully express their discontent. There are several possible reasons for this.

Some researchers posit that workers are making adjustments to their work situation and, therefore, are becoming integrated into the present system. However, such theories often fail to account for the social structural conditions surrounding the workers. In many situations, discontent and the will to organize exist; however, social structural obstacles are equally present at the same time. The data indicate that sales clerks are discontented, yet they face numerous structural obstacles which inhibit any formal, organized expression of these feelings. These obstacles include a low level of social organization, high atomization and a lack of resources. Gender is an additional element inextricably tied to the above factors.

These social structural obstacles are *fundamental* in explaining the passivity of the sales clerks in this particular store. Historically, there has been no correlation between negative feelings which the workers experience and the organized, open expression of discontent. No matter how frustrated any workers *feel*, if the structural conditions surrounding them are not conducive, they tend not to protest collectively. It follows logically, then, that even if these psychological adjustments were absent, workers would still not organize. Adjustive behaviour — in the form of consumerism, social interaction, and attempts to create work and appear busy — is a necessary consequence of the inaction caused by structural obstacles. It is a coping response to the grim realities which the female sales clerk must face from day to day.

Notes

1. See, for example, Robert Blauner, *Alienation and Freedom* (Chicago: University of Chicago Press, 1964); Charles R. Walker and Robert H. Guest, *The Man on the Assembly Line* (Cambridge: Harvard University Press, 1952); Donald Roy, "'Banana Time' Job Satisfaction and Informal Interaction," *Human Organization* 18 (1960), pp. 155-168.

2. As of May, 1982, the total employed labour force in Canada was 10,704,000. Of this, 1,964,000 were employed in the manufacturing sector. (Statistics Canada Labour Force Survey, Catalogue 71-001.)

3. Between the years 1965 and 1975, in particular, there was a dramatic increase in the number of females entering the paid labour force. The figures rose from 2,066,000 women to 3,697,000. This constitutes a rise of 79%. (G. Hartman, "Women in the Labour Market," 1974 cited in The Women's Bureau Ontario Ministry of Labour fact sheets, No. 3, 1981).

4. James W. Rinehart, *The Tyranny of Work* (Don Mills, Ont.: Academic Press, 1975) discusses many of these behaviours in the chapter entitled, "Blue-Collar Work."

5. For example, in 1975 slightly more than one out of every three workers was a woman, but only one out of every four union members was female. Proportionately fewer women than men are organized. In 1975, 31.8% of the male Canadian workforce was unionized whereas only 19.2% of the female work force was unionized. (Women's Bureau Ontario Ministry of Labour fact sheets, No. 3, 1981.)

6. C. Wright Mills, *White Collar: The American Middle Classes* (New York: Oxford University Press, 1956).

7. Harry Braverman, *Labor and Monopoly Capital* (New York: Monthly Review Press, 1974), pp. 371-372. Braverman argues that the "proletarianization" of white-collar work has so speedily occurred, that the white-blue-collar distinctions are insufficient to explain actual working conditions.

8. Rinehart, op. cit., p. 52.

9. Ibid., p. 76.

10. Ibid., p. 37.

11. Ibid., p. 37

12. Ibid., p. 76.

13. Donald Roy, op.cit., pp. 158-168.

14. Henri De Man, *The Psychology of Socialism* (1927; rpt. New York: Arno Press, 1974).

15. Elinor Langer, "The Women of the Telephone Company," in *The Capitalist System*, eds., R.C. Edwards, Michael Reich, T.E. Weisskops (Englewood Cliffs, N.J.: Prentice-Hall, 1972), pp. 14-22.

16. Ibid. p. 21.

17. Ibid., p. 21.

9/Moving the Mail*

David MacFarlane

There came a moment in our conversation when I thought he was about to cry. He had an intelligent, mathematical look — he told me more than once that he was a university graduate — but there was something unsettling about him. Even his occasional smiles were mournful, and his view of the post office, where he had

---

* Abridged from David MacFarlane, "Moving the Mail," *Saturday Night* (July) 1982, pp. 22-30. Reprinted with permission of the author.

worked for five years, might have been Kafka's. He spoke with bitterness of proposals he had made that had been ignored by the many levels of management above him, or, more infuriating still, stolen. He told me of shadowy plots and intrigues, and even of Ottawa's master plan to destroy the post office as we know it. "They deliberately keep us in the dark," he said, "but I've made it my business to know these things."

It was nine o'clock in the evening, more than halfway through the afternoon shift, and we had just come back from our lunch. We had walked from South Central's cafeteria, across the main foyer where the security guard sits each night staring blankly at his reflection in the glass doors that lead out to the parking lot and Eastern Avenue. In the foyer, three young men who were candidates for the local executive of the Canadian Union of Postal Workers were handing out election pamphlets. They didn't give any to us. He was a supervisor, and I was with him.

Past the guard, at the entrance to the plant itself, the clattering of mechanized sorters and the humidity increase abruptly. Here, the 1,400 people who work the busiest shift of the biggest mechanized letter-processing plant in Canada leave daylight behind and step onto "the floor," ten flourescent acres of belts and machines and computers and mail. We walked down the blue-tiled aisle that runs along the west side, past rows of machines that are known, as almost everything in the post office is, by their initials — the GDSs, the OCRs, the LSMs — then beneath the rolling noise of the central buffer zone, past the undeliverable mail office, and past a cluster of metal monotainers where a lovely young punk in her leathers calmly sorted bulky, oversize mail.

"The mail is all concentrated in here," he was saying, "and the experts are all out there. Oh, the odd time they'll walk through and make their usual cursory comments."

We passed the two inclined conveyors that carry the 3,500 mailbags, half the take of the afternoon shift, from the dock up to the three primary buffer lanes. About 1.4-million pieces of mail — raw mail, good mail, bad mail, originating mail, incoming mail, all of which is called code 1 or code 2 depending on whether it is stamped or metered — passes up these belts between 3:30 p.m. and 11:30 p.m. each day. Most of this shift's mail had passed up already, and had been sent across on another line of belts to the four bag-induction centres, the first stage in the enormous and complex process by which letters are sorted into their destinations at South Central. "Ottawa," he said, "just doesn't understand the system."

The dock was quiet. In the long, grey receiving area that runs beside the teamway, a few handlers, standing on their tow-motors, cut across the cement with the graceful swirls of figure skaters. . . .

Construction of the South Central plant began in 1972 as part of a $1-billion mechanization programme that would eventually affect twenty-two major cities in Canada. The programme had its origin in a 1969 report, tabled by the then-minister of communications, Eric Kierans, which called for a mechanized postal system based on a national postal code, and for the transfer of the post office from the department of communications to the status of a crown corporation. In the Toronto area, mechanization meant the construction of three massive plants: Gateway, a letter, parcel, and bulk-mail processing plant in Mississauga; the Scarborough letter-processing plant; and South Central, a letter-processing plant that draws its take from downtown Toronto and Don Mills, and became fully operational in 1977. These three, barren, modern buildings represent the height of technological sophistication, and process almost half of Canada's mail each day. Everything outside the area they serve is known as "the universe."

From the time the mechanization programme was announced in 1971 to the time employee orientation was completed at South Central in 1977, postal service in Canada had been interrupted by a string of strikes — legal, wildcat, and rotating. Six separate unions are represented at South Central. There was a five-week strike called in the winter of 1975 by the Public Service Alliance of Canada and a forty-three-day strike by the Canadian Union of Postal Workers that ended that December. Sporadic work stoppages continued from the day in March, 1977, when South Central went on-stream to the day in October, 1981, when the post office finally became a crown corporation. One rotating strike in 1978 led to a jail term for Jean-Claude Parrot, the CUPW president, and last year the inside workers he represents were off the job again for forty-two days. The latest two-year contract, signed last August, includes seventeen weeks of paid maternity leave and an hourly wage that amounts, for most inside workers on South Central's afternoon shift (once their cost-of-living catch-up and and shift differential are included), to almost $12 an hour. From the time in 1969 that Eric Kierans recommended that the post office become a crown corporation to the day last October when Michael Warren became president of the Canada Post Corporation, the hourly wage of most inside workers had increased by almost 200 per cent. During the same period, Saturday deliveries were cancelled, letters began taking longer to get from A to B, stories emerged from urban postal stations of drug dealing, theft, and vandalism, and the postage rate increased from six to thirty cents a letter. These are the things most people talk about when they talk about the post office.

Inside South Central, the size of it is what everyone talks about — the size, and the fact that no one on the outside has any idea what it's like on the inside. Every conversation about the problems — the boredom, noise, the bottlenecks, mis-sorts, the management, and the union — comes down finally to that — "Just the *size* of it." It is one of the few things on which everyone agrees.

Marg works in mail prep with Angie and Margot, and together they are everything postal workers are not popularly supposed to be. Marg has a BA and attractive, steady, brown eyes, and usually wears blue jeans and a comfortable shirt. She is twenty-eight and often works with headphones and a pocket-sized radio at her hip. She applied to the post office in August, 1981, and started work last January.

Like most of the people in the mail prep, she is a part-timer, working 6:30 p.m. to 11:30 p.m. Monday to Friday, and every third Sunday.

Marg spent seven years in community social services in Kitchener, and came to Toronto to look for a job when government cutbacks finally became too severe. She applied at Manpower in the summer and was called to South Central for tests, along with sixty other applicants, in the fall. The memory tests were conducted in the staffing office with the kind of you-may-begin and pencils-down-please punctiliousness that is generally associated with elementary school. "For most people," Marg remembers, "they were incredibly hard. Maybe fifteen of us passed from that sixty."

Eight of the people who passed were asked back the next day for a dexterity test. The applicants punched postal codes into keyboards that, for most of them, called to mind the face of an adding machine. Out on the floor, they would later realize, there are machines called the group desk suites — the GDSs — where keyboard operators sit at rows of consoles and punch the alpha-numeric-alphas of the postal code onto letters that thunk monotonously in front of them like stamped and addressed guillotine blades. Working on the group desk suites is generally regarded as the most numbingly boring of a good many boring jobs at South Central. But apparently the post office had decided that if you were dexterous enough to punch a postal code on the GDS, you would be dexterous enough to heave a tray in the mail prep, feed cardoxes of pure LVMs into the optical character readers, or slot letters into the wooden cases of pigeon holes in manual sort. Of the eight applicants who appeared for the dexterity test, only one failed.

One week later, Marg was called back to South Central. She was interviewed by two people whom she would probably never see again. Their questions were either general — "Why do you want to work at the post office?" — or of the ethical variety about which people applying for jobs do not have to think very carefully — "If your supervisor shows you one way to do something and another worker shows you a short-cut, which method will you choose?" At the conclusion of the interview, Marg's fingerprints were taken.

For Marg, and for anyone new to South Central, the place is a rattling confusion of directions and purposes. The mail flow, which the people who measure, plan, and worry about it call the "through-put," is not readily discernible. Letters don't simply come in and go out. By the time they reach the mail prep they have already travelled, in their dingy canvas bags, from the primary buffer lanes to the four bag-induction centres. From there they are sent on a groaning carousel, clockwise, and deposited in one of the eighteen lanes of the secondary buffer. After the bags have been opened and the mail has gone through its initial preparation, it can go through the rest of the plant by any number of routes. Few workers at South Central understand any outside their own area. "You may have noticed," said one sixteen-year veteran drily, "they don't enourage us to visit other parts of the plant." A supervisor of the mail-prep area said "It's pathetic. We sometimes get nine or ten

new people in a two-week period. That's the problem. They don't know the difference between first- and third-class mail, let alone code 2 and 3. By the time they
do, they're transferred." One of the keys to understanding South Central is that
everyone seems always to be up against a "they."

When Marg started she was introduced to the supervisor of the mail prep area
and taken on a tour. She was introduced to her shop steward — the CUPW representative working in her area — and was told that she could go to the washroom
when she wanted and that she should have a shop steward with her whenever she
had to discuss anything with management. She was given a copy of the collective
agreement, which informed her, among other things, of what would happen
"where a part-time employee dies, otherwise terminates his employment, or is appointed to a full-time position." It was, she recalls, all very strange. "At first I felt
very isolated and very alienated. Even the initial tour was fairly brief and just of
our area, so I still have no real idea what happens after us. Some of the stuff makes
no sense, some does. Fortunately, the variety of people I work with is enough to
keep my mind alive."

The mail prep, where Marg works, is on a mezzanine of scuffed orange tile. It
extends from the dock over the south end of the floor. The mailbags are shaken
out here. Up in the system of conveyors, twenty feet above the orange tile, the
bluejeans of the young men who pass their shifts on the bag-shake-out machine
can be seen as if through the branches of a tree. Raw mail tumbles down through
layers of conveyors that are watched by closed-circuit cameras and controlled by
two computer systems and a bored-looking console operator who sits in a room
nearby. In a fusty bunker the operator sits, smokes cigarette after cigarette, and
watches nine black-and-white monitors, each one giving the monotonous mounds
of letters a brief and curious celebrity. Once the bags have been shaken out, the
mail drops down through two layers of belts and a curved chute to the line of men
and women who, standing on either side of the culling belt, begin the sorting; the
continual motion of the belt sometimes makes people feel seasick. The stamped
mail is separated from the metered mail. Small packages — which are called, for
reasons no one can remember, *autres objets* — are sent down to the AO sort. Registered mail goes down to registration. Third- and fourth-class mail is culled out,
and stamped mail gets sent on to the culler-facer-cancellers. . . .

The cameras have lost sight of the mail by the time it cascades down to the
people on mail prep, but there are other cameras. According to the collective
agreement, the cameras behind the black, dome-shaped bulbs in the ceiling
throughout the plant are not to be used unless "there is a reasonable and probable
cause for their use in order to protect the mail." Anyone who has waded through
the meticulous dullness of the collective agreement recognizes this as language of
the loosest sort, and most people assume that the security and investigations
people are always there.

"Oh yeah," said a young, emphatic Chinese mail handler who works afternoons in the mail prep and goes to school during the day, "they're watching us. We don't know who, or where from, exactly, but they're doing it to keep us honest. You see a lot of things in the mail — money, cheques, credit cards. Sometimes they'll plant some money in the mail, a twenty-dollar bill or something, just to see whether we turn it in."

Marg and Angie and Margot usually work the first part of their shift on the culler-facer-cancellers. On the orange tiles, here and there around the CFCs, are letters like scattered leaves. Some of them have been stamped with foot-prints. . . .

There is no means of measuring progress in the mail prep. The mail left behind at the end of a shift looks the same, and is just as abundant, as the mail that was there at the beginning. Angie used to work at the post office in Chilliwack, and was overwhelmed by the size of South Central when she moved to Toronto. She has an almost angelic face, and wears white peasant blouses, corduroy pants with suspenders, and hiking boots. Sometimes she has to make up games: "I'll see if I can do so much in a certain period of time, just so I can get into it." Marg and Margo work together on the pre-cul, they either talk or listen to their headphones while they sort.

On the culler-facer-cancellers no one does much talking. The noise, like the noise throughout the plant, is not terribly loud, but it is terribly constant. Working on the CFCs is not unlike having water trapped in your ears. Designed and built in Japan by Toshiba, the eight CFCs cull out any over-sized or overly thick letters and then shoot a stream of stamped envelopes, at a rate of eight per second, across a course of scanners, flippers, shuttlecocks, and cancelling printers. The letters stand horizontally on edge, caught between the facing palms of rapidly running belts. Watching the mail's blurred passage from hopper to canceller to stacker is like watching a crazy electric train pass at breakneck speed through a landscape of strange device, only to run headlong into a wall. The stack of letters grows very quickly, and any letters that have not fared well during the journey — there are always a few — look very much the worse for wear. Oddly enough, having been flipped, manipulated, and directed across the surface of the CFC with dazzling mechanical dexterity, the letters always end up in the stacker upside down.

Angie rights the stack of letters, drops them in a black, magnetically coded tray, and then heaves the tray on the rollers behind her. The trays run fifty metres down the edge of the mezzanine, take a sharp left just beyond Harry Stoneham's station, and head off to the gallery of dozens of aisles of clanging rollers: the primary buffer zone. Stacked up like jets above O'Hare, the trays will remain there until the computers that feed the machine area call the mail down to be processed.

In the old days, back in Terminal A, beside Union Station on Front Street, in the dusty, un-air-conditioned facility that had once so depressed Eric Kierans, people used to say that they "worked the mail." Today, at South Central, they process it. Through the doors of the main foyer, the first area you come to, rat-a-tatting like a room full of teletype, spartan and bright and dustless, is the machine area. The first machines you see are the long, shiny carriages of the group desk suites. There are eight rows of them, and each row has twelve operators on black swivel chairs at coding desks. A few supervisors steadily roam the area. As they pass up and down the aisles, most operators glance away from their desks in order to see who is looking over their shoulder. At such moments the facial expression of the operator is always vaguely defensive, and here a curious fact of South Central becomes apparent: it is almost impossible to approach anyone at any job in the plant, without coming upon them from behind.

The mail, which management hopes and prays will be machinable, is called down from the central buffer zone by the computers. It descends to the floor in the black, plastic, magnetically coded trays, and is fed into the loading stackers at the end of each GDS row. The keyboard operators — middle-aged men and women in slacks and Wallabies; frizzy-haired youths plugged into Sony Walkmans; statuesque black women with gold bracelets and high heels; earnest-looking Chinese; and swaggering, tight-jeaned gays — take turns feeding the stackers. With a sound like the burst of a muffled machine gun, the mail shuttles through a singulating valve, and in a rapid single file shoots across the tops of the desk to the twelve operator positions. The letters stack up just above the operators' heads, and are dropped, one by one, to a viewing window at eye level. The operators read the postal code on each of the letters — if, indeed, there is one — and, with one hand, punch the code into the keyboard. Abruptly, as if yanked by an off-stage cane, the letter, now bearing a printed yellow bar code that the letter-sorting machine can read, is whisked away as another letter drops into place.

Encoded letters pass down a long steel chute of conveyors, deflectors, and pre-sort channels to the end of the group desk suites where they are separated according to general categories of destination. Trayed once again, the mail goes back up to the buffer until the letter-sorting machine needs more mail; then the mail descends again and is automatically sorted, by way of the yellow bar codes, into more particular pigeon holes. From here it will eventually go to despatch unless, some steps back, it was rejected because it had no code or because the computer determined the code was in error. Non-machinable mail — of which there is always a great deal — gets sent over to the row upon row of pigeon-holed cases where letters are sorted by hand.

Kenny is one of the handlers who makes sure that the group desk suites are kept supplied with mail. He usually wears a large, clean T-shirt, suspenders, jeans, and construction boots. He has worked with the post office since 1956, and says "nay-ho-mah" to the Chinese people on the GDS. His beard and constantly askew glasses give him something of a poetic, absent-minded look, although his supervisors all agree he does his job extremely well. "People who work here," said one supervisor, "are either interesting and eccentric, like Kenny, or they're incredibly boring — the Laverne and Shirley set."

Soft-spoken and shy, Kenny usually keeps his eyes trained on his work. Like many postal workers, he has developed the knack of knowing who is watching him without ever looking directly their way. His language is halting and nervous, but has a thoughtful, pleasant formality. One night, coming across a photograph that had been stamped and used as a postcard, he eyed the speedy rigours of the GDS for a moment and said, "I'm rather inclined to send this to manual sort." He's not the kind of person to complain about his work, but he does wonder sometimes why mail bags can sit un-opened on the belts in the mail prep when, on occasion, the GDSs are desperate for mail. In the old days, back at Terminal A, someone would just walk over and get them.

Like a good many people who work the machines, Kenny is skeptical about the efficiency of much of the mechanization; the rejection rate from machines to manual sort is sometimes as high as sixty per cent. He suspects that when mail goes into the rattling lanes of the buffer zone from the mail prep, comes down to the machine area, goes back up to the buffer zone, and then comes back down again to the LSMs, it is following a route that allows the computers to record its passage and volume, but which may not be the quickest way out of the plant. "Sometimes," he says, "I think management is more interested in statistics than in getting the mail delivered."

South Central's statistics are recorded, measured, and analyzed by production, planning, and control, a department that has its office adjacent to the group desk suites. Tom Urban, who works afternoons for PP and C, is probably the only man on the shift who consistently wears a jacket and tie; he is certainly the only man who wears narrow ties. He roams through the plant each evening, clipboard in hand, making notations, eating almonds from his pocket, and leaving momentary whiffs of Aramis in his path. Eventually he returns to his desk and computer terminals to do some calculating. Young, dapper, and bright, he fields the objections raised against PP and C with a certain equanimity. The people in operations persistently inform him that "you can't move the mail with a slide rule," but Urban maintains, as Ottawa does, that the problems now besetting the post office will be solved only with the kind of analysis PP and C provides.

Predicting the mail flow, identifying bottlenecks, up-dating the computer programmes, and co-ordinating work areas are Tom Urban's general concerns; unfortunately, he often ends up dealing with isolated crises. One night, for example, Urban was called up to the mail prep, where a large load of mail from Carling O'Keefe had blocked one of the feeds into a hopper. The belts, supposedly controlled by the computer, seemed to be functioning arbitrarily. When Urban questioned one of the mechanics, the reply was quaint but unhelpful: "Sometimes the belts do funny things." Urban scribbled a few notes. Once the feed had been cleared he climbed down from the catwalk, crossed the floor to the facing table, and picked out a handful of letters that had caught his attention. They had been mailed in Lachine, Québec, and were destined for addresses in Lachine. "I don't know what the hell this is doing here," he said, and sighed. "By the time you put out one fire, another one's smoldering."

Sometimes, after visiting the mezzanine, Urban returns to the main floor by the east staircase. Barren and cut off from the noisy air of the plant, the east staircase is rarely used by anyone. It is one of the depressing architectural nowheres in South Central. At floor level, the door leading out to the curbless nothingness of Woodfield Road is called the "Christmas door," and is used only during the few weeks when temporary help comes in for the Christmas rush. A door to be used only by Christmas help seemed, this past year, even more of a drawing-board caprice when the Christmas rush failed to bring its usual onslaught of mail. It was a funny thing, and people at South Central still shake their heads about it the same way people would if one spring, inexplicably, there were no robins.

The east staircase is not a cheery route for someone in production, planning, and control. At the foot of the stairs, Urban steps back onto the floor at a point where a few tired-looking, slow-moving men fold the empty mailbags that have travelled down by belts and chutes from the bag shakeout in the mezzanine above. Crossing the floor toward the PP and C office, Urban passes through rows of pigeon-holed cases where postal clerks, mostly women, sort mail the way the mail used to be sorted — slowly and by hand. That so much of the mail that comes into South Central should be non-machinable is depressing for anyone who spends his working life in calculation; perhaps even more depressing are the monotainers full of mail lined up behind the cage of the undeliverable mail office. Mail that bears incomplete addresses or no addresses at all, mail that has been shredded by the machines, letters with no envelopes, envelopes with no letters, wallets that have been dumped into street mailboxes — all wait to be sorted at the undeliverable mail office. Sometimes the UMO performs postal miracles; lost letters find lost envelopes; hopelessly vague addresses are pinpointed; money orders that have floated through the flow like wandering souls are returned to their banks of issue. Inevitably, a few cardoxes of perfectly good mail, sent to the undeliverable mail office by mistake, have to be sent back to the machines or over to manual sort. The process is slow at the UMO — it seems a tranquil oasis amid the frenzy and bustle — and anything that moves slowly is not good mail.

Just beyond the UMO, the mail moves very quickly. Machines called optical character readers, designed in Japan, process the large-volume mailers — the cartons of thousands of pieces that come from the likes of Visa and Consumers' Gas. The OCRs are, as one mechanic put it, "the saviours of the post office." In other words, the kind of mail that people find the least interesting to receive is the mail that the post office encourages and is best-suited to handle. Hand-written birthday greetings from grandmothers and perfumed love letters that have been S.W.A.K. are something of an inconvenience when you're trying to move 4.5-million pieces of mail every twenty-four hours, and the post office does not exactly lament the decline of the personal letter. Good mail comes from the LVMs, and the best is from Bell and the Royal Bank. The laser printing those companies use on their envelopes gives good definition, and when the definition is good the OCRs can index 100 per cent acceptance at a rate of 30,000 pieces an hour.

Every second, eight letters are sucked, one at a time, from the optical character readers" in-put stacker and fed to the whirling track of belts. Each letter passes before a pre-scanner where 128 light-sensitive diodes sweep the envelope and identify the location of the postal code. (In fact, the pre-scanner makes a grid of the envelope's surface and merely identifies an area, called a mask, where there happen to be six characters divided by a space. The location of the mask is transmitted, just ahead of the letter's passage, to the main scanner.) As the letter reaches the main scanner, the light of a cathode ray is reflected back from the envelope to four photo-multipliers, which amplify the signals and transmit the patterns of light and dark to the Nippon Electric computer. Comparing the patterns to its memory of alpha-numeric characters, the computer chooses the most likely postal code and transmits the information to the A.B. Dick Video Printer. As the leading edge of the letter passes before the printer's light beam, a stream of pink, fluorescent ink — which looks like a suspended line of silk thread and which costs more than $60 a litre — is broken into tiny dots, each drop charged with specific voltages corresponding to the postal code, and printed in a series of bars across the envelope. Passing from the printer to the ultra-violet light of the bar-code reader, each letter has its postal code deciphered and is then channeled and sorted accordingly. During this process the computer has up to ten programmes operating simultaneously. Each letter of the 500 the OCR can process in a minute has its postal code located, identified, printed, and read in what might be described with some precision as the blink of an eye.

The manual sort and the optical character readers could hardly be more dissimilar. In one, the postal clerks sit in front of their cases, chat with their colleagues, and methodically slip letters into pigeon holes, glancing at their watches every few minutes to see how much longer until their break. In the other, letters are shuffled and dealt across a table of belts and scanners with a speed that the tireless computer measures in nano-seconds — 1×10^{12} of a second.

Oddly enough, this juxtaposition does not trouble Tom Urban as much as one might expect. When asked about the biggest bottlenecks in the plant, he first mentions the group desk suite. Nobody in PP and C worries very much about the manual sort because the mail moves about as quickly there as hand-sorted mail can move. The GDSs, on the other hand, move mail much faster in theory than they do in fact.

A good operator can punch in the postal codes of almost 2,000 letters an hour on the GDS. Few do. The job demands close attention, is a strain on the eyes, can be hard on the back, and sometimes hurts the fingers. Beyond these minor irritations, the work is relentlessly, oppressively, even maddeningly boring. Operators on the group desk suite talk a lot with their neighbours. Sometimes they inspect their nails. The most enthusiastic worker will, within days of starting on the GDS, detest the sight of a postal code. Nobody disputes this, but aside from rotating workers from the group desk suites to the letter-sorting machines to the optical character readers, nobody knows quite what to do about it. "I don't think I could do it," one supervisor said. "I don' think I could stand it."

Workers at South Central are allowed to go to the washroom whenever the need arises, and people tend to go to the washroom frequently when they're working on the group desk suite. It is a sore point with the floor's mechanics that the machines they strive to keep 100 per cent operable are sometimes fifty per cent empty. On the GDS, people still remember the worker who punched in one postal code too many one night; for weeks afterwards he sat down each shift and keyed in the same code, again and again, until he was fired.

When it's time for a break there are no bells or whistles. The signal to stop work passes through the people on the machines invisibly, like the instinct that wheels a flock of pigeons in the sky. There are instances of a common, unspoken consciousness around the machines — Gary Irvin, a frenetic, industrious supervisor, says he can "feel something in the air sometimes when the mail isn't moving as quickly as it should — but the area only really becomes a single unit at breaks or at the end of a shift. People leave their work in unison, abruptly. There is never anything to tidy up or finish off. In some cases, people actually run across the rust-coloured carpet of the machine area, on their way to lockers or telephones or card games in the cafeteria, or perhaps to the parking lot for a joint.

One night, a young, female supervisor stood stoutly in the midst of the rush for the doors and shouted, "No running!" in a voice that at once transposed the scene to the hallways of a school at recess. A few workers slowed their stride for one or two steps and then, irresistibly, like school children, again broke into a run for the doors. . . .

10/Professional Career Patterns in the Oil Industry*

J.D. House

The Initial Years
The typical Calgary oilman studies engineering or geology at a western-Canadian university.[1] He gets his first exposure to the oil industry by taking a summer job with a Canadian major, which usually involves some field experience, such as working in a gas-processing plant if he is an engineering student, with a seismic crew if he is a student in geophysics, or on a drilling rig if he is a geology student.

---

* Abridged from J.D. House, *The Last of the Free Enterprisers: The Oil Men of Calgary* (Toronto: Macmillan of Canada, 1980), chapter 5, "Careers: The Luxury of Choice." Reprinted with permission of the publisher and the author.

Since the last two operations are done by contractors, he may act as a company representative although his main task is simply to gain some practical experience in the industry.

Upon graduation, the young professional goes to work for one of the Canadian majors (or a large independent), which, as we have seen, serve as the training centres of the industry. His first year is mainly a training year and may involve a trip to Houston or some other international oil centre for a course in some aspect of petroleum technology. He is then assigned to a technical task group. Initially, his task assignment involves some fairly mechanical operation such as geophysical processing, well-logging, or computer simulation of particular oil and gas reservoirs. Later, if he shows promise, he is assigned to more challenging technical work like geophysical interpretation or the design of secondary recovery methods for producing wells. If he shows leadership potential, he may become a group leader after a few years.

After working for four or five years in such a technical capacity, the young oilman reaches a crucial phase of his career. On the basis of his own and other people's assessments of his abilities and of the career opportunities open to him, he must make a decision about what kind of long-term career he wants to pursue. There are numerous possibilities. If he decides to remain with his present company (a strikingly large number of Canadian oilmen have spent their whole careers with a single Canadian major), his basic choice is whether to opt for a technical or managerial career.

Technical Careers

Technical careers appeal to people who like solving challenging technical problems, and who feel uncomfortable with having to co-ordinate and make decisions about personnel — to cope with "people problems" as oilmen put it. Successful professional technologists can enjoy interesting work, good salaries, job security, and a fair measure of prestige from those who depend on their technical expertise. Technical careers themselves are of two types. Most professional technicians continue to work upon technical problems of immediate practical concern, such as where to drill the next well to best effect in the Beaufort Sea, or how to maximize recovery from a declining field in southern Saskatchewan. But some people shift to longer-term technical problems and are known as researchers. Imperial Oil runs a fairly large exploration and production research laboratory in Calgary which works on such problems as improving knowledge and expertise in ice engineering for the north, or finding the best means to recover the heavy oils from the Cold Lake region of Alberta. The following comments by a researcher illustrate aspects of the contingencies and satisfactions of those who opt for long-term technical careers within the majors.

Immediately before I was here I was in graduate school. Before that I worked for three years in eastern Canada, as an engineer in a research lab. I came back to do my master's degree at the University of Alberta, and doctorate at the University of Calgary. Graduate degrees are helpful for getting into the research area but, as far as the work I'm doing goes, I'm not really using it that much. I applied to Imperial because I wanted to stay in Calgary where I could work while I finished off the degree. I prefer the west, I have no desire whatsoever to go to Toronto. That means I probably can't go too far in the management line. I had no exposure at all to the oil industry before I came to Alberta for my master's and doctorate. That's definitely a disadvantage now when I'm dealing with production problems. Our major project is trying to investigate the thermal damage that can be done through permafrost, mainly in the Delta area; and we have done some design for possible gas-plant development in the Delta area. We don't have one project as such, but are involved in a number of projects.

I guess I'll probably be here five years from now. I would guess my work would have something to do with Arctic development. If I did move, it would probably be as a consultant, but I don't think so, particularly with my lack of experience in the oil patch. In a big organization like Imperial, you get exposed to many people, conferences, meetings, trips; and there are an awful lot of support facilities to make the job much easier. And you have the freedom to work with the larger research group in Houston. These are conveniences you don't get in a smaller company. Of course, you can get lost in a big company, shuffled off into some job. . . . This doesn't happen too much, they keep moving people around.

This point clearly illustrates the context within which oilmen make their choices. This man gained higher degrees to pursue a research career. He enjoys the technical challenges of his work, and sees that a big company can provide superior opportunities to be involved in frontier research with other experts and with the best possible support facilities. Despite the possibility that one might become lost in a big company, he prefers it to a small company which provides less technological challenge. He has thought about going into consulting work, but does not feel familiar enough with the Calgary oil community to take that career risk. And his decision not to move to Toronto means that he has effectively locked himself out of a managerial career.

Not all technical careers, however, are chosen from this wide a variety of options. Those whom management consider to be lacking in promise either as administrators or as high-level technical experts may be kept on for years doing the more routine kinds of geological, geophysical, and engineering work. . . . These constitute the most dissatisfied sub-group of professional oilmen. Often they may be laid off, or may decide to leave the company or even the industry, although such professional drop-outs seem to be an exception.

Managerial Careers

In order to make it to the top in the corporate sector of the oil industry, young oilmen must opt for managerial careers by making the crucial shift from the technical to the administrative organizational ladder. The option to attempt this move is not, of course, entirely up to them; but those with managerial aspirations can let these be known and, if they are considered to have promise, will usually be given a chance to prove themselves. The lowest level of administrative job, as a leader of a project group, still involves a lot of technical work. This link helps ease the transition to the administrative ladder, where purely administrative and business concerns become proportionately more important as people move up. As they progress, their university and early training in the industry become more and more irrelevant. Except for a few in-house training courses, Canadian oilmen must learn their managerial and business skills on the job.[2]

The following is one man's account of his successful managerial career.

I took a general science degree in Manitoba. I was a kid from the farm. As far as aspirations were concerned when I was growing up, well I did well enough in school to keep on going to college. I just took the courses that came easiest. About the time I was ready to graduate I didn't have any firm ideas, although I had worked one summer in hard rock geology — enough to come to some understanding of geology. I found the natural sciences quite fascinating. An uncle of mine suggested that geophysics might be a good field, so I went to Toronto for a year of graduate school. Then I spent one summer in the seismic business in Alberta.

Actually, how I was drafted into Imperial, my uncle was working for Imperial at the time; I would have to say that he influenced me. I should have looked at other offers. That was back in the early fifties. Our training program at that time involved a moderate amount of time on a seismic crew, six weeks in my case; and then I had a six-week formal lecture-workshop type of course. Then I went to the Regina district as a trainee for a year or so. At that time we were putting interpreters back on geophysical crews; and I was on a crew for about a year and a half, and wandered around: Saskatchewan, Fort MacLeod, Red Deer, Calgary, Fort St. John. That was probably a low point in my career.

Then I went to the Edmonton office as a junior interpreter. At that time I think I took a real serious responsibility for doing what was assigned to me as well as I possibly could, and perhaps a little more broadly than I thought. I was fairly competitive. Then we had a bit of an internal reorganization within the Edmonton division and went to an area system — four areas with a junior technical man assigned to each. I didn't immediately get an assignment like that and it bothered me; I began to worry that obviously I'd been slotted and other people were going to get more responsibility. But then I got the responsibility for a specialized geophysical program. Then I got an assignment as an area geophysicist; I found that quite satisfying. Really, since then I've never had time to get concerned about whether I could take on more responsibility than what I already had.

I later had a transfer from that job as an area geophysicist to our research department. I reoriented myself into more academic approaches to things; I liked that role, it gave me a chance to prove that I could be a scientist I guess. After that I got into a straight staff job for about five years; I found it satisfying and exciting.

I moved to Toronto on the staff there, and then came back here as an area-exploration manager, and now I'm manager of all our exploration operations. When the job was offered to me, it never occurred to me to consider turning it down. Not that I expected it at that time or at any particular time, but it was the next logical step in the system. In a big corporation, there's no such thing as standing still on the main line. In the future, as far as the main-line path is concerned, that leads to Toronto. . . .

This man was a confident manager, and others in the department believed that his next move would indeed be to an executive position at the corporate head office in Toronto. The logic of a successful managerial career leads, as he points out, to a senior-executive position and eventually a seat on the board of directors.

This man's career vision, like that of most Canadian oilmen, is largely restricted to Canada. But there is also an international flavour to the industry which, although less pronounced in this country than in most oil-producing areas, nevertheless contributes significantly to the breadth of choice that oilmen enjoy. Many older Albertan oilmen spent a number of years with parent affiliates in South America and the Caribbean before returning to Alberta after the major discoveries in the 1950s. Nearly all Canadian oilmen in the majors go on training programs to the United States. And a notable minority of senior managers who have started out with the Canadian majors have moved up to senior managerial positions with their American parents, the most notable example being the former chief executive of Exxon.

There is also a new breed of young professionals and managers. . . . These individuals consciously view their careers in international terms. They see themselves as employees, not of Imperial and Shell Canada, but of Exxon Corporation and the Royal Dutch/Shell group.

I could see myself in, well, there's one job in the corporation, a guy in New York who works in producing co-ordination which is sort of a world-wide co-ordinator job. He's an ex-Canadian and a real salty explorationist. I could see myself doing that job very easily and it would sort of complement my love of travel. I think it would be a waste of the company's time to leave me at this desk for the next twenty years, and I think if I saw that coming I'd probably ask them to do something about it. I'm not so sure that my career really belongs at Imperial. It's a little bit of a family-style organization, I think perhaps I'm part of the larger family. I guess I'm telling you that my advancement model would be within the larger corporation.

This man sees himself as shaping his career in international terms within an international company. However, it is evidence of the cohesion of the Calgary oil community that this type is the exception rather than the rule, although many Canadian oilmen do enjoy short-term overseas experience.[3]

Of course, not all competent managers can reach the top, either within the Canadian major or its parent multinational. Positions become scarcer and competition keener the further up the hierarchy one moves. Those who do not quite make it to the top are accommodated by various staff positions, with important but secondary corporate responsibilities. The "main line" is cleared for other promising upwardly mobile managers. Oilmen refer to the career stage when one's maximum level in the organization has been reached as "peaking." This can be a disappointing and disillusioning experience.

One of the trends in industry is the use of younger people in managerial positions, so I'm at an age where I can't look forward to any kind of managerial position — perhaps, I don't know. I guess you could say that once you get to forty-five plus and haven't reached your goal, you're not going to achieve it. It's kind of a downhill slide from that time until retirement I guess. You know that you're over the hump anyway. I blame the company in part for this too, the company's attitude has changed. My goals were never reached within the company that I had set for myself, I had hoped that I might be able to get up into the directors. Successful managers seem to exude some kind of a confidence most people don't have. As far as ability is concerned. . .I don't know.

Personal ease in social intercourse seems to be necessary for managerial career success. This may be displayed in "off-duty" situations — for example, at meetings of professional associations or on the golf course — although few oilmen believe that one can make it to the top through such informal channels alone. Proven managerial and entrepreneurial ability is the main requisite. Another career contingency involves moral choice. Rising managers may have to take courses of action that they do not really believe in. . . . I was told of an unusual case where a promising young manager, who had been prevented from transferring some engineers into a project which he felt would be beneficial to their professional development, resigned in protest and went into farming. Such personal rebellions are rare. As in most businesses, oil managers make moral compromises or, when need be, rationalize their behaviour as being in the best long-term interests of the company, themselves, or their families. . . .

Within the Canadian oil industry, however, barriers to intra-company mobility, whether imposed by others or as a matter of personal choice, are compensated for by the presence of other career opportunities. Once they have gained their basic training in the majors, oilmen can and do leave to take up new careers as consultants, as senior members of small oil companies, or even as independent oilmen. . . .

Conclusion

The western-Canadian oil industry is structured in such a way that it provides a great variety of career opportunities to its members, particularly those with formal training in engineering, geology, and geophysics. Typically, professionals start their careers as workers with major oil companies. But, depending upon their early success, the growth of the industry itself, and their own preferences and choices, a great variety of career possibilities may open out to them. If they continue as professional workers, they can do so as well-paid organization men in the majors or large independents, or they can become technical-specialist consultants working on their own or on a contract or fee basis with a consulting firm. As another alternative, they can pursue an organizational career as a manager within a large company, where success depends upon moving up the organization's hierarchy of formal offices. Or, as yet another alternative, they can leave the majors to pursue entrepreneurial careers as deal-making consultants or as members of small oil companies. Career failure, on the other hand, is found among those who stagnate at low-level technical jobs, peak out at low managerial levels, and run into personal or market-induced difficulties as consultants or small businessmen. . . .

Notes

1. The reader is reminded that I am constructing an ideal/typical career pattern here. There are many individual variations.

2. This purely technical background may help explain why Canadian oilmen seem to experience difficulty, by their own admission, in dealing with governments and the public.

3. By contrast, many oilmen in Britain today view their involvement in the industry as a step toward leaving the country with its (in their view) high levels of taxation and its economic problems.

11/A Segmentation Approach to Poverty and Low-Wage Work in the Maritimes*

Donald H. Clairmont, Martha Macdonald, and Fred C. Wien

Introduction

As many reports have indicated, Canada, like other Western industrial countries, exhibits considerable inequality in earnings and household income, high unemployment, a narrow conception of what constitutes work, and large numbers of working poor. In the Maritimes, the locale for our research on inequality and low-wage work, these patterns are of even greater significance. Here a very large proportion (some 52% in 1973) of the families falling under the poverty line have the head of the family, not to mention other members, working during the course of a year; here, too, the scarcity of good jobs is reflected in high levels of unemployment and, as in the United States, in the significant movement over time between programs such as UIC [Unemployment Insurance Commission], Manpower training or welfare and low-wage work. Thus a sizable portion of the poor are persons either currently working for low remuneration or likely to do so. In this light, a casualty model of poverty which restricts the issue to the infirm, the uneducated, the old or the single parent can be seen to be extremely limited.

The indirect effects of inequality and low-wage work in determining the general level of poverty in Canada are also considerable. Low-wage work imposes constraints on the development of social welfare measures, restricting the levels of social assistance (as in New Brunswick, where support levels are pegged in relation to the minimum wage) and preventing the implementation of reforms because of their presumed threat to low-wage work (e.g., a guaranteed annual income). Social service case workers in Nova Scotia indicate that income supplementation programs are often shrouded in secrecy lest the army of potential claimants ever come forward. . . .

Directly and indirectly, then, inequality and low wages in the work world are integral to the poverty found in advanced capitalist societies, especially Canada. There is little reason to think that these factors are going to diminish in their significance in the near future. Some studies have shown that earnings inequality has in fact increased over the past two decades (Johnson, 1974; Adams, 1970).

Certainly low-wage work continues to be an important characteristic of the Maritimes. For example, if we define low-wage industries as those which, in 1970,

---

* Abridged from Donald H. Clairmont, Martha Macdonald, Fred C. Wein, "A Segmentation Approach to Poverty and Low-Wage Work in the Maritimes," in John Harp and John R. Hofley, eds., *Structured Inequality in Canada* (Scarborough: Prentice-Hall of Canada, Ltd., 1980), pp. 285-315. Reprinted with permission of the publisher and the authors.

had more than 60% of their full-time workers earning less than $120 per week, over 50% of the Atlantic provinces' labour force could be placed in the low-wage sector. . . . Over the 20-year period 1957-1976, the wage gap between low- and high-wage industries grew in both absolute and percentage terms (Smith, 1977). It also appears to be characteristic of industries in the low-wage sector to have had lower rates of increase in nonmonetary compensations in recent years (Wood, 1977). Despite large employment losses in low-wage sectors such as farming, logging, and fishing on the one hand and significant public sector expansion on the high-wage side, the overall employment increase in the low-wage sector was two-thirds that of the high-wage sector. In short, low-wage industries take in a large proportion of the labour force, are growing in absolute terms, and the compensation gap at the very least has not narrowed. . . .

Low Income Work from a Segmentation Perspective

To understand what characterizes a segmentation perspective it is useful to begin with a summary of the competing orthodox economic and sociological view of the labour market and wage/income determination. The orthodox model is based essentially on neoclassical economic price theory. In its assumptions and central ideas, the model shares many similarities to structure-functionalism in sociology (Whyte, 1971).[1] In oversimplified terms, a central tenet of the orthodox position is that in the short run, under conditions of perfect competition and equilibrium in the supply and demand for labour, workers' wages equal their marginal revenue products and one wage rate prevails for homogeneous units of labour.

Productivity is in turn linked to the workers' individual qualities such as the level of general education, training, previous work experience, and natural ability. In the human capital elaboration of the orthodox model, it is argued that individuals invest in improving their stock of human capital (skills), expecting an adequate return on their investment in the form of higher wages. Employers, for their part, facing a labour supply with a higher reservation or asking wage, will employ an individual at the higher wage so long as the wage demanded is not more than the individual's marginal revenue product. Supply and demand considerations affect the investment choice — individuals will avoid situations where an oversupply of labour to a particular occupation, industry, or region has reduced the wage below the cost of the human capital investment, and they will gravitate toward occupations with higher returns.

In the orthodox model, then, wage rates are seen to respond to (and signal) the movement of factors of production, and it is argued that there is a long-run tendency toward equalization of returns. It is suggested that workers have considerable influence and choice over the nature of their employment. Thus, worker sovereignty prevails and present employment situations can be seen as freely chosen (Gordon, 1972). There is little emphasis in the model on how the job structures among which individuals allegedly choose were developed in the first place, and how they affect and limit the range of individual choice.

If equalization in wages has not occurred over the long term, as is demonstrably the case even for workers at comparable levels of education and skills (Bluestone, 1974; Wachtel and Betsey, 1972), some orthodox theorists would argue that the conception of human capital needs to be broadened to include elements which, unfortunately, are more difficult to measure (e.g., the quality of education, the effect of preschool differences in ability, etc.). Alternatively, others would argue that exogenous changes in technology and consumer tastes keep the labour market in a continual state of disequilibrium, though the wage signals still operate to alter the supply and demand for labour in an equilibrating direction.

By way of contrast, a segmentation perspective finds the division of the economy into two or more sectors with unequal returns to be a fundamental feature, which is continuously being reinforced and regenerated, although its characteristics may change over time. The intellectual roots of contemporary segmentation approaches are diverse; for American economists, of significance were the institutionalist school of the 1950s in labour economics (e.g., Kerr, 1954; Dunlop, 1957), the dualistic economic development literature applied to the Third World (e.g., Boeke, 1953; Lewis, 1954) and applied research conducted on race relations (e.g., Myrdal, 1944). The dual labour market model advanced in the late 1960s and early 1970s had, as its immediate reference point, research conducted on ghetto labour markets in several major urban areas (e.g., Bluestone, 1970; Baron and Hymer, 1968; Vietorisz and Harrison, 1970). These studies posited the dichotomization of the labour market into primary and secondary segments on the basis of certain job characteristics:

...the primary market offers jobs which possess several of the following traits: high wages, good working conditions, employment stability and job security, equity and due process in the administration of work rules, and chances of advancement. The. . . secondary market has jobs which, relative to those in the primary sector, are decidedly less attractive. They tend to involve low wages, poor working conditions, considerable variability in employment, harsh and often arbitrary discipline, and little opportunity to advance. The poor are confined to the secondary labour market (Doeringer and Piore, 1971).[2]

At the same time, a somewhat different dualistic perspective was emerging in eastern Canada. Brox (1972), drawing on theoretical literature in economic anthropology (Bohanan and Dalton, 1965; Barth, 1967) examined the Newfoundland fishing industry from a segmentation perspective, in terms similar to that used in the Third World economic development literature:

The most striking feature of Newfoundland's economy is the dualistic nature of its development. On the one hand, there are modern, sophisticated, technologically up-to-date industries. On the other, economic practices and techniques exist that appear to be almost medieval, such as inshore fishing and especially the processing of salt fish, where no innovation whatsoever seems to have taken place, either in tools or work methods. . . . Most noteworthy is the fact that the traditional fishing population is not mobilized for the trawler fleets — the latest innovation in Newfoundland fishing technology. Traditional inshore fishing continues along-side commercial, large-scale trawler fishing in striking contrast to Scandinavia and especially Iceland, where modernization seems to take place simultaneously in all sectors and regions (Brox, 1972).

In our own case, we have drawn on both of these streams in developing a dualistic perspective in which the two segments are labeled the central and marginal work worlds. The latter is defined in terms of work settings (establishments) and occupations (in the case of self-employed individuals) which provide, for a majority of their work force or membership, employment packages characterized by low wages, limited fringe benefits, little job security and restricted internal advancement opportunities, among other characteristics.[3] Under this definition, if an establishment (or self-employed occupational group) meets the above criteria, then all persons belonging to the establishment or occupation, whether low wage or not, are considered to be part of the marginal work world, part of a social reality in which the actors have a shared external environment and, at least on some dimensions, some common attitudinal and behavioural patterns. Generally, small labour-intensive firms and relatively unorganized self-employed groups, serving an unstable or restricted market, fall into the marginal work world category. Common examples in the Maritimes include motels, textile plants, sawmills, fast food outlets, day care centres, taxi drivers, and food processing establishments. Since the definition is based on the actual employment package available at the establishment level, work settings can fall into the marginal sector even though they may be linked, through ownership, to powerful firms in the core of the economy.

Central work world establishments, in contrast, offer (or are required to provide) high wages, extensive fringe benefits, internal career ladders, and job security provisions. They are characterized by the interfacing of powerful actors on both the employer and employee sides, and include the public sector as well as establishments in the large-scale highly capitalized private sector (e.g., coal mining, steel, petroleum refining, auto assembly or pulp and paper production). Well-organized self-employed occupational groups such as the professions and the highly-skilled craft guilds are also included in the central work world category, with the organization of the *occupation* providing the structure that is provided for other workers by their *establishment*.[4]

While the postulate of pervasive work world segmentation appears to be increasingly attractive to social scientists, not all segmentation approaches select the establishment or work setting as the key defining unit. Some researchers have focused upon the *industry-wide* level (Beck, 1978) while others have seen segmentation in terms of core and peripheral *firms* (Averitt, 1968).[5] Dual labour market theorists have defined segmentation in relation to *job* characteristics. The different operationalizations overlap a great deal in terms of the social reality to which they point but the overlap is by no means complete. Much research is necessary to understand the theoretical implications of the diversity. Compared with our emphasis on the establishment or work setting there are some advantages in the alternative operationalizations. The firm rather than the establishment is the decision-making unit (Simon, 1957); technological imperatives are best appreciated at the industry-wide level where, also, secondary data are more available; and low status jobs, wherever they are found, are highlighted in the dual labour market perspective. Nevertheless, we think our focus on establishments is heuristic since work settings are important units of social reality. Our approach suggests that it matters considerably where low status jobs are located (i.e., by type of establishment). Moreover, it enables us to appreciate the persistence of segmentation at the work setting level along with the increasing integration of the work world at the firm level.

There are a number of important themes in a segmentation view of low wage work. Among the most important is the emphasis on the existence of barriers that restrict individuals from making transitions between the segments. It is argued that barriers exist which restrict a significant number of persons to the marginal segment, for reasons unrelated to their preferences or productive capacities. This has at least two important implications. In the first place, it suggests that individuals in the marginal sector will circulate among jobs and work settings within the sector (e.g., from domestic work to waitressing; from inshore fishing to rural carpentry) more readily than across sectors, even within the same industry (e.g., from small sawmills to the pulp and paper industry).

A second implication is that there is a substantial number of persons confined to the marginal sector who are under-employed there, who have the education, skills, and other qualities to perform well in the central sector, or who could easily adapt to employment there if given the opportunity to do so.[6] Segmentation theorists generally reject the orthodox contention that the labour market, as a result of a competitive bargaining process over wages, will serve to assure jobs for all who would like to work; they suggest that the labour market can only determine which individuals obtain the limited opportunities available (Eichner, 1977). Thurow (1975) maintains that the employer, who takes the initiative in determining the number and types of jobs available, is generally indifferent in the short run to the availability of labour at lower wages, particularly in the central sector, where measures have been taken to protect workers from job and wage competition pressures. Job vacancies, rather than wages, signal the reallocation of labour. The point at issue then becomes who, among the large number of qualified individuals, obtains access to the relatively scarce central work world positions, with their attendant mobility and on-the-job training opportunities. Thus, there is a situation where substantial differences in employment rewards exist and persist over time, even among workers with similar attributes of skill, education, or age. . . .

The restricted number of central work world jobs is, consequently, a most important barrier, especially in a region such as the Maritimes. Other barriers that serve to restrict access include unwarranted education requirements (credentialism), licensing and certification provisions, and union restrictions. Ascriptive characteristics such as age, sex, race, or class may also serve as barriers to the mobility of certain groups through discrimination.

Another important theme is the relationship between segments; they clearly cannot be examined in isolation. Examples of both conflict and accommodation can readily be found in the region. Exclusionary practices, for example, have the effect of creating a crowding situation in the marginal sector which serves to restrain wages and attempts at organization; this is particularly evident in open-access occupations such as taxi-driving. Within particular industries such as forestry, there is conflict between small local sawmills which serve a specialized or restricted geographical market (e.g., for lobster traps, fish crates, or housing frames) on the one hand, and the large capital-intensive pulp and paper corporations, on the other, which place vast demands on the limited raw material resources of the region.

The marginal sector continues to persist, however, which suggests that it serves important functions for the larger social system with which it is integrated. A particularly interesting examination of the interrelationship of the two sectors is given by Berger (1973) who, in writing about Italy, argues that the "declining classes survive" and segmentation is maintained rather than eroded because the marginal sector provides an element of production flexibility for central firms (e.g., via subcontracting),[7] and political stability for the society as a whole by soaking up fluctuations in employment. She argues that in North America, unemployment insurance programs contribute to the same purpose.

Researchers operating from a segmentation perspective have, in fact, been careful to specify the interconnections among low-wage work on the one hand and other related systems such as the "training economy," the "welfare economy" and the "irregular or hustle economy" (Harrison, 1972). These are argued to have similar characteristics, such as low remuneration, short-term involvement, and limited potential for future advancement. The extensive and frequent mobility of individuals among these subsystems has also been documented (Ferman, 1967; Harrison, 1978; Butler and Buckley, 1978).

Finally, another distinctive feature of segmentation models is that employer and worker behaviour and attitudes are said to differ across segments, and therefore that a uniform model cannot be applied; the rules of the game are different within each sector.[8] In contrast to the orthodox model where the causes of a good deal of worker and employer behaviour and attitudes are relegated to exogeneous factors, segmentation models tend to stress the effect of job structures and the work context on individual behaviour and attitudes. Thus low motivation and low job stability on the part of workers in marginal establishments may well reflect a sensible adaptation to employment where stable, long-term, more highly trained employees earn little more than new recruits. The *opportunities* for stable employment and for on-the-job training may also be quite limited by the nature of the jobs available in the marginal sector. A similar argument can be made for the reluctance of entrepreneurs in the marginal sector to adopt new technologies.

Thus, rather than taking labour market structures as given and examining individual "choices" within this context, there is considerable interest among segmentation theorists in understanding the historical and theoretical roots for the development of particular labour market structures — the conditions under which segmented labour markets develop, and the role that factors such as class antagonisms, the nature of product markets, or the labour force requirements of particular firms play in the development of technology and job structures. . . .

Attempts to Transform the Marginal Sector

With respect to the organization of occupational groups whose members are largely self-employed, we have seen considerable change taking place in the region over the last decade and a half. A number of occupations whose members are in the low to middle range are becoming better organized, either through their own initiative or through the intervention of external actors. While organizational developments are not automatically translated into the achievement of CWW status (reflected in higher incomes, more stable and secure employment, etc.) and while the process of organizing is not an easy one, there have been some significant developments. In rural occupations such as inshore fishing, for example, licensing and quota regulations as well as occupational organizations have been advanced; dairy farming has seen the development of marketing boards and commissions. Among urban service occupations such as hairstyling and day care services, there have also been organizational and certification developments.

A variety of strategies are used in these attempts to achieve greater institutionalization, as Kerr (1954) would call it. In our research program we have undertaken case studies of seven occupations, including those mentioned above, and are inclined at this point to divide the strategies into two major categories: associations grouping together persons who regard themselves as independent producers, and unionization strategies. There are various subtypes within each category; for example, association strategies may take a semi-professional form, or involve non-professional organizations which nevertheless have licensing or certifications procedures. Cooperatives and marketing boards also fit into this category. On the unionization side, craft, white collar and other union models are found. Often there is debate within an occupational group about the relative merits of association or union strategies, as in inshore fishing and taxicab driving, or a shift from one strategy to another over time as conditions change. One of the interesting questions being pursued in the research is to establish the determining conditions by which a particular organizational strategy is selected.

While some occupations have become more institutionalized, two of the cases we have examined, taxicab operators and woodlot owners, have faced substantial obstacles. In addition, the advances made by one group (e.g., hairdressers) may well be made at the expense of another (e.g., barbers) as the clientele shifts from one to the other.

It is also the case that as occupational groups organize, the process of transformation means the exclusion of residual members of the occupations (e.g., part-time fisherman), or the achievement of gains by reducing membership in the occupation, thereby feeding surplus labour into other parts of the marginal sector where access barriers have not been erected.[9] Again, segmentation persists in the absence of an overall strategy directed at its elimination. On the basis of our case studies, it is clear that provincial and federal governments are important actors in these efforts at collective occupational transitions, and their support is a crucial variable in whether or not a successful transformation is made — whether day care workers become certified, or whether small woodlot owners are able to establish a pulpwood marketing board in the face of opposition from the pulp and paper companies. The only alternative source of institutional support for these movements would appear to be the resources of the organized labour movement.[10]

In addition to these case studies of attempts to organize occupational groups, we have also begun some research on the transformation of marginal work settings through the unionization of employees within establishments. . . . It appears that more than half the work force in Atlantic Canada can be classified as being in the MWW. Only about 10% of MWW workers are unionized, as compared with at least 35% of the total work force (Nova Scotia Department of Labour, 1976). If these figures are accurate, then a majority of those working in the CWW — and, of course, an even larger proportion if one excludes groups like management and the armed forces — are members of unions, and the union movement is largely constituted by CWW employees. There are some MWW work settings with a long history of unionization, as in textiles, and there are some large MWW-based unions such as the retail, wholesale, and department store workers. Even the larger, more established MWW-based union locals in the Maritimes, however, do not have the resources and bargaining power of their CWW counterparts.

From the standpoint of unionism, the MWW remains primarily a "frontier land," difficult to settle, secure, and transform. Union organizers face stiff opposition from both independent or family-owned establishments where the ability to pay may be in question, and from large corporations which may have set up an establishment locally to secure cheap or non-unionized labour. They have to organize work settings where there may be a tradition of independence (e.g., rural craftsmen) or a more paternalistic style of employer-employee relations (e.g., small or modest size manufacturing concerns, retail trade operations). They have to win over low-income persons who may be justifiably skeptical of what a union could accomplish. Part-timers and women, who are disproportionately in the MWW and who may define themselves as secondary household earners, are difficult to organize, as are those who have self-selected non-union work settings. And this organizing has to be done with few resources, with competition rather than cooperation from other unions and on an establishment basis where the size of each unit is rather small and where turnover is often high.[11] Finally, once having organized an MWW concern, the union representative will generally have to put up with settlements that fall below the collective bargaining average and will be threatened occasionally by "raiding" or decertification.[12]

The significant growth of unionization in Atlantic Canada in recent years has primarily occurred in the areas of public administration and community services (Wood and Kumar, 1977). Industries most likely to spawn MWW establishments — trade, light manufacturing, personal and business services — have witnessed little growth in unionization. The fact that there is relatively little unionization in the industries where MWW-based unions are found sets severe constraints on the effectiveness of collective bargaining in the MWW. In effect, the predominance of non-union establishments means that the strike threat there has few social and economic implications beyond the establishment, an especially vital consideration given the often considerable imbalance in power between companies and workers, the limited strike funds available to union locals in the MWW and the usual problems of mobilizing and maintaining appropriate commitment in MWW establishments.

Preliminary interviews with union officials, perusal of collective agreements and more detailed examination of the MWW in specific regions of the Maritimes (e.g., metropolitan Moncton) indicate little difference in wages between unionized and non-unionized MWW establishments in the same industry. The most obvious advantage of organized MWW workers is in the area of fringe benefits, but perhaps the most important union benefits relate to the regulation of employer-employee relationships and of working conditions generally.

Our research thus far indicates profound differences in collective bargaining clout between MWW-based and CWW-based unions. Sharp differences are also evident in the important union activity of contract administration. Business representatives of locals servicing MWW workers not only have fewer financial and organizational resources, but what they do have is further thinned by the spread of the relatively small membership of the local over a number of distinct establishments or bargaining units. Thus one could not expect the same level of service and contract administration provided by the typical CWW local nor perhaps, in the "composite locals" common in the MWW, the same level of identification by members with their local. It should be noted too that the situation does not appear much different in those instances where a CWW-based union (i.e., a union drawing its core membership from CWW establishments) has organized MWW workers. Finally, our research indicates that CWW-based unions are much more active in the field of social policy and in labour federations and district labour councils.

There appears to be considerable skepticism among union people whom we have interviewed regarding the prospects of unionization in the MWW and the significance of the unionization that might occur there.[13] Furthermore, the fragmentation of the labour movement and the prevalent business-unionism orientation do not suggest the transformation of MWW work settings via unionization under present conditions. However, in other advanced capitalist societies where segmentation is less significant (e.g., Sweden, Australia) the work force is more heavily unionized and significant collective bargaining, guided partly by a strong equality principle, takes place on an industry-wide basis and at the national level (Robinson, 1972).

In North America, strong unionism is thoroughly implicated in the creation and maintenance of segmentation. The widespread contention in the segmentation literature is that the combined forces of monopolization and unionization in the oligopolistic or core sector of the economy have produced segmentation or divergent development as an unplanned outcome (Kahn, 1975). The strong or CWW-based unions shelter the employment of their members, contributing to the process of shifting the costs of societal economic organization onto those workers who are either unorganized or weakly so (Piore, 1973). Their success here has depended as much if not more on the capitalization and monopoly character of CWW operations as upon trade union struggle (Aronowitz, 1973). Without a fundamental change in union ideology and organization, accompanied by an equally basic change in certification and collective bargaining, the transformation of MWW work settings will depend upon similar considerations and, perhaps, extensive government regulation of market forces and working conditions.

Clearly mergers among several MWW-based unions competing for similar workers would have an important effect, and in the limiting case where virtually an entire MWW industry (e.g., fishing) is organized by a single union, MWW-based unionization could be very important in attenuating segmentation. But apart from possible quantitative changes in work world segmentation, the historical pattern of strong unions not having gained a larger portion of the pie for labour in society, and having their gains at the expense of those still unorganized or weakly organized, would continue (Johnson and Miekowski, 1970). Our analysis and research indicate that profound changes are necessary, changes directed at the heart of current power imbalances. There is serious question concerning the extent to which the labour movement can or will pursue such changes. Segmentation is quite compatible with the corporatism characteristic of most western societies. As Janowitz (1976:75) observes, class goals have less and less significance and "the politics of an advanced society is a reflection of its own system of inequality which is characterized by intensive occupational and economic interest group competition." In this situation it is not surprising to find, as Goldthorpe discovered, "a general appreciation (among workers) of the extent to which their individual prosperity depended upon the economic fortunes of the firms in which they were employed"; nor is it surprising that CWW workers and their unions could adopt "an increasingly particularistic approach to industrial relations, giving rise to a new corporatism and the consolidation of a new labour aristocracy. . .oriented to sectional rather than class objectives and eschewing any commitment to radical change in the wider economic or social order" (Goldthorpe, 1974: 157).

The Value of the Framework: Low-Wage Work in the CWW versus the MWW

. . . In a preliminary way the data which we have obtained strongly support the suggestions made above. Low-wage workers in CWW establishments in metropolitan Moncton have been found to earn more, have greater fringe benefits, higher overall job satisfaction, and less relative deprivation and alienation than counterparts (matched on occupation, age, sex, ethnicity, and area of residence) drawn from MWW establishments. It also appears from longitudinal data currently being collected that the low-wage CWW workers are more likely to experience wage and occupational mobility.

For example,. . . low-wage CWW workers have gained on the provincial average income over their work careers much more than have their MWW counterparts in this Moncton sample. Particularly significant is the finding that the income mobility pattern for females differs profoundly depending on the sector of employment. Also supportive of the hypothesized segmentation effect is the upward mobility found with a change from the MWW to the CWW and the downward mobility found in the reverse movement, though the number of cases is small.

It can also be argued that the situation of the low-wage worker in the CWW should improve over time relative to other CWW workers. Given the social reality constituted by the establishment, low-wage work may well be incongruent with the control and compliance objectives of management, which depend somewhat upon the image of work organization projected to and assimilated by employees (Edwards, 1975). Hence management in CWW establishments might be more inclined to meet demands of their low-wage employees. Also, given the establishment-specific nature of most skills and the ever-present threat of technological change (greater in CWW work settings) it may well be in the interests of the more advantaged workers to delicately balance status claims with solidarity behaviour (Sabel, n.d.); thus there would be reinforcement of those considerations which incline collective bargaining to favour, relatively, the least advantaged. If there is anything to this argument, then one might expect not only a different future for the individual low-wage CWW worker compared with her or his MWW counterpart but also some relative gains vis-à-vis the more well-paid strata of CWW workers.

Our most detailed observations on these relative gains within the CWW are with reference to the public sector in the Moncton area. Within the past few years the low-income workers there such as maids, clerks, caretakers, and laundry workers have experienced very significant improvement in wages and working conditions. Both union and management officials with whom we discussed this situation referred to the "pre-election bonus" of 1974 when the provincial government, faced with both a general strike of its non-professional/technical/managerial workers (virtually all of whom are in the same union) and a provincial election, settled generously with the union. Low-wage workers were particularly favoured under the new contract; their wages jumped by almost $70 a week over a two-year span and their working conditions and fringe benefits became comparable to other public sector employees (e.g., maids received four weeks' paid vacation after seven years of service). Not unexpectedly, these changes were accompanied by sentiments of "distributive injustice" on the part of lower level supervisory personnel; one payroll supervisor, referring to the similarity of wages between cleaning and supervisory work, exclaimed "Why should I take all this responsibility then?" That the 1974 occurrence was not simply idiosyncratic is attested to by the fact that the more recent pattern of "cash-across-the-board" wage settlements has effected a further flattening of the wage and salary scale. According to union officials the working policy of the union is to narrow the gap between low-wage and other workers, while maintaining an absolute differential between them.

It appears, then, that the situation of the wage workers in the public sector in New Brunswick — and probably throughout the Maritimes — has improved in both relative and absolute terms in recent years. At the same time, keeping down compensation costs remains an important objective of CWW firms and job-sheltering remains a major priority of the CWW workers. Thus, along with the above implications may well go the emergence of a new and more important kind of inequality — the difference between regular employees and those designated as part-time, casual, and temporary. Yet even here it appears to be against the long-term interests of those regularly employed to allow a significant gap in the wage rate component of the compensation package (i.e., this could have the effect of job devaluation); so to the extent that part-time temporary personnel are involved in CWW establishments, the inequality there would be based more upon employment status, and possibly fringe benefits, than upon wage differentials.

In our research on the public sector in Moncton, we encountered a significant number of part-time and casual workers, especially in the hospitals. According to management officials, part-timers and casuals are generally covered by union contract, draw similar wages and have preference for available full-time positions; officials also were of the opinion that these persons for the most part preferred their current work arrangement to full-time, regular employment.

Finally, if the theoretical argument developed earlier has merit, then despite the peculiarities of the above example (i.e., public sector, pre-election bonus), similar patterns should be found elsewhere in CWW work settings with respect to the compensation of low-wage workers over time and the relative wage gains among different categories of workers. Recently Velk (1976) has suggested that the working poor have found their position improved considerably over the past decade; in support of this contention he presented a table showing that since 1967 the average annual increase in wage rates for new settlements has been significantly greater than the annual rate of change in the consumer price index. Interestingly, the wage increase data are based on averaging overall collective bargaining units of 500 or more, excluding the construction industry; such units would in our terms represent the CWW, and consequently we interpret the Velk article and more generally the well-known "union effect" (Rees, 1973) as supportive of part of our hypothesis. Also we have found in assessing the position of labourers in the construction industry in Nova Scotia, that over the recent past this category of workers experienced considerable improvement in their compensation package both in absolute terms and relative to the skilled tradesmen. One union official representing construction labourers noted that there is a conscious consensual "agreement" to keep wages roughly 75 cents per hour below that of the tradesmen; as wages have steadily improved this has meant of course that the position of the labourers (the lower-wage employees) continually improved relative to the other workers. If these implications of the segmentation model are valid, it would further direct attention to the nature and structure of work settings rather than to the characteristics of workers and occupations. Further it would suggest that micro stratification processes are conditioned by a segmentation effect. Indeed Tolbert, Horan, and Beck (1978) have found in the U.S. that the status attainment process is *not* uniform across economic sectors and they contend that "any attempt to analyze the process of attainment of occupational prestige without reference to the industrial structure of the American economy. . .will result in estimates of basic parameters and interpretations of major findings which are open to question." . . .

Notes

1. Structure-functionalists posit that the functional importance of work roles (measured largely by the human capital investment required) is the prime determinant of stratification differences (measured by rewards and benefits). Further, Parsons (1971), sees a mobile, homogeneous labour force as increasingly characteristic of modern society. In the Whyte formulation, technological change primarily determines changes in functional importance.

2. In the dual labour market analysis, an important feature of establishments operating in the primary sector is their development of internal labour markets. The term is defined as a set of structured employment relations within the establishment, embodying a set of rules (formal and informal) that governs each job and their interrelationship in such matters as job content, wages, opportunities on the promotion ladder and grievance procedures. Access to the establishment for employment is restricted to a few low-level entry points, and beyond entry-level positions, jobs are filled from within the ranks, often on the basis of seniority, along well-defined mobility structures (which also facilitate on-the-job training). It is argued that much of orthodox theory is not applicable within the internal labour market, but may have some relevance for explaining the characteristics of entry-level positions.

3. We do not mean to imply a negative characterization of the marginal work sector, however. There may well be positive compensating factors that offset the characteristics mentioned above (e.g., greater flexibility in the organization of work, or more control over the work process in some occupations such as fishing or shipbuilding). Nor do we see the central sector in uniformly positive terms. To some extent, our survey data covering employers and workers in both sectors will shed some light on how the participants evaluate different work structures. We expect to find a good deal of variation within each segment.

4. The two types of organization may well overlap for some occupations (e.g., accountants working in central establishments).

5. In referring to *firms,* we mean the total corporate entity of a company, while the term *establishment* refers to one particular location of work.

6. The resolution of this inequity need not necessarily be achieved through individual mobility out of the occupations and work settings characteristic of the marginal sector. It can also be achieved by restructuring existing work settings through unionization, marketing boards, cooperatives, etc, in order to provide more stable and remunerative employment opportunities.

7. To continue with the forestry example, in the Maritimes, subcontractors in trucking and logging serve to absorb the instabilities in the supply of and demand for logs, thereby cushioning the effect on the corporate sector (Marchak, 1977; Wien and Comeau, 1978).

8. Specific predictions on such factors as the wage determination process and the role of education are developed by Doeringer and Piore (1971), Gordon (1972), and Harrison (1972), among others. A critical review is provided by Wachter (1974), Cain (1976) and Smith (1976).

9. An especially vulnerable but expanding area of employment is the service sector where jobs are particularly likely to be low-wage, part-time and unprotected. The Atlantic region generally has the largest proportion of persons employed in the service sector of any Canadian region and the smallest in manufacturing, with the exception of the Prairies (Statistics Canada, 1974). Using U.S. data, Freedman (1976) finds that the proportion of persons employed in the least sheltered jobs has increased from 36 to 46% between 1960 and 1970, with much of the growth taking place in the service sector.

10. The current attempt to organize inshore fishermen in Nova Scotia involves a struggle between a fishermen's association funded until recently by the provincial government and a fishermen's union supported in part by the Canadian Labour Congress. The task of the union organizers is made more difficult by the refusal of the provincial government to change legislation which, at present, excludes fishermen from the provisions of the trade union act.

11. Attempts at unionization at the establishment level may be challenged by the firm on the grounds that it represents too limited a base for an appropriate bargaining unit, as in the case of bank branches.

12. In Nova Scotia since 1974, all but three of the 15 cases of revoked certification involved MWW-based union locals.

13. One union official who represents workers at several MWW establishments stated that the high rate of unemployment in the region acts as a brake on aggressive unionism; otherwise, he added, "I believe if you can't trade, get out! I have come to the conclusion that by negotiating and keeping such companies alive, all you are doing is prolonging the agony. You are not doing the workers any good."

References

Adams, Ian, *The Poverty Wall* (Toronto: McClelland and Stewart, 1970).

Aronowitz, Stanley, "Trade Unionism in America," in B. Silverman and M. Yonowitch, eds., *The Worker in Post-Industrial Capitalism.* New York: The Free Press, 1974, pp. 410-23.

Averitt, Robert, *The Dual Economy.* New York: Norton, 1968.

Baron, Harold and Bennett Hymer, "The Negro in the Chicago Labor Market," in Julius Jacobson, ed., *The Negro and the American Labor Movement.* New York: Doubleday Anchor Books, 1968.

Barth, F, "Economic Spheres in Darfur," in R. Firth, ed., *Themes of Economic Anthropology.* ASA Monographs, No. 6, London: Tavistock, 1967.

Beck, E.M., P.M. Horan and C.M. Tolbert, "Stratification in a Dual Economy: A Sectoral Model of Earnings Determination," *American Sociological Review* Vol. 43 (Oct. 1978).

Berger, Suzanne, "The Uses of the Traditional Sector: Why the Declining Classes Survive," Massachusetts Institute of Technology, Dept. of Economics, Cambridge, Mass., 1973.

Bluestone, Barry, "The Tripartite Economy: Labor Markets and the Working Poor," *Poverty and Human Resources Abstracts,* Vol. 5, No. 4 (July-Aug. 1970), pp. 15-35.

Bluestone, Barry Alan, *The Personal Earnings Distribution: Individual and Institutional Determinants.* Boston: Social Welfare Regional Research Institute, 20 (Nov. 1974).

Boeke, J.H., *Economics and Economic Policy in Dual Societies.* Haarlem, Netherlands: H.D. Willink and Zoon, 1953.

Bohannan, P. and C. Dalton, *Markets in Africa.* New York: Northwestern University Press, 1965.

Brox, Ottar, *Newfoundland Fisherman in an Age of Industry: A Sociology of Economic Dualism.* St. John's, Newfoundland: Institute for Social and Economic Research, Memorial University, 1972.

Butler, Peter and Pam Buckley, "Work and Welfare: A Closer Look at Linkages between Income Security and the World of Work." Working Paper, Institute of Public Affairs, Dalhousie University, 1978.

Cain, Glen G., "The Challenge of Dual and and Radical Theories of the Labor Market to Orthodox Theory." Institute for Research on Poverty, Discussion Papers, Jan. 1976.

Doeringer, P. and M. Piore, *Internal Labor Markets and Manpower Analysis.* Lexington: D.C. Heath, 1971.

Dunlop, John T., "The Task of Contemporary Wage Theory," in George W. Taylor, ed., *New Concepts in Wage Determination.* New York: McGraw-Hill, 1957, pp. 117-39.

Edwards, Richard C., Michael Reich and David M. Gordon, eds., *Labor Market Segmentation.* Lexington: D.C. Heath, 1975.

Eichner, Alfred S., "The Human Resources Approach to Labor Economics." Conservation of Human Resources Project, Columbia University, Feb. 1977.

Ferman, Louis A., "The Irregular Economy: Informal Work Patterns in the Ghetto." Dept. of Economics, University of Michigan, 1967.

Freedman, Marcia, *Labor Markets: Segments and Shelters.* Montclair, N.J.: Allanheld, Osmun and Co., Universe Books, 1976.

Goldthorpe, J.H., "Affluence and the Workers' Work World," in B. Silverman and M. Yanowitch, eds., *The Worker in Post-Industrial Capitalism.* New York: The Free Press, 1974.

Gordon, David M., *Theories of Poverty and Underemployment.* Lexington: D.C. Heath, 1972.

Harrison, Bennett, *Education Training and the Urban Ghetto.* Baltimore: Johns Hopkins University Press, 1972.

————, "How Americans Mix Work and Welfare." *Challenge* (May-June 1978).

Janowitz, M., *Social Control of the Welfare State.* New York: Elsevier, 1976.

Johnson, H. and P. Miezkowski, "Effects of Unionization in the Distribution of Income," *Quarterly Journal of Economics*, 84(1970).

Johnson, L.A., *Poverty in Wealth*, 2nd ed. Toronto: New Hogtown Press, 1974.

Kahn, L., "Unions and Labor Market Segmentation." Ph.D. Dissertation, University of California, Berkeley, 1975.

Kerr, Clark, "The Balkanization of Labor Markets," in E. Wright Bakke et al., eds., *Labor Mobility and Economic Opportunity.* Cambridge, Massachusetts Institute of Technology Press, 1954.

Lewis, W.A., "Economic Development with Unlimited Supplies of Labour." The Manchester School of Economic and Social Studies, May 1954.

Marchak, Patricia M., "Corporate and Non-corporate Labour in a Hinterland Economy: The Case of Interior Forestry Workers in British Columbia." Draft paper prepared for the Polish-Canada Exchange Seminar, May 1977.

Myrdal, Gunnar, *An American Dilemma.* New York: McGraw-Hill, 1944.

Nova Scotia Department of Labour, *Labour Organizations in Nova Scotia.* Halifax: Province of Nova Scotia, 1976.

Parsons, T., *The System of Modern Societies.* Englewood Cliffs, N.J.: Prentice-Hall, 1971.

Piore, M.J., "Union Rules: The Changing Character of Work," *Social Policy*, 14, 1 (July-Aug. 1973).

Rees, Albert, *The Economics of Work and Pay.* New York: Harper and Row, 1973.

Robinson, D., *Solidaristic Wage Policy in Sweden.* Paris: Organization for Economic Cooperation and Development, 1972.

Sabel, Charles F., "Industrial Conflict and the Sociology of the Labor Market." Unpublished paper, Max Planck Institute, West Germany, n.d.

Simon, Herbert A., *Administrative Behaviour*, 2nd ed. New York: MacMillan, 1957.

Smith, David C., "The Dual Labor Market Theory: A Canadian Perspective." Research and Current Issues, Series #32, Industrial Relations Centre, Queen's University, Kingston, 1976.

Smith, Ron, "The Marginal Work World in the Maritimes: Preliminary Statistical Analysis." Halifax: Institute of Public Affairs, Dalhousie University, 1977.

Statistics Canada, *Perspective Canada: A Compendium of Social Statistics*. Ottawa: Information Canada, 1974.

Thurow, L., *Generating Inequality: Mechanisms of Distribution in the U.S. Economy*. New York: Basic Books, 1975.

Tolbert, Charles, Patrick Horan and E. Beck, *The Dual Economy in American Structure*. Athens, Georgia: University of Georgia, 1978.

Velk, Tom, "Good News: Changes in Income Distribution," *Canadian Forum* (May 1976).

Vietorisz, Thomas and Bennett Harrison, *The Economic Development of Harlem*. New York: Praeger, 1970.

Wachter, Michael L., "Primary and Secondary Labor Markets: A Critique of the Dual Approach." *Brookings Papers on Economic Activity*, 3(1974).

Wachtel, H. and C. Betsey, "Employment at Low Wages," *The Review of Economics and Statistics* (May 1972).

Whyte, Donald, "Sociological Perspectives on Poverty," in John Harp and John Hofley, eds., *Poverty in Canada*. Scarborough, Ont.: Prentice-Hall of Canada, 1971.

Wien, F.C. and Louis Comeau, "The Socio-Economic History and Structure of South-West Nova Scotia." Working Paper, Institute of Public Affairs, Dalhousie University, 1978.

Wood, W.D. and Pradeep Kumar, *The Current Industrial Relations Scene in Canada*. Kingston, Ont.: Industrial Relations Centre, Queen's University, 1977.

12/Chinese Immigrants on the Canadian Prairie, 1910-47[*]

Peter S. Li

This paper examines the job histories of a group of first-generation Chinese immigrants who have been living in Canada from 50 to 70 years. The study focuses on the working experience of the Chinese prior to and during the exclusion era between 1923 and 1947, when they were barred from immigrating to Canada, and were subjected to numerous legal restrictions in Canada. The purpose of the analysis is to draw some general conclusions about the economic survival of an ethnic minority which has historically encountered severe discrimination and other structural barriers. The use of case histories in the study provides some detailed insights into the organization of an ethnic group, which survey data often fail to capture.

[*] Abridged from Peter S. Li, "Chinese Immigrants on the Canadian Prairie, 1910-47." Reprinted from *The Canadian Review of Sociology and Anthropology*, Volume 19:4, 1982, pp. 527-540 by permission of the author and the publisher.

Ethnic Competitions and Segmented Economy

The recent literature on ethnic inequality suggests two basic approaches regarding the treatment of ethnicity in the process of stratification. The first approach considers ethnicity as an ascribed individual attribute, which, depending on the ethnic group, may be an asset or a liability in the career of the individual. The second approach views ethnicity as a shared characteristic for members of the same ethnic group which provides the basis for economic and other organizations in response to a segmented or segregated labour market.

Status-attainment models (Blau and Duncan, 1967; Duncan and Duncan, 1968; Featherman, 1971; Duncan, Featherman, and Duncan, 1972; Featherman and Hauser, 1978) provide a good illustration and summary of the first approach. Ethnicity or ethnic origin in these models is treated in the same way as other variables such as education, family background, aspirations, and I.Q., measuring individuals' abilities and resources in the competitive labour market. Critics of this approach (Horan, 1978) point out its theoretical proximity to the structural-functional theory of stratification (Davis and Moore, 1945), in which a single unified and open market is assumed, and the effect of labour market structuration on the process of attainment is ignored.

More recently, a second theoretical approach has emerged in the literature. This approach focuses on the way in which racial minority groups are incorporated into the industrial structure of the capitalist economy (Bonacich, 1972; 1976; Baron and Hymer, 1968; Burawoy, 1976). Ethnicity in this context is viewed as a group characteristic which often provides grounds for labour segregation. Migratory labourers, immigrant groups, and racial minorities (Bach, 1978; Burawoy, 1976; Edwards and Gordon, 1975) provide a cheap marginal labour supply to enable faster accumulation in the capitalist economy's core sector.

Aside from a basic difference in the treatment of ethnicity in the process of stratification, the second approach also differs from the first in the way the capitalist economy is described. According to this view, the capitalist system consists not of a single, unified economy, but a dual economy in which a monopolized core sector of large firms co-exists with a competitive marginal sector of small firms (Averitt, 1968; Gordon, 1972; Edwards and Gordon, 1975). The job market in the core sector is characterized by high pay, security, and promotion opportunity; the marginal labour market is insecure and unstable, with little incentive to human capital investment as schooling and training.

More recently, Wilson and Portes (1980) have suggested a third structural dimension to the dual economy to include the enclave economy associated with immigrant firms. The full implication of the enclave economy is not known, aside from the suggestion that it fulfils the role of middlemen in exploiting immigrant labour for the benefit of the firms in the core sector (Wilson and Portes, 1980). Using a somewhat different terminology, Light (1973) writes about the success of some immigrant groups in establishing the ethnic enterprise as a viable alternative in the American economy.

By identifying the ethnic business sector as a third dimension to the dual economy one can better understand the way in which immigrants are incorporated into the market structures. Although some attempts have been made to explain the emergence of ethnic enterprise (Light, 1973; Li, 1976; 1979; Siu, 1953; Yancey et al., 1976), most of the discussion has to do with arguments over institutional versus cultural explanations. Little remains known about the structure of immigrants' work world and the organization of ethnic business. In subsequent sections, I shall describe the case of the Chinese on the Canadian prairie between 1910 and 1947, focusing in particular on the work world of the Chinese and how some of them managed to move back and forth between marginal employment and the ethnic business. The job histories of these Chinese provide further understanding of the rise of ethnic business, and the way in which an oppressed minority adjusted to the economic structure of Canada. . . .

Chinese Immigration to Canada

The Chinese immigration to Canada began around 1858 after gold was discovered in the Fraser Valley, British Columbia. The initial wave of Chinese immigrants consisted of miners from the west coast of the United States, and immigrants from Kwantung province of China. Subsequently, large numbers of Chinese labourers were recruited to Canada to fill a labour shortage, especially between 1881 and 1885 when the Canadian Pacific Railway was constructed. Between 1881 and 1883, for example, the number of Chinese arriving by ship at Victoria was 13,245 (Li, 1979). The wave of Chinese immigration continued after the CPR was completed, albeit at a slower rate. Between 1886 and 1894, the number of Chinese entering Canada and paying a special head tax was 12,197. This number was increased to 32,457 for the period 1895-1904 (Li, 1979).

As early as 1875, the provincial government of British Columbia passed anti-Chinese bills to disenfranchise the Chinese, and to restrict their civil rights. The Dominion Government of Canada had resisted passing a federal bill to control the flow of Chinese immigration before 1885, for fear that it would create a shortage of labourers, and impede the construction of the CPR. The first federal anti-Chinese bill was passed in 1885, in the form of a head tax of $50 imposed upon every Chinese person entering Canada (Statutes of Canada, 1885, c. 71). The tax was raised to $100 in 1900 (Statutes of Canada, 1900, c. 32), and $500 in 1903 (Statutes of Canada, 1903, c. 8). In 1923, the federal government passed the most restrictive Chinese Immigration Act, essentially excluding all Chinese from entering Canada (Statutes of Canada, 1923, c. 38). The act was in effect until 1947 (Statutes of Canada, 1947, c. 19). . . .

Initially, the Chinese were recruited to the west coast as labourers in various pioneering industries such as mining, railroad construction, and later canning and other manufacturing. They were attractive to employers because of low labour cost and large supply. As white workers increased in number in British Columbia, the Chinese were perceived as competitors who were willing to undercut wages, and to serve as scabs in labour disputes. As organized labour began to grow, the Chinese became increasingly the target of labour exclusion. Organized labour demanded the exclusion of the Chinese from trades, and eventually their total exclusion from the country. The anti-Chinese sentiments received political support as politicians saw the advantage of adopting a platform to exclude the Chinese. By 1880, for example, all political parties found it necessary to take such a platform to gain popular support.

As a result of anti-Chinese movement and subsequent legislative control, the Chinese found it difficult to compete with white labourers in the core labour market. Many were forced to take up employment in the marginal sector. The hostile labour market also accelerated the growth of ethnic business among the Chinese, first concentrating in laundry operations, later in restaurants. The marginal sector and the ethnic business provided an occupational refuge for many Chinese when opportunities were restricted in the core labour market. . . .

The statistics indicate that in 1921, 24 per cent of the Chinese were labourers and unskilled workers, and 35 per cent were employed as store employees, servants, cooks, laundry workers, and waiters.[1] These percentages reflect the concentration of the Chinese in the marginal and ethnic business sectors. The figures for 1931 show an increase in such a concentration. Labourers and unskilled workers constituted 21 per cent of the employed Chinese, while store employees, servants, cooks, laundry workers, and waiters made up another 42 per cent.[2] These figures illustrate in part the restrictive employment opportunities open to the Chinese. . . .

Opportunities and Constraints in the Labour Market

The job histories of the thirty-one pre-war immigrants have a number of characteristics in common. For example, all the jobs were menial in nature and poorly paid. They often worked as domestic servants, laundry workers, and restaurant workers. As Chinese laundries declined in the thirties, the restaurants, both Chinese and non-Chinese owned, provided the main source of employment for many Chinese. All the respondents had a working history of high turnover from job to job. The mobility was frequently from one prairie town to another, but the line of work remained the same. The following two cases illustrate well the typical job history among the Chinese.

Case 1: "I came to Moose Jaw in 1913. . . . First I washed dishes, making $35 a month. I worked for 14 to 16 hours a day. I knelt down on the floor and washed the floor and washed the dining room every morning. I had a potato bag to make it easier for my knees. Then after that, I went to work for a Japanese owner of a restaurant. That was 1914. . . . After a while, I went to Simpson, at harvest time, up north, it was the CPR line. I worked in a farm. I got up 6 o'clock in the morning, milked the cow, and came back to the house to cook breakfast for my boss. . . . He was not a very friendly person. . . . It was no good, so I quit. I came back to Moose Jaw to work for my brother for $50 a month for 12 hours a day. At night I scrubbed the floor and waited on tables. Then in 1918 I went back to China to get married."

Case 2: "When I arrive at Saskatoon (1918), I rested for a couple of days, and went to wash dishes for an Englishman in a hotel. . . . I didn't work there long, and went to Biggar to work. I was also washing dishes in Biggar. . . . I worked for long hours, 10 hours or so a day. I worked with Mr. _____, and then the boss was transferred to Lethbridge from Biggar. . . . So I followed him to Lethbridge. I went there to work as a night cook. At night when the train come in I would have to make 100 sandwiches and coffee. . . . I made $50 a month. It was in the 1920s. I worked there for a couple of months. I didn't like it, and so I came back to Saskatoon. My relative was working at a hotel as a cook. The hotel went broke, and he asked me to be his partner. . . ."

Jobs among the Chinese have all the features typical of employment in the marginal labour market. These features include long hours of work, little security, low pay, and low skill. The employment opportunity open to the Chinese was limited mainly to laundries and restaurants in the service sector. One respondent described the job situation for the Chinese in Moose Jaw around 1913 as follows: "At that time there were about 450 (Chinese) men and two women. . . . In Moose Jaw, there were about 35 to 38 Chinese laundries and three cafes. . . . All the Chinese worked there."

On the surface, it would seem that lack of occupational and language skills would explain why so many Chinese had low-status jobs in the service sector. Although skills in general enhance the market value of employees, jobs open to the Chinese required little skill. As long as employment in other sectors was not available to the Chinese, improvement in language and other skills would help little in enabling the Chinese to gain higher paying jobs.

There is strong evidence to indicate that the Chinese faced a discriminatory job market even in cases where Chinese employees had the necessary skill to perform the task. Although none of our respondents had university training, we spoke to a few Canadian-born Chinese who described the difficulties in their job searches prior to the Second World War.

Among the Canadian-born Chinese, there were a few of us who went to university. Some of them, like my two brothers, got their degrees at UBC. But none of them was able to find work. One of my brothers was a civil engineer, who graduated in 1933. He wasn't able to get anything, so he had to go to Quebec. . . . My other brother got a degree in dairying. He wasn't able to find anything, so he went back to China around 1935. . . .

Ethnic Business
Since employment opportunities in the labour sector were highly restrictive, many Chinese immigrants ventured into an ethnic business to preserve a job and to maintain a living. The Chinese first entered into the laundry business, and later into the restaurant business. The Chinese restaurants in the prairie towns in the twenties and thirties, however, were very different from the post-war Chinese restaurants in metropolitan centres. These earlier restaurants were small in scale, poorly decorated, and labour-intensive. The hours of operation were long, and the profit margin was small. The restaurants simply provided a business venture for many Chinese whereby they could put up a small amount of capital to secure a guaranteed

place to work and live. The case histories clearly indicate that in those cases where the respondents became part owners of a restaurant, they were doing the same kinds of work in their own restaurant as they did when working for somebody else. The restaurants provided an economic refuge for the Chinese in a restrictive labour market.

Twenty-two of the respondents had the experience of holding a partnership in a restaurant sometime in their career. In many cases, the respondents reported a history of moving back and forth between employment and self-employment in restaurants. There was little doubt in the minds of the respondents that self-employment in one's restaurant was just as much a job as employment in another restaurant.

Partnership was a viable means for many Chinese to start a restaurant because it allowed meagre capital and labour to be pooled. Given the kinds of jobs most Chinese had, the capacity to save a large amount of capital for investment was limited. Partnership provided a means of joint venture with little capital. The business partners also worked as a team in running the restaurant to reduce the cost of hiring other workers. . . . During the Depression, the restaurants provided a means of survival for many Chinese. As one respondent described the situation of a restaurant during the early thirties: ". . .there were 4 partners and 10 others who just stayed there because there was nowhere else to go. . . . There was no work to do elsewhere, and they looked after the restaurant.". . .

A number of factors probably facilitated the formation of business partnership among the Chinese immigrants. The fact that many respondents came to Canada by way of relative sponsorship means that they had certain kinship ties that could be used as a basis for business partners. Indeed, partnerships were frequently formed between fathers and sons, uncles and nephews, and brothers. In some cases, the partnership may be extended to more distant relatives and friends. Since the Chinese immigrants emigrated from predominantly the same region, common lineage and clanship ties provided the Chinese immigrants with a web of both close and distant relatives from which partners could be drawn. The prevalence of business partnership was confirmed by all the respondents. As one of them described it: "In the old days, it was partnership. . . we all worked partnerships. . . . In my case, I worked together with my brothers.". . .

The partnership business among the Chinese declined after the war as more Chinese were allowed to bring their families to Canada. The family members provided additional labour power to operate the restaurant. Many partnership businesses broke up as the post-war immigration altered the demographic pattern among the Chinese community.

Mobility Dream

To many Chinese immigrants before the war, the only hope of success was to work hard in Canada, and save enough money to retire in China. Meanwhile, during their stay in Canada, they aspired to visit China periodically, where they could unite with their families for a short period of time. This mentality, sometimes described as a "sojourner's orientation" (Siu, 1953) or a "marginal personality" (Park, 1928; Stonequist, 1937), basically results from a clash of two cultures, leading to the immigrants' inability to identify with the host community. In the case of the Chinese in Canada, there is every indication to suggest that their mobility aspiration to return to China was greatly influenced by a number of structural factors.

For example, the restrictive immigration laws against the Chinese meant that most Chinese men in Canada before the war were unable to bring their families (Li, 1980). Before 1923, the law stipulated a head tax of $500 for practically every Chinese person entering Canada. After 1923, the Chinese Immigration Act precluded the Chinese from admission to the country. Aside from the restrictive immigration laws, the social atmosphere was very unfriendly to the Chinese as a group. They were excluded from many aspects of life in Canadian society. Their ties to the host community were maintained in a symbiotic relationship in which the Chinese provided cheap labour and service in the marginal and ethnic business sectors in exchange for meagre pay to support themselves and their families in China. The position of the Chinese in the economy was similar to that of many migrant workers in industrial societies. . . .

It is difficult to estimate how many Chinese immigrants actually retired in China, and how many stayed in Canada. For those who stayed, their way of thinking changed radically after the war as the treatment of the Chinese improved, and their families were allowed to immigrate to Canada. The 1949 socialist revolution in China may also have discouraged overseas immigrants from returning. The difference of the pre-war and post-war mentality was clearly explained by one respondent: "After the war, they allowed us Chinese to bring the wife, and then the children here. . . . Now you are ambitious to teach the children to go to school so others wouldn't look down on you. . . . Before, it was not the same. . .even if you were educated, even if you knew how to do the job, the government wouldn't hire you because nobody wanted Orientals."

Summary and Conclusion

The oral history of the Chinese shows that immigrants before the war found a limited number of jobs in the service industry. These jobs have many of the features common to marginal labour, such as long hours of work, menial labour, low pay, and lack of promotion opportunity. The Chinese also reported a history of changing from one menial job to another, including a movement between employment and self-employment in the ethnic business.

The predominant Chinese business was the restaurant which provided a viable employment opportunity for many in a restrictive labour market. Limited by capital and manpower, the Chinese made use of partnership investment to build their restaurant business. The organization of partnership enabled a maximum use of labour power among partners to reduce labour cost, at the same time providing enough flexibility to cushion business risks and uncertainties. The popularity of the restaurant business among the Chinese before the war represents a successful attempt on their part to adapt to the structural constraints of the labour market.

Aside from the general restrictive employment opportunity which encouraged many Chinese to seek alternative avenues in the ethnic business sector, a number of other factors also facilitated the formation of business partnership among the Chinese. Partnerships were largely formed on the basis of kinship ties. Since most of the Chinese immigrants came to Canada through the sponsorship of relatives, the kinship ties which were instrumental in their immigration remained important for the subsequent stage when partnerships were struck. The web of kinship ties was also enriched by the fact that most of the immigrants came from the same place of origin. The absence of Chinese wives and young children as a result of the restrictive immigration law compelled young Chinese men to rely on business partners for additional labour in their business operation. The success of Chinese restaurants as survival vehicles was related to Chinese immigrants' ability to mobilize kinship assistance.

This study suggests the importance of studying the conditions of the labour market as well as the adaptive responses of an ethnic group for an understanding of its structural position in the economy. The development of ethnic business among the Chinese calls for further attention to the enclave economy in theories of a dual labour market.

Notes

1. The figures are based on all gainfully occupied Chinese in Canada, ten years of age and over (Census of Canada, 1931: vol. VII, Occupations and Industries, Table 69, pp. 988-97).

2. The figures are based on all gainfully occupied Chinese in Canada, ten years of age and over (ibid., Table 49, pp. 430-3).

References

Averitt, Robert T.

   1968   *The Dual Economy: The Dynamics of American Industry Structure*. New York: W.W. Norton.

Bach, Robert L.

   1978   "Mexican Immigration and the American State." *International Migration Review* 12:536-58.

Baron, Harold M. and Bennet Hymer

   1968   "The Negro worker in the Chicago labour movement." In J. Jacobson, ed., *The Negro and the American Labour Movement*, pp. 232-85. New York: Doubleday.

Blau, Peter and Otis D. Duncan

   1967   *The American Occupational Structure*. New York: John Wiley and Sons.

Bonacich, Edna

   1972   "A theory of ethnic antagonism: the split labour market." *American Sociological Review* 37: 547-59.

   1976   "Advanced capitalism and black/white race relations in the United States: a split labour market interpretation." *American Sociological Review* 41: 34-51.

Burawoy, Michael
1976   "The functions and reproduction of migrant labour: comparative materials from southern Africa and the United States." *American Journal of Sociology* 81: 1050-87.

Davis, K. and Wilbert E. Moore
1945   "Some principles of stratification." *American Sociological Review* 10: 242-9.

Duncan, Beverly and Otis D. Duncan
1968   "Minorities and the process of stratification." *American Sociological Review* 33: 356-64.

Duncan, Otis D., David L. Featherman and Beverly Duncan
1972   *Socioeconomic Background and Achievement.* New York: Seminar Press.

Edwards, R., M. Reich and David M. Gordon
1975   *Labour Market Segmentation.* Lexington, Mass.: D.C. Heath.

Featherman, David L.
1971   "The socioeconomic achievement of white religio-ethnic subgroups: social and psychological explanations." *American Sociological Review* 36: 207-22.

Featherman, David L. and Robert M. Hauser
1978   *Opportunity and Change.* New York: Academic Press.

Gordon, David M.
1972   *Theories of Poverty and Underdevelopment.* Lexington, Mass.: D.C. Heath.

Horan, Patrick M.
1978   "Is status attainment research atheoretical?" *American Sociological Review* 43: 434-541.

Li, Peter S.
1976   "Ethnic businesses among Chinese in the U.S." *Journal of Ethnic Studies* 4: 35-41.
1979   "A historical approach to ethnic stratification: the case of the Chinese in Canada, 1858-1930." *Canadian Review of Sociology and Anthropology* 16: 320-32.
1980   "Immigration laws and family patterns: some demographic changes among Chinese families in Canada, 1885-1971." *Canadian Ethnic Studies* 12: 58-72.

Light, Ivan H.
1973   *Ethnic Enterprise in America.* Berkeley, California: University of California Press.

Park, Robert E.
1928   "Human migration and the marginal man." *American Journal of Sociology* 32: 881-93.

Siu, Paul
1953   "The Chinese laundryman: a study of social isolation." Unpublished Ph.D. dissertation, University of Chicago.

Statutes of Canada
1885   An Act to restrict and regulate Chinese immigration into Canada. Chapter 71.
1900   An Act respecting and restricting Chinese Immigration. Chapter 32.
1903   An Act respecting and restricting Chinese Immigration. Chapter 8.
1923   An Act respecting Chinese Immigration. Chapter 38.
1947   An Act to amend the Immigration Act and to repeal the Chinese Immigration Act. Chapter 19.

Stonequist, Everett V.
1973   *The Marginal Man.* New York: Scribner.

Wilson, Kenneth L. and Alejandro Portes
1980   "Immigrants enclaves: an analysis of the labour market experience of Cubans in Miami." *American Journal of Sociology* 86: 295-319.

Yancey, William L., E.P. Eriksen, and R.N. Julian
1976   "Emergent ethnicity: a review of reformulation." *American Sociological Review* 41: 391-403.

Part III/Working Women

Editors' Introduction

The work of women has historically gone unrewarded and unrecognized, largely because they have toiled within the confines of the home as wife and mother. At the turn of the century, only 16 per cent of Canadian women worked outside the home for pay. With the exception of the two world wars, when women temporarily filled the jobs of men who had gone off to fight, it is only since the 1950s that we have witnessed a dramatic increase in female labour-force participation. Highlighting this trend has been the employment of married women, to the point where now over half of all wives hold paying jobs. The chapters in this part focus on the experiences of women in the workforce, especially the barriers they encounter to achieving the same conditions and opportunities as men. Despite the influence of the women's liberation movement during the 1970s, the five chapters that follow make it abundantly clear that little has changed.

Pat and Hugh Armstrong set the stage for our investigation of the problems and issues surrounding women's work today. In Chapter 13, they graphically portray how the majority of working women are trapped in low-level, dead-end, and poorly paying jobs in the clerical, sales, service, and light manufacturing sectors. They document how the labour market is divided into segments, with the more desirable professional, managerial, and skilled manual jobs being defined as "men's work." Through their socialization experiences, the streaming process in schools, as well as the operation of the labour market, women are channelled away from these male preserves and into a small number of female "job ghettos," which have all the negative connotations the term implies. Furthermore, the ways women adapt to their poor working conditions (high absenteeism and quit rates, or a lack of job commitment) confirms in the eyes of management that they simply are not suitable for more responsible positions.

Remarkably, the same job ghettos have accounted for the bulk of female employment since the early twentieth century. This fact underlines the formidable hurdles women encounter when trying to improve their work situations. Clerical work is a good example of a typically "female" occupation. By the 1920s menial office tasks had been permanently labelled as "women's work," with the result that only women were hired for these jobs. The label has persisted, and even today women with university degrees are likely to be recruited into clerical positions instead of more challenging administrative posts. In contrast, male office recruits often begin as management trainees and look forward to upward career mobility. True enough, we can now point to some "high profile" women in corporate and government organizations and in male-dominated occupations and professions, but they are usually the exception.

Most new jobs that have been created in the last few years are part-time. Lacking the security, pay and benefits of full-time work, these jobs are accounting for a growing share of the female labour force. But even if women are employed full-time, chances are that they will earn only about 60 per cent of what the average male earns. This great disparity between male and female earnings is only partially due to wage discrimination where women perform the same work as men but for a lower wage. The fundamental problem, emphasized by all the chapters in this part, is that the labour market is comprised of unequal segments with little movement between them: there is men's work where pay, security, and advancement opportunities are good; and there is women's work where conditions are generally poor.

Given the growing prevalence of part-time work among women, it is worth asking why employers often prefer this type of arrangement. In Chapter 14, Wendy Weeks examines managements' views of the advantages of part-time employment. Involved in a constant struggle against rising costs, management sees reduced wage and benefits costs as the primary inducement to hire workers part-time. Greater flexibility and efficiency in utilizing personnel is also an advantage, especially for employers whose business comes in peak periods. On the other side of the coin, it is also true that this flexibility in hours appeals to many women, particularly if they have young children. But the attractiveness of the part-time option could be significantly enhanced if these workers, instead of being treated as "second class" employees, received the same wages, benefits, and status as those working full-time.

In Chapter 15, Wendy Johnston draws on her experience as an aircraft assembly worker and a member of the United Auto Workers' union women's committee to illuminate the difficulties women face when attempting to break into blue-collar employment. She argues that the voluntary affirmative action guidelines initiated by governments in the last decade are ineffective. Her experiences have led her to conclude that only mandatory hiring quotas will bring about greater opportunities for women. This is certainly a contentious proposal, mainly because it would require hiring women less qualified than men in some cases. Yet advocates of hiring quotas claim that they are necessary to allow women, a disadvantaged group, time to catch up and establish themselves in previously inaccessible occupations.

Chapter 16 offers an insightful commentary by a management consultant on a puzzling situation often encountered by large corporations. Even though some organizations allocate half of their management training positions to women, very few actually enter the program. Thus, while on paper these training programs appear to offer "equal opportunity," in practice they do little to improve women's representation in management ranks. Furthermore, the fact that many women actually turn down the opportunity only confirms to senior male managers that women are less ambitious than men. The ten reasons Edita Kowalski gives for this situation can be traced to the nature of the training programs and the stereotypical views of women deeply engrained in top corporate circles. In short, management is still very much a male domain, with subtle mechanisms operating to keep it that way.

The last chapter on women's work draws some important links between the world of paid employment and the family. Meg Luxton's research in the single industry resource town of Flin Flon, Manitoba, richly documents the experiences of forty wives who must juggle the responsibilities of their family roles with paid employment. Luxton is especially interested in why the wives she interviewed, all of whom had young children and working husbands, went to work in the first place. By comparing women from working-class and middle-class families, she traces the decision for both groups to financial need, but is quick to note that the definition of need varies according to class. In middle-class families, the wives took jobs to help out during a financial crisis. By contrast, in working-class families it was when things were running smoothly that wives sought paid employment because they were then better able to cope with the added strain. In addition, the relatively greater financial contribution of working-class wives to family income meant that, compared to middle-class families, both spouses placed greater value on the wife's labour-force activity. One thing did unite the women whom Luxton interviewed: all had to carry the double burden of family duties and job.

In sum, men and women experience different realities in the work world because they perform different kinds of work. The reasons for the glaring inequalities between the sexes in terms of opportunities for challenging and rewarding work are many and complex, but essentially they are rooted in the structure of the labour market. The barriers to women's full and equal participation in the labour force cannot, however, be viewed in isolation. They mirror inequalities in the larger society, which is male dominated in most spheres of activity. Changes have been slow, but perhaps the pace will quicken as women form increasingly effective lobby groups in the political arena.

Suggested Readings

Pat Armstrong and Hugh Armstrong, *A Working Majority: What Women Must Do for Pay* (Ottawa: Canadian Advisory Council on the Status of Women, 1983).

M.S. Devereaux and Edith Rechnitzer, *Higher Education — Hired? Sex Differences in Employment Characteristics of 1976 Postsecondary Graduates* (Ottawa: Statistics Canada and Labour Canada, Women's Bureau, 1980).

Rosabeth Moss Kanter, *Men and Women of the Corporation* (New York, Basic Books, 1977).

Graham S. Lowe, "Women, Work and the Office: The Feminization of Clerical Occupations in Canada, 1901-1931," *Canadian Journal of Sociology* 5, 4 (1980), pp.361-81.

Meg Luxton, *More than a Labour of Love: Three Generations of Women's Work in the Home* (Toronto: Canadian Women's Educational Press, 1980).

Marlene Mackie, *Exploring Gender Relations: A Canadian Perspective* (Toronto: Butterworths, 1983).

Martin Meissner, E.W. Humphreys, S.M. Meis and W.J. Schue, "No Exit for Wives: Sexual Division of Labour and the Cumulation of Household Demands," *Canadian Review of Sociology and Anthropology* 12, 4, part I (1975), pp. 424-39.

Paul Phillips and Erin Phillips, *Women and Work: Inequality in the Labour Market* (Toronto: Lorimer, 1983).

S.M. Trofimenkoff and A. Prentice, eds., *The Neglected Majority: Essays in Canadian Women's History* (Toronto: McClelland and Stewart, 1977).

13/The Structure of Women's Labour Force Work: Everywhere and Nowhere*

Pat and Hugh Armstrong

The woman who wrote the Dick and Jane stories read by generations of Canadian children died recently. The fictional homemaker she created to bake cookies, feed Spot and mind the children has also passed away. But images are hard to bury.

When we ask our college students to describe a mother, they draw a picture of a housewife who differs little from the one in the old elementary school textbook. At home for the children after school, cook to the neighbourhood, protector of her family, she is in turn protected from the demands of paid employment by her wage-earning husband. When we ask the same male and female students to describe a day in their lives at age 35, they conjure up images of family life that the author of the old children's reader would easily recognize. They too expect to cook, clean, and care for a family, or marry a woman who will do these things.

If our female students say they will "choose" to work in the labour force, the jobs they will look for are interesting, highly paid, and have short hours which do not interfere with their work at home. They will start work late enough in the day to get their children off to school before they leave, come home early enough to prepare the evening meal, and earn enough to have domestic help. According to these students, they will be lured back to the labour force when their children start school because the jobs are good and the pay is better now. As far as they are concerned, the issues raised by "women's lib" have been largely resolved. Like the woman in the cigarette ad, they have come a long way.

But the reality is different. The majority of women in the labour force are married, and most do clerical, service, sales, and factory work, often at very low pay. Only a minority of women in Canada today are full-time housewives, and with prices rising faster than wages, fewer and fewer women will have the luxury of

---

* Abridged from Pat Armstrong and Hugh Armstrong, *A Working Majority: What Women Must Do for Pay* (Ottawa: Canadian Advisory Council on the Status of Women, 1983), chapter 2, "The Structure of Women's Labour Force Work: Everywhere and Nowhere" and "Statistical Appendix." Reproduced by permission of the Minister of Supply and Services Canada and the authors.

choosing this option in the future. Many of the women who seek work find no job at all, a large number find only part-time positions, and many are underemployed in terms of their training and qualifications. Many of women's best jobs, in teaching and nursing, are disappearing, while the micro-electronic chip, which has made possible the word processor and the automatic teller, is reducing both the skills and the number of jobs in clerical work.

It is time to draw an accurate picture of the woman working in the labour force, and it is time to change the reality as well. We've still got a long way to go.

Women's Work

1980 marked the first time in Canadian history that a majority of women were officially in the labour force.[1]

And even this statistic, which indicates that more than one out of every two women had a paid job or wanted one, underestimates the actual numbers of both employed and unemployed women. Many more women would take paid employment if the working conditions were better, if the pay increased, if childcare and housework assistance were available, if their husbands' attitudes changed, if their health improved, or if they had more or other training and education.[2] Not only are many of those who want and need work left out of the official statistics, so are many of the women who clean houses, babysit, sew clothes, keep books, type essays, and stick labels on bottles. These women, working at home and paid in cash, are unrecorded in most statistical accounts and are unprotected by most legislation. Given that a significant proportion of women are also in school, it is clear that only a minority of them are full-time housewives, and some of these women do not stay home by choice. A substantial majority of women have or want paid employment.

For both women and the labour force, this represents a dramatic change. In 1946, only one-quarter of Canadian women were employed or looking for employment. By 1966, just over one-third were in the labour force. What started as a trickle in the early 1950s has, since the mid-1960s, become a flood.

Yet rather than signalling a fundamental shift in women's work, the rapid movement of women into the labour force has meant more of the same kind of work. Paid or unpaid, women scrub floors, serve food, sort laundry, mind children, make coffee or clothes, answer the telephone, or wait on people. It is true that more women now work as lawyers, doctors, dentists, and professors than ever before, but then there are more women in all occupations in the labour force. Most women continue to be segregated into the kind of jobs women have done since they entered the labour force. Most women now work for pay, but most still do women's work.

What is this women's work?[3] The most recent data show that, as of 1980, one-third of all women with paid employment do clerical work. A minority of these women are secretaries in the traditional sense of that job, with the variety of tasks it entails. A large number do type, some answer phones and some file, but many are actually bank tellers, mail sorters, library or bookkeeping clerks, receptionists, or telephone or keypunch operators, to name only a few of the jobs in this occupational category. When figures on the increasing number of women in construction, finance, and utilities are presented as evidence of women penetrating traditional male preserves, it should be remembered that more than two-thirds of the women employed in these industries do clerical work. More than three-fifths of the women in public adminstration, fishing, hunting, trapping, and mining are typing, filing, sorting, answering phones, and making coffee. Meanwhile, half the women doing clerical work are concentrated in trade and service, the lowest paid industrial sectors, and another quarter are in finance and public administration.

Not only are women segregated into this kind of work, it is also apparently women's work. Three-quarters of clerical workers are female. In some areas, the segregation is even more pronounced. Nine out of 10 clerical workers in finance and service, four out of five in trade, and three out of four in public administration, construction, and other primary industries are women. Only in the utilities sector is there any significant male presence in this kind of work, and most of these men are reading meters and checking railway boxcars, not typing letters.

Although the proportion of employed women doing clerical work has declined somewhat over the past five years, the proportion of clerical workers who are female has increased. Of the additional jobs that have become available during this period, 99 per cent have gone to women. The number of men doing clerical work full-time has actually declined. This may mean that women are competing more successfully with men, but it more likely means that men are finding clerical jobs less attractive. It certainly means that the occupational segregation of clerical work has increased.

So has the amount of part-time work in this occupation, which may help to explain why men are not entering it. A quarter of the women with clerical jobs in the post office and in doctors' offices have only part-time employment, as do one in ten of those in finance.

While the proportion of employed women doing clerical work is declining, the proportion in service jobs, the second most important female occupational category, is increasing. Between one-fifth and one-sixth of all women with paid jobs do service work. Included in this group are domestics, waitresses, cooks, janitors, hairdressers, building superintendents, hospital workers, and childcare workers. In other words, many more women are cooking, cleaning, and washing clothes for pay in 1980 than were doing so in 1975, and many of the women doing this work are not included in the official statistics. When women do daily cleaning in private homes, babysit for the woman next door, or sew clothes for the people down the street, they are often paid in cash, under the table and outside the scope of official numbers. They hide their employment from interviewers and record keepers because they (or their employers) want to avoid paying taxes, and pension and unemployment insurance contributions, or to avoid regulations related to welfare, immigration, and their husbands' taxes.[4] If these hidden employed were added to those already counted as service workers, the proportion of women recorded in this kind of work would increase significantly.

During the last five years, women have become the majority of those in service work. Nine out of 10 domestics, for example, are women. Three out of five people providing personal services like childcare and hairdressing are also women, and so are a growing share of those doing janitorial jobs.

Although service work is the fastest growing occupation in employment terms, more than half of the additional jobs made available here between 1975 and 1980 were part-time, and more than twice as many of the new full-time jobs went to women as went to men. As in clerical work, the workers here are increasingly female and increasingly part-time.

When the women employed in sales occupations are added to those doing clerical and service work, the total represents over 60 per cent of all women who have paid jobs — a working majority. One-tenth of the women in the labour force do sales work, and four-fifths of these women can be found in the trade sector of industry. In other words, most of the women in sales are behind the counter selling candies or women's underwear, and running the cash register in grocery or department stores. The rest of them are concentrated in the finance sector, selling services in banks and selling houses in real estate. Male sales workers are more widely distributed amongst the industrial sectors, with a higher proportion in finance and manufacturing where the pay is better and the required skills are recognized.

Sales workers, too, are increasingly female and increasingly part-time. In retail trade, half the workers are now women, although they make up less than one-fifth of those employed in manufacturing and less than one-third of those in finance. Between 1975 and 1980, there was a decline in the number of men working full-time in sales and a large increase in the number of their female counterparts. The trend towards more female sales employees is likely to continue as the proportion of part-time jobs increases. Well over one-third of the women who do sales work are employed only part-time. In retail trade, two out of five jobs created during the last five years have gone to women working part-time. In the trade sector as a whole, employers seem to have decreased the number of full-time males in favour of hiring the cheaper, more temporary, part-time female help. More of the sales workers are women and more of them fail to find full-time jobs.

A large number of women also work in factory jobs, that is, in the processing, machining, and fabricating occupations. Most are in the manufacturing industries, producing food and clothes in the lower-paid jobs in labour-intensive industries where people rather than machines do most of the work.

Unlike clerical and service work, "factory" work is not primarily women's work, if the broad occupational categories of the Labour Force Survey are used as the basis for analysis. [Editors' note: The Labour Force Survey is conducted each month by Statistics Canada among a large sample of adult Canadians to determine labour market trends.] However, as our interviews clearly indicate, just as women, not men, sell candies and women's underwear, so do women rather than men eviscerate chickens and sew baby clothes. Within particular industries and within each plant, the jobs are usually divided by sex — there is women's work and men's work. Here, too, the number of women doing the work is under-estimated, since some of the women who do home work — gluing seals on liquor bottles, sewing skirts, pressing clothes from factories — are hidden from the official records.

Women have increased their share of the jobs in processing and fabricating, but not in the more highly skilled and paid machining occupations. In contrast to the clerical, service, and sales fields, however, the majority of new jobs in processing and fabricating have gone to men working full-time. Only a small proportion of these jobs have gone to women working part-time. While more than 7 per cent of all employed women do factory work and while the jobs they do are mainly traditional female tasks, as a whole, processing, machining, and fabricating work is still primarily men's work.

The industrial sectors where women work are also the ones with the largest number of small establishments. Except for finance, the trade and service industries have the highest proportions of female workers and the largest numbers of establishments employing 20 or fewer people. Many of the unrecorded workers are also in very small operations, in corner stores, small neighbourhood salons, and business offices. These small establishments usually offer less opportunity for prestige, promotion, protection, and security than do larger ones.

Taken together, these statistics show that more than 70 per cent of all women who work for pay are in clerical, service, sales, processing, and fabricating jobs, doing "women's work" in offices, banks, stores, private homes, and factories. Although women have moved into almost all jobs in the labour force, most continue to do women's work. In addition, they are becoming even more dominant in these traditionally female areas.

Since 1975, women have lost ground in just two occupational categories, teaching and machining, both of which are relatively well-paid and skilled jobs. Although more women are factory workers than are teachers, in this century teaching has been one of the few relatively prestigious and well-paid jobs open to a large number of women, and one of the two female-dominated professions. During the last five years, however, there has been a significant decrease in the number of full-time teaching jobs going to women. The teaching jobs that have been created have gone equally to men working full-time and to women working part-time. In the education industry as a whole, well over half the additional jobs have provided only part-time female work, and another third have provided full-time male employment. None of the limited job growth in education has benefitted women working full-time.

The pattern in medicine, the other occupational category where a large number of women find professional work, is somewhat different. In 1980, more women were employed in medical occupations than in factory jobs, although they represented a smaller number than those doing any of clerical, service, or sales work. Of course, not all women in the medical category have professional jobs since many are nursing assistants, for example. A large number, nevertheless, are nurses and technicians who have training and skills that are recognized in terms of pay and prestige. Looking after the old, the young, the sick, and the pregnant has traditionally been women's work, and has provided more rewards than most other female occupations. As with teaching, however, a smaller proportion of employed women were doing this work in 1980 than in 1975. More of the workers in medicine are female, over three-quarters of them now, but in the last five years the overwhelming majority of additional jobs have gone to women working part-time. More of the jobs here are women's jobs, but once again more women work only part-time and a smaller proportion of employed women are in this relatively good occupation.

Teaching and nursing, then, traditionally the two best jobs for women, account for a declining proportion of the women who work for pay. An increasing number of those who do manage to capture jobs here find only part-time work. The picture is not simply one of increasing segregation, however, with more and more women locked into the worst of women's work. A higher proportion of both women and men were managers in 1980, and a higher proportion of managers were women than ever before. However, men's share of additional full-time employment in this occupation was greater than women's, and a quarter of the new female managers were part-time. Three-quarters of the women, as compared to fewer than half of the men, were managers in the service industry, which represents an increase here in the concentration of female managers. In other words, while some women have improved their position by moving into managerial jobs, these jobs are likely to be at the bottom of the pile, directing small beauty salons rather than large factories.

Women have been flooding into the labour force, leaving a minority working as full-time housewives. Although women have moved into virtually all occupations and industries, they continue to be highly concentrated in traditional jobs in clerical, service, sales, and factory work, Indeed, the proportion of women in these occupations has increased. And although women have managed to capture the majority of additional jobs in many occupations and industries, a large proportion of these jobs are in unprotected, low-paid, and often part-time work. In teaching, women have been losing ground to men; in nursing, relatively fewer women have found jobs, particularly ones that are full-time.

There has been a dramatic shift in women's daily lives. A majority of them now have or are searching for paid employment. But there has been depressingly little change in the kind of work they do. At home, and in the labour force, the majority of women still do women's work. . . .

Women's Wages

There are not only men's jobs and women's jobs, but men's wages and women's wages. While the most recent data available on earnings by occupation and sex are from 1978, we do know that women's average earnings in 1979 were $7,673 compared to $14,981 for men. Some of this difference can be explained by the shorter work weeks of women who are employed part-time, but even when only full-time employees are considered, women average $11,741 to men's $18,537.

Table 1. Average Annual Earnings, Canada, 1978 and 1979

Earner group	Women	Men	Women/Men
All earners, 1979	$ 7,673	$14,981	51.2
Full-time workers, 1979	11,741	18,537	63.3
Full-year workers by occupation, 1978			
Managerial	13,250	24,337	54.4
Professional	13,484	21,865	61.7
Clerical	9,592	14,403	66.6
Sales	7,193	16,456	43.7
Service	6,372	13,258	48.1
Primary occupations (1977)	4,230	9,805	43.1
Processing and machining	8,698	16,271	53.5
Fabricating	8,179	15,728	52.0
Transportation	10,424	15,575	66.9
All occupations	10,008	17,404	58.0

Sources: For 1979, calculated from Statistics Canada, *Income Distribution by Size in Canada*, 1979 (Cat. no. 13-207), Ottawa, 1981, Tables 70 and 72. For 1978, Labour Canada Women's Bureau, *Women in the Labour Force 1978-79, Part II Earnings*, Ottawa, 1981, Tables 1A and 2B.

Averages often hide more severe disparity. The occupational breakdown of earnings provided in Table 1 indicates more clearly the wage difference between men and women. The table also suggests that the greatest inequalities are in the worst jobs and in the occupations that account for the greatest increases in women's employment. In clerical and transportation jobs, women are paid, on average, two-thirds of what men receive. Compared to women in other occupations they are relatively better off, but few women work in transportation and the micro-electronic revolution will make clerical work increasingly hard to come by. The largest pay gaps can be found in sales, service, and primary occupations where women earn half as much as men in these jobs. Almost a third of the women in the labour force are employed in jobs where men earn twice as much. Given that the majority of service workers are female and that this is the fastest growing sector in job creation terms, it seems unlikely that pay differences will soon disappear.

Notes

1. A more detailed explanation of the data, including sources, used in this chapter may be found in the Statistical Appendix. Any figures not included there are calculated from the annual averages for 1980 found in Canada, Statistics Canada, *The Labour Force, December 1980* (Ottawa: Supply and Services Canada, 1981). For a more thorough discussion of the historical trends, see Pat Armstrong and Hugh Armstrong, *The Double Ghetto: Canadian Women and Their Segregated Work* (Toronto: McClelland and Stewart, 1978); Patricia Connelly, *Last Hired, First Fired: Women and the Canadian Work Force* (Toronto: The Women's Press, 1978); and Morley Gunderson, "Work Patterns," in Gail Cook (ed.), *Opportunity for Choice* (Ottawa: Information Canada, 1976). For an excellent discussion of a single occupation, see Laura Johnson with Robert E. Johnson, *The Seam Allowance* (Toronto: The Women's Press, 1982).

2. The importance of these factors in counting the unemployed is clearly shown in Robert Stirling and Denise Kouri, "Unemployment Indexes: The Canadian Context," in John A. Fry (ed.), *Economy, Class and Social Reality* (Toronto: Butterworths, 1979). For additional discussion of these hidden unemployed, see Hugh Armstrong, "Job Creation and Unemployment in Post-War Canada," in R. Marvyn Novick (ed.), *Full Employment: Social Questions for Public Policy* (Urban Seminar Six), (Toronto: Social Planning Council of Metropolitan Toronto, 1979); Cy Gonick, *Out of Work* (Toronto: Lorimer, 1978); and The People's Commission on Unemployment in Newfoundland and Labrador, *"Now That We've Burned Our Boats. . ."* (Ottawa: Mutual Press, 1978).

3. A detailed account may be found in the Statistical Appendix.

4. Under the current federal income tax system, women with net incomes of more than $2,990 cannot be declared as dependents by their husbands.

14/Part-Time Work: The Business View on Second-Class Jobs for Housewives and Mothers[*]

Wendy Weeks

Part-time workers have accounted for an increasing proportion of the Canadian labour force since the nineteen-fifties. Whereas 3.8% of the labour force worked part-time in 1953, this figure had increased to 6.7% by 1960 and 13.1% by 1978. Two-thirds of part-time workers have consistently been women, although by 1978 this had risen slightly to 71.6%. The majority of these workers in 1978 were over the age of twenty-five. Looking at the figures from a different perspective, almost one-quarter (23.8%) of Canadian women in the paid labour force in 1978 worked part-time.[1]

Part-time employment has been defined by the International Labour Organization as "work on a regular and voluntary basis for a daily or weekly period of sub-

[*] Abridged from Wendy Weeks, "Part-Time Work: The Business View on Second-Class Jobs for Housewives and Mothers," *Atlantis* 5,2 (1980), pp. 69-86. Reprinted with permission of the publisher and the author.

stantially shorter duration than current normal hours of work."[2] This widely accepted definition suggests regular and continuous work. However the views of businessmen present a very different conception of part-time employment.

This article analyzes the recorded views of businessmen on part-time work since 1960. The purpose of such a study is to explore the extent to which ideas about part-time employment reflect the actual conditions and experience of part-timers. Part-time work has been pre-dominantly "women's work," and in fact it appears to be the female form of casual and seasonal labour which is usually conceived of as a male activity. Because of this, ideas about part-time work will perhaps contribute to an understanding of prevalent ideology about women and the paid labour force.

Method

Articles on part-time employment listed in business periodicals indexes were the major source used to examine views and conceptions of part-time work.[3] Other publications used as supplementary sources include: studies of part-time employment reporting employer attitudes; views presented by business representatives at Government-sponsored consultations on alternative work schedules;[4] and collective agreements in Canadian industry. The sources of data were Canadian and American with the exception of Hallaire's study of part-time employment, sponsored by the Office of Economic Co-operation and Development.[5] The choice of sources rests on the assumption that business operates in an era of multi-national corporations and on Miliband's assertion that business has "a basic ideological consensus, which is of fundamental importance in [its] representation and impact."[6]

To examine ideas expressed in business periodicals and records of businessmen's views, is to use only one gauge to explore the "ideology of part-time work." However, given the power of employers in the labour market, it is assumed that their views will be central to understanding the ideology of this type of work. It is assumed here that the ideas about part-time work held by businessmen, will reflect the circumstances of part-time workers in the labour market. . . .

Advantages of Part-Time Employment

In the context of concern to maintain profits and resist inflation in the face of rising labour costs and the increasing expense of fringe benefits, cost saving has been seen as the major advantage of part-time employees. Other frequently mentioned advantages to the use of part-timers such as "flexibility and efficiency in manpower utilization," productivity and filling gaps caused by peak loads or shortages of qualified full-time staff also contribute more indirectly to cost saving.

1. *Cost saving*
"Paying only for the actual time worked."[7]
This 1974 *Business Week* article quoted Elmer Winter, president of one of the

multi-national temporary help companies, as saying "Today's economy is helping to expand what has already become a burgeoning business — supplying part-time office, factory and professional help." The article reports that "in industry after industry, inflationary pressure on profit margins is forcing companies to re-examine their total manpower needs. Many are replacing under-utilized full-timers with part-time 'temps' and paying only for the actual time worked."

Direct cost saving is achieved by lower wage rates and fewer or no fringe benefits. Bossen noted that lower starting rates keep wage costs down,[8] and Nolen quoted employers as finding part-timers useful because they could pay lower wages.[9] Fringe benefits, assessed to be the fastest growing component of labour costs, are the major expense saved by using part-timers. In 1976 fringe benefits were estimated to be "gobbling up 31% of payroll costs" so their absence provides substantial saving.[10]

Costs of absenteeism and lay-offs, turnover and overtime are all said to be reduced by the use of part-timers. Absenteeism is less expensive because part-time workers are paid only for the time worked. Werther observed that "Unlike full-time personnel, who can (and often do) miss work without a reduction in pay, part-time help has a special interest in reporting to work: pay. Even when absent, at least the firms costs are held down."[11] Lay offs are cheaper and less likely to damage the morale of other workers. In direct employment of part-timers, the company can cease to call in a particular employee without any required notice of termination or pay in lieu. If employers are using a temporary help service, a *Business Week* journalist comments, "You can send back a person who doesn't work out, and you don't have to give notice."[12] Over-time costs, often involving double wage rates can be avoided by using part-time staff. According to Winter: "Getting regular employees to work overtime doesn't work. As the hour gets later the workers wears out. Salary costs soar and so do errors."[13] Turnover costs can be reduced, both by actual decrease in turnover among part-timers (in skilled occupations) and by retaining some of the benefits of previous experience and training if full-time workers (typically married women or retired persons) move to part-time schedules.[14]

2. Flexibility and efficiency in manpower utilisation
"Flexible personnel for flexible workloads."[15]
To prevent costly under-utilization of workers, employers attempt to balance the demand for work and the supply of workers as efficiently as possible. This benefit of part-time employment has been applauded in articles such as "Part time help boosts staff flexibility" (*Administration Management*, 28:38, Dec. 1967) and "Engineering part-timers — how they can help you" (*Modern Power and Engineering*, 70:5, May 1976). According to Werther, "The most useful aspect of part-time personnel is the tremendous scheduling flexibility they offer to managers."[16] Bossen also found this to be the most frequently mentioned example in her Canadian

study.[17] This flexibility is seen as useful for varying situations. Peak periods in demand for workers is the most obvious example: annual peaks, such as Christmas and summer sales; hotel and resort work and seasonal work such as parks maintenance; weekly peaks such as in food sales, banking and meat packing plants; and daily peaks, such as in transportation. Other jobs are considered to require less than a full-time work commitment; for example, cleaning, certain clerical tasks and professional services in hospitals and correctional institutions, or activities such as market research, and are thus open to part-time workers.[18]

Part-time employees have been described as useful to fill monotonous jobs not attractive to full-time workers. Shell Canada, for example, reported the use of part-timers for opening envelopes, a task for which they considered they could not employ full-time workers.[19] In a different context, organizations with continuous operations use part-time employees to fill weekend and evening hours, for example, in hospitals, hotels and motels, and department stores. They can also be used as general categories of shift workers to prevent closing down plant operations.[20] As Werther concluded: "The case for part-time manpower must certainly be viewed as a significant tool of effective management,"[21] from the business point of view.

3. A solution to the shortage of qualified staff
"Half a librarian is better than none."[22]

Part-time employees have been described as meeting business's need for skilled and qualified labour in areas of labour shortage. In 1960, the *Labour Gazette* observed that in North America "industry has made relatively little use of part-time workers except in times of labour shortage."[23] Schwartz reported the use of part-time employees to fill manpower shortages in social work and health services but she found that even where widespread shortages existed the "part-time" solution was unacceptable to some employers.[24] Hallaire observed that the major economic argument in favour of part-time employment was that it provided a source of supplementary manpower and that it had developed "because the manpower shortage was impeding or paralysing growth."[25] He added that in all cases "Part-time employment was looked upon as scraping the barrel for manpower recruitment."[26]

Married women have typically been the major source of labour used to counteract labour shortages. In 1967 the solution to the shortage of secretarial and clerical workers was reported to be "found among housewives who have had previous experience in this area and who have since left work."[27] *Business Week* reported a project in which Control Data Company developed "mini-shifts" for "morning shift mothers" and "afternoon shift mothers."[28] Apparently sharing the concerns of the Canadian Royal Commission on the Status of Women for the "alienation which housewives occasionally suffer,"[29] Control Data reported that "The plants serve a constructive social purpose, but they also fill a crying need for workers."[30] "Mature women" on a part-time employment basis were found to be "an answer to the computer programmer shortage" in 1970, and offered additional benefits in that they demonstrated increased productivity and a reduced turnover rate in comparison with full-time programmers.[31] . . . .

4. Increased productivity
"The answer to coffee breaks."[32]
Part-time workers have been described as the "least fatigued, least error-prone workers."[33] Highly skilled part-timers, such as married women not otherwise available for full-time work (given a traditional division of labour in the home) add quality to the workplace.[34] Not surprisingly, therefore, the productivity of part-time employees has been found to be greater than that of full-time workers.[35] Schwartz, who also noted that positive attitudes in employers correlated with experience of part-time employment, quoted one employer as saying "We have been so successful with part-time workers we would not reject anyone solely for lack of full-time availability."[36] Such a view is an interesting diversion from the usual analysis of the value of part-time workers.

5. A minority view -- the benefits of permanent part-time employment
"If Madame Curie were alive, but could only work from 9:30 to 3:15, would you hire her?"[37]
A small number of articles such as the one discussed in the previous section did stress the benefits of permanent part-time work to women and families.[38] *Industry Week*, for example, interviewed Ina Torton, director of Newtime, a division of Ribolow Employment Agency, New York, which specializes in permanent part-time positions. She deplored the lack of opportunities for permanent part-time employment, and added that "it seems to be taking hold faster on the West Coast than in the East, in academe, and in small companies, because they can see the (positive) results immediately without waiting for them to filter through layers of management."[39] Lazer proposed "job sharing as a pattern for permanent part-time work," and concluded that the impetus for this change would be likely to come from young people and those professional women interested in non-traditional family and alternative work roles.[40]

These contributions emerged as a minority view in the business discussion and were mainly expressed by women writers and by some male professors of business administration.[41] This view rests on the assumption that part-time employment, while being far shorter than normal hours of work, could have all the attributes typically associated with full-time work: adequate wages and benefits, job satisfaction, some security, productivity, a serious attachment to the labour force. The supporters of the minority view have suggested job-sharing and job-pairing, they are interested in non-traditional roles within the family and favour a formalized flexibility in the allocation of time between work and leisure, or paid work and family work, arrangements which would be preferable if one is concerned to allow people to meet their total family obligations more fully. . . .

The Social Function of Part-Time Work

The key to understanding the social function of part-time work is the conception and use of part-time workers as unregulated, flexible, and temporary workers. Temporary and unregulated workers are cheaper, useful, and disposable when the demand has passed. They provide a reserve supply of cheap labour. It appears that to regularize the working conditions of part-time employment would defeat the purposes for which part-timers are attractive to business.

Part-time work is one form of peripheral or marginal work. In fact it appears that "part-time" is the female equivalent of "casual" and "seasonal" labour which are terms usually used to describe male marginal workers, but which equally well describe part-time work. Morse's theory of peripherality developed to explain part-time and intermittent employment,[42] is supported by Canadian data. In an extension of dual labour market theory, he asserted that peripheral work experience, characterized by intermittent employment, is usually performed by low-status social groups, and noted that "in contemporary America these groups are females, younger and older workers and the non-white."[43] Morse also suggested that: "Part-time and intermittent employment on a significant scale are inherent characteristics of dynamic economies and economies in which personal services constitute an important part of final demand."[44] Why is this so? In capitalist economies, marginal workers in a split and hierarchical labour force provide a reserve supply of cheap and flexible labour to maintain profits and maximize control of labour.[45]

Part-time and other marginal workers appear to be both marginal and yet essential to the economy. Part-timers are marginal by virtue of their lower status and earnings, their lack of job security and their position as a reserve supply of labour. They are marginal even to the female labour force. Figures relating to women and the labour force are infrequently presented showing the percentage of part-time work and part-year work — an indication of its invisibility. Yet it has been noted here that nearly one-quarter of women in the Canadian labour force are working part-time.[46] The marginal economic relationship of part-timers to the means of production is reflected and reinforced in the language of social relationships. Part-timers are persons whose social status is primarily defined by characteristics other than their working life or capacity: housewives, mothers, students, retired persons. . . .

What is the significance of the overwhelming majority of women among part-time workers? Part-time jobs have been taken by people, usually women as secondary family income earners, who occasionally or regularly sought paid work to supplement family incomes. (The other major group of part-timers — students — require income to support their education.) Part-time work offers a focus on women's work at the intersection of women's two jobs: their work in the home and their work in the paid labour force. In the fifties, in Britain, Myrdal and Klein observed that part-time work was a solution to "the widespread desire of married women to enter gainful employment in Britain."[47] Women, still grateful for a job at all, let alone a well-paid secure job, are all too willing candidates for temporary and insecure jobs. Furthermore, part-time work fits conveniently (in one sense) with traditional family roles. In a society in which a traditional division of labour in the family prevails, part-time work, in spite of its second-class employment status, might be a feasible solution for women with children who want or need to work to supplement the family income. It is a compromise solution in a situation of limited options for women. As Young and Willmott suggested, part-time work allows the demands of the (traditional) family and the (traditional) workplace to be reconciled.[48] It reinforces traditional sex-roles and division of labour in the home, because married women can, as part-time workers still fulfil their family service and maintainance roles.

Earlier in the seventies, part-time work was proposed by the Royal Commission on the Status of Women as a potential step toward equality for women.[49] An expansion of part-time work on a temporary and unregulated basis, as it presently exists for the most part, will not lead to equality, but will reinforce traditional sex roles in the family and perpetuate the practice of segregated men's and women's work. Armstrong and Armstrong's conclusion about women workers and their segregated work is equally applicable to part-time workers: "Women workers are essential to the economic structure in that desegregation of the labour force would require fundamental changes in those sectors which rely on a cheap and/or flexible labour supply. It is therefore in the interest of many employers to maintain the division of labour by sex."[50]

In view of the support this analysis of part-time work offers to Connelly's theory of women as a reserve army of cheap labour,[51] and to Armstrong and Armstrong's analysis of women's segregated labour force participation as essential both to the economy and to maintaining family incomes, why would some writers have pointed to the advantages of part-time work? The key difference in their conception of part-time work is that they were proposing permanent, on-going, secure and serious work, for women and men, with shorter than normal working hours. Their view reflects the same ideal as the International Labour Organization definition of part-time work quoted earlier. Permanent part-time work would not be cheap and flexible labour to benefit employers, but would offer time and flexibility for families, for example, those with young children. Perhaps this is utopian in a society where married women are entering the labour force full-time to supplement and maintain family incomes. However, with equal pay for work of equal value and better paying job opportunities for women, two adults could perhaps work fewer hours outside the home and still support their family's income needs, and neither would have to do two full-time jobs.

At present, however, the "business view" of part-time work both reflects and reinforces the circumstances of part-time workers. Part-timers are part of the cheap and flexible reserve labour force. Part-time work appears to be the female equivalent of casual and seasonal labour. It parallels the circumstances of women's work generally, and part-time workers appear to be both marginal and yet essential to the economy. Part-time work reinforces women's low status in an occupationally sex-segregated labour force, and perpetuates a traditional division of labour in the home.

Notes

1. Statistics Canada, *The Labour Force* (December 1975), p. 68; (December 1978), p. 36.

2. "An International Survey of Part-Time Employment: Part 1," *International Labour Review* (October 1963), p. 383.

3. *The Business Periodical Index*, vols. 3-17 (1960-75); *Canadian Business Periodicals*, vol. 1 (1975-6); and the *Canadian Periodicals Index* (1960-74) were systematically examined. The extent to which discussions of part-time work has occurred at Conferences and Board meetings has only been monitored if it was recorded in the sources listed. No systematic attempt was made to monitor the views of business recorded in the media. The *Toronto Star* reported one article in a clipping file and the *Globe and Mail* reported a small (unspecified) number of articles in their clipping file.

4. For example, Jane Schwartz, *Part-Time Employment* (New York: Alumnae Advisory Centre, 1964); Marianne Bossen, *Part-Time Work in the Canadian Economy* (Ottawa, 1975); Ontario, Treasury, Economics and Intergovernmental Affairs, "A Survey of Attitudes Towards Part-Time Permanent Work in the Ministry of Treasury, Economics and Intergovernmental Affairs," Women's Advisory Committee, 1975 (xeroxed); Nollen and Eddy's findings are reported in *An Introduction to Alternative Work Schedules*, Proceedings of New York State Temporary Commission Conference (August 1976).

5. Jean Hallaire, *Part-Time Employment: Its Extent and Its Problems* (Paris: Organisation for Economic Co-operation and Development, 1968).

6. Ralph Miliband, *The State and Capitalist Society* (London: Werdenfeld and Nicolson, 1972), p. 157.

7. Elmer Winter, "A Boost for Temporary Help," *Business Week*, 3 August 1974, p. 60.

8. Bossen, op. cit., p. 52.

9. Nollen, op. cit., p. 51.

10. *Financial Times*, 26 July 1976.

11. William B. Werther, "Mini-Shifts: An Alternative to Overtime," *Personnel Journal* 55 (March 1976), p. 131; Nollen, op. cit., p. 51.

12. Winter, op. cit., p. 61.

13. Ibid. See also Werther, op. cit. and Bossen op. cit.

14. See Nollen, op. cit. pp. 46, 51.

15. "Flexible Personnel for Flexible Workloads," *Personnel Journal* 49 (January 1970), pp. 61-62.

16. Werther, op. cit., p. 132. See also Werther, "Part-Timers: Overlooked and Undervalued." *Business Horizons* (Feb. 1975), pp. 13-20.

17. Bossen, op. cit.

18. See Bossen, op. cit., pp. 50-1; Schwartz, op. cit., p. 28; Nollen, op. cit.

19. Winter, op.cit., p. 62.

20. Werther (1976), op. cit., p. 132.

21. Ibid., p. 133.

22. J. Hooper, "Half a Librarian is Better Than None," *Canadian Library*, 24 (January 1968), pp. 338-40.

23. "Women as Part-Time and Part-Year Workers," *Labour Gazette* (July 1960), p. 668.

24. Schwartz, op. cit.

25. Hallaire, op. cit., p. 40.

26. Ibid. See also Australia, Department of Labour and National Service, Women's Bureau, *Some Aspects of Part-Time Work* (Melbourne: 1970); Alice Cook, *The Working Mother: A Survey of Problems and Programs in Nine Countries* (New York: Cornell University, 1975); Werther (1975), op. cit.

27. J.R. Corey, "Part-Time Help Boosts Staff Flexibility, " *Administration Management* 28 (December 1967), p. 38.

28. "Plant for Part-Timers (Control Data)," *Business Week*, 29 November 1969, p. 108.

29. *Report of the Royal Commission on the Status of Women* (Ottawa: Queen's Printer, 1970), pp. 104-5.

30. "Plant for Part-Timers (Control Data)," op. cit.

31. W.A. Thompson et al., "An Answer to the Computer Programmer Shortage," *Adult Leadership* 18 (1970), pp. 213-14. See also Bossen, op. cit., p. 52.

32. W.B. Collins, "Answer to Coffee Breaks," *Financial Post*, 22 September 1962, p. 63.

33. Werther (1976), op. cit., p. 132.

34. Carol Greenwald and Judith Liss, "Part-Time Workers Can Bring Higher Productivity," *Harvard Business Review* (Sept.-Oct. 1973), p. 21.

35. Nollen, op. cit., reported higher productivity and fewer accidents; the Catalyst study showed part-time social workers to carry 84% of the load carried by full-time workers; Greenwald and Liss, op. cit.; Werther (1976), op. cit., p. 132; Schwartz (1964), op. cit., p. 28; Robert Lazer, "Job Sharing as a Pattern for Permanent Part-Time Work," *Conference Board Record* (October 1975), pp. 57-61.

36. Schwartz, op. cit., p. 29.

37. "Part-Timers in the Managerial Ranks?" op. cit., p. 44.

38. Carol Greenwald, "Working Mothers: The Need for More Part-Time Jobs," *New England Economic Review* (Sept.-Oct. 1972); Kathie Graham, "Part-Time Employment: Another Alternative to the Traditional Work Week," *Canadian Personnel and Industrial Relations Journal*, 8,1 (January 1974), pp. 35-38; Greenwald and Liss, op. cit.

39. "Part-Timers in the Managerial Ranks?" op. cit., p. 44.

40. Lazer, op. cit.

41. Cf. footnote 38.

42. Dean Morse, *The Peripheral Worker* (New York: Columbia University Press, 1969).

43. Ibid., p. 66.

44. Ibid., p. 65.

45. See Patricia Connelly, *Last Hired, First Fired* (Toronto: Canadian Women's Educational Press, 1979) for a discussion of women as a reserve army of labour.

46. Canada, Health and Welfare, Policy Research and Long Range Planning (Welfare) Report, No. 5. *The Changing Dependence of Women: Roles, Beliefs, and Inequality* (April 1978), p. 21. A study completed in 1973 showed that less than one-third of working mothers were working in full-time, full-year jobs.

47. Alva Myrdal and Viola Klein, *Women's Two Roles* (London: Routledge and Kegan Paul, 1968), p. 83.

48. Michael Young and Peter Willmott, *The Symmetrical Family* (Middlesex: Penguin, 1975), p. 284.

49. Royal Commission, op. cit., p. 105.

50. Pat Armstrong and Hugh Armstrong, *The Double Ghetto: Canadian Women and Their Segregated Work* (Toronto: McClelland and Stewart, 1978).

51. Patricia Connelly, op. cit.

15/Women's Struggle for Non-Traditional Jobs[*]

Wendy Johnston

Although unionization of women and equal value legislation would help close the wage gap between men and women workers, desegregation of the workplace is an important part of this battle. Desegregation would objectively challenge numerous myths about women. At the same time women would be located in the powerful industrial unions which have the potential leverage to alter radically the conditions of all workers.

Desegregation would break down the material division in the workforce which at present serves only the interests of the bosses. Wherever a section of the working class is used as a source of cheap labour this exploitation threatens all workers. For example, in the southern "right to work" states in the United States where blacks are used as cheap labour, the wages of white workers tend to be lower than in the northern states.

The Fight for Affirmative Action — Where Are We Today?
Influenced by the feminist movement, many women have acquired the necessary confidence to do "heavy" jobs traditionally done by men. In addition, spiralling inflation and unemployment have forced many women to look beyond the traditional "female" occupations for better paying jobs. Many attempts to enter non-traditional occupations are waged by individual women. It is almost impossible to gauge the extent of these attempts; for example, the Women Back into Stelco campaign discovered that 10,000 women (10% of all applicants) had applied at Stelco during the last ten years. None of these women was hired. Who knows how many women have unsuccessfully applied to work at CN, de Havilland Aircraft, Ford, GM, Steel Car, etc.?

At the same time there is increasing evidence of organized and collective efforts to desegregate the workplace. The INTO (Introduction to Non-Traditional

---

[*] Reprinted with permission of the publisher and the author from Wendy Johnston, "Women's Struggle for Non-Traditional Jobs," *Resources for Feminist Research* 10,2 (1981), pp. 16-17.

Jobs) courses co-sponsored by Canada Manpower and the community colleges in Ontario are overwhelmed by applications. Groups such as WITAI (Women in Trades and Industry) are springing up across Ontario. In April 1981, 200 women participated in the Ontario Women in Trades and Industry conference, coming from as far away as Red Lake and Elliot Lake.

Campaigns organized co-operatively by women and unions in Hamilton, Fort Erie, and Sudbury have succeeded in getting some women into non-traditional jobs. Recently the Women Back into Stelco campaign forced the company to hire around 130 women. In 1974 activities by USWA local 6500 led to 100 women being hired by INCO in Sudbury. At Fleet Industries in Fort Erie, the union local fought together with women workers recently laid off from another plant to get a 10% quota of women hired. Women across the country have fought to gain access to non-traditional jobs in CN. The result is that 30 women have been hired in Montreal and Toronto. These efforts by women, supported by the trade union movement, have won some modest victories. During these organized campaigns certain areas for discussion have emerged.

Equal Treatment Does Not Equal Equality
To some people, real equality simply means that women should be treated equally. If a woman applies for a non-traditional job and has the same qualifications as a man, she should be hired. This is not a bad beginning, but it is not real equality.

Women face enormous disadvantages in the job market. Historically women have had inequitable access to "qualifications"; they bear the brunt of sex-role stereotyping in the school system; and on the job many employers refuse to hire or train women. In order to compensate for years of discrimination and to ensure equitable distribution of industrial jobs in the long run, women need preferential treatment in hiring. This means that a woman with fewer qualifications than a male applicant should be hired and trained. Although this creates a new set of problems, *without* preferential hiring women will never acquire the necessary skills and experience to compete with men.

Government Programs and Affirmative Action Legislation
According to Julie White, an Ottawa researcher, the federal government's Affirmative Action Program, established in April 1979, is responsible for providing technical advice and assistance to companies wishing to institute a voluntary affirmative action program. Between 1979 and 1981 only 15 companies had asked for advice and no programs had been implemented. Julie White also noted that the federal government did a survey of employers across Canada asking if they would institute affirmative action programs on a voluntary basis. The companies responded that they would not, unless they were forced to. In addition to "encouragement" to institute voluntary programs, the government also offers companies subsidies if they hire women in non-traditional jobs. According to White, however, the funds allo-

cated two years ago have not yet been spent. Employers are not interested, even when they are paid to hire women.

Julie White's research supports an argument for obligatory quotas. If we don't move in the direction of demanding obligatory quotas, then we face the prospect of never making substantial gains for women in non-traditional blue-collar jobs. In the future, a total integration of women into non-traditional jobs would mean that women workers in a given plant would equal the percentage of women in the workforce in that particular locality.

In terms of fighting discrimination, obligatory quotas will put the onus on the companies. As it stands now the one-by-one approach of fighting every single case of discrimination through human rights commissions puts the onus on individual women. The other result of the one-by-one approach is that a tiny minority of women remain isolated in industrial workplaces. This substantially weakens the efforts of women on the shop floor and in the union to convince male workers of the legitimacy of women's presence in non-traditional jobs. In the long run the isolation and harassment can lead women to quit.

Through specific campaigns we may get certain companies to hire women. Some unions may negotiate some kind of affirmative action programs. But in the final analysis affirmative action legislation which contains obligatory quotas will be necessary to ensure an end to discriminatory training and hiring policies.

Lay-Offs and Affirmative Action

Undoubtedly the fight for affirmative action is more difficult today because of the economic crisis and the inflation and unemployment that it causes. Working people everywhere are being hit with increasing ferocity. Gains that women workers make in getting non-traditional industrial jobs will be eroded by lay-offs. At Inco in Sudbury and at McDonnel Douglas in Toronto, the already small female workforce has been substantially reduced by lay-offs. If women workers are ever to gain a secure foothold in these jobs, women and their unions will have to deal with the difficult question of the seniority system which, in fact, serves to perpetuate discrimination against women. Because women have been excluded from these jobs for decades, we have the lowest seniority. As the "last hired," we are always the "first fired."

Some in the union movement argue that fighting against the lay-offs of recently hired women goes against the seniority system. The seniority system represents a major gain for the working class. It protects workers against arbitrary firings based on the favouritism of the employer, or on age, race, or political beliefs. However, the seniority system is not ideal. It grew out of a different set of circumstances in the workplace, and it is inadequate to deal with the problems women face in non-traditional jobs.

To overcome the discriminatory aspects of seniority systems, we need to fight for double seniority lists or preferential seniority for women. During the world wars, preferential seniority was sometimes given to men who got drafted, so that they could continue accumulating seniority during the fighting and come back to their original jobs after the war. Women need preferential seniority to compensate for past discrimination. This would demonstrate to women workers that unions can really defend them against the sexist hiring policies of the bosses. If unions allow the bosses to discriminate against women and to exploit us doubly, then the fundamental tenet of the union movement "an injury to one is an injury to all" becomes meaningless. Unless unions are able to take up broader social issues, which range from the industrial strategy of governments (which create unemployment), to priorities of budgets (which create social service cutbacks), to the discrimination against women, they will be increasingly unable to protect the interests of their memberships and to further improve the conditions of working people.

In conclusion, there will be numerous fronts where the fight for affirmative action will be waged. There will be more campaigns that target particular companies or industries that will involve women workers and their unions. Increasing numbers of women will demand access to skilled trades apprenticeships and industrial jobs. Unions will negotiate affirmative action plans into their collective agreements. There will be pressure to institute affirmative action legislation. Essentially, the fight has just begun.

16/Why Women Are Not Going Into In-House Management Training Programs*

Edita Kowalski

Corporation XYZ, is one of the largest communications and computer companies in the world. It has facilities in the United States, Canada, and Western Europe. This enormous multi-national offers to its employees enviable benefits: life insurance, medical coverage, dental, share purchase opportunities, and access to education programs. Among the more spectacular education programs is one whereby, every quarter, supervisors from a variety of departments, both line and staff, select certain employees for management training. Those employees selected spend the following week in intensive management training sessions. They are taught the fundamentals of delegation, motivation, communication, and time management. The entire program revolves around turning employees into future corporate managers.

---

* Abridged from Edita Kowalski, "Why Women Are Not Going Into In-House Management Training Programs," *Canadian Personnel and Industrial Relations Journal* 26,6 (1979), pp. 17-24.

Corporation XYZ does not discriminate. Each quarter almost the same number of women as men are selected for the management training program. However, each quarter 60% of the women who are selected turn down the opportunity. In the past six years only *one* man has turned the program down! This phenomenon is noted every quarter, and yet to date there has been no interest in why such a situation exists. No one in personnel, human resources management, or training has questioned the women who declined beyond the usual one-line reason given on the form: "family commitments will not permit."

These statistics are not unique to Corporation XYZ. They are repeated almost identically across Canada in every organization from the public sector right through to the private sector. No industry or company is exempt. Even those organizations which publicly boast advanced equal employment opportunities find that between 40% and 70% of their female corporate resources never take advantage of their in-house management training programs.

The reason is in fact rooted in many of the training methods and social presuppositions about women and management that every corporation and organization is labouring under. . . .

Historically, the concept of industrial training for women is a non-issue. Women were never expected to remain in the labour force on a permanent basis and hence were considered interim and unskilled labour. This has now radically changed. The high cost of living, the availability of higher education and the changes brought on by the feminist movement have rocketed women into the permanent labour force. In fact, recent Canadian statistics indicate that 48% of all women in Canada work outside the home. This figure is not likely to decrease in the future.

Industry has been slow to recognize this trend and has not made adequate preparation for it on the organizational level. This is reflected in the general dissatisfaction of women with available training in-house.

In my conversations, correspondence, and research, women themselves answered the question of why they don't take part in in-house training programs. And their answers go well beyond the superficial ones of "home" and "family" responsibilities and general feminine timidity.

The Reasons Why

Women don't take advantage of in-house training programs for the following reasons:

1. *There is a lack of female resource people in the training programs themselves.* The bulk of training programs for management level personnel are conducted by male trainers and resource people. Rarely is a women chosen to train, the feeling being that women lack credibility and authority as industrial trainers. Some government supported training programs are making attempts at turning this situation around. However, the private sector still has a long way to go.

While this may seem a picayune point — after all, skills are skills and a teacher is a teacher — women are left with the distinct impression that there are only men in management, that vocabulary is geared to the male manager, and systems are designed for the male manager exclusively, and that the female trainee is somehow encroaching on territory to which she has no right. This theme was very aptly expressed in the book, *Games Mother Never Taught You*, by Betty Lehan Harrigan.

2. *Few on-the-job role models.* The majority of women in organizations today are working below the middle management level. They are not represented equally throughout the organizational hierarchy, particularly in senior and executive levels of management. Women, seeing this ceiling, feel so frustrated and inhibited that no amount of training can tempt them. They conclude that training is being offered to them, not as a valid step to executive positions, but as a sop to ambition.

3. *Management responsibility and involvement is not explained to the new female manager.* When an organization invites a candidate to enter into a management training program, the male candidate sees this as the realization of his earliest ambitions. He has had contact with other males, both in his own peer group and above, and is well versed in the duties and responsibilities of management. He knows that the job requires not *more* work but a different kind of work. He knows that there is a strong management team of which he will be a part, a team that will stand behind him through every level of the organization at a low, task-oriented level. . . . Women have no experience, either through peers or superiors as to the actual ramifications of management, and hence, turn down management opportunities.

4. *Mobility as a factor of productivity.* Mobility not only through the ranks of the organization, but also through the various locations of the organization is recognized as as necessary maneuver to keep management productivity high. Women, on the other hand, tend to learn their job so well, that they are less productive with each passing day. This mobility factor is never explained to women entering the organization. Hence women feel that the better they do the job, and the more experience or longer they stay in the job, the more responsibly they will be treated. This of course is a fallacy that is rarely clarified to female personnel.

5. *Mentors and the Queen Bee.* Much has been written about the male network that exists in organizations and across industry lines. This old boy network has as one of its objectives to select promising candidates from the ranks of the lower level managers and groom them for future senior positions. Each junior man is then locked into a senior male mentor, who informally advises, smooths the upward path, and points the junior on the right path for senior management.

The female junior has no such mentor. Often, women senior enough to give young ones help take the attitude that "it took me so long to get here, I'll be damned if I'll help you!" This Queen Bee attitude, while relenting a bit, is still rampant enough to hinder the faltering steps of the neophyte organization woman.

6. *Senior male managers' mythology.* The senior levels of management today are populated by males in their late fifties and early sixties. Men who grew up with a certain female role model; namely, their mothers, sisters, or secretaries. These are the roles that men in positions of power associate with women. These are not roles they are going to change easily. For a senior male to suddenly be confronted with a female peer is a shock. It is tied up in a male/female mythology about abilities, place in the overall scheme of things, and sexuality. It will take a long time to change, but it must change before women will feel comfortable or even welcome in the senior levels of the organization.

7. *Lack of facilities for women.* This issue does not arise in the service industries, which have had women in lower level management and supervisory level positions for some time. But in the manufacturing areas, training programs often involve the additional cost of providing adequate facilities where none exist. Washrooms, showers, change areas must be installed to accommodate female personnel. Rather than incur the expense many companies discourage women from applying.

8. *Traditional societal role.* While the work place is changing, society still has some adjustments to make regarding the traditional male/female roles. By and large, domestic arrangements, although the media would have us believe the contrary, are still traditional. The male is considered the major breadwinner, and decides family policy. The female is responsible for running the household, bringing up the children and fulfilling a "helping" function. This societal role places women at a disadvantage on the job, and in any training program they may be requested to take. Since their main job is still seen as a domestic one, that must take priority. Consequently training programs must be weighed in light of additional domestic responsibility. Particularly those intensive week-end training sessions in isolated lodges or camps, where the real job training takes place. Women can't leave their families for overnight training stints, or often can't stay late to exchange informal decision-making experiences with other managers because of their domestic responsibilities. This situation is widespread and, until some provision is made to free women from their dual roles, will not change.

9. *Entry-level.* Women by and large enter the organization at levels well below that of their male counterparts. Clerical, lower level administration, secretarial, these are the starting levels for most women. Men, on the other hand, start their organizational life several levels above that. They enter directly into a management training program, or a few months below one. Men go into the company hoping to get ahead; women go into the company hoping to get and keep a job. Here lies the difference. For most men, an invitation to join a management training program is a long-awaited moment; for women, the invitation is a sudden and in many cases unexpected offer. She becomes disoriented, confused and is rarely given time to sort out her reaction to this new role. Her initial reaction is to turn down the opportunity — and so she does.

10. *Male-Female Group Dynamics.* The group dynamics between male and fe-

male in a learning environment are a significant reason why many women decline joint educational opportunities, particularly at work. Women, since grade eight, have learned informally, that when in a group learning situation it is better not to shine in academic situations. Better to let the men get the kudos. In terms of an industrial training program this is even more critical. Women inherently feel that they must not outshine their future peers or even bosses as management material. This feeling precludes many from seriously considering management training for themselves.

Conclusion

These then are the real reasons for women to hesitate when management training is offered to them. They are not lazy, they do not lack ambition, nor do they want to remain at low level jobs. However, until management does something about these ten fears, women will always hesitate when offered an opportunity for advancement, and their hesitation will always be misinterpreted.

17/Taking on the Double Day: Housewives as a Reserve Army of Labour[*]

Meg Luxton

Canadian women's work is ghettoized in the home as domestic labour and in "women's jobs" in the paid labour force. Most married women end up in both ghettos — holding down two jobs and working a double day. At home, they work long hours at very difficult, highly responsible work that receives very little social recognition and is, of course, unpaid. Within the paid labour force, they face a series of discriminatory practices, the most important of which is the low wages most women receive.[1]

As a result, women working the double day carry an extraordinarily heavy load and the price they pay is enormous. They work long hours and have virtually no leisure time for themselves. They are subject to high levels of stress and they get paid about half of what men receive. Given this situation, why are women with children entering the paid labour force in ever increasing numbers? Why do women take on this double day?

[*] Abridged from Meg Luxton, "Taking on the Double Day: Housewives as a Reserve Army of Labour," *Atlantis* 7,1 (1981), pp. 12-22. Reprinted with permission of the publisher and the author.

It is generally argued in the literature that married women take on paid work for two reasons. The primary one is economic: women do paid work because they need the money. The secondary reason is closely related to the first. Like other workers, married women derive independence, satisfaction, sociability, and a sense of pride from their paid jobs. More recently, investigators have begun to analyze the structural imperatives that underly the work patterns of Canadian women.

In *Last Hired, First Fired* Pat Connelly addresses these questions by arguing that women in the home constitute a reserve army of labour and, as part of that analysis, she considers "the pressures that push housewives into the paid labour force" (1978: 63). Connelly demonstrates the existence of underlying structural imperatives which constrain and mould women's decisions of whether or not to take on paid labour. For Connelly, "women's participation in wage labour is not a matter of immediate situational factors but rather of prestructured alternatives which direct the decisions that women are compelled to make." (1978: 76)

Most studies of women's work in Canada have concentrated, as Connelly does, on the general category "women": "This view distinguishes women as members of a special group" (1978:6). While such general studies are vitally important, it is also necessary that we begin to refine our analyses by distinguishing patterns specific to particular categories of women. We need to know how the large-scale "macro" social processes are translated into individual behaviour.

So, while we have studies which show that the percentage of married women in the paid labour force is steadily increasing, we do not yet know whether this means essentially the same thing for all married women or whether some women have significantly different experiences from women in other circumstances. For example, are there important differences between married women with young children and those with no dependent children, or between married women whose husbands do not contribute to their wives' and childrens' support and those whose husbands do.

Of particular interest are those women who have young children and whose husbands have steady incomes which they contribute to supporting their wives and children. Domestic labour for these women is at its most intense and demanding. This, plus the appalling lack of adequate child care, coupled with all the social pressures which assert that women should stay home with their preschool children, exerts enormous pressure on women to do domestic labour full-time and to remain out of the paid labour force. When they have husbands with regular incomes, the potential for them to be financially dependent is maximized. Therefore, it is particularly significant when these women take on paid labour. In addition, we need to know whether working-class women have significantly different experiences from middle-class women. How does women's class position both structure the alternatives available to them and affect the way they respond to the structural imperatives which impell their lives?

The Study

This study is based on a comparison of two groups of twenty married women. At the time of the study, all forty women had been married for at least five years and had at least one preschool child at home. The first group of twenty were working class; that is, they were members of family-based households which depended, for the major portion of their income, on hourly wages earned by the men. The second group of twenty were (loosely defined) middle class; that is, they lived in family-based households which received the major portion of their income from the salaries earned by husbands in professional occupations or in business. All of these women had, for at least one year in the five years prior to the study, worked as full-time domestic labourers and had been financially dependent on their husbands. All of them had full-time paid jobs outside the home and in addition, retained primary responsibility for the domestic labour in their households.

It is important to stress at the outset the unique features of this case study.[2] Flin Flon, where the study was conducted, is a small, single industry, northern, working-class community. While there is a middle-class component to the town's population, it is relatively small, elite and in circumstances quite unlike those in which the majority of middle-class Canadians live. Therefore, as I have argued elsewhere, while the working-class households in Flin Flon are typical and representative of working-class households elsewhere in Canada, the middle class is unique and therefore cannot be considered typical (Luxton, 1980).

Increasing Household Income

All of the women interviewed were married to husbands who were earning a regular wage or salary, which had been, at some point in the five preceding years, sufficient to support a non-earning wife. Nevertheless, all the women maintained that their main reason for taking on paid work was because "we need the money." This raises a very difficult question of how "need" is determined. In some cases need was apparently obvious. The household was in debt, and the husband's earnings alone would not be sufficient to sustain the household and pay off the debt. However, while the debts were indeed real, they had often been incurred for different reasons. . . .

Middle-class households obviously had more disposable income than working-class households and thus had access to a wider range of social and material comforts. All of the households, however, had an established standard of living which was, by the mid 1970s, being visibly eroded by inflation. The majority of these women, regardless of class, took on paid jobs to acquire the income necessary to sustain their households' standards.

Their class position affected the types of jobs these women got and how they experienced their paid work. Employment for women in Flin Flon is severely limited, as it is in most primary industry communities. There were many more women wanting paid work than there were jobs available. What jobs there were, were mainly traditional "working-class female jobs" — sales and clerical work. While most of the working-class women resented the job ghettos and wished they could break out of them, for the most part they assumed that this was the only type of work they could expect to get anywhere. Eight of the middle-class women had jobs that were slightly better paying, or were higher status than most — teachers, administrative assistants, social workers. They expressed relative satisfaction with their work. In contrast, the rest of the middle-class women were unable to find such jobs. They ended up in low-paid, low-status jobs, expressing frustration and anger at their situation. They resented being unable to use their education and training. They felt they had been forced to take jobs "beneath my position." One middle-class woman pointed out very forcefully that the "crummy job" she had proved how desperately her household needed the "pittance" she earned: "No one would do this job for this pay unless she was absolutely strapped." These differences are illustrated more clearly when we consider what impells women into the paid labour force when their households are not in a state of immediate economic crisis.

The majority of the middle-class women, regardless of what type of job they had, maintained that, if they did not need the money, they would prefer to stay at home. Fourteen out of the twenty women interviewed, including six who had "good" jobs, said that they were working for money because they had to. They argued that they had entered the paid labour force when their households were in an economic crisis and they insisted that they intended to leave as soon as possible. Six middle-class women, including four with "crummy" jobs, said they were working outside the home because they preferred their paid jobs to domestic labour and they maintained that they would keep their paid jobs regardless of the economic situation of their households.

For the majority of working-class women, the exact opposite was the case. Thirteen of these women maintained that they had taken on paid work at a point when their households were not in crisis. They maintained that when their husbands had regular employment, the household was not seriously in debt and things were running smoothly, that was the time when it was easiest for them to take on paid work. These women made their decision to enter the paid labour force based on two assumptions. The first was that if their households were running smoothly, it was possible for them to take on the added stress of the double day. The second assumption was that while things might be good at the moment, disaster was to be expected in the future and so they took on paid work to build up a nest egg of security for the hard times they anticipated ahead.

One woman described her understanding of this situation:

I'd take on a job either if we really needed the money real bad or if things is [sic] going good at home, then I'd get a job so we could save up a little extra. When my husband's having a rough time at work, then I like to be at home so I can take care of him....

The different motivations that women have in taking on paid work may be re-lated to the fact that proportionately, the amount that working-class women con-tributed to their household incomes was considerably greater than the amount contributed by middle-class women. Again it is important to reiterate here the point that the middle-class women of this study may not be typical. It would be useful to examine household incomes for women who hold professional jobs to see whether such income discrepancies occur for their households as well. The average earnings of the working-class husbands was $11,375.00 and of the wives $5,275.00. By taking on paid work, these women increased their household in-comes by 32%. In contrast, middle-class husbands earned an average of $29,568.00 while their wives earned an average $7,456.00. Thus, while the middle-class women earned on an average 29% more than the working-class women, their contribution increased their household incomes by only 20%. . . .

All of the working-class women felt that their earnings were an essential part of the household income and most of them expected that they would probably have paid jobs for most of their lives. Even those who anticipated leaving the paid labour force at various periods knew that such absences were only temporary and that what they were earning at the time was necessary.

It may be that there is a correlation between the type of increasing expenses a household is forced to offset and the women's decision to take on paid work.[3] In other words, when household expenses increase in those areas where it is possible for housewives to intensify their own labour, women may choose to work harder at home, rather than take on the double day. So, for example, when food and clothing costs increase, women may offset those expenses by shopping more care-fully, making more from scratch and mending more often. However, when house-hold expenses increase in areas where women cannot intensify their labour, they often have no choice but to earn money so that the household has the necessary fi-nances to meet the increased costs. For example, when the cost of home heating increased dramatically in the mid 1970s, most women had no way of intensifying their domestic labour to meet increased oil costs. In one exceptional case, the fam-ily installed a wood-burning stove and the housewife added chopping wood and stoking the fire to her domestic labour. This is not an option readily available to most households who must instead find more money to pay the oil bills. . . .

If the cost of work-related expenses is subtracted from the amount of money women earn, the result gives some indication of the real contribution women's earnings make to the household income. On an average, the earnings of working-class women increase their total household income by 34%. In contrast, because their husbands' incomes are so much higher, the earnings of middle-class women, on an average, increase their household's income by just 16%. The impli-cation of these figures is that, proportionately, working-class women are able to make a larger economic contribution to the subsistence of their households. It may be that there is a correlation between the relative importance of a woman's economic contribution and the respect and value that she and her husband attribute to her paid work.

Reduced Domestic Labour

When a woman takes on paid work, she usually does not relinquish her domestic labour. However, the amount of time and energy she has available for domestic labour is sharply reduced. Various time budget studies have suggested that married women working at two jobs in fact do less domestic labour than full-time housewives. However, when their paid work time and their domestic labour time are added together, the woman doing both jobs puts in about 12 hours more than full-time housewives each week.[4]

In comparing the way time was allocated by the two groups of women, a number of interesting observations emerged. On an average, the working-class women worked about 2.4 hours more than full-time housewives on a typical work day and about the same amount of time on weekends. In other words, this group corresponds to the findings of comparative time budget studies by working about 12 hours more than full-time housewives each week. In contrast, the middle-class women worked about 3.7 hours more than full-time, middle-class housewives on a typical work day and they worked 2.2 hours more on weekends. Thus these women were putting in about 22.9 hours per week more than full-time housewives or 10.9 hours more than working-class women! . . .

All the middle-class women felt very strongly that they had to continue improving the quality of their houses through activities which required their own labour. Where working-class women recognized that they could not keep up their former standards, middle-class women felt compelled to do so.

The second factor which contributes to the increased labour time of middle-class women is the extent to which husbands contribute to domestic labour. Cross class time budget studies have shown that husbands rarely increase the amount of time they spend doing domestic labour when their wives take on paid work. In this case, the working-class men did not increase the amount of time they spent on domestic labour on work days but on weekends they did half an hour more, spread over two days. In contrast, with one notable exception, the middle-class men actually reduced the amount of time they spent on domestic labour when their wives took on paid work![5]

One of the requirements of professional and commerical work is that a considerable amount of entertaining and social life must go on within the family household. Wives of professional and business men subsidize their husbands' jobs by maintaining an appropriately furnished home, by producing acceptable social events such as dinner parties and by accompanying the husband to social occasions organized by others. This conspicuous consumption and display behaviour is an essential part of maintaining social status. Regardless of what the wives may be doing elsewhere, they are expected to continue playing hostess for their husbands.

In contrast, the majority of working-class households, regardless of whether or not the woman was employed outside the home, did very little entertaining at home. Most of their social activities occurred outside the home, and the fact that the women were earning money meant that it was possible for them to increase the amount of socializing they did. Several of these women noted that by taking on paid work they were able to spend more money on organized leisure activities and therefore were able to do more: "Before I had a job I couldn't afford to get a sitter and go drinking . Now I can get out at least once a week.". . .

Conclusions

The case study that I have presented here is very small and the class-based comparisons I have drawn may not be typical for Canada as a whole. What the study does show is that while many women experience a similar process, the content of their experience may well be very different depending on their class background and current class position.

While it is important to understand the general underlying patterns of women's work and to untangle the implications of the sexual division of labour for women as a whole, it is also important to understand how women, as a group, are stratified. While structurally all married women constitute a reserve army of labour, we need to conduct further, indepth studies to determine how this is experienced by different types of women.

Notes

1. Pat Connelly, *Last Hired, First Fired*; Pat Armstrong and Hugh Armstrong, *The Double Ghetto*.

2. The research on which this paper is based was carried out in Flin Flon, Manitoba. An extended analysis of the working class material is presented in Meg Luxton *More Than a Labour of Love*. I have just begun to analyse the middle-class data and this is the first time I have presented it.

3. I would like to thank Pat Armstrong for suggesting this line of research.

4. See Luxton, 1980, chapter 6 for a discussion of time budget studies.

5. The exception to this pattern occurred in one household where the couple were profoundly influenced by feminism. In this case, the husband did almost half of the domestic labour and the woman estimated that she did about six hours a week more than the working-class women but about 4.9 hours less than other middle-class women. In this household, both the wife and husband believed that when the woman worked outside the home, the domestic labour should be shared by both of them. The husband argued that such a system was only "fair."

References

Armstrong, Pat and Hugh Armstrong
    1978   *The Double Ghetto: Canadian Women and their Segregated Work*. Toronto: McClelland and Stewart.

Connelly, Pat
    1978   *Last Hired, First Fired: Women and the Canadian Work Force*. Toronto: The Canadian Women's Education Press.

Luxton, Meg
    1980   *More than a Labour of Love: Three Generations of Women's Work in the Home*. Toronto: The Canadian Women's Educational Press.

Part IV/Approaches to Management

Editors' Introduction

With industrialization and the development of contemporary capitalism, business enterprises have grown in size and complexity. The activities of government in industrial capitalist society have also expanded dramatically. Hence, coordination of many workers performing a variety of different tasks has become the role of management. Managers have thus become a new and important occupational group within business and state bureaucracies.

Management involves more than the rationalization of the division of labour, although early management experts such as Frederick W. Taylor (whose "scientific management" techniques are discussed in several chapters in this part) believed otherwise. Managing also involves motivating workers who, unlike the owners of business enterprises and their managerial representatives, may not consider higher productivity and profits as primary goals. For the individual worker, satisfaction of personal material and psychological needs is more important. Several different management approaches intended to align the interests of employers and employees have evolved in the last century, and are considered below.

One should not go too far, however, in emphasizing the role of modern managers in building cooperation and consensus in the workplace. A number of writers featured in this part argue that a central preoccupation of management has been the removal of control over work from workers themselves. Through the careful planning and regulation of all activities in the productive process, management attempts to achieve greater efficiency, productivity, and profits. These critics conclude that new methods of management, including recent strategies of "industrial democracy" and "quality of work life" programs, are merely window dressing that disguise the latest assaults on employees' ability to regulate their own work. Thus, Part IV of this reader continues to explore key themes — power relationships and issues of control — first introduced in Part II.

In Chapter 18, Graham Lowe describes the rise of modern management in Canada, focussing on the first few decades of the twentieth century when industrialization fully took root in this country. He distinguishes between "soft" approaches to management, such as welfare work and the introduction of joint industrial councils, and "hard" approaches, best exemplified by Taylor's scientific management. In the former, managers attempted to involve and integrate workers in the enterprise, while in the latter the primary goal was the rationalization of the work process to obtain more output from each worker. However, in both approaches, Lowe identifies the same dual goals of management — improving efficiency and removing control of work from those performing it.

Taylor firmly believed that deliberate worker laziness was the source of all industrial ills, an assumption which became engrained in some management circles. In Chapters 19 and 20, Roland Frazee (a banking executive) and Reg Baskin (a union official) point out that productivity is not simply a function of the efforts of labour, as Taylor believed. Frazee writes: "Canadian productivity is low. I can think of at least six reasons why, but lazy workers are not on the list." Productivity may be influenced by investment practices, organizational designs, technological changes, and future-oriented research and development programs, as well as by techniques of managing and controlling labour. Such techniques are the subject of the remaining articles in this part, but Basken and Frazee's reminder that other factors also affect productivity must not be lost sight of.

T.F. Cawsey and P.R. Richardson present our first case study of management practices in Chapter 21. They describe the job enrichment techniques used by management of a large and modern Canadian mine. Workers are paid well, enjoy good working conditions, and have a reasonable amount of autonomy in deciding how to do their own work. Management attempts to be approachable, and emphasizes safety before productivity. The authors believe that the goals of this management strategy — increased productivity, reduced employee turnover, and increased employee satisfaction — are being reached. They also suggest that such benevolent management tactics eliminate the need for unions and, consequently, allow management greater flexibility in its planning and decision making.

Chapter 22 documents the unique organizational design and the innovative union-management contract created for a new petro-chemical plant in Sarnia, Ontario. Louis Davis and Charles Sullivan counter the argument that unions create rigid organizations and invariably place themselves in an adversary position with management. They describe how union and management together designed an efficient and productive "post-bureaucratic organization" in which the quality of work life was high, and in which individual workers had considerable scope for decision making. In Chapter 23, John Clarke describes the rescue of an inefficient (because of out-dated technology) Vancouver plywood factory, about to be closed by its owners. Here we also find evidence of a union working with management to increase productivity. However, as Clarke notes, the jobs were saved because the union challenged management's traditional right to shut down a plant — the ultimate act of controlling the labour of employees. Thus, he argues that unions are still essential and useful, a subject considered in more detail in Part V.

Donald Nightingale's study of twenty Canadian enterprises in Chapter 24 provides a systematic assessment of the effects of "formal participation" or "industrial democracy" on workers' psychological responses to work. In those organizations where employees are able to formally participate in the decision-making process, they are more committed to the organization and more satisfied with their jobs. Nightingale also demonstrates that "job enrichment" positively affects workers' attitudes. He concludes that in some work organizations job enrichment may be impossible, but introducing some form of industrial democracy may still have positive outcomes for both workers and their employers.

In short, these examples of Canadian work organizations make the case for both job enrichment and industrial democracy. Efforts to improve the quality of working life by involving workers in decision making appear to enhance organizational and individual effectiveness. However, in Chapter 25, G. Levine and G. Hunnius return us to the initial criticism of these "new" management techniques. Hunnius describes the common elements in Taylorism, job enrichment, and industrial democracy, arguing that the new management strategies are only further attempts by owners and managers to control labour and increase profits. He admits that job enrichment and industrial democracy may increase worker satisfaction, but suggests that even greater worker control may also result. This, in turn, might lead to the restoration of more hierarchical traditional forms of management. Levine is also pessimistic about the prospects for industrial democracy in Canada. He argues that North American unions will not really be interested, since they have traditionally focussed principally on wage and benefit issues. His conclusion is that "real" industrial democracy would require a complete transformation of capitalist society so that workers could totally control productive enterprises. For many this will have a utopian ring. Nonetheless, it is certainly worth considering just how far current work arrangements can be reformed in a quest for genuine improvements in the quality of working life.

Suggested Readings

Rinehard Bendix, *Work and Authority in Industry* (Berkeley: University of California Press, 1974).

Alfred D. Chandler Jr., *The Visible Hand: The Managerial Revolution in American Business* (Cambridge, MA: Harvard University Press, 1977).

Stephen Hill, *Competition and Control at Work* (London: Heinemann, 1981).

Theo Nichols, "Management, ideology and practice," in Geoff Esland and Graeme Salaman, eds., *The Politics of Work and Occupations* (Toronto: University of Toronto Press, 1980).

Donald Nightingale, *Workplace Democracy: An Inquiry into Employee Participation in Canadian Work Organizations* (Toronto: University of Toronto Press, 1982).

Charles Perrow, *Complex Organizations: A Critical Essay*, 2nd Edition (Glenview, Ill: Scott, Foresman, 1979).

Michael Rose, *Industrial Behaviour: Theoretical Development Since Taylor* (New York: Penguin Books, 1975).

Joseph Smucker, *Industrialization in Canada* (Scarborough: Prentice-Hall, 1980), Chapters 6 and 7.

18/The Rise of Modern Management in Canada[*]

Graham S. Lowe

In Canada the framework of a modern industrial society was laid down by the end of the First World War. Small-scale local enterprises which characterized the National Policy era were supplanted by large corporations in major manufacturing and service industries. Between 1896 and 1914 manufacturing received a tremendous boost from the wheat boom and western settlement. The net value of manufacturing production jumped more than 250% during the first decade of the century.

The First World War provided a further economic stimulus, and the continued prosperity during most of the 1920s helped to firmly entrench corporate capitalism. Indeed, manufacturing investment reached a peak in 1929 which would not be surpassed until the 1950s! Service industries — especially transportation and communications, retail trade, finance, and government — grew rapidly in response to the demands of the emerging industrial society. But it was manufacturing that formed the basis of the new economic order. There was a ten-fold increase in manufacturing production between 1900 and 1929, much of which can be attributed to the growing number of US branch plants dominating the economy.

Accompanying industrialization was the concentration of capital into a relatively small number of giant organizations. In 1890 only about 20% of Canadian manufacturers employed more than 75 workers. Mergers occurred in textiles and agricultural implements during the 1890s, but it was not until after the turn of the century that the consolidation process got fully underway. There were two major waves of merger, one between 1909 and 1913 and another more pronounced wave which peaked in 1928. By the late 1920s the giant corporation was a central feature of the Canadian economy. Employment conditions became increasingly bureaucratized. The growth of the central office was part of this trend, as exemplified by the swelling of Sun Life Assurance Company's headquarters' staff from 70 in 1900 to 2,856 in 1930.

It was the administrative problems precipitated by this trend that led to a range of reforms which formed the basis of modern management in Canada.

Welfare work, or industrial betterment, is one of the earlier programmes implemented by management to rationalize the work place. Welfare work schemes were concerned with manipulating the "human factor" in production, making them a forerunner to the Human Relations School of Management.

---

[*] Reprinted with permission of the publisher from Graham S. Lowe, "The Rise of Modern Management in Canada," *Canadian Dimension* 14(3) 1979, pp. 32-38.

The Canadian welfare work movement derived much of its inspiration from the American experience, especially the model welfare programme implemented in the 1890s at National Cash Register's Dayton Ohio plant. Canadian and American factories faced a similar range of programmes related to the work force. By the 1920s in both countries the "welfare secretary" of the turn of the century had given way to a new managerial speciality, the personnel expert. The National Association of Employment Managers was formed in 1919 in the U.S. Similar institutionalization occurred the following year in Canada with the formation in Toronto of the Employment Managers' Association. The Association's aim was "to promote and foster interest in employment and industrial relations problems in Toronto and elsewhere; to discuss problems of employees, including selection, training, management and working conditions; to encourage closer cooperation between industrial relations executives and to work with municipal and governmental bodies to bring about close cooperation concerning employment problems."

In one of the first public discussions of welfare work in Canada, *Industrial Canada* of June 1902 argued that "pleasant surroundings are conducive to the economical production of good work, while at the same time they attract a much better class of working people." Pretty factories with well manicured lawns and healthful working conditions were thought to induce higher moral standards and better work habits among employees, thereby reducing class tensions. These concerns fostered programmes such as pension plans, stock plans, company newspapers, cafeterias with subsidized meals, athletic facilities, educational programmes, and medical departments. Profit-minded employers justified the additional expense on both moral and pragmatic grounds.

While welfare work was defined as "embracing any effort by an employer on behalf of his employees, over and above the payment of wages, towards making them more comfortable and contented with their present work," its ultimate aim was to reduce overt employee discontent and increase managerial control. So in January 1907 *Industrial Canada* argued "that care for the physical, intellectual, and moral welfare of ... employees had a direct return in increased output and better work."

Williams, Green, and Rome Company, a Berlin, Ontario manufacturer of shirts, collars and cuffs was at the vanguard of the Canadian welfare work movement. Upheld in the business press as a model, the company's welfare plan was introduced in 1903 "for the purpose of securing mutually satisfactory relations at all points with its working people." What most impressed observers was the cooperative spirit of labour relations based on a humane concern for the well-being of the workman. The company president was portrayed as a great humanitarian dedicated to achieving the ideals of democracy and harmony in industry. Beneath this ideology of a new industrial spirit of order and cooperation lay the businessman's pragmatism: "It is good business, that human beings, like machines, give best service, and require less time and expense for repair when carefully treated for."

Welfare work had an ameliorative side — cleaner, safer and generally more humane working conditions. It was a soft tactic, involving little overt coercion. But persistent attempts at creating a unity of interests between labour and management, a feeling of "one big happy family," should not mask the way welfare work coopted worker resistance to managerial authority.

The company magazine was a major vehicle for propagating the ideology of cooperation. House organs were a logical development from the welfare work movement. Employers thought that by creating a feeling of community they could mollify the economic strains and labour-management tensions of the post World War I period. By the early twenties, house organs were a standard tool in modern management's repertory. In 1921 the federal Department of Labour analyzed forty such publications. It linked the company magazine to the general concerns of modern management: "Efficient work, contented employees, safety and a low labour turnover are conditions which every modern manufacturer is anxious to secure. In fact, once they are secured, the problem of industrial relations may be considered as solved. At these ultimate results all welfare work is aimed, and in such work the company paper plays a part by no means unimportant."

The soft tactics of welfare work and the harsher strategies of scientific management are complementary and were often combined. Progressive managers saw both as useful for countering labour and organizational problems. Both approaches extended management control so that inefficiency, waste, uncertainty, and worker "laziness" and unrest could be eliminated. Both were directed by a new cadre of expert managers. The "welfare secretary," the complement of the stop-watch wielding efficiency expert, was considered a necessary adjunct to corporate welfare plans as early as 1910. By then firms such as Williams, Green and Rome and McClary Manufacturing of London, Ontario had established welfare departments headed by these quasi-professionals.

Whether producing goods or providing services, bureaucracies increasingly faced problems requiring multifaceted solutions. The Consolidated Mining and Smelting Company, to give one example, established a comprehensive plan in 1930 based on the "cooperative principle." Included were scientific efficiency measures, such as wage incentives and employment aptitude tests, as well as welfare provisions, ranging from pensions and insurance to a home building fund and a safety department.

A survey conducted in 1928 by the federal Department of Labour revealed that "scientific management" was wide-spread among a sample of 300 manufacturing firms and public utilities. The study used the term scientific management broadly, including joint councils and other industrial relations plans, welfare work as well as the doctrines of Taylorism. In short, welfare work became part of a multi-pronged strategy to infuse efficiency and managerial control into large-scale organizations.

Joint Councils in Industry

Joint Councils are an example of how management imposed a formal structure of control on their relations with labour. For a number of reasons, the modern concept of employee relations took shape during the First World War. Unions were growing more powerful, the rise of bureaucracy was widening the rift between workers and managers, educational facilities had to adapt to the increasingly diverse technical requirements of industry, and the war conditions created a general sense of urgency in all matters relating to industrial relations. Conditions were ripe for the development of a coherent approach to labour relations.

It was against this background that William Lyon MacKenzie King's Colorado Industrial Plan of 1915 spread throughout the Rockefeller empire and into other industries. King was one of the first major ideologues of modern management in Canada. He was representative of an ascendant group of corporate technocrats who utilized science in the interests of industry. King's work — as first editor of the *Labour Gazette*, first federal Minister of Labour and renowned labour relations expert — exemplifies two central themes in management: scientific investigation of labour and organizational problems and cooperation between labour and capital. Commissioned by John D. Rockefeller to make "an academic and scientific study of labour relations in general" after the 1914 Ludlow Massacre, King devised the "Rockefeller Plan" of joint industrial councils. These councils were essentially a sophisticated form of company union and they established the pattern for industrial relations schemes in many large Canadian and American companies.

The end of the First World War marked an upsurge in joint councils on both sides of the Atlantic. By October, 1919, 225 firms in the U.S. had implemented the councils, all but 18 having done so after 1918. In Canada the first councils were set up by Bell Telephone, Imperial Oil and International Harvester in 1919. Within the next few years 17 large corporations had instituted full-fledged joint councils. Other factories and offices followed suit during the twenties. By 1930, for example, Imperial Oil had 90 such councils coast to coast, 11 in major offices. The scheme is still operating today.

The war crisis made capitalists face up to the fact, had they not already done so, that greater control over the labour process and its social organization was called for. Unhindered production, essential in war industries, demonstrated that the absence of industrial strife boosted profits and aided the expansion of corporate empires. Furthermore, a potentially volatile industrial relations climate had been created through rampant wartime inflation, growing union strength, and the productivity demands of the war effort. Employers seized upon the possibility that the opposing classes could cooperate in the factory to the same high degree as they did on the battlefields in Europe.

Massey-Harris thus heralded the introduction of its joint council plan in these terms: "Cooperation is the basis of all success. Without it, the allied armies would have been ineffective against a ruthless enemy. It also applies to the commercial and industrial world as greatly as to any group of armies. The cooperation of employees with employers, the cooperation of the mechanic and foreman, and last but not least, the cooperation of various departments, all tend toward a successful firm, a contented workman, happy in the knowledge of work well done and an assured pay envelope."

The federal government contributed to the formation of the employee relations component of modern management. The 1918 Royal Commission on Industrial Relations supported the idea of joint councils. The Department of Labour sponsored a National Industrial Conference on Industrial Relations and Labour Laws in September 1919. Prime Minister Borden's message to the conference stressed the need for greater cooperation between labour and capital echoing the Royal Commission's recommendation that joint industrial councils be established "with a view to promoting harmony and better relations between employers and employees."

Another government-sponsored conference in 1921 registered the success of the Joint Council movement in Canada. Ten large corporations, all with joint council plans, attended. Guest speakers were brought in from two American pioneers in the field — International Harvester and United States Rubber Company. The Canadian Manufacturers' Association was impressed by the success of the councils, voting at its 1922 convention to encourage their adoption. The C.M.A.'s policy reflected a growing concensus among business leaders that there must be "the development of a spirit of mutual good will and cooperation between employers and employees, instead of one of antagonism." Underlying this was the recognition that the ideology of cooperation was central to the extension of managerial control.

Around the time of the First World War progressive managers reached a common understanding on labour relations matters. Direct frontal attacks on unions were still common, but a more sophisticated remedy had developed. By urging the cooperation of labour in the pursuit of corporate goals, managers ultimately hoped to lessen worker resistance to managerial controls. This, of course, would ideally bring higher productivity, lower costs and more profits.

The ideology of cooperation was institutionalized through joint councils. Even more significant, though, was the advent of the employee relations manager at the end of the War. A new management speciality was created, carrying the logic of efficiency and control into the arena of labour relations.

Vocational Education

Industrial development after 1900 accentuated the division of labour and brought about the decline of the craftsman. As old occupations disappeared new jobs and skill requirements were created. Capitalists, however, were unwilling to become saddled with the costs of training the expanding army of factory and office workers. The old apprenticeship system could not meet the mounting demands for vocational education. It also became increasingly clear that the labour market was no longer self regulating. These factors pushed the state into an interventionist role, forcing it to accept responsibility for vocational education. Behind the initiatives to establish educational programmes lay another key feature of modern management: the rationalization of the labour supply.

Early vocational programmes were often privately run, reflecting the lack of suitable public educational facilities. Nine Ontario cities had private business colleges by 1901. The Canadian Pacific Railway set up its own school in 1904 to teach employees telegraphy, stenography, typing and railway operations.

By the start of the War, the Insurance Institute of Toronto and the Canadian Bankers' Association were offering extensive educational courses to workers in the financial sector. These courses may have met some of the requirements for white-collar workers. However, businessmen harboured the more basic concern that the supply of trained operatives would lag behind the expansion of production. The Canadian Manufacturers' Association, through its Technical Education Committee set up in 1904, thus began lobbying for a comprehensive plan of industrial education.

The C.M.A. argued for educational reforms on the grounds of industrial progress and efficiency: "Efficient workmen are absolutely essential if industries are to prosper. If one man can increase the speed of a machine, even to the smallest extent, the shop in which he works is placed in an advantageous position in the industrial race.... The Labour Convention (Trades and Labour Congress), the Canadian Manufacturers' Association, and the heads of important educational institutions, all agree that technical education is a necessity for a country which expects to win the industrial race.... Too much emphasis cannot be laid on the importance of efficient work. On it depends the whole industrial life of the country."

Public vocational education made slow progress prior to World War I. The federal government appointed a Royal Commission on Industrial Training in 1910, but a national plan for the development of industrial education had to await the 1919 Technical Education Act. Under the Act, 139 vocational schools had been set up by June 1920. The state had formally committed itself to ensuring industry a supply of trained workers. By 1920, the groundwork for a modern vocational education system had been laid.

These developments are further evidence of the diffusion and institutionalization of modern management. Ideologically, managerial discussions of vocational education emphasized industrial progress, a cooperative and competent labour force and the rationalization of all components of the productive process. Large corporations, facing high risk factors and strong competition, could leave little to chance. The scope of managerial control had to be extended. Waste, inefficiency and anything not rational, calculable and planned were abhorred by managers. A regulated, trained industrial work force was thus a palliative: human resources were not wasted, efficiency of production was more likely and a tutored worker was more easily regimented.

Complementing the trends in technical and vocational education was the growing prominence of management education during the 1920s. In 1919 the University of Toronto mounted the first specialized course on the new science of management. Geared mainly for employment managers, it ranged over a broad terrain covering topics such as scientific management, welfare work, employee training and industrial relations. The course symbolizes the formal status management had achieved as a distinct body of knowledge. It is evidence of not only the ascendancy of modern management ideology, but also of its practical application.

Scientific Management: "The New Gospel of Industrial Progress"

Taylorism and its variants stand in contrast to the "soft" approaches to management problems discussed above. Taylorism had gained a foothold in Canadian industry by the start of the First World War. The Lumen Bearing Company of Toronto had adopted the Taylor system by 1911. An official of the firm spoke for his fellow businessmen when he claimed that "efficiency management is the biggest problem in manufacturing today." The company's efficiency drive determined piece work rates through time study and eliminated work planning by mechanics. The firm no doubt attracted considerable attention in management circles when its casting production rose from 28 to 65 units per day. To give another example, in June 1909 the Canadian Pacific Railway hired H.L. Gantt, an associate of Taylor, to scientifically reorganize locomotive repair work at the Montreal Angus Shops. Gantt's changes included a piece work system, standardized job routines governed by instruction sheets, standardized tools, an elaborate scheduling method for repair work and the physical reorganization of the shop.

In 1911, Gantt advised Canadian manufacturers on "the straight line to profit." Preaching that "scientific management is the new gospel of industrial progress," he advised businessmen to prune unnecessary costs rather than raise prices. This was a fundamental element of the Taylor system and it became quite popular with Canadian managers. Gantt argued that cost-cutting required the elimination of chance, or, in other words, the application of managerial control: "To eliminate this blind by-play with chance and substitute methods based on technical inquiry and proved results, is the task of scientific management. Every element in a business should come under this searching inquiry, from shop to office. And whenever it strikes, it means the elimination of waste time, waste energy, waste materials."

Any doubts Canadian businessmen still harboured about these claims may well have been allayed by the three articles F.W. Taylor himself published in *Industrial Canada* during 1913. Yet seldom was the complete Taylor system adopted. Manufacturers seemed to prefer tackling inefficiencies through less rigid, more eclectic reforms. Piece work was especially popular, for it allowed management to control production output, relocate decision-making regarding production from the factory floor to the front office and reduce labour costs.

The use of mechanical time recording devices is further evidence of the extension of tight control over the activities of workers. Employee time recorders were introduced into Canada in 1902 as a scientific way to regulate labour costs and worker productivity. By 1915 the International Time Recording Company of Canada, a predecessor of IBM and the major distributor of these punch clocks, listed fifty large Canadian organizations among its customers. Ads appearing after the war for the devices were often directed specifically at office managers. The sales pitch reflected modern managerial thinking, underlining the need to control clerical overhead by careful measurement of working time. This indicates the ease with which scientific management made its way from the shop floor into the office....

The reduction of labour costs was a top priority for businessmen. The *Monetary Times* of September 1919 elaborates: "Cost systems are an essential part of modern scientific business management. For the capital invested in a business proves just as efficient as are the brains employed to handle it; and the best guide for brains is analysis. That is the function of a cost system — to give the manufacturer a detailed knowledge of his business — and to give him this detailed information regularly and automatically." The institutionalization of cost accounting as a specialized branch of management followed from the widespread recognition that "the secret of efficiency, after all, is costs." An early textbook on the topic claims that "organization, management and cost accounting are so intimately related that it is almost impossible to consider them separately." Cost accounting records and analyzes what each component of the production process (all input factors) contributes to final profits. The ultimate objective is "to provide data for the control of the business."

The spread of cost accounting in Canada paralleled post-1900 industrialization. Extolling the "practical value" of cost accounting, *Industrial Canada* argued that the new science provided overall managerial control in addition to reducing expenses. Cost accounting was seen to offer two distinct advantages to firms in an increasingly competitive and complex economic environment. First, accurate cost estimates of proposed work could be made and second, the effectiveness of managerial techniques, production methods and labour efficiency could be evaluated.

These measures were readily integrated with other efficiency methods. For example, one of Canada's largest bookbinding establishments combined costing with Taylorist production methods. All production workers were required to submit a daily work ticket recording work completed. Accounting clerks would compare these output data with work to be done, thereby providing a check on rising labour costs. On another occasion, an accountant argued that the best way to reduce factory overhead was to keep careful production records for each worker and monitor the flow of work so that men and machines would be consistently busy.

The Science of Management and the Office

Given the growing application of modern management techniques to industry, it was to be expected that inefficiency in the office would also fall under the critical scrutiny of management. Businessmen at first accepted the disproportionate growth of administrative jobs as an unavoidable side-effect of the scientific approach to factory management.

A 1905 gathering of Hamilton manufacturers was cautioned that the elimination of overall waste and inefficiency through cost accounting would result in higher office overhead: "of course it must be understood that to have an accurate Cost System will increase the expense of the office or accounting, though not to a great extent, but with a proper system the results will more than pay the extra expense, while the ways of saving waste, etc., will show up so clearly that the extra clerical expense will be saved again and again in the factory."

But as administrative costs continued to mount, they threatened to undermine the effectiveness of the office as an administrative control centre. The recording, analysis, and storage of a growing array of information on costs, worker productivity, market conditions, customer accounts and so on was necessary for effective managerial decision making. Large, multi-departmental office structures evolved in services and manufacturing as the means of handling the mass of paper work accompanying industrial expansion. Soaring administrative costs were in part a result of the basic inefficiences of office bureaucracies, especially their structural fragmentation and growing task specialization.

One of the earliest administrative systems for dealing with these problems was introduced in banking. Around the turn of the century Canadian banks were expanding their horizons to national and international dimensions. Facing management problems similar to those found in large-scale factories and shops, the Bank of Nova Scotia devised a sophisticated method of controlling clerical productivity. Called the Unit Work System, it was introduced in 1901 as the basis of the bank's cost accounting system and service charge schedule. By comparing the number of standardized work units handled by a particular branch with the efficiency ratings of its staff, head office management could determine manpower requirements, salary increases and promotions throughout the branch system.

Some large bureaucracies employed American efficiency experts to rationalize clerical procedures. Just prior to World War I, for example, the Land and Collection Branch of the Canadian Pacific Railway's Department of National Resources in Calgary was handling a larger volume of business than any loan company in the Dominion. After conducting a survey of office methods used in Canadian and American loan companies, the railway hired "a thoroughly competent efficiency expert" from the U.S. to reorganize the branch and simplify its methods.

Scientific Management in the Civil Service

Even more sweeping reforms were instituted by American management consultants in the Federal civil service. The Ottawa bureaucracy had a long history of inefficiency largely due to rampant patronage. The problems reached crisis proportions with the swelling of civil service ranks during the First World War. "Efficiency in government" became the rallying cry of the Borden government's attack on the evils of patronage. The result was an elaborate civil service classification and salary scheme developed by Arthur Young and Company, a team of Chicago management consultants.

The Civil Service Commission oversaw this massive reorganization, probably the most extensive in any Canadian organization during the pre-World War II period. Enshrined in the 1918-1919 Civil Service Act were the most advanced ideas in U.S. management circles.

The consultants advocated "a business-like approach to government." One way in which they achieved this was to apply the full weight of Taylorism to the Department of Public Printing and Stationery, one of the most inefficient parts of the bureaucracy. Records and procedures were standardized, staff requirements formalized, plant and office lay-outs stream-lined, new equipment introduced and 400 "unnecessary" employees eliminated on the basis of their relatively low efficiency ratings. The results brought resounding approval from the Civil Service Commission, which at the time was recruiting a resident expert in "industrial management work."

Word of Arthur Young and Company's successful rationalization of the federal civil service spread. To take advantage of this, in 1920 the firm separately incorporated its industrial engineering department in Canada as Griffenhagen and Associates. The new firm was subsequently hired for organizational work by the Province of Quebec, Massey-Harris and Canadian Cereal and Flour Mills Ltd.

Ontario appointed its first Civil Service Commissioner in 1918 and, like his federal counterpart, he also embraced scientific management as the cure for the ills of bureaucracy. The new Commissioner was not unlike many industrial managers of the time, being driven by the ideals of greater economy and efficiency in administration. The major reform, completed in 1927, was a merit-based system of job classifications and salary scales. The Commissioner argued that "the merit system is concerned with the selection and the maintenance of an efficient personnel and with the application of sound and scientific principles.... Its uniform application to employment problems would ensure efficiency and economy in the Public Service and eliminate irregularities and anomalies." The government's occupational structure was thus rationalized by job analysis, one of the basic tools of scientific management. Jobs were graded, re-classified and in some cases subdivided. Efficiency ratings were taken for each employee in order to determine his or her status in the new hierarchy. In short, the civil service had grown large, uncoordinated, and sluggish by the end of the war. "Scientifically determined standards by which to gauge efficiency" were therefore a key aspect of reorganization.

The decades from 1900 to 1930, then, constitute the formative stage in modern management in Canada. This does not mean, however, that the concepts of efficiency, control, scientific investigation and labour-management cooperation found their way into all or most firms. The trends described here more accurately suggest what occurred in those giant organizations at the forefront of industrialization. Even today, smaller firms or those in less competitive industries continue to rely upon traditional management techniques. Nonetheless, by the Depression, the managerial quest for efficiency and control had become a major force in Canada's new industrial order.

19/Working Smarter: Improving Productivity in Canada[*]

Rowland C. Frazee

The definition of productivity is simple: it is output per unit of input, or what you get out for what you put in, in labour, capital, and resources. Productivity figures are most often expressed in terms of labour input — for example, in Canada we produce a ton of steel in 8.2 man hours; in Japan they do it in 6.1 man hours.

Figures like that can lead to a pernicious misunderstanding. Too many people take them as "proof" that Canadian workers are lazy. Such a conclusion is not justified.

Canadian productivity *is* low. I can think of at least six reasons why; but lazy workers are not on the list. Statistics like the steel production figures just quoted not only reflect labour input but also inputs of capital and technology, such as the age and efficiency of steel mills in each country. In addition, the numbers are not strictly comparable due to differences in product mix and work week in the two countries. Canada's steel industry, in fact, is a bright spot in our productivity picture.

Productivity is not a judgment on how hard people are working. It *is* a measurement of efficiency — how cleverly and innovatively industry uses each of the elements that go into creating a product or service. Overall, that measurement — GNP per worker — determines total income. It is what a nation lives on, and it is *all* it lives on.

It is not just the absolute level of productivity that is important. In a competitive, changing world, the *rate* of productivity improvement is what counts. That

[*] Reprinted, with permission of the publisher, from Rowland C. Frazee, "Working Smarter: Improving Productivity in Canada," *Canadian Business Review* 8:4, 1981, pp. 17-20.

rate fluctuates, sometimes dramatically, from quarter to quarter and year to year. While short-term changes are often the subject of debate, the real determinant of long-term prosperity is the average productivity growth over a period of years. The Canadian results should be causing us grave concern.

Productivity growth in this country averaged 2.5 per cent a year from 1960 to 1973 and only 0.2 per cent for the next six years. For the last two years productivity has actually declined. The twenty-year trend is down.

Even more important, in the last fifteen years Canada has done one third as well as Germany and one fifth as well as Japan — and we have significant advantages over both countries in resources.

Is there any *good* news? Well, sort of — but only short-term. This year the rate of decline will not be quite as big as last year's drop. In other words, we are still bleeding to death, but not as fast.

Canada is paying the price now for decisions made, or not made, ten years ago. That loss is not recoverable. Nothing can be done to significantly change efficiency this year. A great deal can be done to improve it over the next decade. It is what is done now that will determine how well we will live, and how well our children will live, in 1990 and beyond.

There is already a serious gap between what this country is likely to achieve and what it is capable of achieving. Here are two projections, both in 1980 dollars.

Let us assume that the average productivity increase during the coming decade will be 2.3 per cent a year. That happens to be the actual average for the 26 years from 1946 to 1972. If that rate were achieved, by 1990 average disposable income per employee would be $4,600 more than what is earned today.

On the other hand, what if the average productivity rise is only, say, 0.2 per cent a year? That also happens to be an actual average for Canada — from 1973 to 1979. If that were the figure over the coming decade, then by 1990 disposable income per employee would have risen by only $400. That is a large order of difference — $4,600 per employee versus $400. Raising Canadian output so that employees will have that extra $4,600 a year by the end of the decade means making some major changes in performance, and starting now.

Let us begin by recognizing that it is the quality, rather than the quantity, of inputs to productivity that has to change. Rather than working harder, we have to start working smarter. There are at least six major ways of doing that.

The first has to do with the country's overall economic policy climate — the approach to inflation, fiscal and monetary policies, the degree of government intervention — but *especially* it has to do with the environment of business-government and inter-government relationships.

Serious attention to the challenges we face requires an atmosphere of purposeful calm and a degree of political stability. In a number of crucial policy areas, business, labour, the provinces and the federal government appear to have their heels dug in, all pulling in opposite directions.

Compromise is overdue. This is not to suggest that Ottawa and the provinces should or will have identical views. They have different mandates. The important thing is a mutual acceptance of the necessity to resolve the differences within a reasonable period of time. Whatever the *details* of the energy-pricing agreements between Ottawa and the provinces, we are all going to pay the costs of the *delay* in reaching them.

I don't wish to be simplistic. All of these issues — energy, inflation, constitutional reform, federal-provincial cost-sharing — are complex. In fact, we delude ourselves if we think they can be solved, in the usual sense of that word. They do have to be dealt with, and compromise is the key word. But a relative degree of peace and harmony among labour, business and government and among levels of government is not an end in itself; it merely provides the essential atmosphere in which policy can be made.

If creating the atmosphere is the first step toward improving productivity, the second step has to do with the attitude toward sources of capital. Canada has enormous capital needs in the decade ahead, and yet we seem to have arrived at a philosophy that Canadian capital is good and foreign capital is bad. I'm not referring solely to government. There are businessmen, labour representatives and media commentators — even, I suppose, an occasional banker — all of whom have encouraged this myth of the superiority of Canadian capital.

That kind of nationalism is economic nonsense.

Canada cannot meet its capital needs from within its own borders. Unless we want a steady decline in our living standards, there is *no choice* about importing capital. Provided that the bulk of those funds are productively invested, there is little reason for concern.

Nevertheless, the debate about increasing Canadian ownership cannot be ignored. In fact, the debate now has more to do with the methods and degree than with the goal itself, to which I am generally sympathetic. But as we develop these methods, I think there are some important points to consider.

First, if there is a choice between investing a dollar here to build new Canadian enterprise and create new Canadian jobs or sending it abroad to buy back ownership of existing enterprise in Canada, common sense should indicate the former.

Next, foreign owners must obviously abide by any legal requirements Canada make of them. They may also need to be told that good corporate citizenship goes well beyond simple adherence to the law. As a nation we can regulate and we can recommend — but in both cases let us be very specific about what we are going to require. Broad prohibitions, particularly those that have a retroactive effect, are not only discriminatory against foreign investment, a majority of which has been beneficial to Canada, but they also increase the likelihood of retaliation against Canadian investment abroad.

Finally, capital flows coming into Canada are a sign of economic strength, not economic weakness. They are a tangible vote of confidence in our future prospects and an affirmation of our past success. It is not difficult for people outside Canada to understand our desire to increase Canadian ownership in certain key sectors over time. But it is difficult for them to deal with us if our attitude is one of generalized suspicion and hostility, and *particularly* if they do not know what the rules are going to be.

A third area where Canadians could be working smarter is in industrial relations. As a country we have a miserable record, and the blame is not all on one side. Organized labour doesn't want to be loved; it does want, and it does deserve, respect for its contribution. Increased productivity is as good for labour as it is for management, stockholders and the country. It is the only route to real job security and to real and sustained increases in wages. The search for improved efficiency can, of course, cause short-term disruptions in employment patterns, and that reality must be dealt with if we are to enlist labour as a full partner in the fight for increased productivity. The basic point, which labour understands full well, is that unemployment results not from technology, but from a lack of it.

A fourth example has to do with people skills. It seems incredible that industry is short of skilled workers — that Canadian business must continue to import tool and die makers, for instance, while the better part of one million people are out of work. There are dozens of other examples. Canada has too few foresters. We are also short of engineers and accountants. There is a need to create jobs. There is also a need to create the skilled people who can fill them.

On the management side, the challenge is even greater. We need new approaches to the organization and motivation of people, new methods for the structuring and control of tasks in the work place. It is individuals, energetic and committed, who will provide continuing productivity improvement. As business looks for better ways of turning on the machines, we must also find better ways of turning on the people. There are many who would suggest that enlightened management is essential to productivity improvement.

A fifth area in which we should be working smarter is our approach to investment. Managers and investors have too often been guilty of looking for a quick profit at the expense of long-term investment. It is an understandable fault. Management is under continuous pressure to do two things simultaneously: maximize profit in the short run and build for the long run. The two are often difficult to reconcile — but that is the challenge. Investments in modernization, particularly in new technology, present an agonizing choice. If we do invest, the payback can be slow and is never certain. If we don't invest, international competitiveness moves farther out of reach.

In that context, it is encouraging to see the pulp and paper industry, for example, putting such a high percentage of earnings back into plant and equipment, particularly after a decade of relatively low return. Canada's steel industry has also undertaken the expensive task of modernization. Doing that across the board in

Canada, more successfully than we have in the past decade, is the fifth step to increased productivity.

Number six, and by far the most vital, is increased investment in research and development. The record is poor. In 1968, as a nation we were spending 1.4 per cent of GNP on research and development. The government felt that was too low, so it set a target of 2 per cent. Ten years later, spending was *down* by well over a third, to 0.9 per cent, where it rests today. So new target figures were set — 1.5 per cent of GNP. This year the government changed the target *date* from 1983 to 1985.

The bad news does not end there. Canada provides employment for fewer industrial R & D workers than almost any industrialized nation. Sweden, with one third, and Holland, with only half our population, each have more researchers in absolute numbers — and they look like pikers compared to the world leaders, West Germany and Japan.

It is too easy to suggest that government should be doing more. In point of fact, government both federally and provincially is already doing a fair amount. If Ottawa isn't spending enough through, say, tax incentives, at least one major reason is that tax-paying companies aren't making the investments in the first place.

If we want a healthy private sector R & D effort in Canada, we in the private sector have to create it ourselves. Blaming Ottawa and the provinces can be just another excuse for inaction.

There is one particularly valuable aspect of R & D government support — purchasing policy. A government contract to develop and build a particular piece of high technology can be the most effective stimulant of all. Government gets a direct benefit; the company gets not only support for the research involved but experience and credibility in the marketplace.

That's how it worked for a company that is today one of the high technology super stars in Canada — MacDonald-Dettwiler and Associates. From 1971 to 1974, they operated under three federal government contracts, developing and selling systems for digital processing of satellite-originated data. The total cost to the taxpayer was $251,000, modest enough.

In the seven years since, that government contract has resulted in sales by MacDonald-Dettwiler of $36 million — more than three quarters of it to export markets. The multiplier effect of the original contract is in the order of 150 to 1; the company that started in a basement eleven years ago now has 200 employees, annual sales well into eight figures and is a world leader in its field.

That success story is worth remembering when we hear suggestions government could do more to encourage research and development. Yes, they could do more — but so could the private sector. We have some winners. We need a lot more.

A parallel concern has to do with the amount of foreign-originated technology now in use in Canada. A common figure is that only 20 per cent of our technology is our own. Increasing that percentage will take time. In the interim, the important thing is not the nationality of the technology but the rate at which it is adopted and built on. There is every sign that we are not quick enough to use other people's best ideas.

Importing technology is not the answer by itself, any more than importing capital is. In fact, the two often come as a package. It is what we do with them once they are here that is important.

Japan offers some useful comparisons. Most Canadians remember when "made in Japan" meant a low quality copy of some other country's product. The world that used to laugh at the Japanese propensity for making cheap, quick copies is not laughing any longer. The huge Japanese microelectronics industry didn't even exist in 1953, when the Sony corporation paid Western Electric the vast sum of $25,000 for non-exclusive rights to manufacture the transistor — a bit of imported technology the Japanese have done reasonably well with since. A more recent example is the industrial robot, invented in the United States. Three thousand robots are at work in American plants. Very commendable. But Japan, with half the population, now has 10,000 robots in industry fourteen years after they imported the first ones from the United States.

If there are real productivity benefits from developing our own technology, there are equally real and probably quicker benefits from importing and then expanding on other people's technology.

Taking the steps outlined above will set us on the road to realization of our potential ten years from now: 4,600 additional dollars per employee, versus 400.

In Newfoundland today, fishermen catch an ugly little creature called the lumpfish. At certain times of the year, its body weight is nearly one-third roe. The yellow fish eggs are separated and packed in small kegs and sold to buyers from Europe. There, lumpfish eggs undergo a modest amount of processing — they're dyed black and packed in little glass jars — and then they are shipped back to Canadian delicatessens to be sold as lumpfish roe caviar. The Newfoundland fisherman gets $70 a keg; once processed, the contents of the keg are worth $4,000.

That is an *extreme* example of our national tendency to let others benefit from value-added processing while we sell raw resources.

If we accept that situation on a broad scale and take the easy route of yielding the high technology ground to other nations, we condemn ourselves to an ever-diminishing share of our own wealth.

And Canada *can* do it. We have a world lead in telecommunications research, cold-ocean engineering, long-distance hydro transmission and earth resources satellites, to name only a few examples. We can build on those strengths, and add others.

We have the opportunity to become what we have always told ourselves we were — one of the world's most-favoured nations. If we develop the resolve to make it happen and the self-discipline and long-term view to allow it to happen, then it can and will happen.

20/Labour's Role in Productivity[*]

R.C. Basken

Productivity, by definition, is the output of the average worker over a stated period of time — an hour, a day, a week, or a year. Most careful observers would refer to this as "labour productivity." But the word labour is frequently dropped in the heat of discussion.

Somehow, the impression is left that Canada's productivity would increase if we could only get that average worker to work a little bit harder. Certainly what a worker can produce in any given period of time depends on skills as well as on how hard the employee works. But there are a substantial number of other factors that affect productivity and are beyond the control of any worker or even any group of workers.

During periods of a downturn in the economy, plants function at less than capacity and management frequently develops "make-work" projects, reasoning that it will be cheaper than laying workers off only to rehire them later. While in theory this should be good for the worker, in practice it generally just provides an excuse for economists to blame low productivity on workers not working hard enough. In the long haul, the development of a corporate and a national industrial strategy should permit the type of planning that would alleviate such problems.

Productivity is greatly influenced by the efficiency of machinery; it also depends on management's effectiveness. Workers cannot produce if they are required to wait around for supplies. Nor can a worker produce if he is required to switch from one task to another by supervisory direction or because of lack of materials.

Most manufacturing installations are designed to run most efficiently when producing at or near capacity. Inefficiency because of economic downturn opens industry to the charge of low productivity, with the blame inevitably falling upon the worker.

Oversupervision can affect labour productivity by stifling worker incentive. It should not be surprising that if workers are so supervised that they are told when to start work, when to stop for coffee, when coffee break is over, when to go to the bathroom, when to increase the speed of a machine, and when to slow it down, the workers cease to offer much ingenuity.

Workers must be given the opportunity to have some say in the planning and implementation of the production schedule. Canada today has the best educated and most highly skilled work force in its history. It is wasteful to educate and train

---

[*] Reprinted, with permission of the publisher, from R.C. Basken, "Labour's Role in Productivity," *Canadian Business Review* 8:4, 1981, pp. 15-16.

people and then treat them at the work place as if they knew nothing. It is time that we consider workers as responsible and trustworthy. Most workers can work well as individuals and also work effectively together as members of a group if they feel they have the right to develop their own methods and be permitted those little idiosyncrasies that all individuals have. Workers are capable of making proper and useful decisions when given the necessary information.

Work place design must reflect efficiency; otherwise time is wasted and materials are used ineffectively. Proper training of engineers and architects is necessary so that they will design for improved productivity, not just convenience. It is clear that job design should be fitted more to the individual than the individual fitted to the job design.

Work rules must permit employees to learn on the job and continue learning. They must permit them also to develop to their own level of ability as they desire. Often an individual who turns down a promotion is denied future opportunities of advancement. This is a foolish policy that gives no consideration to the individual's current desires or circumstances.

While incentive pay and payment according to piece work have long been viewed as increasing productivity, both methods are actually counter-productive. They give little or no regard to the quality of work, and they assume that all workers work at the same speed and are only interested in financial return.

Another long-held myth is that unions and strikes reduce productivity. Current productivity studies indicate that this is not and has not been the case. Strikes get a tremendous amount of attention, but strike time loss is extremely low. Over the past 20 years not more than 1/2 of 1 per cent of total work days were lost as a result of strikes in any given year, and the average over that time is something like 2/10 of 1 per cent. Also, strikes do not affect the productivity calculation, because when no one is working no output exists and neither are there any working hours to use in the calculation. I also believe that sometimes a strike clears the air, and following its conclusion work rules change, attitudes change, equipment changes and the new understanding between workers and employers actually leads to increased productivity.

According to new research by a North Carolina State University economist, unionized construction workers are more productive than non-union construction workers. Output per employee was found to be at least 29 per cent greater in unionized building firms and up to 38 per cent more productive if the extra productivity is attributed to labour. Dr. Steven G. Allen, who conducted the study for the Center to Protect Workers' Rights, said that it is impossible to say exactly why unionized building trades workers are more productive, but they are. His research follows other recent studies by Charles Brown, from the University of Maryland, and James Madoff, of Harvard University, who found output per working hour to be 24 per cent greater in unionized manufacturing plants.

Madoff points out that "employees of the group may work more efficiently, cooperate more, be more willing to train others when they know their place in the hierarchy, when they don't feel threatened." He explains that there is not much featherbedding in the major U.S. companies attributable to unions. "Featherbedding does exist, but it exists both in union and non-union settings. There is no reason to assume that non-union companies don't have implicit work rules that could be labelled featherbedding. It is said that a non-union firm has the power to change implicit work rules. Well, there is no evidence that this is the case." Madoff goes on to argue that "concern about work force morale and the possibility that workers may join the union" were the two most significant reasons why the non-union management were ineffective in increasing the productivity — false economy, to say the least.

In highly capital-intensive industries, such as energy, labour is kept on — stockpiled, in essence — over long periods to have a ready work force on hand in anticipation of future shortages. In such industries the pricing of the product has little or no relationship to the cost of production, and workers are sometimes literally encouraged to be totally unproductive. I know of cases where workers were required to do such useful functions as play cribbage for days on end; then, all of a sudden they were expected to be motivated and highly efficient when work became available. Such situations are often unavoidable, but the workers affected cannot justifiably be blamed for reduced productivity as a result.

Restrictive work practices and rules play an important role in productivity and are factors that workers have little or no control over. One of the worst of a group of stupid rules is exemplified in the 1981 case of an American postal worker who was disciplined for not holding the letters he was sorted at a 45-degree angle. The worker took the case to arbitration and explained that because of both the lighting and his poor eyesight it was much more convenient to hold the letter at a substantially different angle than required by the work rule. The arbitrator ruled in favour of the worker.

It certainly appears that rather than focusing on labour, one of the best ways to increase output is to get unused productivity capacity into production. Beyond that, the very structure of the economy needs improvement. If we were to build world-scale plants and manufacture more materials for export instead of shipping raw materials to other countries, productivity would increase, particularly now with the lower value of the Canadian dollar in relation to our outside markets. An industrial strategy by industry and company that permitted year-round work, rather than switching from one small amount of output for local market to another, also would significantly improve overall productivity.

Without denying that labour is a factor in the calculation of productivity, it seems that simply urging workers to work harder is shortsighted and ineffective. It only serves to make them angry. Many of them believe that there is little or nothing the average worker can do about productivity in their own location and much less that they can do in the context of the overall economy. Very little time is now available in the work place to explain the worker's relationship to the production system.

We have the best educated and trained work force in history. There is reason for optimism. Part of the training program can be used to explain that improved productivity is a direct benefit to all and not only used to maximize profit. I believe that we must allow this training and education to be reflected in greater participation by workers in workshop decisions. We can expand the role of workers to permit a more complete utilization of their training and experience.

21/Employee Relations at the Kidd Creek Operations of Texasgulf Limited[*]

T.F. Cawsey and P.R. Richardson

Introduction
"Kidd Creek is a good place to work." This was a typical response from operators interviewed during a visit to Texasgulf's Kidd Creek mine and metallurgical complex near Timmins, Ontario.[1] The operations have won the John T. Ryan trophy for the last three years, having experienced the lowest accident frequency of any Canadian mine. Labour turnover and absenteeism are low compared to other mining operations, and managers maintain that productivity consistently meets the goals of the company.

At Kidd Creek, Texasgulf has a comprehensive and internally consistent employee relations program. Senior managers emphasize the importance of communication with the work force, and ensure that this communication is facilitated by competent, well-trained supervision. However, according to one senior manager: "The key to the entire program is attitude."

Both operator and supervisory attitudes are carefully monitored, and are seen as important indicators of the management-operator relationship. Other important elements in the program are concern for the welfare of employees, salaries (rather than wages) and associated benefits for all employees, and the opportunity to have an ownership stake in the company.

Both management and operators appear to view the program as a success. This paper describes the program, and attempts to show why this success has come about.

---

[*] Abridged from T.F. Cawsey and P.R. Richardson, "Employee Relations at the Kidd Creek Operations of Texasgulf Limited," in *Employee Relations Initiatives in Canadian Mining*. Proceedings of the 4th CRS Policy Discussion Seminar, November 22-24, 1978, Proceedings No. 5. (Kingston, Ontario: Queen's University Centre for Resource Studies), pp. 45-59. Reprinted with permission of the publisher.

Company Background

Texas Gulf Sulphur Incorporated was originally formed to produce sulphur for agricultural and industrial uses. From the firm's inception, it adopted a policy of providing employees with a level of benefits designed to eliminate any need for unionization.

Texasgulf has been able not only to provide these benefits, but also to ensure that employees are never subjected to lay-offs. As a result, none of the company's operations has been organized.[2]

After the Second World War, the corporation started a program of diversification away from sulphur products into other natural resource industries. Exploration for minerals in the Canadian shield was considered as early as 1952. Aerial exploration commenced in 1959 and early in the program a magnetic anomaly (denoting the existence of a mineral deposit) was recorded around Kidd Creek, 15 miles north of Timmins. Following extensive drilling, the existence of the Kidd Creek ore body was announced in 1964. Construction of facilities for an open pit mine began in 1965, and by 1967 a mine and concentrator were in full operation. The mill building was located 17 miles east of Timmins, and was connected to the mine by a railroad.[3]

A second phase of construction started in 1969, when development of an underground mine and building of a zinc plant commenced. These operations came into production during 1972, at which time the permanent work force of the operation increased from approximately 900 to 1,700. A third construction phase was underway during 1978 as a mine expansion program necessitated the sinking of a new shaft and the building of a copper smelter at the metallurgical site. These projects were delayed by the company because of weak markets for zinc and copper, the two major products of the operation. However, they are expected to be completed in the near future. By 1978, the total work force numbered 2,100, of which 1,000 were employed at the mine site and the remainder in the metallurgical complex. . . .

Because of the high degree of mechanization of the mine and metallurgical plant at Kidd Creek, efficiency of the operations is largely process controlled. Individual employees have relatively little influence on the rate of production. However, the operators do have significant impact on the effectiveness of the operation, as they control sophisticated and costly process equipment. Poor utilization could lead to a significant increase in operating costs.

The Employee Relations Scheme at Kidd Creek[4]

The employee relations scheme is intended to provide two major benefits to the company. First, the object is to motivate employees to operate in a way that maximizes company profits in the long run. As one manager commented: "We want operators to feel that it's their job and their company." Accordingly, as well as a share in company profits, the company offers job security to satisfactory employees. Secondly, by providing operators with benefits that eliminate the need for unionization, the firm aims to increase the flexibility of supervisors in making operating decisions. Superintendents stated that they felt able to make decisions without having to consider if they were setting precedents. In return, the corporation attends to the safety and concerns of all employees on an individual basis.

The management at Kidd Creek has modified the worldwide Texasgulf program to meet the unique needs of their operation. At present there are five major elements:

1) management attitudes towards the workforce
2) executive visibility and communication
3) the salary and benefit package
4) bonuses
5) attitude surveys. . . .

Management Attitudes Towards the Workforce

Members of the senior management at Kidd Creek believe that their attitudes towards the employees form the cornerstone of a successful program. They devote a great deal of energy to ensuring that employees are treated as individuals. This philosophy views individuals as adults who deserve to be treated accordingly. It has led to a significant level of openness, trust, and camaraderie between organization members. These values pervade the organization and individuals accept them quickly. There seems to be significant peer group pressure to adopt these values, and individuals who resist this process generally leave Texasgulf of their own volition.

Treatment as an adult comes about in many ways at Kidd Creek. Individuals are given significant responsibilities and expected to meet them. All employees are salaried and when an employee is sick or late he is treated in a manner which relies on his integrity. Management understands and accepts the right of the employee to have needs which differ from those of the company. Furthermore, the fulfillment of job-related needs is perceived to be important (thus safety in the work place becomes a prime concern).

Senior managers at Kidd Creek believe that this philosophy must be reflected in the attitude of first line supervision. Consequently, considerable care is taken in the selection and training of shift foremen. They are usually chosen from within the workforce, so that they are already imbued with the attitudes and values that pervade the operation. Assessment centres are used to identify individuals with high potential, and once selected, new supervisors are given a course on the Neil George Safety system, as well as a one-week American Management Association supervisory training course.

The responsibilities and authority of first line supervisors are clearly defined. Within these limits they are granted complete autonomy of decision making. Senior managers allow that mistakes will be made in the exercise of judgement, but tolerance of such errors is viewed as a part of supervisory development. This deliberate delegation of decision making is consistent with the overall view of the individual adopted by company management. Thus, while supervisors are restricted in areas of discipline (e.g. control of firing is the general manager's responsibility), they have direct responsibility for the organization, operation, and safety of their work group.

Policies exist which direct first line supervisors to place individual safety above all other considerations. In posted minutes of monthly crew meetings, supervisors could be seen to be stressing safe practice, sometimes at the expense of production. As one supervisor put it: "If I don't care about the safety of an individual, I don't care about the person."

Along with this concern for individual safety, there is evident concern about the overall welfare of operators. Job security is accepted by management as an issue to be dealt with carefully. While first line supervisors must approve of any new employee in their own crew, they are not allowed to dismiss subordinates. Supervisors are encouraged to understand and work with operators who are not performing adequately, and operators who abuse work rules can be suspended by their supervisor without pay. However, the supervisor must prove his case to the management group. Dismissal is seen to be a last resort, and has to be approved by the general manager of the Kidd Creek operation.

Supervisors are well-rewarded financially. There is a significant salary differential between them and other employees. As well, they can earn overtime pay. However, because of the key role the first line supervisor plays in the Texasgulf employee relations program, the job has not developed into a sinecure.

The demands on and management expectations from supervisors are considerable. At times, some do not perform adequately, even with the training and guidance provided. When this occurs, they are moved to less critical positions. As one supervisor pointed out:

In most mines the supervisory group is stable, and there is high turnover among the operators. At Kidd Creek turnover rate among supervision may be high also. This care for the quality of our supervisors helps to convince operators that we are serious about employee relations.

Although first line supervisors are encouraged to identify with the problems of their crew, they feel that they are part of the management team. Accordingly, although performance requirements are high, the social and financial benefits ensure that the position is viewed as desirable for ambitious operators.

Executive Visibility and Communication

The Kidd Creek operations operate on a first-name basis throughout. Executives are visible, and make frequent visits to working places. The chairman of the corporate board visits the operation between two and six times each year. The president, located in Stanford, Connecticut, makes regular visits to the operation and attempts to attend the annual picnic.

A formal grievance procedure exists, with grievances usually passing through an operator's immediate superior. Nevertheless, employees can take questions, problems, and grievances directly to executives at the operations, or even to the president of the company. A "hot-line" telephone number for this purpose is conspicuous on most notice boards throughout the operation.

Employee meetings held in company time play an important role in communications. Monthly crew meetings are held by each first line supervisor to discuss safety, company news, and his crew's own problems. Minutes of those meetings are posted on bulletin boards, and also widely circulated. The general manager reads all of them, and will investigate a persistent problem that does not appear to have been resolved. He follows up on one or two issues per week which arise from these minutes. Supervisory personnel have their own monthly meetings in which current concerns are voiced, plans are discussed, and the company's management philosophy is reinforced.

All employees are invited to semi-annual general meetings. Senior corporation executives attend, talk about important company news, respond to questions, and afterwards meet with employees for informal discussion. Executives also attend the employees' annual picnic.

The Salary and Benefit Package

All Texasgulf employees are salaried. However, this fact is not seen by the company to be important for its own sake. Rather, there are significant benefits to both employees and the company from the salary system. Managers note that they probably spend more time on employee relations concerns than if the operations were unionized. However, this time is not spent in unproductive bargaining sessions.

Annual salary increases are determined by Texasgulf's board, based on recommendations from operating management. Consequently, high performance can be recognized through merit increases, a feature which is difficult to implement within a collective bargaining framework. A basic cost of living increase forms part of the annual salary review. However, clerical, technical, and supervisory personnel receive individual merit awards, while production and maintenance staff receive group merit awards.

Texasgulf maintains a comprehensive benefits plan including medical and dental benefits, life and accident insurance, retirement plans, as well as other benefits for leaves of absence, educational assistance, and the employee share ownership plan. Management believes that one purpose of the benefits plan is to treat everyone equally (except for salary). Employees perceive one of the most important benefits to be the medical plan provided in the case of sickness. Full salary is received from the first day of illness or injury for six months, at which time a long-term disability program comes into effect. Medical notification of illness is not required for the first three days. In spite of this freedom, absenteeism is not a problem, averaging only about 3 per cent annually. Employees appear to avoid abuse of this privilege, for fear of losing it. For many years Texasgulf has maintained a benefits package which was superior to most other companies, although recently this competitive edge has eroded somewhat.

Bonuses

The share ownership scheme apparently reinforces the perception among employees that they have a stake in the company. On the first anniversary of employment, one share of stock is received by each employee. On the fifth anniversary, a further five shares are awarded; thereafter, every five years, employees receive one share of stock for each year of employment. Employees do not feel that they work any harder because of these awards. In fact, some of the younger employees tended to regard their one share (approximate value of $30.00 Canadian) with some disdain. However, employees approaching ten or fifteen years with the company look forward to these awards. Few employees sell their shares, but instead keep them as some small capital for the future.

No individual incentive schemes are maintained by the corporation. This reinforces the emphasis on safety before production. For instance, unlike other metal mines in Canada, Kidd Creek has no mining bonus. Instead, an annual bonus is awarded to all employees. The amount of the bonus is determined by the board of directors, and each individual receives an amount proportional to his annual salary. The bonus is intended to reflect the performance of the firm during the preceding year. Because of the cyclical nature of markets for Texasgulf's products, the bonus cannot be directly proportional to profitability as this depends to a great extent on prices beyond the control of the company and its employees. However, the employee still knows that his bonus is related to the company's performance.

There is also a safety bonus awarded to Kidd Creek employees. For every 100,000 hours worked by each crew without a lost time accident, prizes are awarded. These are distributed monthly, and are usually items such as work gloves and dance tickets. Supervisors commented that as a crew neared the required total of hours, tension became apparent, and there would be general disappointment if a lost time accident occurred. Operators viewed the bonus as further evidence of management's concern for safety.

Attitude Surveys

Management remains in communication with the workforce through a variety of informal mechanisms. In addition, formal attitude surveys, on a number of general and company specific indicators, are taken periodically across the entire workforce, covering fifteen general items. A modified form of the survey is administered to supervisory personnel.

The survey provides information on attitudes which can be directly compared with norms for other companies in which the general survey is administered. One drawback to this comparison is that these companies are not Canadian and not in mining, so there is no indication as to how the attitudes at Kidd Creek compare to those in other mining and metallurgical operations in Canada. However, some idea of trends in attitudes can be drawn from a historical analysis, by comparing data from past surveys at Kidd Creek.

The surveys complement informal means of gathering data on employee attitudes, and provide information on key areas of management concern. They may provide concrete evidence to support management beliefs on what is occurring in particular departments. They occasionally provide the basis for changes in employee relation policies. For instance, one survey indicated that there was substantial dissatisfaction with the informal grievance procedure then in effect. Consequently, after a management study of the problem, a more formal, clearly defined system was introduced. . . .

Why Has the Program been Successful?

The employee relations scheme at Kidd Creek has benefited from several favourable underlying factors. First, the operation is located near Timmins, the centre of one of Ontario's largest gold mining districts. When Kidd Creek opened, the gold mines were declining, and wage rates were depressed. Consequently, prospective employees perceived an opportunity for higher income, job security, and good working conditions. As a result, the operation drew upon a large pool of skilled, relatively stable labour. Furthermore, because of the high grade deposit, the company could afford to invest heavily in equipment and facilities that would provide good working conditions for employees. For instance, underground restrooms are painted, contain flush toilets, and have both hot and cold running water. These facilities are not found at many other mines in the area. For a number of years, the operations were constantly growing and changing. Consequently, there were always developments to keep employees interested, and expansion created new job opportunities for career development. However, these factors alone do not explain the exceptional operating results.

We believe that the most important factor in the program's success has been the attitude of management and supervision. All other factors can be related to this factor. As a result of management attitudes and philosophy, money was spent to improve working conditions, the benefits package was established, and the focus was put on first line supervision. These factors led to favourable attitudes on the part of employees, and subsequently to the impressive results which have been outlined. . . .

The underlying management philosophy at Kidd Creek is a belief in a rational, rather than authoritarian, style of management. Executives believe in the worth of individuals. As one manager puts it:

Executives believe that operators can be motivated to do a good job by aligning their interests with those of the company. This depends on high levels of trust and communication within the company.

If this trust were to be lost, the program would falter. Accordingly, management policies ensure complete fairness in dealings with individuals. For example, the firing of an employee is seen as a last resort and, as mentioned earlier, only the general manager has this authority. Furthermore, the program is not intended to "keep the union out." This motive would be perceived negatively by workers, with the attendant consequences. Instead, the purpose of the scheme is to treat the human resources of the operation in the way management believes individuals should be and want to be treated. Concern for the safety and careers of individuals are hallmarks of Texasgulf. To some, this statement might sound like a platitude. We believe it reflects enlightened management appropriate to a skilled and loyal workforce.

A second important factor in the program's success is the satisfaction which people achieve. Herzberg identified two types of influence on human behaviour: hygiene factors, and motivating factors.[5] Hygiene factors will not motivate people to do a good job, but must be satisfied before motivating factors can be effective. Hygiene factors can play a major role in affecting turnover and absenteeism. At Texasgulf, the hygiene factors are taken care of by the basic policies in the employee relations program. These factors are perceived by the majority of workers at Kidd Creek to be satisfactory. They include: company policy and administration, relations with supervision and peers, working conditions, security, salary, and fringe benefits.

With the hygiene factors met, workers can be motivated by the nature of the work itself, achievement, recognition, as well as opportunities for advancement and personal growth. At Kidd Creek, these motivators have been acknowledged in a number of ways. Expansion created many opportunities for career advancement. Recognition is provided in the form of financial rewards, by social status through company publications, but most importantly by Texasgulf's reputation as a fine place to work. The employees are proud of "their" safety record. The nature of the work is challenging, and the individual attention by management reinforces the desire to perform and do well.

A third critical factor in the success of the program has been the recognition of the key role played by first line supervision. Enlightened management attitudes will not be perceived by operators if first line supervisors do not mirror them. Trust and rationality can be rapidly dissipated by poorly trained supervisors. At Texasgulf, however, the care given to selection and training of, and communication with, first line supervisors provides them with the skills to act effectively, and positions of status. The monthly crew meetings provide an opportunity for supervisors to show concern for their operators while providing leadership in a number of issues.

Many factors play a part in the success of the program. Working conditions, salaries, meetings, and executive visibility all contribute significantly. However, these factors would not be effective without the three key elements we have just described. In short, the success of the Kidd Creek scheme in the past can be ascribed to its integrity and comprehensiveness. . . .

Notes

1. The research was made possible by the cooperation of employees of Texasgulf Canada Limited.

2. Ascertained from company records.

3. Clarke, P.R., "The Ecstall Story — Introduction," *CIM Bulletin*, May 1974, vol. 67, no. 745, pp. 3-5.

4. Grenville, D.F., "The Employee Relations Department," *CIM Bulletin*, May 1974, Vol. 67, no. 745, pp. 89-94.

5. Herzberg, F., "One More Time: How Do You Motivate Employees?" *Harvard Business Review* vol. 46, 1968, pp. 53-62.

22/A Labour-Management Contract and Quality of Working Life[*]

Louis E. Davis and Charles S. Sullivan

Introduction

In the North American tradition of evolving theory from practice, this paper reports what may become a significant innovation in union-management relations. This pragmatically evolved development may be crucial to the evolution of new forms of union-management collaboration. Reported are the extremely rare events of union participation in the design of a new chemical plant organization and the evolution of a new form of union-management contract developed through collective bargaining and responding to the organizational philosophy that guided the design.

During the past few years suspicion and distrust have surrounded the issue of union-management collaboration in the development of work environments and conditions that could provide a rewarding relationship between work and the needs, expectations, and goals of those who do the work. Both unions and managements were and largely are immobilized by the uncertainties of departing from the 200 year old tradition of (1) instrumentalism, i.e., work as an instrument to support the goals of satisfying personal needs of individuals outside the workplace and (2) the external behaviour control of workers to achieve the goals of the organization or of its managers. This immobility characterizes all Western societies at

[*] Abridged from Louis E. Davis and Charles S. Sullivan, "A Labour-Management Contract and the Quality of Working Life." *Journal of Occupational Behaviour* 1980, pp. 29-41. Reprinted with permission of the publisher and the authors.

this stage in their evolution. It has led to partially appropriate responses that are either political — (*mitbestimmung* or union representation on boards of companies in Western Europe) or economic — (Scanlon Plans, earned time bonuses, etc. in the United States, Davis, 1979). In deep and meaningful ways such responses to the new realities of demands to enhance the quality of working life (Yankelovitch, 1979) can be seen as either avoidance of the need to develop a new relationship between union and management responsive to the evolving new demands in the workplace, or recasting of the expressed needs and expectations into conventional responses of more money, fewer hours, etc. All this is taking place in the face of deep changes in Western societies surrounding the meaning and purpose of work and the relation between society's members and the work of society. Such challenges signal the transition of modern societies from the historical period of the last 200 years, the industrial era, to an evolving post-industrial era.

The attempts of a future-oriented union and a future-oriented management to develop a new relationship between worker and work confronted both of them with the need to evolve a new and more appropriate relationship pushing beyond the terms of historical union-management relations. Both the union (Oil, Chemical and Atomic Workers International Union) and the management (Shell Canada, Ltd.) came to perceive the formal collective agreement as an instrument that would support or hinder the evolution of new workplace relationships, i.e., the collective agreement as a part of the "social support system." The collective agreement that emerged from the process of free and open collective bargaining was informed by the shared perception that the contract, as an enabling instrument, would become the central social system support instrument or general constitution supporting the evolution of specific adaptive and collaborative practices.

The joint design in Canada of a complex chemical plant for the manufacture of polypropylene and isopropyl alcohol and its organization and followed later by the bargained labour-management contract serve as a crucial learning opportunity. The reasons are that this design is a triple first, i.e., the first joint technical and social design of a highly complex, continuous, automated process plant and its interrelated social system or organization; the first joint design undertaken with participation of both union and management; and the first labour-management contract bargained in response to an organization (and job) design which is an alternative to bureaucracy (Davis, 1977). As with other firsts crucial to the evolving post-industrial era such as the engineering design in Volvo's auto assembly plant at Kalmar, Sweden (Gyllenhammer, 1977), this development will intrude and have to be considered in all future union-management efforts directed to forming union-management relationships based on other than adversarial relationships.

To aid our learning from this signal development, we want to explore the background to the organization design of this new plant, the specifics of the design and the content of the labour-management contract. A detailed report of the design is being prepared for publication as a case report. . . .

Background to the Design

The background to the design starts in the early 1970s when the manufacturing division of Shell Canada, Ltd. began studies of its own way of managing its workers and utilizing their capabilities. Substantial recommendations were made, some of which were implemented and many of which seemed to be waiting for 1975 when the design of the polypropylene-isopropyl alcohol plant was to begin. The sum of the recommendations of the earlier studies pointed to the need to enhance the quality of working life of refinery and chemical plant workers. Such workers, with good pay and working conditions, were found to be seeking greater control over the decisions affecting their lives in the workplace and were inhibited from fully utilizing the considerable skills and experience they had acquired. The usual roles of a traditionally operated organization, enlightened though it may be, imposed needless restrictions on workers. Typical of their comments were: "I operate a 5 (or 10) million dollar machine but have to obtain approval from the foreman for an overtime meal when I am asked to stay at work beyond my usual departure time." "I have to wait for the foreman to arrive to sign off on a maintenance request. All he does is add his signature to the form after he asks me if the work is needed." The primary concern of Shell management and a major concern of OCAWIU was the physiological and psychological problems associated with shift work.

In the early 1970s the worker issues of remuneration, security, control over workplace decisions, shift work, development of self, participation in governance of one's work life taken together came to be called the quality of working life. By the time the design began the participants were well aware of this concept and that it could be strongly affected by organization and job designs. . . .

Union-Management Joint Design Process

There was considerable discussion regarding union jurisdiction. Some expected that the refinery union would have jurisdiction over the new plant when completed; others thought the union would not. Some said this did not matter since it was management's prerogative to design and organize work. Others were concerned with the negative consequences of placing a completed design before the union as a *fait accompli*. The consultant to the design team questioned whether excluding the union was contrary to the organization philosophy and to the congruency principle of socio-technical systems design which calls for design methods to be congruent with the features of the organization (Cherns, 1976). All came to see that success of the future operation of this costly, leading edge technology plant was in various ways bound up with participation by the union.

Finally, following considerable examination, the design team recognized that the union would represent the future members of the plant and invited it to join as a partner in developing the design of organization, jobs, rewards, training and controls. Such participation of the union as a basis for successful operation is contrary to conventional wisdom about advanced technology, large corporations, and engineering and management processes.

The union accepted with two stipulations — (1) that it be a full partner in the design process and (2) that it would maintain a high profile. This was quickly accepted. The participation of the union representatives provided the means for capturing and utilizing organizational learning at the shop floor level. Initial concerns were quickly forgotten as the high quality of union contribution unfolded and managers congratulated themselves for their statesmanship.

Later the external consultant had opportunity to interview the Canadian national director of the union. He was asked to indicate why he supported his union's participation in the design process in the face of the history, in North America, of rejection by many unions of quality of working life activities. His reply is very instructive. He said that

We would be poor union leaders indeed if we did not utilize the opportunity given us by management to participate in providing for satisfaction of quality of working life needs for workers. If you think that only managers have problems with our members as their workers, then you are unaware that we have many similar problems with our members, particularly younger members. We must grasp each opportunity that becomes available to learn how to find the means of responding to quality of working life issues raised by our members if we are to be a strong viable union.

What was the role of the union in the design process? What was their contribution to the design? Would the design have been the same without them? How were they beneficial to future union members who would be joining the new organization? These questions are difficult to answer because of the relationship that evolved. Quickly managers accepted the union leaders as equals and vice versa. Each contributed as an individual whose membership on the Design Team was highly valued. The team called on its members as experts on the basis of their reputations, knowledge, and experiences. Many proposals were generated through synergistic interaction among team members, whether union or management. Proposals for features of organization and jobs were examined by both union and management for secondary and unintended effects on members at all levels. The union representatives' greatest contributions seemed to be centred on proposals regarding the knowledge and skill modules for advancement, maintenance, working hours, shift teams and their rotation. Additionally the union representatives helped develop the team coordinator role, shop steward role and the Good Work Practices Handbook. The details of the structure of the organization and jobs will be described in a separate publication.

Design Process and Outcomes

. . . .The design selected treated the entire plant and its processes as one organizational unit. One team of 18 people plus a team co-ordinator operates the entire process including laboratory, shipping, warehousing, and many aspects of maintenance on each shift. The teams needed for 24 hour, 365-day operation would be supported by some planners, engineers, and managers as well as a team of 14 maintenance craftsmen-instructors and two laboratory specialists on days. The organization design was further influenced by societal issues stemming from strong negative pressures about shift work. The design team sought to minimize shift work and to share equally the positive and negative aspects of working life. The design provides for six shift teams, each consisting of 18 people plus a co-ordinator. Each team rotates and controls, in turn, all the work activities of the plant. Based on the 37.5 hours per week schedule of the plant, 4.5 shifts are required for continuous around-the-clock operation. The design selected calls for 1.5 shift teams, on average, to join on days, with the following groups: 14 maintenance craftsmen-instructors, 2 laboratory specialists, and 2 warehousemen-schedulers. The shift team joins with the maintenance craftsmen to become the maintenance work force while obtaining cross-skill training in maintenance crafts. In this manner, a maintenance response capability becomes available on all shifts for emergency situations, with a concentration of maintenance capability during days. The six shift team arrangement provides the means whereby the members of all shift teams spend 53 per cent, approximately, of their work time on days. Should a future experiment with the 12-hour day work out then 72 per cent of each member's work time would be spent on days as compared with 33 per cent on days in a conventional shift arrangement.

Thus a team of 18 with its team co-ordinator operate the entire plant including its administrative, laboratory, shipping, warehousing and maintenance activities. Not unexpectedly the organization structure is flat, having three levels — the shift teams and their co-ordinators, operations managers, and plant superintendent. The day foremen level present in conventional refineries and chemical plants is omitted since these people are now staff technical advisors. Within the teams the structure is deliberately amorphous, permitting the team to assign tasks to its members as required. Additionally, for organizational continuity, various leadership functions including planning and co-ordination have been assigned to the team members. Team members have received training to perform a variety of social system maintenance functions including problem solving, confrontation, conflict resolution, norm setting, etc. Each team has a shop steward who is one of its members. This is particularly useful since very few rules exist and the labour-management contract language is permissive, leaving to team members the determination of their day to day working lives. A Good Work Practices Handbook was developed, with union input, which serves as an administrative guide governing specific job-related activities such as overtime-meals etc. What is frequently described in labour-management contracts, making them rigid and subject to legal quibbling, concerning work-related activities, is now in the Good Work Practices Handbook. The collective agreement thus remains as the enabling document it was originally intended. The team co-ordinator, who stays with his team as it rotates through the shifts, serves as the intershift team link and the link with management. His major functions are to provide boundary protection for the team acting as a mediator or buffer between his team and demands from the environment; to provide technical expertise and training on the processes; and to serve as the management representative on the shifts when he may be the only such present. In addition to the shop stewards, the union structure has a five-person executive committee including the union officers in the plant.

Members of the team do not have specific job titles or assignments but rather grade levels or competence levels based on the knowledge and skill attained. Advancement depends on qualifying examinations and performance tests covering specific groups of knowledge and skill modules. This arrangement supports open progression and satisfaction of individual differences through the many career paths available to an individual. Each team member must acquire all the process or operations knowledge and skill modules. Some are present in every wage grade level. Beyond this there are choices available for individuals to combine knowledge and skill modules from six specialty areas with operations modules to make up each individual wage grade level. The specialty area skills include maintenance crafts, quality laboratory testing, warehousing and production scheduling. The various combinations provide six career paths along which an individual can choose. The specifics of the path chosen depend on joint organization needs and individual desires. The interests of the plant and of the individual member come together in the provision and support of training which is always available, reinforced by the system of wage payment and reward. The more groups of knowledge and skill modules learned, the higher the wage level and each member may move at his or her own pace right to the top level. While there is an expectation that everyone would attempt to reach the top level that each individual is capable of achieving, time limits are not imposed for doing so. No one, however, is forced to move and failure to learn and advance cannot impede anyone else's progress. These are norms developed by team members at the start of plant operation.

Collective Agreement

As the organization design was completed (some specifics were later added) recruiting, selection, and training were designed. At this time, the union representatives took on dual roles — continuing their work on the design team and engaging in the collective bargaining process for a labour-management contract for the new plant. Participating in the bargaining for management was the manager of the manufacturing centre, the chemical plant superintendent, and the employee relations manager. The union negotiating committee was composed of the local and regional officials who were serving on the design team joined by five of the craftsmen-instructors who had been transferred from the refinery to the chemical plant to form the maintenance team.

After hard bargaining, a first-of-its-kind labour-management contract was developed. As indicated earlier, this contract is unique in that it is the first labour-management agreement developed in consonance with the design of a post-bureaucratic organization giving specific emphasis to achieving high quality of working life for its members. Both union and management representatives at the bargaining table understood the central nature of the new organization with its emphasis on self-control, learning and participation, its flexible work assignments, and its evolutionary structure based on specifying only what is critical to organizational functioning, i.e. minimal critical specification (Cherns, 1976). They understood that the design was in effect a skeleton structure that would be further evolved from subsequent experiences. This learning was the opposite of their prior experiences in living in a bureaucratic organization where all aspects of structure and relationships were completely specified. They agreed that the survival of the organization and enhancement of the quality of working life for its members would come from the detailed structures and practices that would be evolved by those living in the organization, from the participation of members in solving the problems of the organization and from the feedback and utilization of organizational and individual learning.

Both union and management appeared to conclude that protecting and developing the organizational form would best discharge their responsibilities and advance the satisfaction of their own needs and the needs of those they represented. Their shared understandings led to agreement that flexibility and support should be the central features of the labour-management contract. The contract emphasizes and reflects flexibility and is itself an evolutionary document providing enabling conditions consonant with the organization design. It was as if the principle of minimal critical specification had been applied by the negotiators. Both sides made some signal concessions in support of developing the collective agreement. Management did not insist on the customary management rights clause in the contract accepting general rights stated in law. At the same time it accepted mandatory deduction of union dues as necessary for continuity of the union. Not as a concession, the union for its part did not require a seniority clause, except for lay-off, since open progression was one of the central features of the organization. With provision of continual training and objective qualification examinations each worker has an equal opportunity to advance to the highest level the individual's aspiration, capacities and energy will take him or her. Under these conditions, the union saw no need for the usual seniority clause.

An examination of the agreement indicates how flexibility and support were translated into contract language. The agreement unconventionally begins with a unique foreword that sets the tone for what follows. The complete text of the foreword is as follows:

The purpose of the agreement which follows is to establish an enabling framework within which an organizational system can be developed and sustained that will ensure an efficient and competitive world-scale chemical plant operation and provide meaningful work and job satisfaction for employees. Recognizing that there are risks involved and that there are many factors which can place restraints on the extent to which changes can occur, both management and union support and encourage policies and practices that will reflect their commitment to the following principles and values:

Employees are responsible and trustworthy, capable of working together effectively and making proper decisions related to their spheres of responsibilities and work arrangements — if given the necessary authorities, information and training.

Employees should be permitted to contribute and grow to their fullest capability and potential without constraints of artificial barriers, with compensation based on their demonstrated knowledge and skills rather than on tasks being performed at any specific time.

To achieve the most effective overall results, it is deemed necessary that a climate exists which will encourage initiative, experimentation, and generation of new ideas, supported by an open and meaningful two-way communication system. . . .

Social System Support

The first year of the collective agreement was taken up largely by training of new employees, team formation, equipment testing and some plant commissioning. Actual operation of plant by work teams looks as if it will begin during the second year of the collective agreement. Late in the first year of the agreement, when all workers were on site, the stresses of not having rules or norms and no specific contract language led to some extended developmental meetings between the union executive committee and plant management. One of these meetings evolved a collaborative social system support mechanism to deal with grievances as called for in Section 3 of the collective agreement. Established was a Team Norm Review Board composed of seven employee representatives, one from each team, three management representatives and the union vice president. Consensus is required in reaching recommendations by the Board and in introducing new norms. The Board audits team norms. It cannot discipline. In the event that a team member's problem is not resolved at team level, i.e., face to face with the Team Coordinator and Shop Steward, the member may appeal to the Team Norm Review Board to adjudicate the issue. To date the Board has been an effective vehicle for problem solving and for developing guides at shop floor level.

Later in the first year a Joint Information Committee was established to aid with the very considerable task of communicating and sharing of information among teams who operate around the clock every day of the year. The Information Committee is composed of one Team Co-ordinator and one Team Member from each team making 14 members. This committee should also prove to be an important part of the social system support mechanism by which the organization maintains itself.

The union's view of developments that took place during the first year of the collective agreement is revealed in part of an article written for publication by the National Director of the union. Reimer (1979) states:

Our program with Shell Canada, Ltd., at the Sarnia Chemical Plant has received much notice. Programs of this nature and others of course require continuing attention. However, one can already observe that in this "open society" operation, where people speak up more frequently, there is less fear in the plant and indeed higher attendance at Union meetings. The nature of the operation tends to keep people more informed and the meetings where decisions are made affecting their welfare have a higher priority. I understand there is very little absenteeism and the quality of training and the versatility in the plant are concrete attainments. The more the worker is trained, the higher is his income and management can put him to better use. Our Collective Agreement has a statement of purpose and is about five short pages in length. We expect that nothing will be written into the Agreement arbitrarily and that if anything is added, it will have stood the test of time. It is interesting to note that in this Agreement, management does not incorporate the traditional Management's Rights clause.

The first year under the collective agreement came to an end and negotiations for renewal are completed. Management and union agreed that, with the exception of changes in salaries, the contract finally signed remains the same as the collective agreement described above.

Conclusion

The design process and the resulting organization design as well as the collective agreement for this non-bureaucratic chemical plant indicate that there is another path available better suited to the post-industrial era. This path is marked by a co-operative process and by the objective of a high quality of working life for all members of the organization. Once again we see a demonstration of the powerful outcomes of substantive collaboration as compared with confrontation in union-management relations. It may be that only by such collaboration will a high quality of working life be truly provided for the members of organizations.

The collective agreement informs us that the "contract as an enabling document" is essential to evolutionary design and thus to a post-bureaucratic form of organization. Counter-intuitively we are instructed that high technology increases dependence on workers for economically successful operation. Increased reliance on workers further emphasizes the obligation during design to examine the needs, aspirations and goals of members, i.e., their quality of working life. The joint union-management process more easily satisfies this examination and the development of useful responses. It also demonstrates that shared responsibility for the development of a new organization evolves through union-management collaboration.

We may well close by examining a duality of questions. First, would this innovative collective agreement have been developed without the prior experience of the joint union-management design process? Second, would the new form of organization have survived without the collective agreement as an evolutionary and enabling document?

The answers to these questions are inferential. The long period of working together, the trust developed, the shared experiences, the agreement on organizational philosophy, and the early-on exposure to socio-technical systems concepts and quality of working life concepts had their effects. Undoubtedly union and management had likely developed a substantial set of shared understandings which served as a base for considering their individual and joint needs as well as those specific to this new form of organization. At this period in the life of the new organization, given both the fragility of any new social system and the open evolutionary form of the design, it would appear doubtful that this new form of organization can survive for very long without the collective agreement as an enabling and supporting instrument.

References

Cherns, Albert (1976). "The principles of sociotechnical design." *Human Relations*, 29(8), 783-792.

Davis, Louis E. (1977). "Evolving alternative organization designs: their socio-technical bases." *Human Relations* 30(3), 261-273.

Davis, Louis E. (1979). "Individual-organization conflict." *California Management-Review*, Winter.

Gyllenhammer, Per (1977). *People at Work*, Addison-Wesley, Boston.

Reimer, C. Neil (1979). "Oil, chemical and atomic workers international union and quality of working life — a union perspective." *Quality of Working Life: The Canadian Scene*, Winter, 5-7.

Yankelovitch, Daniel (1979). "Work, value and the new breed." In: Clark Kerr and Jerome Rosow (Eds), *Work in America: The Decade Ahead*, Chapter 1, Van Nostrand-Reinhold, New York.

23/The VanPly Affair: New Directions in Worker-Management Relations[*]

John Clarke

By virtually all the rules of economics the Vancouver Plywood Division operation of MacMillan Bloedel Ltd. of British Columbia should be closing down. In fact, that is what the company wanted to do and had announced its intention to do. But as a result of an agreement with the International Woodworkers of America (IWA) union, supported by the B.C. provincial government, it will be kept open.

The decision is expected to have a major impact on labour relations not only in B.C. but throughout Canada generally. It's the first time a large international corporation has been prevented by union intervention from closing a clearly uneconomic operation.

The unilateral right of the management of a corporation to make the economic decisions affecting its operations has been significantly eroded. Other unions will now expect, as their right, to be consulted before the final economic judgments are made.

The VanPly division, after nearly 50 years, is one of the oldest of MacMillan Bloedel's operations. The plant is rundown and the equipment is outdated and discouragingly inefficient.

The market for the high quality sanded plywood it produces has been dimin-

---

[*] Reproduced by permission of the Minister of Supply and Services Canada from John Clarke, "The VanPly Affair: New Directions in Worker-Management Relations," *Labour Gazette* 78(7) 1978, pp. 296-298.

ishing and competition from the lower-wage southern United States, together with recent inventory-reduction policies of Scandinavian countries, has made it quite uneconomic for VanPly to keep going. It has been losing money at the rate of $3 million a year.

But the closure would have meant the loss of 700 jobs, according to company figures, or nearly 1,000 according to the IWA. It also would have sent shock waves through the entire logging industry.

The Truck Loggers' Association, made up primarily of independent logging companies, called the VanPly affair the tip of the iceberg. TLA president Dave O'Connor said: "VanPly is only part of the story of near bankruptcy of MacMillan Bloedel's coastal operations in logging lumber, plywood and shingles. The side effects of this disaster (would be) so sweepingly significant that it is not appropriate that Calvert Knudsen (MacMillan Bloedel president), IWA regional president Jack Munro and Forests Minister Tom Waterland meet in a back room to arrange a petty trade-off for VanPly's closure."

What O'Connor meant was that if the VanPly decision was indicative of MacMillan Bloedel's future plans for plywood production, it could set off a chain reaction dislocating independent logging producers and throwing not just 700, but thousands of men out of work.

As it happened, the backroom work was done primarily by the company and the union, although Premier Bill Bennett had made it known that the closure was unacceptable to the government.

Under the settlement they worked out the union agreed that the 42-year-old "A" mill is too old to be saved and it will be closed with the loss of 200 jobs. Most of the men affected will be placed in other MacMillan Bloedel operations and those that can't or don't want to continue working for the company will be given either early retirement or substantial severance pay. A joint planning group comprising representatives from the company, the union and the provincial department of labour will supervise the arrangements.

The younger "B" mill will be kept operating for at least the next two years. The company will spend $1 million to modernize the lathes used in peeling the logs and to improve other equipment. For its part, the union undertakes to co-operate in increasing the productivity at the mill. This will save just over 500 jobs.

Whether the mill can be made economic within the next two years "remains to be seen," in Knudsen's view. The IWA, however, has no doubts about the success of the operation.

It is, however, the second part of the agreement that is the most significant. The forest industry on B.C.'s coast has many operations not unlike VanPly in condition and expectation. They have become rundown while the industry has concentrated on developing the younger and more efficient sector of the industry in the interior. A few years ago the province changed its logging regulations to allow the harvesting of smaller-diameter trees. This meant the industry was able to go in there with virtually brand-new plant and machinery and the returns immediately looked more attractive than on the coast.

But it's on the coast where the bulk of the IWA's 35,000 members are employed. If the VanPly decision was, in fact, the tip of the iceberg, many more mill closures could be expected and thousands of workers faced with the eventual loss of their jobs. This would not happen overnight, of course. But it was the prospect the IWA saw over the next several years.

For MacMillan Bloedel the choice was extremely difficult. Faced with competition from the southern U.S., European countries and, to some extent, the B.C. interior, it had to decide whether to abandon an uneconomic plant in favour of capital investment elsewhere in its operations, or try to keep VanPly going as best it could. The economics indicated closure.

But pressure from the provincial government and the union really denied it that option and the resulting "agreement" has set a number of precedents.

The first is that the closure of major operations affecting significant numbers of workers will in future be subject to negotiation. It still isn't clear how far negotiations can be taken. For instance, if the company had held to its decision to close, could the union have staged an extensive strike against MacMillan Bloedel operations generally, as seemed to be implied in some of its initial threats? Such a strike would probably have been illegal under the province's Labour Code. So the negotiations to that extent were permissive on the part of the company. Nevertheless, the precedent has been set which other employers, and no less the government, will have to follow.

The crucial point in any such negotiations is the extent of the private corporation's authority to make the economic decisions its shareholders expect it to make. That authority has been very significantly compromised by the VanPly case which underscores a point the trade unions have been trying to make for years — that employees have an equal right with shareholders and management to a role in determining the company's future.

The key point for the company is the IWA's undertaking to work with management in devising procedures to improve productivity at the plant. And that is the second precedent.

Trade unions in Canada have, with some exceptions, traditionally considered productivity a matter for management. The great majority of technological change clauses in contracts, for instance, have more to do with the protection of working conditions, wages and so on, than with efforts to improve productivity resulting from the changes themselves.

Management has taken the contrary view. Because of restrictions favouring workers in labour contracts, management has tried to involve the trade unions in the productivity issue. At VanPly the IWA has categorically agreed to work with the company to improve output.

The IWA's regional president Jack Munro says: "We are going to look at everything. The object is to make that place more productive." That won't be easy because the union will have to work around clauses in the contract that have had to do with everything but productivity. But the 700 workers at VanPly, many of them with 20 years' service with MacMillan Bloedel, got a rude shock when the mill closure was announced and are clearly now in a mood to help make the operation more efficient. And that will be a key to the union's approach. The union wants to bring the individual workers as much as possible into the productivity discussions. How that will be done is not yet clear, but no doubt it will involve the filtering up of ideas from the shop floor through a union committee dealing with management at higher levels.

How the two sides work out a design for productivity improvement within the existing contract will be closely watched by other unions and other companies. That design will, of course, have a significant bearing on MacMillan Bloedel's future capital investment programs. The company will obviously be more prepared to spend money renovating older plants if there are reciprocal productivity initiatives by the union.

So MacMillan Bloedel and the IWA could well set a pattern for industry generally if they produce a successful blueprint for greater efficiency.

The VanPly case also reveals the model Canadian unions will clearly prefer in handling worker input in managerial decision making. They will stick with collective bargaining, suitably modified, rather than adopt the European system of union-worker representation directly on corporate boards of directors.

Jack Munro calls worker directors "mere tokens," not to be trusted to truly carry the workers' interests into the boardroom.

Industrial democracy is very much a buzz word in labour relations circles these days. Federal Labour Minister John Munro is known to favour much greater worker involvement in the running of corporations, although he has never been specific. But he has a report on the German system of co-determination from Charles Connaghan, former president of the Construction Labour Relations Association in B.C. and now an administrative vice-president at the University of British Columbia.

The IWA has poured scorn on the German system which, according to union leader Munro, hasn't worked nearly as well as North American-style free collective bargaining to improve the lot of the ordinary worker.

For the IWA, having a worker on a board of directors compromises the union at contract negotiating time. If the capital investment decisions, or decisions about closing down operations, are made at the director level under the German system, there isn't anything left for the unions to negotiate about. The union therefore is effectively squeezed out of the process.

But under procedures indicated by the VanPly agreement, the union will be involved *before* the decisions are made. It will be able to retain its independence and therefore exercise a greater influence in the consultative process.

MacMillan Bloedel did not, of course, invite anybody from the IWA to join its board of directors. Nor did the IWA seek a seat there. But the point is that the VanPly agreement is a mightily significant first step toward the remoulding of free collective bargaining to accommodate broader sharing of management responsibility with the unions.

Whatever happens at the national economic planning level to the idea of tripartism, the IWA in B.C. has made it clear that individual unions want no part of it at the company level.

24/Work, Formal Participation, and Employee Outcomes[*]

Donald V. Nightingale

The modern work organization faces mounting pressures from within and without to meet the challenge of employee alienation and dissatisfaction. Evidence of growing employee disenchantment comes from large-sample surveys of working people (Cooper, Morgan, Foley, and Kaplan, 1979; Fenn and Yankelovich, 1972; Sheppard and Herrick, 1972; "Work in America," 1973) as well as from in-depth case studies (Terkel, 1974; Schrank, 1978).

There is a search for new and effective forms of work organization. This search has taken two major directions: improvement in the nature of the work itself and extension of decision-making rights to employees at lower hierarchical levels. Work improvement (commonly called "job enrichment") was first popularized in North America by Frederick Herzberg (1959, 1966); recent research and practice has tended to focus on the redesign of entire work systems (e.g., Susman, 1976).

Employee participation has been of long-standing interest to behavioural scientists as a way of improving morale, satisfaction, and commitment at the workplace. In recent years, European initiatives and experimentation with a new form of employee participation — "formal participation" — has sparked a revival of interest in North America in the concept "participation."

Organizations which give rank-and-file employees the right to participate in decision making are called "formally participative." The decision-making rights governing employee participation are contractually binding on all parties. These rights may be codified and sanctioned by legal arrangements outside the organiza-

---

[*] Abridged from Donald V. Nightingale, "Work, Formal Participation, and Employee Outcomes," *Sociology of Work and Occupations* 8(3) 1981, pp. 277-296. Reprinted by permission of the author and Sage Publications, Inc.

tion — as in Yugoslavia and the Federal Republic of Germany (Tannenbaum, Kavcic, Rosner, Vianello, and Wieser, 1974), or the decision-making rights may be codified in the organization's charter or collective agreement. Although there are relatively few formally participative organizations in North America, they are growing in number and are attracting the attention of scholars (Tannenbaum, 1974; Jones, 1979; Whyte, Gurdon, Hammer, Stern, and Long, 1978).

"Formal participation" is to be distinguished from "informal participation." Informal participation is a supervisory style characterized by participativeness, supportiveness, and openness. Informally participative supervisors are under no obligation to share decision-making power with their subordinates (they do so for reasons that are largely their own), and the issues subject to participation concern the shop floor and not organizational policy. Informal participation is based on organizational norm or custom and has no legal standing.

The distinction between "formal" and "informal" participation has been made by Tannenbaum (1974), Dachler and Wilpert (1978), and Nightingale (1979), and is similar to Walker's (1976) "structure" and "living" participation; French's (1964) "objective" and "psychological" participation; Emery and Thorsrud's (1969) "real" and "apparent" participation; and Bass and Shackelton's (1979) "industrial democracy" and "participative management.". . .

Method[1]

Sample of Organizations

The sample consists of 20 industrial organizations in Canada: 10 organizations are formally participative and 10 are of conventional hierarchical design. Each formally participative organization is matched with a conventional counterpart on six criteria: number of employees, geographic location, products, union-nonunion status, ethnic composition of the work force, and plant type (parent or branch plant).

Among the 10 formally participative organizations are producer cooperatives, firms with worker representatives on the board of directors, and firms with works councils which give employees the right to set wages, hire workers, determine work assignments, hours of work, pace of work, and participate in matters of organizational policy. The 10 formally participative organizations are among the most participative in Canada.

Sample of Employees

Within each of the 20 organizations, 50 respondents are selected randomly to represent three hierarchical levels: (1) upper — the chief executive officer and all his immediate managerial subordinates; (2) middle — all other managerial and supervisory personnel; and (3) lower — rank-and-file employees, including both white and blue collar employees. In this sample of 1000 organization members, approximately 450 job titles are represented. The sample design is described fully in Nightingale (1978).

The matching of organizations on the six criteria and the random sampling of respondents within organizations is designed to provide comparable samples of respondents in the two types of organizations. The respondent samples in the formally participative and conventionally managed organizations are compared by hierarchical level (upper, middle, lower) on six criteria: age, sex, income, education, company seniority, and job seniority. Of the 18 comparisons (two-tailed), 3 are statistically significant.[2] Middle-level respondents in the formally participative organizations have more formal education than their counterparts in the conventionally managed organizations (12 years compared to 11 years, respectively); lower level respondents in the formally participative organizations have more formal education than their counterparts in the conventionally managed organizations (11 years compared to 10 years, respectively); and there is a higher percentage of females at the lower hierarchical level in the formally participative organizations than in the conventionally managed organizations (28% compared to 11%, respectively).

The average number of respondents at upper, middle, and lower hierarchical levels is 7, 12, and 31, respectively, in the formally participative organizations and 6, 11, and 33, respectively, in the conventionally managed organizations.

Measures

The measures of work, formal participation, and member outcomes are obtained by three operationally independent methods. Characteristics of work are obtained from field observations; the measure of formal participation is obtained from company documents; employee outcomes are obtained by questionnaires completed at the workplace.

The field observation instrument is based on Turner and Lawrence (1965) and the Michigan Organizational Assessment Package (1975) and includes 31 dimensions of work.

Field observations for production workers typically required 20 minutes each while interviews/observation for supervisory and managerial personnel typically required 45 minutes each. The split-half reliability of the field observation instrument corrected by Spearman-Brown is .84. The test-retest reliability is .80. (There were 100 observations repeated by another member of the field observation team. Half of the observations were completed at the same time by both observers, half at different times.)[3] . . .

A 122-item questionnaire provides measures of a broad range of outcomes such as job satisfaction, general life satisfaction, alienation, loyalty, commitment, and motivation. The split-half reliability of the questionnaire, corrected by Spearman-Brown, is .83. Four outcomes were selected — alienation, life satisfaction, organizational commitment, and job satisfaction. These outcomes are only moderately correlated and represent diverse dimensions of the construct "outcomes." . . .

In addition to these standardized measures, a detailed examination of organizational procedures and politics was undertaken by means of a semistructured interview with the Personnel Industrial Relations Manager and the union/employee association President.

The use of operationally independent sources of data for the measures of work, outcomes, and formal participation overcomes the problems of "halo responding" (Nightingale and Toulouse, 1977) and "priming" effects (Salancik and Pfeffer, 1977) which may lead to spurious associations between measures of the concepts.[4]

Results

Relations among Dimensions of Work

. . . .Most dimensions of work are significantly interrelated. Work which is unattractive in some respect — such as poor physical working conditions — tends to be unattractive in most other respects as well. Conversely, work which offers opportunities for the exercise of initiative, work which is varied, and work which provides freedom from immediate supervision also tends to allow frequent social interaction, is characterized by good physical working conditions, requires a complete cycle of work, and tends to have fewer conflicting demands placed on the incumbent.

This pattern of relationships is identical in the formally participative and conventionally managed organizations. These relationships are also invariant by hierarchical level, although the relationships are strongest at the lower hierarchical level and weakest at the middle hierarchical level.

A factor analysis (varimax rotation) of the nine dimensions of work yields four factors: (1) a task enrichment factor, consisting of autonomy, skill, mental effort, variety, and uncertainty; (2) a task completion factor; (3) a social interaction factor consisting of required interdependence and conflicting demands; and (4) a physical conditions of work factor. The factor structure is identical in the formally participative and conventionally managed organizations.[5]

Nature of Work in Formally Participative and Conventionally Managed Organizations

The four factors (and the dimensions of each) are compared in the formally participative and conventionally managed organizations. . . . Among the 12 comparisons of factor by level, 4 are statistically significant, but 2 are significant in the nonpredicted direction. Among the 21 comparisons of dimensions of each factor by level, 7 are statistically significant, and 2 of the 7 comparisons are significant in the nonpredicted direction.

At the upper hierarchical level, tasks of managers in formally participative organizations require less completion of a full cycle of activities and are characterized by poorer physical working conditions than the tasks of their counterparts in conventionally managed organizations. Tasks of managers in formally participative organizations may involve less closure than the tasks of their counterparts in conventionally managed organizations because they work more frequently in teams and conduct less work on their own. The physical conditions of the work of managers in formally participative organizations may be less attractive because they tend to spend more time on the shop floor than their counterparts in conventionally managed organizations.

At the middle hierarchical level, there are no differences between formally participative and conventionally managed organizations on any of the four factors. Two subdimensions of factors, however, are significant. The work of managers in formally participative organizations is less varied and involves fewer conflicting demands than the work of their counterparts in the conventionally managed organizations. The greater variety of tasks for upper level managers may eliminate some of the variety from the work of their subordinates. The similarity of work for middle-level managers in the two types of organization is surprising. The frequently expressed fear that greater worker participation in decision making will mean that middle management will be circumvented and their work diminished in importance is not supported by this study.

At the lower hierarchical level, workers in the formally participative organizations, compared to their counterparts in conventionally managed organizations, have more enriched tasks (and greater autonomy from immediate supervision) and greater social interaction with others (more conflicting demands placed on them and greater required interdependence with co-workers and supervisors).

Although Trist and Bamforth (1951), Davis (1971), Susman (1976), and others have shown that work can be redesigned to be more rewarding to the individual performing it without impairing economic efficiency, economic and technological constraints may well limit the extent to which tasks can be redesigned — even in organizations in which employees can alter the nature of work if they so choose. The data from this study suggest that the movement toward industrial democracy may not necessarily be accompanied by work which is more attractive and enriched.

The Full Model
The path model linking type of organization, work and outcomes is tested with four outcomes — alienation, job satisfaction, life satisfaction, and commitment.[6]

Two of the four path coefficients linking type of organization and work are statistically significant. Formally participative organizations have more enriched tasks and tasks requiring greater social interaction.

All four path coefficients linking type of organization and outcomes are statistically significant. Employees in formally participative organizations are more committed, less alienated, and express greater satisfaction with their jobs and their lives in general than employees in conventionally managed organizations.

All four dimensions of work are significantly related to at least three of the four outcome measures. The task enrichment and social interaction measures of work are most strongly related to outcomes, and physical conditions and task completion less strongly related to outcomes. Type of organization and the four characteristics of work account for 12% of the variance (on average) in the four outcome measures. Though the adjusted explained variance is small relative to several other studies of job outcomes, these results are more reliable as ordinary method bias has been eliminated. The variables are operationally independent.

The regression analysis suggests that work in the formally participative organizations differs in some respects from the work in the conventionally managed organizations. When the data from the 10 formally participative organizations are disaggregated, the results show that workers in 3 of the 10 organizations have used their power to change some aspects of their work but, in the remainder, no changes have been made.

In one organization, union representatives on the board of directors pressed for significant improvements in work areas which were hazardous and unpleasant. A multimillion dollar redesign has been undertaken to improve these conditions. However, the nature of the product — fine paper — requires a technology which permits little enrichment or change. The worker representatives on the board are now attempting to reduce the number of first-line supervisors and to allow workers more self-control — perhaps the only way that the work can be enriched.

In a second firm which designs and manufactures office cabinets, the wood cabinets continue to be handmade by skilled craftsmen, although an automated process (requiring semiskilled workers) is employed by most of the firm's competitors. The product is of superior quality when made by craftsmen, but it is also considerably more expensive. However, in the judgment of employees in this firm (workers make all quality control and production quota decisions without management intervention), the workers prefer to perform skilled work than to obtain higher wages.

In the third firm, the production process is highly automated (continuous process in the manufacture of "waferboard"), and alterations to the technology are virtually impossible. The workers — who operate without supervision — have decided to rotate all jobs among workgroup members every two hours and to enrich the work by combining machine maintenance and repair with the operation of the machines. The workers also hire members of their team, elect a team leader, discipline team members for infractions of rules, and determine work schedules and work assignments.

Significant worker control over decision making does lead to positive outcomes, and this relationship is found when the nature of work is controlled. In other words, attitudes can be improved even in organizations in which major task redesign is impossible. Apparently, uninspiring work can be tolerated if employees have the right to exercise influence over other areas of their work lives.

Enhanced employee participation in decision making and improved work itself

— the two strategies currently popular in North America for improving employee outcomes — have been found in this study to be significantly related to employee outcomes as predicted. Both characteristics of work and formal participation are found to have independent and significant effects on diverse outcome measures. The pattern of results suggests that two characteristics of work — enrichment and social interaction — are more strongly related to outcomes than type of organization or physical conditions of work and the extent of task completion.

When employee outcomes are compared in the different forms of formally participative organizations, the most positive outcomes are found in organizations which have combined a program of job improvement with enhanced employee participation in decision making. Least positive outcomes are found in producer cooperatives in which employees express little interest in participating in the affairs of the organization and in which jobs are difficult to improve because of technological and economic constraints.

As the modern work organization becomes more democratic and as employees continue to gain control over significant areas of their work lives, the nature of work should not be expected to change dramatically. However, in organizations in which technological and economic constraints limit the freedom to redesign the work technology, formal participation may be an effective means of creating a satisfying and rewarding work climate.

Notes

1. Author's Note: This research is part of a larger study supported by grants from The Canada Council (S77-1111), Canada Department of Labour-University Research Program, the Associates' Workshop in Business Research, School of Business Administration, University of Western Ontario, and the School of Business, Queen's University. Pierre Daragon and Gilbert Tarrab of the Université de Québec à Montréal assisted with data collection.

2. Editors' Note: Comparisons of the characteristics of individuals employed in formally participative and conventional organizations are necessary to counter arguments that it is the type of worker, rather than the nature of work and form of organization, which lead to different outcomes. The author finds few statistically significant differences — differences large enough to conclude that they did not merely occur by chance — between the workers in the two types of organization. This strengthens his subsequent conclusion that the form of work organization makes a difference for workers' psychological responses to work.

3. Editors' Note: In general, reliability refers to the consistency of measurement. If measurement is unreliable (inconsistent), research findings are difficult to believe. In this study, the issue is whether different observers would similarly evaluate work characteristics and work outcomes in a specific organization. Professor Nightingale reports statistical tests which demonstrate a high degree of measurement reliability.

4. Editors' Note: An important strength of this research design is the independence of measurement of work characteristics, organizational design, and workers' psychological responses to work (the outcomes). An alternative would be to ask workers to describe their work, to evaluate the degree of formal participation allowed, and to also report their level of job satisfaction. This might lead to what the author calls "halo reporting," the tendency, for example, of workers to say they are satisfied with their work because they have just finished evaluating the work and the organizational design positively. Using different sources of information eliminates such problems.

5 Editors' Note: As the author noted earlier, work characteristics in these organizations were described on a total of 31 characteristics which can be combined into nine somewhat broader dimensions. Factor analysis is a complex statistical procedure which aids the researcher in further reducing large amounts of such information into a limited number of statistics. In this case, each organization could now also be ranked on four very broad factors, rather than on the nine more specific dimensions and the 31 very specific work characteristics.

6 Editors' Note: Path analysis, based on regression analysis, is a statistical technique which allows a researcher to examine the effects of one or several variables (e.g. organizational design) on another (e.g. job satisfaction of employees in the organization), and to make inferences about causal relationships between them. A statistically significant path coefficient identifies a relationship of strength sufficient to convince the researcher that it is not merely a chance occurrence.

References

Bass, B. M. and Shackleton, V. J.
(1979) "Industrial democracy and participative management: A case for a synthesis." *Academy of Management Review* 4: 393-404.

Cooper, M. R., B. S. Morgan, P. M. Foley, and L. B. Kaplan
(1979) "Changing employee values: Deepening discontent?" *Harvard Business Review* 57: 117-125.

Dachler, P. and B. Wilpert
(1978) "Conceptual dimensions and boundaries of participation in organizations: A critical evaluation." *Administrative Science Quarterly* 23: 1-39.

Davis, L. E.
(1971) "Job satisfaction research: The postindustrial view." *Industrial Relations* 10: 176-193.

Emery, F. E. and E. Thorsrud
(1969) *New Designs for Work Organization.* Oslo: Tannum Press.

Fenn, D. H. and D. Yankelovich
(1972) "Responding to the employee voice." *Harvard Business Review* 50: 82-91.

French, J.R.P.
(1964) "Laboratory and field studies of power," in E. Boulding (ed.) *Power and Conflict in Organizations.* London: Tavistock.

Herzberg, F.
(1966) *Work and the Nature of Man.* Cleveland, OH: World.

Herzberg, F., B. Mausner, and B. Snyderman
(1959) *The Motivation To Work.* New York: Wiley.

Jones, D.
(1979) "U.S. producer cooperatives: The record to date." *Industrial Relations* 18: 342-357.

Michigan Organizational Assessment Package
(1975) *Progress Report II.* Ann Arbor: University of Michigan, Institute For Social Research.

Nightingale D. V.
(1979) "The formally participative organization." *Industrial Relations* 18: 310-321.
(1978) "Beyond human relations: For participation in work organizations." Kingston, Canada: Queen's University, School of Business.

Nightingale D.V. and J. M. Toulouse
(1977) "Toward a multilevel congruence theory of organizations." *Administrative Science Quarterly* 22: 264-280.

Salancik, G. R. and J. Pfeffer
(1977) "An examination of need satisfaction models of job attitudes." *Administrative Science Quarterly* 22: 427-456.

Schrank R.

    (1978) *Ten Thousand Working Days.* Cambridge, MA: MIT Press.

Sheppard, H. L. and N. Q. Herrick

    (1972) *Where Have All the Robots Gone? Worker Dissatisfaction in the 70's.* New York: Free Press.

Susman, G. L.

    (1976) *Autonomy at Work: A Sociotechnical Analysis of Participative Management.* New York: Praeger.

Tannenbaum, A. S.

    (1974) "Systems of formal participation," in G. Strauss et al. (eds.) *Organizational Behavior: Research and Issues.* Belmont, CA: Madison Industrial Relations Research Association.

Tannenbaum, A.S., G. Kavcic, M. Rosner, M. Vianello, and G. Wieser

    (1974) *Hierarchy in Organizations: An International Comparison.* San Francisco: Jossey-Bass.

Terkel, S.

    (1974) *Working.* New York: Pantheon.

Trist, E. L. and K. W. Bamforth

    (1951) "Some social and psychological consequences of the longwall method of coal getting." *Human Relations* 4: 3-38.

Turner, A N. and P. R. Lawrence

    (1965) "Industrial jobs and the worker: An investigation of requisite task attributes." Harvard University, Boston: Division of Research, Graduate School of Business Administration.

Walker, K. F.

    (1976) "Workers' participation in management — Problems, practice and prospects." Geneva: International Institute for Labour Studies.

Whyte, W. F., M.A. Gurdon, T. H. Hammer, R. N. Stern, and R. J. Long

    (1978) "Employee owned organizations: Processes and productivity." Presented at the meeting of the American Psychological Association, Toronto.

25/Prospects for Industrial Democracy in Canada[*]

1) Industrial Democracy is Workers' Control

Gilbert Levine

Judging by the articles and statements that have appeared recently in the popular and financial press, one might be led to believe that the prospects for industrial democracy in Canada are extremely good. Most of the articles cite favourable experiences with experiments in industrial democracy in several European countries, notably West Germany. Let me quote a few examples: *The Toronto Star* in an article entitled "Worker democracy is creeping into the boardroom" in March, 1975 states:

[*] Abridged from "Prospects for Industrial Democracy in Canada: Four Views." *Labour Gazette* 76(8) 1976, pp. 436-445. Reproduced by permission of the Minister of Supply and Services Canada.

To both its ardent supporters and its most bitter opponents, industrial democracy is a kind of passive industrial revolution. At the least, it is a changing order in industrial relations which is moving into a new phase in Europe and attracting growing interest in North America. It is held at least partly responsible for the enviable record of industrial harmony in most Western European countries.

A senior editor of *The Financial Post* specializing in labour-management relations studied moves towards industrial democracy in Europe and reported on April 10, 1976 that:

> The slow-burn debate in the European Community over worker participation in corporate decision making is fascinating in its own right — but it is also highly relevant to Canada's troubled labour scene. There is widespread agreement that labour relations in Canada need more than band-aid treatment.

Last November 24, at the point he was doing everything possible to smash the Canadian Union of Postal Workers, Postmaster General Bryce Mackasey told the Rotary Club of Ottawa:

> Instead of fighting society for a bigger slice of the pie, and thus preventing the pie from being baked, I think the unions should be fighting for a hand in the baking. They should be fighting the root cause of worker discontent. The primary need of the worker today is job satisfaction, a chance to develop his skills and abilities, his initiative, his individuality. The unions should be fighting for a more democratic workplace.

John Munro, federal Minister of Labour had his department conduct a study of the German model of industrial democracy, euphemistically called "co-determination." Instead of choosing someone with a labour background to conduct the study, the department chose Charles Connaghan, the former president of the British Columbia Construction Labour Relations Association. Connaghan's report was highly enthusiastic, particularly about the very low incidence of days lost through strikes, and he recommended that major elements of West Germany's successful industrial relations system be incorporated into Canada's economic structure.

Before embracing the West German model of "co-determination" for Canada, a few things must be kept in mind:

1. The concept of "co-determination" or industrial democracy did not come about because of a demand from workers or unions. It was imposed in West Germany by the U.S. Army of Occupation as a means of minimizing the effectiveness of a labour movement already smashed by Hitler.

2. There is an obvious connection between the fact that Germany has the most timid labour movement in Europe and that German industrialists have consistently earned the highest return on investment of any country in Europe.

3. The "co-determination" of West Germany reminds me of the "co-prosperity" that the Japanese army of occupation was going to bring to the Asian colonies under Japanese rule during World War II. The people in the colonies ended up having all the "co" while the Japanese had all the "prosperity." In the same manner, under the German system of co-determination, the unions have all the "co" while the employers have all the "determination."

When corporations and their spokesmen in government call for worker participation in decision making, the average Canadian worker is suspicious, and rightly
so. He feels his company is trying to find a new wrinkle to increase its profits and
to restrict the scope of collective bargaining. He feels it has nothing to do with his
economic, social, or psychological betterment.

Therefore, in spite of the enthusiasm within certain sections of management
and government officials for industrial democracy, I am convinced that any form
of true industrial democracy will certainly not come from these sources.

True industrial democracy, as is the case with political and economic democracy, will not come from pressure from above, but from pressure below — in the
workplace. Industrial democracy cannot be imposed by the boss.

The enthusiastic supporters of industrial democracy in the ranks of business
and government are not calling for *workers' control*. What they want is *control of
workers* — and the workers know that.

The U.S. labour movement, from which international union leaders in Canada
derive their philosophical inspiration, shows little support for industrial democracy.
Typical of the U.S. labour attitude is a statement by William Winpisinger, general
vice-president of the International Association of Machinists, who stated to a U.N.
symposium in 1974 that U.S. unions feel that representation on the board would
create a conflict of interest and would compromise the union. He stated:

There is no major perceptible demand by American workers today for participation in the decision making process. . . . You must be on one side or the other to maximize your effectiveness. . . . That is the way
we will continue to do it in the U.S. for a long time to come.

The labour movement in Canada and the United States has traditionally laid
much greater stress on business unionism with its emphasis on short-term economic goals. In contrast, European unions have stressed social unionism, that is,
social and political goals, including the question of industrial democracy and
workers' control. Therefore, the tradition of North American unionism is not a fer-
tile ground to plant the seed of industrial democracy.

There is virtually no support for the concept of industrial democracy among
Canada's trade union leaders. A special conference of the Canadian Labour Congress four years ago concluded that a further extension of the present adversary
form of collective bargaining was the most effective method of achieving any
form of industrial democracy in Canada. The CLC does not want a role in major
management decisions, but instead its unions will continue to whittle away at
management's rights through the traditional system of collective bargaining.

Speaking at Carleton University last winter at a New Democratic Party meeting on industrial democracy, Joe Morris, president of the CLC stated:

This emphasis on collective bargaining, with participation viewed as an extension of joint regulation of
work, is still the keynote of the [British] Trades Union Congress view and remains the kernel of the approach of the CLC. Some of the most basic aspects of the work situation and the security of that employment, stem from decisions taken at extremely remote levels. The type of decisions I have in mind con-

cerns closures, redundancies, major redeployment and mergers in particular. It is to obtain a voice in decisions such as these that the CLC supports ideas of participation, and where we differ from others, surely, is in how to implement it.

Elaborating on this final point, Morris used as an example, a planned layoff in a forest products industry plant. He stated he never questioned the right of the employer to lay off workers. What he was mainly concerned about was the method by which the layoff was carried out. He was concerned essentially that the layoffs were conducted fairly, that is, on the basis of seniority.

Judging by the recent CLC convention, the leaders of organized labour in Canada appear to be moving away from the concept of democratic control at the plant level to advocating a system of corporatism. The CLC endorsed a "Labour Manifesto for Canada" which, in effect, calls for limiting the democratic role of rank and file plant and office workers and would place power in the hands of a few top labour officials whose function it would be to manage the economy as part of a tripartite planning body that would include business, labour and government. Not much room for industrial democracy in the set-up.

With a few business leaders and some government leaders calling for a phony kind of industrial democracy, which I prefer to call "control of workers," and with leaders of organized labour showing a marked disinclination to promote the concept of workers' participation in the industrial decision making process, what then are the prospects for real industrial democracy in Canada?

About five years ago I gave a paper at a conference on industrial democracy sponsored by the Woodsworth Foundation in which I held out high hopes that universities as employers would become models of industrial democracy for others to follow. The fight that faculty and students were waging at the time for representation on governing bodies seemed to be a good example that other public bodies and industrial enterprises might follow in the future.

In the intervening years, however, the faculty and students — and in some universities, even maintenance staff — who have won their token seats on the board of governors, have been co-opted into the "system" and the fight for industrial democracy is virtually dead. The fight that the students waged in the 1960s is over and the faculties are turning to unionizing and collective bargaining in order to have a voice in the affairs of the university. I am therefore very disillusioned about any possibilities of the university as a model for industrial relations in Canada.

We have recently had two rather unusual forms of industrial democracy — or worker ownership and control — in Quebec. In both instances they were cases where workers, who would have otherwise been laid off as a result of plant shutdowns, pooled their resources, bought the plants and are operating them as co-operative enterprises. I speak of the Temiskaming paper mill and the St. Jerome knitting mill now both very successful commercial enterprises. Both have run into tremendous difficulties with governments and banks who were determined to discourage a successful example of a worker-owned operation.

To improve the possibilities of real industrial democracy in Canada, a complete change in the traditional approach to this question will be required. We will have to reject completely the reformist view of industrial democracy, which seeks to transform unions from organizations fighting on behalf of workers to unions that would become agents of managerial control, a view now being promoted by some governments.

I see the fight for real industrial democracy in industry as a process and as a tactical goal, not only for transforming the worker-employer relationship, but as a means of transforming society itself. I foresee workers in Canada using their experience in the fight for control of the workplace to gain control of society and government. The lessons learned in attempting to gain control of industry will be valuable to workers who, in the future, will have to control society, if it is to be a truly democratic society.

Industrial democracy, or workers' control, is incompatible with the capitalist system, with its emphasis on ownership of private property and all of the "management rights" which flow from that ownership. True industrial democracy can exist only under a system of public ownership where the workers own the means of production. This is not to say that unions and workers should not fight for industrial democracy under our present system. In the fight for real industrial democracy, workers will learn the lesson of who exercises the power in the plant and in the state.

Success in achieving real industrial democracy will further require a combining of the struggle for workers' rights in the shops and offices with a similar struggle at the political level. Coupled with the fight for industrial democracy, labour would have to call for a transformation of the capitalist system into a socialist system.

Unfortunately, labour in Canada today is not moving in the direction of transforming society. With its "Manifesto for Labour," the CLC is not requesting a change in society, it is not even asking for the election of a New Democratic Party government. It is asking for the right to co-manage the present iniquitous system in co-operation with business and government.

Such a goal does not bode well for the achievement of true industrial democracy in Canada.

2) Co-determination — A Capitalist Innovation

Gerry Hunnius

Employer-initiated innovations which aim to modify or change the so-called adversary system of labour-management relations historically have taken a variety of forms, but there has been a certain consistency in terms of the expected results of all such innovations.

The questions we should raise include the following:

What functions are initiatives of this kind expected to perform?
Why are they made now?
What responses are open to workers and organized labour and what are the likely consequences of each alternative response?

After studying a series of waves of such initiatives by the state and by the owners of capital, one can come to only one conclusion as to the expected function of each and all such innovations: to maintain or increase production and profit while simultaneously retaining control over production and capital accumulation.

The tactics of course are continually changing and range from the largely successful attempt at the end of the last century to smash the power of the Amalgamated Association of Iron, Steel and Tin Workers in the Homestead strike of 1892, to the more sophisticated tactics culminating in the currently popular initiatives in the direction of job enlargement, job enrichment, and "industrial democracy."

Let us look briefly at one of these mechanisms which capital has used historically to cement power over the productive process and thus over capital accumulation. Certain aspects of "Taylorism" stand out as particularly relevant. The stated rationale of the systematic minimization of skills is that it gets the worker on the job as quickly as possible, cutting down training costs. The separation of physical work from mental work — taking knowledge of production away from the skilled worker — was greatly aided by the scientific principles of Frederick Winslow Taylor, who recognized that knowledge about production means power.

In his *Principles of Scientific Management* (1905) he stated that workers possessed a collective knowledge which management did not possess. Total control over production demanded that this knowledge be "transferred" to management. In his manual, *Shop Management*, he insists that all possible brain work should be removed from the shop and centered with the planning or laying-out department.

The "transfer" of skills was carefully worked out in the methodology of scientific management and soon spilled over into the educational system and other institutions of socialization.

Once we understand that the underlying reason for the changing tactics — as well as the innovations themselves — rests with the determination of corporate capital to maintain ownership and control of productive resources and processes, the nature and timing of various capitalist innovations is relatively easy to comprehend.

Let me illustrate briefly one example of such an innovation during the early years of this century, largely restricted at that time to the United States: It was called variously *welfare work, welfarism* or *industrial betterment* and it was the forerunner of the later *human relations approach to management* and the current initiatives in job enrichment, and co-determination.

They dealt with the same issues and were introduced for the same reasons: to forestall "labour troubles," to maintain control over the process of production and the work force, and to increase production and profits.

The humanitarian philosophy was publicized at the time when welfarism emerged, although its managerial assumptions were seldom articulated publicly. The essence of this approach was intended to instill virtues and values in workers which would promote an attachment to work and a sense of loyalty to the enterprise.

This approach came about on the heels of a concerted capitalist offensive to halt or destroy the growth of unions and it coincides with the Homestead strike where the power of the steelworkers was smashed. By the end of 1904, the growth of unionization appeared to be checked and the following year showed the first decline since 1897.

Welfarism included the installation of hygienic facilities, introduction of a banking system within enterprises to encourage workers to save their earnings, wage incentives, and various minor employee representation schemes. What is more relevant is to determine why these policies were introduced by employers. Two factors emerge very clearly: It was profitable to the employer. It tended to reduce the turnover of employees and the occasional outbreak of open conflict. The slogan "it pays," publicized by the president of National Cash Register, was repeated by many senior managers from coast to coast.

Even more significant is the fact that welfarism was used by employers to eliminate labour unions or to undermine their formation by providing management-sponsored employee benefits.

In many cases, employers encouraged the creation of worker committees as part of their welfare policies. This particular tactic proved temporarily successful in preventing the growth of unions. Powerless as these committees were, they functioned as vehicles through which management exerted more effective control over the work force. Welfarism — or welfare work — was thus not only a method to bust unions, it also offered the employer an alternative to unionism and collective bargaining.

Unionization, despite its initial setbacks, recovered, and collective bargaining as it is practiced today became the dominant model of labour-management relations in the U.S. and Canada. This model, has on the whole, served the interests of the employer class well. Today, at least in Canada, we are warned of a crisis in collective bargaining. One of the essential links in the sophisticated chain of collective bargaining has weakened to the point where it is feared that it may burst asunder. That link is the disciplining function of management and unions over the workers. It is in this context that I am viewing the recent employer-initiated offensive in "industrial democracy."

There are at least two general directions which current employee/government initiatives are likely to take. They are not alternatives and will probably both be pursued:

1. An attempt to involve organized labour, particularly at the level of the CLC as well as at the level of national and international union headquarters, in a tripartite system of consultation and limited decision making beyond what presently exists.
2. In the large unorganized sector, it will likely take the form of a more sophisticated "industrial betterment" approach.

In either case, in quite different ways, the outcome is likely to be the following: A blurring of the present adversary system in union-management relations, followed gradually by the replacement of collective bargaining as we know it in Canada by some kind of institutionalized mechanism which in all likelihood will unite employees and management in one organizational framework. If two strong partners unite organizationally with *one* somewhat weaker partner the ultimate outcome is not too difficult to imagine.

In Canada, starting with the *Woods Report*, employers, politicians and civil servants have discovered a "crisis in collective bargaining." Prime Minister Trudeau was most outspoken about what bothered the government. He has been quoted as saying collective bargaining is no longer fulfilling its function in a situation where unions negotiate an agreement, but the members then go out on wildcat strikes.

The solution, according to Trudeau, has to be faced by unions and employers together. But how? The solution emerged quite clearly at the last national convention of the Liberal Party in a resolution which urged, "the government to establish a royal commission to study and recommend ways of bringing some measure of industrial democracy to Canada as a way of replacing the adversary system of labour-management relations with something more co-operative and productive."

During the past two years, there has been a series of comments by senior officials of the federal department of labour pointing in the direction of a system of industrial relations with stronger emphasis on the "mutuality of interests" of all parties (labour, employer and government).

Organized labour in Canada, as well as in the United States, has always been hostile to proposed innovations of this kind. The change in the policy of the CLC, documented in "Labour's Manifesto for Canada" makes the introduction of some form of co-determination in Canada a near certainty.

Since the two models most frequently mentioned are those of West Germany and Sweden, I would like to make a few observations on these models regarding their relevance to Canada.

1. Unions are much more powerful in Sweden and West Germany than in Canada. This is due to a number of factors including the fact that a larger percentage of the Swedish and German workforce is unionized. Both countries' Social Democratic governments have been an important factor.

2. In Germany in particular, it is clearly understood by all parties — labour, capital and the state — that co-determination is a mechanism meant to maintain the smooth functioning of the capitalist mode of production. A statement by the executive board of the German Trade Union Federation (D.G.B.) states bluntly that, "A general conception of co-determination of this type presupposes a system of free enterprise based on the principle of free market economy."

3. Both countries, but particularly West Germany, have used large numbers of foreign workers, a factor of great significance.

What about the results of the West German and Swedish innovations? First, co-determination:

1. It has been instrumental in maintaining a high degree of labour peace, production, and profits.

2. It has enhanced the prestige and influence of the central union federations.

3. Contrary to recent newspaper reports, it has not appreciably affected the rank and file worker at the point of production. It does not, therefore, deal with the wide-spread dissatisfaction and rebellion of blue- and white-collar workers that has been the target of innumerable studies and reports.

3. It has probably played a part in improving the extensive social security and benefit system available to employees in West Germany.

The situation in Sweden is more difficult to evaluate, partly because it is very much in flux and is undergoing continual change. One major difference between the Swedish and West German models is the position of the Swedish trade union movement. LO in particular has been very sensitive to the "blue-collar blues" of its members and has insisted that any placement of workers or union officials on the board of directors of corporations must be accompanied by the introduction of aspects of industrial democracy on the shop floor. There is little indication of interest in *this* aspect of industrial democracy among employers or government in Canada.

In sum:

1. Nearly all successful innovations in job enrichment and industrial democracy have led to an immediate decrease in worker dissatisfaction and a corresponding increase in production and profits.

2. In most instances, these innovations have been altered or discontinued.

3. Today, under pressures briefly touched upon earlier, these innovations have been given the green light again.

It would seem there is a compelling explanation for the hesitancy on the part of employers and government to pursue such innovations in the past.

The introduction of aspects of industrial democracy, particularly at the level of the shop floor, requires changes which would return to the worker a limited amount of autonomy. Semi-autonomous work teams — one of the features of many such innovations — allow for rotation of tasks. Supervision is often replaced by self-direction, and individual competition by co-operation. Former managerial functions have to be partly surrendered to rank and file workers. Such changes have produced instances, particularly in Europe, of revolutionary demands by those semi-autonomous groups of workers. That however, is another topic.

Part V/Unions and Industrial Relations

Editors' Introduction

One of the most hotly debated subjects in contemporary society is the role of unions. Supporters of unions argue that worker organizations are essential in a healthy democracy as a countervailing force to the power of employers. Critics respond that unions have outlived their usefulness and now inhibit economic progress. The seven chapters in this part document that the issues involved are far too complex to warrant a simple "for" or "against" response. Unions are a fundamental part of the capitalist system and are here to stay.

The rise of the modern factory and office was parallelled by the development of workers' organizations dedicated to improving working conditions. Presently about 38 per cent of the non-farm labour force in Canada belongs to unions, although the level of unionization varies widely across industries and occupational groups. The growth of unions in this century also entailed a dramatic shift in membership composition, from largely blue-collar industrial workers in the 1900s toward white-collar public sector employees today. Despite these changes in the size and character of the union movement, and major gains through collective bargaining, we shall see below that many of the problems surrounding the emergence of unions still persist.

Our system of industrial relations is aptly described as adversarial. Unions and management, representing different communities of interest, attempt to resolve their differences through the process of collective bargaining. Ideally, the goal of bargaining is to resolve differences and thereby avoid conflict. In reality, some disputes over bargaining issues culminate in strikes and lockouts (where management denies workers entry to the place of employment), and such conflicts irritate the Canadian public. This prompts Professor Brookbank to ask, in Chapter 26, whether the adversarial system is out of date. Reviewing data on worker days lost due to work stoppages, he concludes that the system in fact is functioning well. It may come as a surprise that the great majority of union-management negotiations are settled in this country without open conflict. From an international perspective, however, Canada is near the top of the list of countries with the most time lost due to work stoppages. Brookbank observes that part of our problem stems from the relative immaturity of our industrial relations system. Complicating this is persistent government interference with the "free" collective bargaining process through such means as wage controls — the 1975-1978 Anti-Inflation Board and now the "6 and 5" restraint program. Such controls undermine the whole bargaining process by predetermining its outcomes, and may lead to increased union militancy.

When contemplating the future of Canadian industrial relations it may be use-ful to draw some lessons from our labour past. The next two chapters illuminate formative events in the early decades of this century, events that have a direct bear-ing on contemporary labour problems. In Chapter 27, Craig Heron and Bryan Palmer analyze the causes underlying strikes in southern Ontario industrial centres between 1901 and 1914. The historical record reveals that these disputes involved much more than wages. At stake was the degree of control craftsworkers could ex-ercise over their labour — an issue that cuts to the core of power relations in the workplace. Our previous discussion of the rise of scientific management and bu-reaucratic workplaces must now be qualified in an important respect: workers did not stand idly by and watch the deskilling and routinization of their jobs. Many of them, at least when unionized, actively resisted these new managerial initiatives.

In a similar vein, in Chapter 28, Stuart Marshall Jamieson provides a blow-by-blow account of one of the most tumultuous episodes in Canadian labour history. The 1919 Winnipeg General Strike is a rare example in Canada of violent class conflict. The issue that, more than anything else, sparked the strike was the right of metal trades workers to have their unions recognized by management. But many employers were firmly opposed to the principle of unionism. Coming as it did only two years after the Russian Revolution, the Winnipeg General Strike was immediately labelled by employers and politicians as a Canadian version of a bol-shevik uprising, and as a radical challenge to the constituted government. Police and army were ordered in, violence erupted, and the strike was soon broken. Despite this surge of worker militancy, organized labour in Canada has largely operated along fairly conservative "business unionism" lines — concentrating on economic rather than broader political issues. Instead of challenging the system, unions have typically worked within it trying to maximize gains for their members.

One basic lesson to be learned from the Winnipeg experience is that the state plays an often decisive role in shaping union-management relations. Because it has the power to establish the legal framework for industrial relations, the state can either facilitate or hinder free collective bargaining. The federal government's 1967 Public Service Staff Relations Act, which extended collective bargaining to its em-ployees, is a good example of the former. The Nova Scotia Michelin Bill, de-scribed by Michael Bradfield in Chapter 29, represents an unfortunate instance of the latter. Michelin, a multinational tire manufacturer, traded promises of jobs in an economically disadvantaged region in return for government guarantees that the firm would be protected against unionization. Such blatant manipulation of the legal framework regulating union-management relations is bound to breed dis-trust among unions and, quite possibly, lead to an escalation of conflict. Recalling our previous discussion of industrial democracy, it is interesting to note that Bradfield proposes worker ownership of enterprises as an alternative strategy for economic development.

Chapters 30 and 31 highlight the debate over whether unions cause more harm than good. John van der Feyst leads off with "management" arguments for why unions are obsolete. While it is unclear how widespread such views are in corporate circles, they undoubtedly have been diffused to the general public through the media. Beliefs that unions cause inflation, undermine the "free enterprise" system, take advantage of their members, or create civil unrest are held by many Canadians. But according to Ed Finn, these views are more myth than fact. In Chapter 31 he attempts to debunk the ten central myths about unions.

The final chapter in this part presents an impassioned defence of workers' rights by Jean Claude Parrot, leader of the Canadian Union of Postal Workers (CUPW) and an executive of the Canadian Labour Congress (Canada's central labour body). His central argument is that basic workers' rights, from collective bargaining to decent working conditions, are being seriously eroded by the combined efforts of business and government. Parrot's account of his union's struggle with management evokes parallels with an earlier era. Legislated interventions in the collective bargaining process (back-to-work legislation and jail terms for union leaders) have replaced the strong-arm tactics of those breaking the Winnipeg General Strike. But in many respects the underlying motivation is the same — the emasculation of unions. What results is a labour relations climate of suspicion and distrust. It is thus easy to see why Parrot stands opposed to any form of consultation or cooperation with management, be it in the form of industrial democracy, quality of work life programs, or joint union-management committees. The spirit of cooperation evident in Shell Oil's Sarnia refinery, documented in the previous part, is more the exception than the rule. Many union leaders agree with Parrot that such schemes are entered into only at great peril. In contemplating the future of industrial relations in Canada, one thing is very clear: as long as the fundamental struggles of the past concerning basic rights continue to be fought in today's workplace, the prospects for schemes such as industrial democracy will remain bleak.

Suggested Readings

John Anderson and Morley Gunderson, eds., *Union-Management Relations in Canada* (Don Mills: Addison-Wesley Publishers, 1982).

George S. Bain, *Union Growth and Public Policy in Canada* (Ottawa: Labour Canada, 1978).

David J. Bercuson, *Confrontation at Winnipeg: Labour, Industrial Relations, and the General Strike* (Montreal: McGill-Queen's University Press).

Paul Craven, *"An Impartial Umpire": Industrial Relations and the Canadian State* (Toronto: University of Toronto Press, 1980).

Colin Crouch, *Trade Unions: The Logic of Collective Action* (Glasgow: Fontana, 1982).

Richard Hyman, "Trade unions, control and resistance," in Geoff Esland and Graeme Salaman, eds., *The Politics of Work and Occupations* (Toronto: University of Toronto Press, 1980).

Stuart Marshall Jamieson, *Times of Trouble: Labour Unrest and Industrial Conflict in Canada, 1900-66.* Task Force on Labour Relations, Study No. 22 (Ottawa: Information Canada, 1971).

Robert Laxer, *Canada's Unions* (Toronto: James Lorimer, 1976).

26/The Adversary System in Canadian Industrial Relations: Blight or Blessing?*

C.R. Brookbank

As Canadians, we appear to relish a substantial amount of conflict in our national sport, the game of hockey. We feel that it reflects the ruggedness of our people and the vitality of our culture. In Parliament, likewise, we cherish the principle of a Loyal Opposition whose role is to challenge and criticize government activities. We consider that this "power to oppose" keeps governments honest in motive and sensitive to the common welfare. In short, we tend to believe, as Canadians, that conflict controlled by the rules of the game — or the House — is of fundamental importance to integrity and progress, even though it may sometimes get out of hand in both environments.

How is it, then, that many of us find controlled conflict distasteful in labour-management relations, where it also tends to get out of hand on some occasions? Why is there a considerable body of opinion in Canada to the effect that the "adversary system" in labour-management relations is out of date? In a country whose citizens tend to resent controls of virtually any kind, how is it that a seemingly large number would be quite pleased to see compulsory arbitration introduced as a reasonable alternative to the strike or lockout in many collective bargaining endeavours? . . .

A look at the present state of affairs regarding work stoppages[1] may help in assessing the extent of "extreme conflict," often cited as justification for abandoning the adversary relationship within the industrial relations system. Table 1 illustrates the record of work stoppages due to strikes and lockouts from 1971 to 1978 inclusive. It can be seen that these declined somewhat during the period of wage and price controls (October 1975 to April 1978) but now appear to be on the rise again. The number of man-days lost and of workers involved dropped drastically in 1977, however, indicating work stoppages of much shorter duration that in 1976 and probably of smaller units. For 1977 in particular, it would appear that work stoppages were curtailed where larger unions and employers were concerned.

* Abridged from C.R. Brookbank, "The Adversary System in Canadian Industrial Relations," *Relations Industrielles/Industrial Relations* 35(1) 1980: 20-37. Reprinted with permission of the publisher and the author.

Table 1. Time Perspective on Work Stoppages.

Work stoppages in existence during month or year

Period	Number	Workers involved	Duration in man-days	% of estimated working time
Year				
1971	569	239,631	2,866,590	0.16
1972	598	706,474	7,753,530	0.43
1973	724	348,470	5,776,080	0.30
1974	1,218	580,912	9,221,890	0.46
1975	1,171	506,443	10,908,810	0.53
1976	1,030	1,582,631	10,624,130	0.55
1977	803	217,557	3,307,880	0.15
1978	949	385,405	7,480,030	0.33

These figures are issued by Labour Canada; the data for 1978 are listed as "subject to revision."
Reproduced by permission of the Minister of Supply and Services Canada.

The *number* of stoppages in 1978 has not increased substantially, but the percentage of lost working time has more than doubled over 1977 and the number of man-days-lost has increased almost to the same point. According to figures released by Labour Canada for 1978, much of this increase in lost working time and number of man-days lost can be attributed to a few large altercations. The two largest stoppages under federal jurisdiction in 1978 were at B.C. Telephone and Canada Post Office, accounting for 60% of federal figures. Inco Metals Ltd. in Ontario, iron mining in Quebec and Labrador, and construction carpenters in Ontario represented 27% of all man-day losses under provincial jurisdiction. It would not appear that the departure of wage and price controls has brought any great surge of strikes, but there have been a few severe and serious ones. Removal of the right to strike/lockout might constrain the severe cases but it would also impose controls on the many who settle with little or no resort to stoppage.

Of more concern than the absolute numbers of stoppages, workers involved, and man-days lost is the general increase in percentage of estimated working time lost, since this is relative to all of the others. In this respect, the time lost in 1978 was equivalent to 33 man-days per 10,000 man-days worked, compared to .15 (15 man-days) in 1977 and .55 in 1976.

While these percentages follow a pattern similar to the others, it is worth noting that this is not the first time in the history of Canadian industrial relations that these percentages have reached present levels. In 1919, the percentage of lost working time through work stoppages was .60; in 1946, it was .54. These percentages are based on a ratio of number of man-days lost for every 10,000 man-days worked, e.g. 53 lost per 10,000 in 1975. While there are many more union members in Canada now than in 1919, or even in 1946, the *relative* loss of working time is no more severe. The "system" seems to be functioning normally.

These interpretations of the statistics are not intended to imply that our problems in labour-management relations are of little consequence, but rather to suggest that more refined analysis of the situation can bring more appropriate and feasible solutions than disposing of the adversary system and running the proverbial risk of "losing the baby with the bath water." Even so, it must be acknowledged that in 1976 Canada vied with Italy, on a list of 35 countries, for the most time lost due to strikes and lockouts. Canada had 55 man-days lost per 10,000 worked during that year.

Over the years, the Canadian pattern of industrial relations has consistently brought about peaceful settlements in the majority of cases. Jamieson[2] makes general reference to a figure of 5% or less of negotiations related to collective agreements in Canada that result in strikes or lockouts, but this rate is low for some periods. In 1976, Labour Canada records 637 agreements negotiated in the industrial sector (excluding construction) of the economy in Canada; of those all but 84 (13.2 per cent) were settled without work stoppages. In 1977, all except 33 (5.7 per cent) of 577 agreements in the industrial sector were settled amicably. In 1978, all but 6.5% (44) were concluded without stoppages. A very respectable record, but why is it that we seem unable to overcome the "crisis" syndrome of peaks and troughs in work stoppages? . . .

The adversary system represents the foundation of employer-union relations in this country. It has developed traditionally in Canada with the private sector and it is constituted ideally on the assumption that a strong employer and a strong union, each with a respect for the power of the other, can negotiate a collective agreement which will integrate the interests of both parties more effectively than any method which would give either side (or a third party) the unilateral power to make decisions for both. The confrontation of these two groups in a "balance of power" has revolved around the distribution of the fruits of economic endeavour, with government maintaining a legislative regulation of the bipartite relationship as guardian of the public interest. With the parties sharing control over the process, there is the further assumption that both sides will feel a sense of responsibility for the effective administration of the collective agreement and will possess the detailed knowledge and awareness of its intent, a factor which is often critical in making effective administration of the agreement possible.

As with any other human system, the practice of collective bargaining in Canada has not been a pure reflection of the theory. For one thing, the *balance* of power which undergirds an atmosphere of mutual respect between employer and union is not always evident. This is particularly so when either party cannot "bargain from strength" because of inadequate resources such as financial support, size, strong affiliations and the like. Imbalance of power can create temptations for the *more* powerful to use that power arbitrarily against the less powerful. For another thing, the lockout was intended theoretically to be the employer weapon to counteract the strike weapon of the union, but until recently the lockout has not been used to any extent in Canadian industrial relations. This has contributed to power imbalance on occasion and it has placed added responsibility on government to control arbitrary uses of power.

In spite of such shortcomings, the adversary system was effective enough to cause the Government of Canada to legislate, in 1967 under the Public Service Staff Relations Act, a pattern of collective bargaining for its own employees in the public sector which embraced similar principles of confrontation, insofar as this was feasible. This was a step taken with good intentions and with an implicit faith in the viability of the adversary system. In retrospect, it has produced some unexpected consequences which merit consideration in the light of present circumstances. It is becoming increasingly evident that inconsistencies between theory and practice also exist in the public sector. Government now has a responsibility as an *employer* dealing with unions as well as a regulator of the private sector. This represents a new and significant dimension which has emerged within the past twelve years, meriting depth consideration in any analysis of the total adversary system in Canada. . . .

For one thing, inclusion in the adversary system has given union members in the public sector a steady growth in numbers and in power which is now exceeding[3] that of their counterparts in the private sector. Provincial governments have, for the most part, followed the lead of the federal government in its efforts to provide bargaining rights for public sector employees, with acquiescence if not encouraged by the employer. Private sector unionization, on the other hand, has remained stable[4] or experienced a slight decline over the past decade while further efforts at organization have faced a considerable degree of informal reluctance on the part of private-sector employers. With this trend, it becomes apparent that public sector unions are in the process of accomplishing a degree of organization within a period of 12 years which private sector unions have never been able to achieve in Canada.

Public sector unions negotiating with the Federal Government are embracing the strike option[5] in preference to compulsory arbitration in increasing numbers.[6] In the normal course of events, this will tend to increase the potential frequency of strikes in the public sector. While the design for confrontation between employer and union in the public sector is similar in principle to that of the private sector, the pattern which is emerging in practice reflects some significant differences. In the private sector, an employer may decide to "take a strike" with considerable hardship to himself but with substantially less difficulty for the general public in most instances.

In the public sector, however, it is often the general public which "takes the strike" if the employer decides to stand firm in the face of union demands. At that point, elected members of Parliament tend to find themselves in the position of risking their political future if they do not make concessions which will achieve agreement and restore services. Such political pressures have not been a factor in private sector bargaining where confrontation has traditionally focussed on economic arguments by both sides, and settlements tend to be reached in light of economic constraints rather than political pressures. Where the public interest may be seriously affected, government has intervened to protect it.

Use of the adversary system in the public sector is further complicated by the fact that government as *employer* does not resort to the lockout as a method for countering the strike option of the union. While such is theoretically possible, the idea of government denying services to the tax-paying public by locking out union members is inconsistent with the mandate[7] of government to serve the people.

In further contrast to the private sector, the government as employer has less opportunity to opt for reduction of the work force as a means of reducing costs when pressed into major concessions through collective bargaining. Private sector unions can ensure that procedures for laying off workers are fair and consistent, but they can seldom prevent lay-offs. Many government workers have a form of job tenure, on the other hand, which protects them from public or political manipulation or abuse as "servants of the Crown" but which also does not allow them to be laid off or replaced easily by technology and other "efficiency" measures.

Perhaps the most important unexpected consequence of the emergence of public sector bargaining is the increasing tendency of major public sector confrontations to be perceived as pace-setters for subsequent negotiations. Those familiar with the industrial relations scene in Canada will acknowledge the traditional role of major employers and unions in the private sector as pace-setters in negotiations. In the steel industry, automobile manufacturing, forest products and the like, strong unions have faced strong employers to argue their cases in the light of economic considerations, including those of foreign trade and international competition. With a strong power balance between employers and unions, settlements in these areas are not achieved without substantial consideration of the facts of economic life, and they have tended to establish a level of wage increase which subsequent negotiators on both sides come to use as a guideline. If this pacesetting function is increasingly assumed by public sector units at the national level, albeit unintentionally, the parameters of bargaining will tend to become increasingly political and economic constraints such as productivity or markets will be less significant in the context of collective bargaining. . . .

Dennis McDermott, President of the Canadian Labour Congress, has publicly stated that unions are still not accepted by a large segment of Canadian employers as full partners in the industrial relations process. If such is the case, can the adversary system be expected to develop as the basic component of a mature industrial democracy in Canada? If the right to union representation can be fully accepted, in practice, in the public sector, resulting in a substantial growth in union membership over the past twelve years, should this right not also be reinforced and not impeded in the private sector?

There is a somewhat similar lack of organization on the employer side in the private sector. Although private sector employers find common cause in organizations such as the Canadian Manufacturers Association, the Canadian Construction Association, and the Canadian Chamber of Commerce, none of these employers' organizations exist for the primary purpose of dealing with unions. This is in sharp contrast to the situation in countries like Sweden where the large majority of both employers and employees are organized for the purpose of making industrial democracy a way of life rather than a theoretical concept.

For present purposes, the significance of the Swedish experience lies in the fact that since 1938 a free system of collective bargaining, built upon the adversary principle, has developed into a full-fledged industrial democracy in the private sector based on the sense of integrity and responsibility — not to mention skill — that has accompanied a high degree of organization on both sides. This has not happened in Canada, and in the light of present trends is not likely to do so in the foreseeable future. As a consequence, the various European formulas for industrial democracy and worker participation, which require elaborate organizational frameworks for effective administration, will not be appropriate here at present. Participation implies involvement, and the *majority* of employers and workers in the private sector in Canada are not involved in our free system of collective bargaining because they are not organized to participate.

In some European countries, adversary systems have matured into industrial democracies; in the private sector in Canada, the adversary system is still in early adolescence. In the industrial adversary system, employers and unions are opponents; they are *not* enemies. The same type of relationship prevails between Government and Loyal Opposition in our political adversary system. Would the critics of the adversary system in industrial democracy also consider the adversary system in political democracy in Canada to be out of date? Would they prefer a more "peaceful" Parliament — without an official opposition? . . .

If there is to be any reasonable and ready reconciliation between those who advocate modification or rejection of the adversary system and those who foresee industrial democracy over the immediate horizon, the *power and integrity* of those employers and unions *in the private sector* who have built the traditional system in Canada — *and made it work effectively* — must be preserved and fostered. The major theme of this paper is that, by accident more than by design, the trend is in the opposite direction. . . .

In the normal process of collective bargaining, each party comes to the table with a set of initial demands on the other party and these are put up for negotiation. At the same time, each side has a general (if not specific) idea of its own point of final resistance, beyond which it will resort to strike or lockout rather than make further concessions. This resistance point, of course, is not presented for immediate public scrutiny because it represents the minimum of achievement rather than the optimum. While bargaining around initial demands, each party is attempting to discover the resistance point[8] of the other, hoping in the process that common ground can be discovered at a point in excess of the minimum and without resort to work stoppage. This is the very essence of a free system of collective bargaining and of the adversary process. It is extremely complex in operation because each concession must not only be negotiated with representatives from the other side but must also undergo some process of ratification by those "invisible committees" whom the negotiators represent at the bargaining table. This is particularly true for union negotiators, who are elected rather than appointed, but reputations and expectations are also at stake on the management side.

What happened to this collective bargaining process when government, through the Anti-Inflation Board, superimposed a maximum final wage settlement before the process began? While this type of intervention did not protect the national economy against inflation, it aborted collective bargaining by a *premature* public declaration of the employer's resistance point on wage increases. The customary bargaining procedures were altered drastically because the adversaries could not perform their customary roles, resorting instead to strategies for dealing with the external control mechanism, the Anti-Inflation Board. . . .

At the same time that the government of Canada was attempting to control, in the interests of the economy, the adversary system as it is reflected in the relationship between private sector employers and unions, it was also concerned for those many unorganized workers in the private sector who do not have the benefit of union affiliation. This concern of government was expressed in amendments to the Canada Labour Code[9] introduced into Parliament in 1978 which provided an additional statutory holiday, additional vacation pay, and other benefits for employees in airlines, railways, banking, trucking, broadcasting, communications, port operations and grain handling. Where these employees were not members of unions with these benefits already available, these developments would be welcomed. By the good graces of government, the wages and working conditions of the less powerful, unorganized workers were brought closer to those of the more powerful, organized workers. The intended results are clear and unequivocal.

Be that as it may, what are some of the *unexpected* results of these legislative changes, particularly for the adversary system in the private sector? Since many of these workers are not organized to represent themselves, the government in effect becomes the "negotiator" for them with their employer. This is a unilateral rather than bilateral process; the employers, although required to accept the increased cost which these extra benefits represent for their operations, are not in the adversary relationship to government. They must therefore absorb these costs, increase the price of their services, or otherwise make adjustments to decisions which are not directly subject to their managerial control. For their part, unions in the private sector will tend to support these trends as progressive, feeling that standards established for organized workers are being used as the model to be emulated. On the other hand, the private sector unions have not been successful in organizing the majority of unorganized workers in the private sector over a considerable period of years.

Is it not reasonable to expect that government acting as "business agent" for unorganized workers will *increase* the disinclination of the unorganized to join unions? Will this not discourage the expansion of private sector unions, in the long term, and serve as a further deterrent to the emergence of the free system of collective bargaining into the maturity of an industrial democracy?

If government is willing to act on behalf of unorganized workers, why should those workers bother to take advantage of their legal right to be represented by unions? Why should they accept the responsibility of paying union dues, attending union meetings, accepting leadership responsibilities which may place them in the adversary role vis-a-vis their employers? Why should they spend time, without pay, as union stewards ensuring that the new concessions are in fact provided by management? It is assumed, of course, that government agents are sufficient — in knowledge and in numbers — and available to perform these functions on behalf of the unorganized. Without the ability to process grievances, the new benefit may not be administered fairly. In the emergent industrial democracy foreseen for Canada, can workers be expected to assume greater authority and control over their work environment without *themselves* accepting some form of responsibility for the system? . . .

In this analysis, it has been the intention to increase awareness of the implications, for the future of industrial relations in Canada, of major developments in employer-union relations over the past decade. It has proceeded on the assumption that the intentions of all parties are sensible and justifiable from their own perspectives. An effort has also been made to illustrate that the "road to Hell" *can* be paved with the unexpected results which can arise from good but over-simplified intentions. The only "villainy" in question here is that which must be shared by those who disregard the longer-range implications of such actions in favour of superficial solutions to current problems.

Given the present trends unaltered and even accentuated, the emergence of industrial democracy as a future method for handling Canadian industrial relations in a balanced partnership with government is improbable. Following the successful pattern of their public sector counterparts, private sector unions will tend to become more political in their strategies and activities. Shirley Carr, executive vice-president of the Canadian Labour Congress, is quoted as stating in New York[10] that "it is becoming evident that labour's share of the national income will be determined less and less by collective bargaining, and more through political decision-making." This view is reinforced by the fact that the national day of protest organized by the C.L.C. on October 14, 1976, resulted in 830,000 man-days lost — as a *political* gesture.

The more the legitimate role of unions as an equal partner in the adversary system declines, the more probable will be the transition to political avenues as a more effective channel of union power. With many private sector employers disinclined to accept organized labour as a full partner even in a bipartite relationship, the union role as anti-establishment "underdog" will be accentuated. In the face of continued employer-union conflict, governments will feel compelled to institute further controls on both public and private sectors or to allow adverse economic circumstances and high unemployment to serve as moderating factors. . . .

There is no simple formula to be found, either in Europe or in the United States, which can be superimposed upon the complex and troubled Canadian scene to resolve all labour-management problems. From the cultural and historical point of view, the Canadian system of industrial relations is more like the American pattern than European models, but government influence and activity in recent years has begun to alter our course. We now stand in the middle of our *own unique dilemma*. The solution, if any, will emerge from an increased awareness of the *strengths* as well as the weaknesses of our own system rather than in emulating any other.

Notes

1. These figures are issued by Labour Canada; the data for 1978 are listed as "subject to revision."

2. Jamieson, S., *Industrial Relations in Canada*, Macmillan Company, Toronto, pp. 78-79.

3. Corporations and Labour Unions Returns Act, 1976, pp. 74-75. In Public Administration, 461,807 of an estimated 685,000 workers were union members. This represents 67.4% of those eligible, and does not include 148,000 members of the Public Alliance of Canada. This sector has the highest percentage of workers unionized and is second only to manufacturing in terms of absolute numbers, the latter sector having 834,844 union members in an estimated potential of 1,919,000 (45.5%).

4. Ibid. "In 1976, 32.2% of an estimated 8,631,000 wage and salaried workers in the major industry groups ... were members of labour organizations reporting under the Corporations and Labour Unions Returns Act."

5. The Public Service Staff Relations Act allows the Union a choice between two options (the right to strike or resort to binding arbitration) in the event that agreement cannot be reached through collective bargaining.

6. Anderson, V.C, and T.A. Kochan, "Collective Bargaining in the Public Service of Canada," *Relations Indutrielles/Industrial Relations* 32, 2, (1977), pp. 234-249.

7. Until fairly recently, work stoppages through the use of the strike have also been rejected as an option by some unions such as the Firefighters. Such principles are in the process of change; in Sweden, the government as *employer* has used the lockout against unions.

8. Walton, R., and R. McKersie, *A Behavioral Theory of Labor Negotiations*, Toronto, McGraw-Hill Book Co., 1965, p. 420.

9. Bill C-8, An Act to Amend the Canada Labour Code, 3rd Session, 30th Parliament, 26 Elizabeth II, 1977, The House of Commons of Canada.

10. "Carr Sees Need for More Labour Muscle," Peter Meerburg, *Halifax Mail-Star*, December 10th, 1977.

27/Through the Prism of the Strike: Industrial Conflict in Southern Ontario, 1901-14*

Craig Heron and Bryan Palmer

The trouble with the heads of many industries is that they become money mad and drunk with the power that money brings. They think that they can do anything and everything in a high-handed and ruthless manner just because they have a fat bank account and gilt-edged securities lying in some safety deposit vault.

When an employer gets that notion into his head he is almost shaking hands with disaster. It is a purely selfish idea and is mainly responsible for strikes.

It is the unbusiness-like attitude that produces unrest among the toilers. It is the tidal wave that will some day engulf the greedy, grasping and gloating galoots who think they can do as they like because they happen to be rich and powerful.

The worm always turns on men like that.[1]

This outburst from the *Bobcaygeon Independent* in 1913 reflected a marked upswing in industrial conflict which accompanied the massive economic expansion in early twentieth-century Ontario.[2] Its dramatic description of the responsibility of the moneyed class for the conflict conveys both the characteristic tone and the analytical weaknesses of the "people's press" of the period.[3] To go beyond such generalized condemnation and probe deeper into the contours and context of industrial strife, we have examined strike activity between 1901 and 1914 in ten southern Ontario cities that were emerging as major industrial centuries.[4] In Berlin [Kitchener], Brantford, Guelph, Hamilton, London, Niagara Falls, Oshawa, Peterborough, St. Catharines, and Toronto, the "toilers" and the "greedy, grasping, and gloating galoots" clashed frequently after the turn of the century. Through an examination of this conflict, in which the strike looms large, we can learn much about class relationships in these early years of a maturing central Canadian capitalism.

What emerges clearly from even the most superficial glance at strike activity in the years 1901-14 is the magnitude of the conflict between labour and capital. Stuart Marshall Jamieson's portrayal of the "relative placidity of labour relations" in Ontario during these years seems strangely misplaced:[5] the ten cities under discussion experienced the trauma of 421 strikes and lockouts in this fourteen-year period and approximately 60,000 working men and women participated in these battles.

---

* Abridged from Craig Heron and Bryan Palmer, "Through the Prism of the Strike: Industrial Conflict in Southern Ontario, 1901-14," *Canadian Historical Review* 58 (1977): 423-458. Reprinted with permission of the authors and the University of Toronto Press.

The pattern of this strike activity buttresses the classic contention that industrial unrest follows closely upon the heels of economic cycles of contraction and expansion. In the boom years prior to 1904 an unusually tight labour market brought about a sharp increase in the incidence of strikes. As years of economic retrenchment, 1904 and 1905 saw the pace of unrest slacken; a resurgence of strikes in 1906 and the early months of 1907 told of the return of more prosperous times. But with the economic downturn of 1908 strike activity came to a virtual standstill, and the severe depression year, 1908, witnessed the least number of conflicts in the entire period. Only in 1910 did the number of strikes begin to rise again significantly, reaching a peak in the early part of 1913. The prewar recession quickly stifled the growing conflict, however, and by 1914 strikes were once again quite uncommon. Strikes, then, were commonly resorted to in times of prosperity when concessions were more easily wrung from recalcitrant employers, and were more sparingly employed in years of recession, most prominently 1908 and 1913-14, when labour's chances of even the most marginal victories were slim indeed. . . .

Perhaps the fundamental feature of the context of industrial strife in southern Ontario between 1901 and 1914 was the accelerating pace of industrial capitalist development. After more than thirty years of economic expansion, the first decade and a half of the twentieth century saw the pace of industrialization quickened and pushed to new heights. Penelope Hartland has argued that the years 1900 to 1914 represented the most rapid growth in the Canadian economy since the decade preceding Confederation, and the 1911 census noted "the gratifying movement of the country's industrial prosperity during the last decade."[6] Finally, the period witnessed the acceleration of the process of concentration and consolidation of business enterprises initiated in the late 1880s. In his study of the Canadian "merger movement," H.G. Stapells documented fifty-six major consolidations in manufacturing industries in the years 1900-12.[7] As a result more and more southern Ontario workers found themselves working in large factories: in Hamilton, for example, 135 firms employed 18,695 of the city's 21,149 industrial workers in 1911.

While this economic development was undoubtedly a national phenomenon, southern Ontario seemed destined to play a leading role: the area offered easy importation of raw materials, especially the coal and iron vital to the development of heavy industry; efficient and lucrative marketing facilities and transportation networks were close at hand; skilled and unskilled labour was long established in the area; cheap hydro, particularly after the turn of the century, was easily obtainable; and local politicians eagerly enticed firms, notably branches of large American corporations, with lucrative bonuses and tax exemptions. Under these conditions southern Ontario cities attracted industry and capital with relative ease, and new factories mushroomed while older concerns expanded. . . .

The impact of the expansion of these years, of course, transcended the figures of aggregate growth and gross output compiled by statisticians and economists. As E.P. Thompson has stressed, "the transition to mature industrial society entailed a severe restructuring of working habits — new disciplines, new incentives, and a new human nature upon which these incentives could bite effectively . . ."[8] Two such disciplines and incentives, mechanization and new conceptions of managerial authority or industrial efficiency, were of particular relevance in capital's quest for "the reconstructing of work habits" and the creation of a new, more pliable, human nature. Although set in motion a century earlier in the first throes of the Industrial Revolution, this process was accelerating rapidly by the early twentieth century.

The disruptive impact of technology and mechanized production on the skilled crafts of the late nineteenth century in advanced capitalist countries is an often told tale, although the Canadian experience has only just begun to receive attention.[9] What has recently been stressed, however, is the other side of the historical coin: the degree to which skilled workers retained much of their craft status, pride, and economic security through a thorough organization and control of the productive process. Gregory S. Kealey has recently demonstrated the lasting power of iron molders and printers in the face of the mechanization of Toronto's skilled trades,[10] while David Montgomery's study of craft workers in the late nineteenth century in the United States regards skilled workers' control of the productive process as the touchstone of their self-conception of manhood: "Technical knowledge acquired on the job was embodied in a mutualistic ethical code, also acquired on the job, and together these attributes provided skilled workers with considerable autonomy at their work and powers of resistance to the wishes of their employers."[11] In many trades, as George Barnett early demonstrated in the case of the printers, mechanization had little disruptive impact, for craft unions were able to "keep tabs" on the new machines by forcing employers to hire only skilled journeymen to run them.[12] Craft workers, as Benson Soffer has argued, cultivated a rich and varied collection of shop floor control mechanisms throughout the course of the nineteenth century. Such devices, assuring skilled workers a degree of autonomy at the work place, exercised a tenuous hold over work relationships in many nineteenth-century trades.[13] Underpinning these mechanisms was a resilient consciousness of pride and self-confidence in their social worth that would carry these workers through many struggles.

Yet, even granting the significant degrees of control over the work processes exercised by many craftsmen to the end of the nineteenth century, by the early twentieth century technology had made real strides in diluting skill and transforming the workers' status on the shop floor. Complementing this propensity of modern machinery, moreover, was another development. Aware of the impediments that the autonomy of the skilled worker had raised against productivity and authority, employers turned to an array of managerial innovations and efficiency schemes after the turn of the century. Ranging from the employment of autocratic foremen, pledged to drive men and women harder and faster, to the utilization of complex systems of task simplification, job standardization, time and motion study, cost accountancy, and piece and bonus systems of wage payment, this amalgam of tactics became known as "scientific management." This pervasive thrust for efficiency, coupled with the impact of mechanization, constituted a concerted assault upon the control mechanisms and customs of the trade embedded within the consciousness and shop practices of the skilled worker.[14]

While the drive to rationalize and intensify the productive process through the agency of scientific management and industrial efficiency had its greatest impact in the United States, the movement's presence was felt to some degree in all industrial capitalist countries.[15] Canada, and particularly southern Ontario, did not escape this generalized experience despite the recent skepticism of Michael Bliss.[16] Much of the efficiency zeal undoubtedly became transferred to Canadian settings via the introduction of branch plants, while the increasing size of corporate holdings, accentuated after 1907 by the accelerating merger movement, lent a logic to the introduction of managers and shop-floor planners. In Hamilton, for instance, where by 1913 forty-five companies attested to US parentage — including such major employers as Canadian Westinghouse, International Harvester, and the Imperial Cotton Company — it is unlikely that managerial personnel were unaware of recent conceptions of techniques gaining such widespread currency south of the border.[17] Frank Jones, of the Steel Company of Canada, described as the best manager of men the young country had yet produced, must have been in direct contact with many of the managerial innovators.[18] But the case of Canadian manufacturers' adoption of the new "science of management" does not rest on inference alone. . . .

Southern Ontario craftsmen lost no time in pointing to the destructive impact of the twin processes of mechanization and modern management upon their callings: specialization, simplification, payment by the piece or on the bonus, the utter disregard of apprenticeship training, and the flooding of the labour market with unskilled, uniformed, "green hands" all contributed to the demise of their skill and the erosion of their craft pride. James Simpson, a prominent trade unionist long associated with Toronto Typographical Union No 91, wrote in 1907 of the "extension of the principle of the division of labour," in which Canadian workingmen were required to specialize ever more narrowly in one small aspect of production. The Royal Commission on Industrial Training and Technical Education, on which Simpson served, received numerous letters from disgruntled workers and stressed in its report the degradation of skilled workers occasioned by modern methods of production.[19] Testifying before an Ontario Commission on Unemployment in 1915 Thomas Findley, Vice-president of Massey-Harris, captured the plight of the modern mechanic when he characterized him as "not a man who understands every process, but a specialist in a single process." Findley's ironic conclusion was that the cure for this social problem lay in an ever larger dose of what must have been part of the cause: "The need is for more supervision than before."[20] Given these developments and sentiments, the strike became an early weapon employed by skilled workers to curb impingements upon their manhood inflicted by the machine or the autocratic manager, superintendent, or arbitrary foreman.

Most trades, of course, by this late date accepted mechanized production as inevitable and attempted to control its ill effects through staunch enforcement of union rules, the introduction of training programmes, petitions for the establishment of technical schools, and, above all else, the thorough organization of their craft. Some workers, however, reacted bitterly when employers sought to utilize machinery to displace skilled labour. Such was obviously the case at the International Harvester plant in Hamilton in 1904, when 125 machinists led a three-month struggle against efforts to mechanize their craft.[21] Similarly, thirty-two stone masons left their Toronto work-place for five days in October of 1905, protesting the introduction of a planing machine. Upon their return they found their places filled by other workers prompting a sympathetic strike of seventy-two of their brothers employed at six other stone-cutting firms.[22] And in February 1912 sixty-five cloakmakers struck the T. Eaton Company of Toronto, refusing to work on new machines installed by their employer. The dispute soon encompassed over 800 employees, but by mid-summer the company appeared victorious.[23] Strikes such as these tended to be the exception and not the rule. Often they ended in defeat and demoralization. More to the point, as the *Industrial Banner* pointed out, was the extent to which the threat of mechanization was utilized to intimidate the skilled worker. In a cigarmakers' strike in London in June 1910, involving 278 members of the trade, "the threat of . . . bringing in machines to replace hand work was brought forth once more to, if possible, intimidate the employees and prejudice the public." The *Banner* concluded that "This old chestnut has grown so stale that it is not even funny anymore."[24]

Hamilton, for instance, witnessed a number of conflicts that appeared to have had their roots in working-class dissatisfaction with various modes of "shop management." Late in 1902 several hundred female employees of the Eagle Knitting Mill objected to a new system of cutting and work classification. Leaving their benches, they claimed the innovations would result in a wage reduction of upwards of $2 a week. The dispute was ultimately "amicably adjusted," management claiming the cutters would soon be doing more work and collecting larger wages. Forty hands at the Chapman-Holton Knitting Mills struck in 1910 against a system of deductions levelled against spoiled work. And in May 1911 one hundred coatmakers at the Coppley, Noyes, and Randall Company successfully blocked the introduction of a piece-work system. Finally, in 1913, workers at the Canadian Westinghouse Company left the plant in an unsuccessful display of opposition to the introduction of time clocks. Like the machinists at the Watertown Arsenal in the United States, these electricians refused to be "put under the clock."[25]

Toronto, too, experienced similar struggles. In the summer of 1902 three hundred carpet weavers waged a protracted work stoppage over the introduction of a "clock system." Nine picture framers left work in 1904, protesting attempts to impose time sheets upon them; the next day they returned to work, the loathsome sheets withdrawn by their boss. From 17 May to 29 June 1905, in an apparently unsuccessful fight with the Canada Foundry Company, sixty-nine machinists opposed the introduction of both individual contracts and the premium system. And in December of the same year, at the Lowndes Company, two hundred garment workers refused to work under a "checking system," designed to keep closer accounts of work output, spoilage, and poor workmanship. The workers regarded such innovations as "a modified form of introducing the sweating system."[26]

But perhaps the most vivid example of the impact of efficiency-conscious managers upon work processes, and the working-class distaste for such developments, was the 1907 Bell Telephone strike, involving women operators. In 1903, in an attempt to undercut unnecessary and inefficient work techniques, the company installed new equipment, demanded the completion of routine tasks in drastically reduced time periods, and cut the hours of work from eight to five per day. Two shifts of women catered to the needs of an "overexacting public." For many the severe nervous tension, heightened by the company's absolute refusal to consider work breaks and the constant flashing of lights and clicking of receivers attendant upon the work, proved unbearable. Maud Orton, Minnie Hanun, Aria Strong, and Laura Rochall later testified that their employment at Toronto's Bell offices had brought about nervous breakdowns and frequent mental discomfort. Shocks from the switchboards were everyday occurrences and the women's seating apparatus, lacking back supports, produced constant irritation. Medical authorities were quick to condemn the unhealthy working conditions prevailing in the offices. Nor was this all that rendered the operatives' work oppressive. Lady supervisors paraded the aisles, making sure the working women violated no rules; talking was strictly forbidden; and a monitoring system, which management deemed essential, intensified the strain and tension seemingly inherent in the job.[27]

Yet from 1903 through 1906 the women at Bell Telephone endured their lot, albeit begrudgingly. Lacking the traditions and practices of control so embedded within the craft consciousness, existing outside the pale of trade unionism and only recently injected into modern work settings, these women had few benchmarks to guide them in their orientation towards an increasingly burdensome and exploitative job situation. If their dissatisfaction grew too great, they left, a frequent occurrence if we are to believe management's complaints of high turnovers in personnel; this process simply exacerbated the problem of inefficiency since trained staff did not always stay on the job long enough.[28] But the women's relatively passive acquiescence was not to last forever.

In March 1906 the company decided to assess the relative merits of the innovative five-hour day. Two studies were commissioned, one by James T. Baldwin and another by Hammond V. Hayes, both employees of the American Telephone and Telegraph Company. Completed late in 1906, the reports concurred in their findings. Through elaborate analyses of the speed and quality of service and minute calculations of the number of seconds allotted per call, as well as the number of calls handled in one hour, both agreed that the eight-hour system, then in effect in Montreal, surpassed Toronto's five-hour plan in the efficient and effective utilization of labour.[29]

From these conclusions the company proceeded quickly. Overly confident of the pliability of its work force, Bell acted as it had in the past, reintroducing the eight-hour day as it had all previous changes in technical and organizational operations: without warning the women at Bell were told that they should once again work eight-hour shifts. Aware of the intensity of work under the old system, and with no assurance that they would receive increased relief or lessened pressures, the employees rightly feared that their new work load would become even heavier. Like their employer, the Bell women acted promptly, striking in January 1907 and soon after joining the International Electrical Workers Union. Within the city the strike was widely reported and discussed, and a Royal Commission consisting of deputy minister of labour William Lyon Mackenzie King and Judge John Winchester conducted a thorough investigation of the issues involved. Although the delay created by the investigation diffused the momentum of the women's protest and ultimately led to defeat for them, the strike serves to remind us that it was not only the skilled who suffered the consequences of managerial drives to perfect human efficiency.[30]

Struggles such as these — built around fundamental changes in the way work was to be organized and carried out — must be seen as efforts by the working class, especially the more skilled sectors, to secure or retain control over their job settings. Although tabulating precise statistics on the issues in dispute in prewar strikes is extremely difficult owing to the sketchiness of much of the Department of Labour's reporting and although the analysis is further clouded by those strikes involving two or more clearly discernible issues, we have concluded that probably more than two hundred strikes involved conflict over some aspect of control of the workplace. It should be made clear, however, that the control we are referring to in this period bore little resemblance to the demands posed in later years by the more consciously revolutionary British shop stewards' movement, or the Western Canadian miners of the One Big Union.[31] These groups went far beyond the limited conception of control embedded within many prewar strikes, demanding workers' control of entire industries on a national basis.

Carter Goodrich long ago distinguished three types of control: restrictive control, shop control, and the more politically conceived control of an entire industry.[32] Restrictive control was widespread among skilled trades in the late nineteenth and early twentieth century, the most common examples of its presence being the limitation of output[33] and the demand for a ceiling on the number of apprentices allowed to enter a trade. It was seen as the bulwark of the wage differential that stood as the badge of craft status and price, separating the skilled from the unskilled. Shop control, also prevalent during the same period, was a somewhat more complex phenomenon, institutionalized in union rules, regulations, and standards: shop committees, controlling hiring and firing, pricing of products, and the hours worked by members of the union were the backbone of this form of control. Some trades, most notably glass-workers, carried this form of control to the point of dictating when production would commence and when it would cease: from July until September every glass factory in North America closed its doors and the workers took their customary summer holiday.[34] The demands for industrial control of entire realms of the economy, raised in the war and postwar years, were an entirely different phenomenon, belonging to the epoch of the twentieth century, where concerns were often moulded by events like the Russian Revolution.[35] Both restrictive and shop control, then, were rooted in the nineteenth-century experience of skilled workers; they thrived as trade customs and were most potent on a localized level. Both were shaken by mechanization but, as we have argued, adapted and revitalized themselves in many crafts. With the introduction of twentieth-century innovative managerial systems geared to rationalize and intensify work processes, however, these forms of control came under severe attack. That is what concerns us in the years 1901-14. . . .

Not all conflicts centred directly on the issues of control of the workplace. Of the 421 strikes and lockouts examined, 212 involved the question of higher wages, and twenty-eight more were the consequence of resistance to wage reductions. Behind this activity undoubtedly lay, in large part, the widely discussed issue of the soaring cost of living in the two prewar decades. In an 1100-page statistical survey of this problem in the period under study, Robert Coats of the federal department of Labour revealed increases in prices of food, fuel, and lighting in southern Ontario cities of 43 to 58 per cent and in rents of 35 to 90 per cent. Wages, he concluded, seldom kept pace.[36] Small wonder, then, that so many workers were prepared to strike over conditions that were eroding their real wages.

Yet it is these struggles which are the most difficult to classify, for as Knowles has argued, wage strikes "tend to be symbolic of wider grievances"; to view them as simply conflicts over the size of a pay packet would be overly reductionist. Certainly disputes which pitted a working-class notion of "a fair wage" against the employer's criteria of efficiency and productivity epitomized fundamentally opposed views of labour in the productive process. Moreover, many of these strikes for higher wages also involved issues that fell more clearly within the sphere of control struggles. And in the case of those conflicts arising out of efforts to impose wage cuts it is clear that many unionists saw such struggles as a defence of their unions, for employers were not above using wage reductions to destroy entrenched craft organizations. Then, too, we have no way of knowing how many workers, conscious of the loss of autonomy occasioned by the drift of modern industry, sought recompense in a higher wage. Nevertheless, it can not be denied that in the context of rampant inflation and declining real wages which, to many workers, became the encompassing reality of everyday life in the modern world, strikes over wage issues were an important feature of industrial unrest in the years 1901-14.[37]. . .

Canadian employers quickly learned important lessons in anti-union practices from their American confrères; strikebreaking in the years 1901-14 became something of an art, involving intricate infiltrations of plants and factories by spies, detectives, and "spotters," as well as massive influxes of often notorious "blacklegs."[38] In a strike at the Canada Foundry Company in Toronto in 1903, a local officer of the moulders' union reported that the company was employing twenty-four to twenty-eight roving professional strikebreakers supplied by the National Founders' Association at $1.50 a day over and above regular moulder's wages; these men had been sent from Duluth and were encamped on company property.[39] The National Metal Trades Association also advised members in the handling of industrial disputes, furnished men and money to break strikes and troublesome unions, and operated an immense labour bureau where the records of hundreds of thousands of men were kept, allowing employers to determine the potential loyalty of prospective employees.[40] Moreover, the resources and expertise of America businessmen often proved quite useful, as in February 1903 when a prominent figure in the American Open-shop drive, John Kirby of Dayton, Ohio, visited Toronto to help employers launch their anti-union offensive.[41]. . .

The stick, however, was not the only means employed by capital to stifle opposition and siphon working-class discontent. A more subtle tactic slowly developed and involved pre-empting the humanitarian appeal of the labour movement by offering employees numerous social amenities associated with the health, safety, recreational, and security requirements of working people. In an article entitled "How About Your Factory," *Industrial Canada* argued that "pleasant surroundings are conducive to the economic production of good work, while at the same time they attract a better class of working people."[42] At the Berlin firm of Williams, Greene and Rome, manufacturers of shirts, collars, and cuffs, the "Right Idea," featuring employee dining-rooms, women's rest-rooms, a relief fund, athletic and benefit associations, a complaint department, and dramatic and literary societies, gained province-wide acclaim. The Frost Wire Fence Company, about to locate in Hamilton's East End in 1904, claimed that in its construction plans, "Space has been set apart for a recreation room, which will be fitted up with pool tables and will be nicely furnished. Current literature will be kept on file for those of a more serious turn of mind. Some vacant property adjoining has been acquired, which will be turned into grounds for out-of-door sports, and the company will encourage their employees to enter a team in local hockey, football and baseball leagues."[43]

Behind provisions like these the *Labour Gazette* perceived a conscious purpose: "The officials of the company anticipate that they will get a return for their expenditure in better service from the man."[44] *Industrial Canada* was even more blunt, arguing in a 1912 article, "Homes for Workmen," that, "Workmen who have comfortable homes are more efficient, contented and reliable than those who have not . . . Out of the slums stalks the Socialist with his red flag, the Union agitator with the auctioneer's voice, and the Anarchist with his torch."[45] To men like the efficiency-conscious H.L.C. Hall, efforts to alleviate the drudgery of modern work settings made good business sense, and he chastized Canadian manufacturers: "You will spend money everytime to increase the efficiency of your machinery. Then why not spend a little time and effort to increase the efficiency of your human machines? It will pay and pay handsomely. It is in some localities quite the fashion to beautify factory buildings and grounds. Civic pride you say. Not a bit of it. Certain wise ones have discovered that it pays to spend a little something on the comfort of the worker. It is a cold business proposition. You get more out of them."[46]

Employer-sponsored welfare schemes for industrial workers were as old as the Industrial Revolution itself, but in the prewar years a new, more sophisticated form of welfare capitalism was emerging throughout southern Ontario.[47] It is crucial to see the development of paternal modes of management as part of a continuum embracing force as well as manipulative coercion. In January 1904 the *Toiler* commented on welfare programmes in an article appropriately entitled "The Wrong Idea": "It can safely be said that the majority of them are designed to protect the firm in a systematic way by keeping the deluded employees under their special care so that they can be more easily robbed of what is their just dues as a return for their labour. These schemes are designed to keep out the trade union or if it is already in to bring about its destruction."[48] Yet we should not be surprised that skilled workers continued to resist the encroachments of industrial capitalism, for their adaptation to the new disciplines of the factory had always been uneven and far from complete.[49] And when startlingly new developments were thrust upon them — such as the innovative techniques of an efficiency-conscious management, or the militantly collectivist response of Canadian manufacturers to craft unionism — skilled workers naturally took refuge in the control mechanisms of the past. It is in this context that we have come to regard control as a vital issue in these years, linking the nineteenth and early twentieth century experience of skilled workingmen.

While the episodic quality of strikes poses problems for wide-ranging generalization, our examination of the contours and context of industrial conflict in the years 1901-14 suggests some conclusions. Skilled workers continued to use the strike to maintain shop-floor control rooted in nineteenth-century work practices, as well as to combat twentieth-century developments in work-shop organization and managerial innovation. At the same time their employers launched a concerted offensive against the institution that harboured and perpetuated much of the craftsman's autonomy, the trade union. By 1914 there was no definite resolution of the conflict between these forces. The cyclical depressions that began in 1908 and

1913 weakened organized labour as an adversary, but each time strikes resumed with the first signs of the return of prosperity. A tight labour market during the war restored strength lost in the prewar slump, and many scenes of the pre-1914 conflict were repeated in the next five or six years, with perhaps even greater intensity.[50]

From this perspective it would seem that the strike was *not* simply a battle over the division of the economic pie. Like Edward Shorter and Charles Tilly, whose massive compilation of data on strikes in France also stresses the role of craftsmen in pre-World War I industrial conflict, we have come to regard the strike as an implicitly political event, a clash over the distribution of power on the shop or factory floor flowing directly from the desire and ability of working people to act collectively.[51] In the same vein, the evidence presented here indicates that the analysis of American historians James Weinstein and Ronald Radosh, stressing "corporate liberalism" as the foundation of a labour-capital alliance, has little relevance for Canada in this period.[52] Like David Bercuson, in his study of the roots of the Winnipeg General Strike, we find the prewar years an age of industrial violence.[53] To end, appropriately, where we began, we must note that if the *Bobcaygeon Independent's* assessment of the causes of strikes lacked sophistication and subtlety, it nevertheless captured one prophetic truth: the worm, in these years 1901-14, had indeed turned.

Notes

1. *Bobcaygeon Independent,* 16 May 1913, 2, from an article "One of the Causes of Strikes," reprinted from *The Windsor Record.*

2. Statistical data on nineteenth-century strikes does not exist. Comparisons between the nineteenth- and early twentiety-century experiences are therefore difficult, and generalization demands caution. Yet it would seem, on the basis of local research currently in progress, that the years 1901-14 saw workers resort to the strike and employers turn to the lockout more often than in preceding years. Bryan Palmer's dissertation research on skilled workers in Hamilton in the years 1860-1914, as well as his previous study of the emergence of a labour movement in London, Ontario, in the years 1867-1914 ["'Give us the road and we will run it': The Social and Cultural Matrix of an Emerging Labour Movement," in Gregory S. Kealey and Peter Warrian, eds., *Essays in Canadian Working Class History* (Toronto 1976), 106-24], suggests this. Kealey's forthcoming dissertation on the Victorian working class in Toronto makes it very clear that the strike was frequently resorted to in the years 1860-92, but it was not as common as it was in this later period, when Toronto experienced 198 such industrial conflicts.

3. On the "people's press" see the viewpoints in Russell Hann, "Brainworkers and the Knights of Labor: E.E. Sheppard, Phillips Thompson, and the Toronto *News,*" in *Essays in Canadian Working Class History,* 35-57; P.F.W. Rutherford, "The People's Press: The Emergence of the New Journalism in Canada, 1869-1899," *Canadian Historical Review,* LVI, 1975, 169-91.

4. The basic source for much of what follows was the *Labour Gazette.* Because this publication provides only an introduction to the many strikes and lockouts of the period, and an often inadequate one at that, we have also turned to numerous local labour newspapers, the regional *Industrial Banner,* and the standard sources on Canadian trade union history and strike activity: Charles Lipton, *The Trade Union Movement of Canada, 1827-1959* (Montreal 1968), 98-161; H.A. Logan, *Trade Unions in Can-*

ada (Toronto 1948); Stuart Marshall Jamieson, *Times of Trouble: Labour Unrest and Industrial Conflict in Canada, 1900-1966* (Ottawa 1968), 62-157. Finally, because strikes involving national or provincial transportation networks often involved cities outside of the regional concerns of this study, we did not include them in our quantitative analysis of the contours of strike activity. Where such strikes illuminated issues of particular relevance, however, we have included them in our impressionistic discussion of the context of industrial conflict.

5. Jamieson, *Times of Trouble*, p. 85.

6. Penelope Hartland, "Factors in the Economic Growth of Canada," *Journal of Economic History*, xv, 1955, 13; Census of Canada, 1911, III (Ottawa 1913), v. Cf, Gordon D. Bertram, "Historical Statistics on Growth and Structure in Manufacturing in Canada, 1867-1957," in J. Henripin and A. Asimakopulas, eds., Canadian Political Science Association Conference on Statistics, 1962-3, *Papers* (Toronto 1964), 93-146; O.J. Firestone, *Canada's Economic Development*, 1863-1957 (London 1958), 209-10; Jacob Spelt, *Urban Development in South-Central Ontario* (Toronto 1972), 150-86.

7. H.G. Stapells, "The Recent Consolidation Movement in Canadian Industry" (unpublished MA Thesis, University of Toronto, 1922).

8. E.P. Thompson, "Time, Work Discipline and Industrial Capitalism," *Past & Present*, XXXVIII, 1967, 57. Cf Herbert Gutman, "Work, Culture and Society in Industrializing America, 1815-1919," *American Historical Review*, LXXVIII, 1973, 531-88; Sidney Pollard, "Factory Discipline in the Industrial Revolution," *Economic History Review*, XVI, 1963, 254-71.

9. See Gregory S. Kealey, "Artisans Respond to Industrialism: Shoemakers, Shoe Factories, and the Knights of St. Crispin in Toronto," Canadian Historical Association, *Papers*, 1973,137-58; David Brody, *Steelworkers in America: The Non-Union Era* (Cambridge 1960), 27-79; Robert Ozanne, *A Century of Labor Management Relations at McCormick and International Harvester* (Madison 1967); George E. Barnett, *Chapters on Machinery and Labor* (Carbondale 1969); Robert A. Christie, *Empire in Wood: A History of the Carpenters' Union* (Ithaca 1956), 80-2; Gregory S. Kealey, ed., *Canada Investigates Industrialism: The Royal Commission on the Relations of Labor and Capital*, 1889 (Toronto 1973).

10. Gregory S. Kealey, " 'The Honest Workingman and Workers' Control: the Experience of Toronto Skilled Workers, 1860-1892," *Labour/Le Travailleur*,1, 1976, 32-68. For a discussion of the experience of skilled workers in Halifax see Ian McKay, "The Working Class of Metropolitan Halifax, 1850-1889" (honours thesis, Dalhousie University, 1975), 53-67.

11. David Montgomery, "Workers' Control of Machine Production in the Nineteenth Century," *Labor History*, XVII, 1976, 485-509.

12. Barnett, *Chapters on Machinery and Labor*, 3-29; Barnett, "The Printers: A Study in American Trade Unionism," *American Economic Association Quarterly*, X (Cambridge 1909), 182-208. Cf. Wayne Roberts, "The Last Artisans: Toronto Printers, 1896-1914," in Kealey and Warrian, eds., *Essays in Canadian Working Class History* (Toronto 1976), 125-42.

13. Benson Soffer, "A Theory of Trade Union Development: The Role of the 'Autonomous Workman'," *Labor History*,1, 1960, 141-63.

14. This paragraph draws on material in Bryan Palmer, "Class, Conception and Conflict: The Thrust for Efficiency, Managerial Views of Labor and Working Class Rebellion, 1903-1922" *Review of Radical Political Economy*, VII, 1975, 31-49; David Montgomery, "The 'New Unionism' and the Transformation in Workers' Consciousness, 1909-1922," *Journal of Social History*, VII, 1974, 509-29.

15. See, for instance, Stearns, *Lives of Labour*, 193-228, for developments in France, Belgium, Germany, and England. On "Taylorist" practices in the French auto industry see Alain Touraine, *L'Evolution du travail ouvrier aux usines Renault* (Paris 1955), 25, 48-53, 107, 115, 156-7; James Laux, "Travail et

Travailleurs dans l'industrie-automobile jusqu'en 1914," *Mouvement Social*, 1972, 9-26. An interesting discussion of the rise of supervisory personnel in the Ruhr is Elaine Glovca Spencer, "Between Capital and Labor: Supervisory Personnel in Ruhr Heavy Industry Before 1914," *Journal of Social History*, IX, 1975, 178-92.

16. Michael Bliss, in an important treatment of the Canadian businessman, has argued that there were few Canadian organization men or managerial specialists prior to 1920. Bliss, *A Living Profit: Studies in the Social History of Canadian Business, 1883-1911*, (Toronto 1974), 11. While our findings, regionally based and preliminary in nature, do not demolish Bliss's argument, they do point to the need for more research in this area.

17. On the rise of the branch-plant in southern Ontario in these years see *Labour Gazette* (Ottawa), III, 1902-3, 138; IV, 1903-4, 1207; *Hamilton, Canada, Its History, Commerce, Industries and Resources* (Hamilton 1913); Herbert Marshall, Frank A. Southard, Jr, and Kenneth W. Taylor, *Canadian-American Industry* (New Haven 1936). For the most recent discussion of the changes in the American management techniques, see Daniel Nelson, *Managers and Workers: Origins of the New Factory System in the United States, 1880-1920* (Madison 1975), 55-78.

18. William Kilbourn, *The Elements Combined: A History of the Steel Company of Canada* (Toronto 1960), 72, 75.

19. Toronto District Labour Council, *Labour Day Souvenir, 1907* (Toronto 1907); Commission on Industrial Training and Technical Education, *Report*, I, 63; II, 173; IV, 2125.

20. Ontario, Commission on Unemployment, *Report of the Commissioners* (Toronto 1916), 227.

21. Canada, Department of Labour, *Report on Strikes and Lockouts*, 1901-1912 (Ottawa 1913), 189.

22. *Labour Gazette*, 1905-6, 673.

23. *Labour Gazette*, XII, 1911-12, 857; *Labour News* (Hamilton), 15 March 1912, I; 22 March 1912, I; 5 April 1912, I; 3 May 1912, 2.

24. *Industrial Banner*, June 1910, 2, 4.

25. *Labour Gazette*, III, 1902-3, 479, 566; X, 1909-10, 1441; XIII, 1912-13, 1000; *Report on Strikes and Lockouts*, 1901-12, 224; Hugh G.J. Aitken, *Taylorism at Watertown Arsenal* (Cambridge 1960), 15.

26. *Report on Strikes and Lockouts*, 1901-1912, 180, 189, 193; *Labour Gazette*, VI, 1905-6, 802.

27. See *Industrial Banner*, May 1903, 2; Royal Commission on a Dispute Respecting Hours of Employment between the Bell Telephone Company of Canada and Operators at Toronto, Ontario, *Report* (Ottawa 1907) 7, 13, 55-60, 98. It is deserving of comparison with Elinor Langer, "Inside the New York Telephone Company," *New York Review of Books*, XIV, 12 March 1970.

28. Royal Commission on Bell Dispute, *Report*, 13.

29. *Ibid.*, 5-7.

30. Cf accounts on the strike in *Labour Gazette*, VII, 1906-7, 922; Alice Klein and Wayne Roberts, "Beseiged Innocence: The 'Problem' and the Problems of Working Women — Toronto, 1896-1914," in *Women at Work: Ontario*, 1850-1930 (Toronto 1974), 244-51; R. MacGregor Dawson, *William Lyon Mackenzie King: A Political Biography*, I: *1874-1923* (Toronto 1958), 144-6.

31. On the British shop stewards' movement see James Hinton, *The First Shop Stewards' Movement* (London 1973); Branko Privicevic, *The Shop Stewards' Movement and Workers' Control* (Oxford 1959); Arthur Gleason, "The Shop Stewards and their Significance," *Survey*, XLI 4 Jan. 1919, 417-22. On the Revolutionary ideology of western Canadian miners in 1919 see Peter Warrian, "The Challenge of the One Big Union Movement in Canada, 1919-1921" (unpublished MA thesis, University of Waterloo, 1971), 52-60.

32. Carter L. Goodrich, "Problems of Workers' Control," *Locomotive Engineers' Journal*, LVII, 1923, 365-6, 415. Cf Goodrich, *The Frontier of Control: A Study of British Workshop Practices* (New York 1920).

33. The most exhaustive treatment of this phenomenon remains Carrol D. Wright, et al, Eleventh Special Report of the Commissioner of Labour, *Regulation and Restriction of Output* (Washington 1904). Restriction of output was extensive in southern Ontario in the late nineteenth century and retained much of its force in the years 1901-14. See Public Archives of Canada [PAC], M.A. Pigott (a Hamilton contractor) to Adam Brown, Esq., MP, 8 May 1888, MacDonald Papers, volume 155, 63160-4; PAC, Department of Labour, Strikes and Lockouts Records, RG 27, volume 296, Strike no 3124, on Hamilton molders and restriction of output.

34. Montgomery, "Workers' Control of Machine Production"; "What One Trade has Done," *John Swinton's Paper*, 23 March 1884, 1; *Report of the Royal Commission on the Relations of Labor and Capital in Canada* (Ottawa 1889), VI, 371-3.

35. While distinguishing between nineteenth-century variants of control and those of the twentieth century, we should not lose sight of the fact that the experience of restrictive and shop control may well have facilitated the rise of the demand for the more revolutionary workers' control of the later period. A shop steward told Carter Goodrich: "People talk as if the demand for control was something that had to be created among the workers by a slow process, but it's there already!" Goodrich, *The Frontier of Control*, 31. Cf Montgomery, "The 'New Unionism,'" 509-29.

36. On the inflationary surge of these years in southern Ontario see Canada, Department of Labour, Board of Inquiry into the Cost of Living, *Report* (Ottawa 1915), II,3, 76, 80, 381; *Labour Gazette*, III, 1902-3, 308; V, 1904-5, 308, 437, 556, 689; VI, 1905-6, 388; VII, 1906-7, 689, 1082; XVIII, 1907-8, 271; X, 1909-10, 864; XI, 1910-11, 49, 53; XIV, 1913-14, 770; *Industrial Banner*, Feb. 1912, 4.

37. Knowles, Strikes, 219. For further discussion of the wider significance of wage strikes see Montgomery, "Workers' Control of Machine Production," 496-7; and Jon Amsden and Stephen Briar, "Coal Miners on Strike: The Transformation of Strike Demands and the Formation of the National Union in the U.S. Coal Industry, 1881-1884," forthcoming in *The Journal of Interdisciplinary History*.

38. On the proliferation of these practices see *The Toiler*, 9 April 1903,3; *Industrial Banner*, Dec. 1903, 3; Jan. 1904, 1; Oct, 1905, 1; May 1906, 2; Sept. 1906,1; May 1908, 1; Aug. 1908, 1; July 1911, 1.

39. *The Toiler*, 10 July 1903, 1.

40. Bonnett, *Employers' Associations*, 109, 117-18.

41. On Kirby's visit and the working-class response to it see *The Toiler*, 6 Feb. 1903, 3; 15 May 1903, 1; *Industrial Banner*, Feb. 1903, 1; May 1903, 1.

42. *Industrial Canada*, 2 June 1902, 354. Cf *Industrial Canada*, April 1901, 205; March 1909, 664.

43. Canada, Department of Labour, *Annual Report*, 1907-1908 (Ottawa 1908), 26; *Industrial Canada*, Dec. 1904, 327.

44. *Labour Gazette*, V, 1904-5, 466.

45. *Industrial Canada*, May 1912, 1064.

46. Ibid., Sept. 1906, 105.

47. See the accounts of various welfare schemes in *Labour Gazette*, V, 1904-5, 136; IX, 1908-9, 744; XI, 1910-11, 1056, 1352; III, 1902-3, 83; XIV, 1913-14, 757. For the best recent summary of the growth of these schemes in the United States, see Nelson, *Managers and Workers*, 101-21.

48. *The Toiler*, 22 Jan. 1904, 1. For an analysis of the management thinking behind welfare capitalism at International Harvester (whose Hamilton plant was one of the city's largest) see Robert Ozanne, *A Century of Labour-Management Relations at McCormick and International Harvester* (Madison 1967),

71-95. See also Daniel Nelson, "The New Factory System and the Unions," *Labour History*, XV, 1974, 163-78. This evaluation of the implementation of welfare schemes at the National Cash Register Company, Dayton, Ohio, buttresses contemporary assessment of corporate motivations.

49. See Gutman, "Work, Culture, and Society," 531-88; Thompson, "Time, Work-Discipline, and Industrial Capitalism," 56-97; Frank Thistlethwaite, "Atlantic Migration of the Pottery Industry," *Economic History Review*, X, 1957-8, 264-73; Sidney Pollard, *The Genesis of Modern Management* (Cambridge 1965), 160-200; Stearns, *Lives of Labour*, 342-3; Stearns, "Adaptation to Industrialization: German Workers as a Test Case," *Central European History*, IV, 1970, 303-31.

50. For example, a massive strike of 1500-2000 machinists in Hamilton's munitions plants in 1916. PAC, RG 27, vol. 304, Strike no 27A.

51. Shorter and Tilly, *Strikes in France*. Cf Charles Tilly, Louise Tilly, Richard Tilly, *The Rebellious Century, 1830-1930* (Cambridge 1975); and a brilliant local study, Peter Friedlander, *The Emergence of U.A.W. Local 229, Hamtrack, Michigan: A Study in Class and Culture* (Pittsburgh 1975). Our conclusions, then, stand counterposed to those of Peter Stearns, who regards the main impetus behind strikes as the struggle for economic gain, realized in higher wages. See Stearns, *Revolutionary Syndicalism and French Labor: A Cause without Rebels* (New Brunswick 1971).

52. James Weinstein, *The Corporate Ideal in the Liberal State, 1900-1918* (Boston 1968); Ronald Radosh, "The Corporate Ideology of American Labor Leaders from Gompers to Hillman," *Studies on the Left*, VI, 1966, 66-88. A recent attempt to apply portions of the above agreement to the Canadian case is Michael J. Piva, "The Workmen's Compensation Movement in Ontario," *Ontario History*, LXVII, 1975, 39-56.

53. David Bercuson, *Confrontation at Winnipeg: Labour, Industrial Relations, and the General Strike* (Montreal 1974), 1-31.

28/The Winnipeg General Strike[*]

Stuart Marshall Jamieson

The mounting labour unrest of the late war and immediate post-war years reached a dramatic climax in the Winnipeg General Strike during May and June, 1919.[1] This event had a strong, indeed almost a traumatic effect upon labour relations in the western provinces, and upon Canada's political life generally, for decades to come. As Kenneth McNaught wrote:

... the Winnipeg strike was a most significant occurrence in Canadian history, if for no other reason than that it was the first and only time in Canadian history that a majority was split clearly into two opposing classes.[2]

---

[*] Abridged from Stuart Marshall Jamieson, *Times of Trouble: Labour Unrest and Industrial Conflict in Canada, 1900-66*. Task Force on Labour Relations Study No. 22 (Ottawa: Information Canada, 1971), pp. 170-180. Reproduced by permission of the Minister of Supply and Services Canada and the author.

. . . . It appears more than likely that the course of the Winnipeg general strike, and the attitudes and actions of organized labour, employers and governments, were strongly influenced by the general climate of 1919. . . . This seems particularly likely in view of the radical orientation of the British Columbia labour movement, the brief general strike in Vancouver in 1918, and the leading role that the British Columbia Federation of Labour had played in the Western Labour Conference and in the formation of the One Big Union. . . .

As the history of industrial relations in Canada prior to the war brings out, employers in this country were for the most part strongly opposed to recognizing and dealing with unions. Where their position was seriously challenged, they were quick to call upon governments to provide police or military protection. There seems good grounds for suspecting, therefore, that much of the apparently hysterical behaviour of various employer groups in the immediate post-war era represented a calculated assault upon unionism as such, rather than any real fear of radicalism or revolution. Other elements in the Canadian community, with their particularly strong aversion to or fear of overt conflict in any form, seemed similarly quick to sanction the use of force to suppress such threats. World War I heightened such tendencies, as evidenced by the special orders-in-council that had been passed to curb or suppress organizations and publications that were deemed to be "dangerous" or "subversive." These regulations remained in effect long after the war.

In the light of these strongly conflicting forces and groups, and their divergent interpretations of events, it becomes extremely difficult to present an impartial and valid explanation of cause underlying the general strike in Winnipeg in 1919, or a reasonably accurate account of the main events that ensued. As Kenneth McNaught summarizes the picture, one view of the situation originated with the "Citizens' Committee of One Thousand." This was a semi-vigilante anti-union organization, on a familiar United States model, that was formed during the strike by a group of prominent business and professional men in the city. The view espoused by this group was accepted by the main governments involved, as well as by such publications as the *Canadian Annual Review* and the *Cambridge History of the British Empire*. It interpreted the strike largely as a conspiracy to establish a Canadian-style soviet government which would "spread forth its power from the banks of the Red River."[3]

An opposing interpretation was expressed in a newspaper published by the strikers during the conflict and by the strikers' defence committee which was set up to combat the government indictments that followed. According to this view, the Winnipeg General Strike, like other major disputes during and immediately after the war, had no basic aims other than improvements in wages, working conditions and labour's bargaining position. The high cost of living, the threat of postwar unemployment, and the hostile attitudes of major employer groups towards unionism and collective bargaining were the main issues provoking the strike.[4] This view found support in the findings of the Robson Commission of July 1, 1919, which had been appointed by the Manitoba government to investigate the cause of the strike.[5] It was also supported by General Ketchen, commanding officer of the armed forces in the Winnipeg area at the time.[6]. . .

The origins of the general strike in Winnipeg were apparently unconnected with the debates and resolutions of the Western Labour Conference in Calgary, such evidence suggests. The strike began with a walkout of workers in the building and metal trades in the city over demands for wage increases, and in protest against the refusal of employers to recognize and negotiate with the Metal Trades Council as a "bargaining unit" for its affiliated unions. The Building and Metal Trades Council then took their case to the Winnipeg Trades and Labour Council. This body ordered a vote among all of its affiliates on the question of a general strike, primarily to secure the principle of union security, and secondly, to achieve general wage increases to meet the soaring cost of living.

The result of the vote was an overwhelming majority in favour of a general strike. On May 15, 1919, approximately 30,000 workers left their jobs, including, significantly, about 12,000 who were not members of unions.[7] Official interpretations of the event sought to prove that the general strike was the beginning of a grand conspiracy of the Calgary Conference and the One Big Union. D.C. Masters, in his authoritative history, however, shows that one man, D.B. Russell, was the sole direct link between the Conference and the Winnipeg Council's Strike Committee.[8]

. . . (A)t the outset were established the two organizations which were to give the strike the aspect of a class conflict: the Central Strike Committee, elected by the General Strike Committee, composed of delegates from each of the unions affiliated with the Winnipeg Trades and Labour Council; and the Citizens Committee, an *ad hoc* group of prominent business and professional leaders, complete with an armed "home guard" to help maintain "law and order."

The Central Strike Committee took official steps to maintain the flow of essential goods and services as the strikers included public servants such as policemen, firemen, postal workers and the employees of waterworks and other utilities, as well as the employees of private enterprises. As had been the case in Seattle, strikers were counselled to stay at home and avoid congregations in the streets that risked conflict with anti-union elements or with military forces.

The Citizens Committee, with the full support of the leading newspapers, the *Free Press* and the *Tribune*, characterized the strike as a revolutionary conspiracy, the work of a small group of red subversives and "alien scum," and thus justifying military intervention and suppression.[9] Indeed, their activities could be construed as a deliberate effort to provoke an outbreak of violence that would justify intervention by the growing reserves of Mounted Police and militia as the strike dragged on.

Efforts to enlist the support of returned veterans to break the strike, the sort of move that was successful in most analogous cases in the United States at that time, failed. The day the strike started a meeting of returned soldiers was called by the executives of the Great War Veterans' Association, the Army and Navy Veterans' Association and the Imperial Veterans of Canada. The purpose of the executives of these organizations was to obtain passage of a resolution condemning the general strike. However, the executive resolution was defeated and another, strongly in favour of the strike, was passed.[10]

Various attempts to conciliate the dispute were blocked by the refusal of most employers in Winnipeg to recognize basic principles of collective bargaining. As McNaught puts it: "The familiar employers' insistence broke all mediation efforts: 'give up the strike, then bargain on our terms.'"[11] Meanwhile the strike was winning sympathetic support across the country, in the form of minor "general strikes" extending from Prince Rupert, British Columbia to Sydney, Nova Scotia. Labour leaders in Winnipeg and some other western cities were beginning to call for a federal strike committee.[12]

These threats brought federal government intervention squarely on the side of employers and of the Citizens' Committee. This finally led to the strike's collapse. Senator Gideon Robertson, Minister of Labour, and Honourable Arthur Meighen, Minister of the Interior and Acting Minister of Justice, arrived on the scene. They confined their conferences to members of the Citizens' Committee and to leaders of the provincial and municipal governments. This demonstration of partisanship brought strong criticism from spokesmen of the official opposition in the House of Commons.[13]

Senator Robertson's first action, on May 25, was to issue an ultimatum to the postal employees to the effect that unless they returned to work and severed relations with the Winnipeg Trades and Labour Council they would lose their pension rights and be barred from future employment in the federal service. Similar measures were taken by provincial and municipal government leaders against public service employees under their jurisdictions.[14]

From then on the forces of government at all levels moved in to defeat the strike, after provoking an increasing level of violence and taking severely repressive measures. On June 6, although there had been no serious violence, the Mayor of Winnipeg banned all parades and forbade the congregation of crowds.[15] The same day Parliament quickly passed an amendment to the *Immigration Act* which extended to British subjects provisions concerning deportation by executive order.[16] On June 9 the Winnipeg Police Commission dismissed the entire police force, save a few top officers and two constables, ostensibly on the grounds that they had refused to sign a "yellow dog contract" agreeing to disaffiliate from the Trades and Labour Council and refuse to participate in sympathetic strikes. Special constables were enrolled to replace them. Their inexperience led to disturbances in which one of their members was injured.[17]

In the early hours of June 17 the Royal North West Mounted Police

(RNWMP) raided various homes in Winnipeg and arrested ten strike leaders. Books, records and "seditious documents" discovered in their homes, and the Labour Temple of the Trades and Labour Council, were seized and kept as evidence at their trials. Newspapers announced that the British-born among the arrested were to be deported without trial, under the newly-amended *Immigration Act*.[18] Execution of the government's policy had been handed over to A.J. Andrews of the Citizens' Committee, who was now, as legal agent of the federal Minister of Justice, in charge of prosecutions of the arrested men.

These developments rapidly built up tension in Winnipeg to a violent climax. McNaught describes it as follows:

June 21 was the "Bloody Saturday" which the Citizens' Committee had been predicting. It was occasioned by an illegal parade of returned soldiers organized as a result of Senator Robertson's alleged conspiracy with the leaders of the Citizens' Committee. The returned soldier supporters of the strike called a parade to form up near the city hall in order to march to the Royal Alexandra Hotel where Senator Robertson was ensconced. Their purpose was to request, through this mass demonstration, an account of the minister's plans with regard to the strike and of his actions since arriving in Winnipeg. [They] were no doubt spurred on by the fear of further governmental action to follow the arrests of June 17. The city was alive with Mounted Police, and all were aware that General Ketchen had alerted the militia units, and that a large number of machine guns had been shipped into Winnipeg.

But the parade was illegal since the mayor had earlier promulgated his order banning such demonstrations. The leaders maintained that the ban was an unconstitutional denial of the civil liberties for which they had recently fought. . . .

On the morning of the parade Mayor Gray issued a proclamation warning that anyone taking part in it would do so at his own risk. As the parade itself was forming up the Mayor read the Riot Act. After that the machinery by which the parade was stopped was put into action. . . .[19]

The parade was broken up with an armed charge by the RNWMP. This action resulted in about 30 casualties, including one death. Sixteen of the casualties were among the public.[20] What happened in the course of this charge has been variously interpreted. The Honourable N.W. Rowell, minister responsible for the RNWMP in his report to Parliament stated that:

. . . the first shots were fired by the paraders, or those associated with them, and the Mounted Police fired only in self-defence. The information that we have is that the police acted with great coolness, great courage, and great patience, as is characteristic of the men of the Royal North West Mounted Police.[21]

An account in the *Western Labour News* gave a more detailed but different version from that given in the Commons. Its description, in part, was as follows:

On Saturday, about 2:30 p.m. just the time when the parade was scheduled to start, some fifty mounted men swinging baseball bats rode down Main Street. Half were red-coated Royal North West Mounted Police, the others wore khaki. They quickened their pace as they passed the Union Bank. The crowd opened, let them through and closed in behind them. They turned and charged through the crowd again, greeted by hisses and boos, and some stones. There were two riderless horses with the squad when it emerged and galloped up to Main Street. The men in khaki disappeared at this point, but the redcoats reined their horses and reformed opposite the old post office. . . . Then, with revolvers drawn, they galloped down Main Street, and charged into the crowd on William Avenue, firing as they charged. . . . The crowd dispersed as quickly as possible when the shooting began. . . . Lines of special police, swinging their big clubs, were thrown across Main Street and the intersecting thoroughfares. Dismounted redcoats lined up across Portage and Main declaring the city under military control. Khaki-clad men with rifles were stationed on the street corners.[22]

.... The riot and its suppression by armed force soon ended all organized resistance in Winnipeg. As described by Masters:

The strike continued for a short time longer in an atmosphere of gathering doom. Most of the leaders, although on bail, had undertaken not to resume activity. Those who had not been arrested were afraid that the blow would fall. The authorities had intervened and were maintaining control of the streets with armed force. Reduced to a state of terror, the Trades and Labour Council capitulated and announced the end of the strike on Wednesday, June 25, six weeks less one day from the beginning of the strike.[23]

The General Strike left a legacy of bitterness and controversy that was to last for decades. The eight strike leaders who had been arrested were brought to trial on charges of "conspiracy to bring into hatred and contempt the governments of the Dominion of Canada and the Province of Manitoba and to introduce a Soviet system of government."[24] After trials that lasted for over a year, one of the leaders, R.B. Russell, was convicted and sent to the penitentiary for two years, five received one-year sentences, one a six-month sentence, and one was freed. The convictions were all based on the dubious assumption that the strike was the result of a conspiracy to overthrow the government, rather than a concerted struggle by organized labour in Winnipeg to secure the basic rights of recognition and collective bargaining.

The Winnipeg General Strike, despite its crushing defeat, provided temporarily a strong wave of unionism and militancy across the country, particularly in the western provinces. Union membership and participation in strikes reached unprecedented levels during 1919 and 1920. . . .

A number of other strikes developed across the country at the same time as the Winnipeg walkout, or shortly after, in a wide variety of industries. These were largely over wages and other direct issues, and not in sympathy with the general strike.

Among the more important of these was an unauthorized strike of 6,266 coal miners in the eastern British Columbia-Alberta district, in protest against a reduction in daily pay incurred by a reduction of working hours from 9 to 8 per diem. The dispute lasted from May 24 to the end of August. It was complicated by the entrance of the One Big Union into the picture, and resulted in jurisdictional conflict with the UMWA [United Mine Workers of America].[25]

Other large strikes included one involving some 2,000 men in several building trades in Montreal, from September 2 to November 24, and one of 525 goldminers at Kirkland Lake, from June 12 to October 16. In both, the main demands concerned higher wages, shorter hours, and union recognition.[26]

All told, then, 1919 was a peak period of labour unrest, with numbers of strikes, workers involved and man-days lost far exceeding any previous year in Canada's history. And, in proportion to the country's total paid labour force and to total union membership, it has never been reached since, even in 1946 or 1966. For the first time also, industries and trades in the "metals, machinery and conveyances" category accounted for the largest number of strikes — about twice those in construction — and for more than one-half the total man-days lost in all industries that year.

An almost equal number of strikes occurred during 1920, namely, 310 as against 322 the previous year. They were much smaller in size and shorter in duration, however, so that total workers involved and man days of employment lost were only a fraction of the previous year. From then on, except for a few prolonged shutdowns in coal mining, the incidence of strikes and lockouts continued on a downward trend until the mid-1930s. It marked the beginning of a long decline in the size, effectiveness and militancy of organized labour in Canada.

Notes

1. Most of the following discussion of this incident has been drawn from D.C. Masters, *The Winnipeg General Strike*, (University of Toronto Press, 1950) and from Chapter 8 of Kenneth McNaught's book, *A Prophet in Politics*, (University of Toronto Press, 1959).

2. McNaught, op. cit., p. 99.

3. Ibid., p. 100.

4. Loc. cit.

5. *Labour Gazette*, 1919, pp. 1-28.

6. McNaught, op. cit., p. 100.

7. Ibid., p. 105.

8. Masters, op. cit., p. 132.

9. McNaught, op. cit., p. 106.

10. Ibid., pp. 107-08.

11. Ibid., p. 110; also see Logan, op. cit., p. 318, and Masters, op. cit., pp. 72 et seq.

12. Logan, op. cit., p. 319.

13. McNaught, p. 112.

14. Ibid., p. 113; Logan, p. 318.

15. McNaught, p. 115.

16. Loc. cit.

17. Ibid., p. 118.

18. Ibid., p. 119.

19. Ibid. pp. 120-21.

20. Ibid., p. 124.

21. *Hansard*, 1919, p. 3845.

22. McNaught, p. 125.

23. Masters, op. cit., p. 110.

24. Ibid., p. 115.

25. *Labour Gazette*, 1919, pp. 1050 et seq.

26. Ibid., p. 792.

29/Michelin in Nova Scotia*

Michael Bradfield

For many people "economic development" means simply job creation. They assume that more jobs automatically increase welfare, regardless of the financial, social or environmental costs of those jobs. The only refinement to the "jobs at any price" mentality is a strong preference for jobs in "high" technology, export-oriented manufacturing. To many, this automatically means jobs in a foreign subsidiary. In this context, the care and feeding of the Michelin company in Nova Scotia is a "natural" proposition, and seems to be an overwhelming success. But is it really? I suggest that the costs of attracting Michelin to Nova Scotia were very high and may well have exceeded the benefits.

Construction of the two Michelin plants at Granton and Bridgewater began in 1970 after two years of negotiation with the provincial and federal governments. Those were years well spent for Michelin since the combined value of the initial government grants and loans plus loans from Canada's chartered banks amounted to the value of Michelin's initial investment in Nova Scotia! In addition, Michelin received tax concessions from the federal and municipal governments who waived import tariffs and assisted in training programmes.

This "foreign" investor received the following grants and loans: DREE grants, $16 million; IEL grant, $8.7 million; low interest loan, $50 million; market rate loan, $14.3 million; Bank loans, $20 million. (DREE is the Department of Regional Economic Expansion. IEL is Industrial Estates Limited, the provincial government's industrial development agency.)

There is no public estimate of the value of the federal and tariff concessions. At the municipal level, both Granton and Bridgewater cut the local tax rate for Michelin, Granton to less than 50 per cent and Bridgewater to almost 25 per cent of standard rates. It is instructive to note that the $68 million in grants to Ford in Ontario also carried tax concessions estimated to be worth over $200 million.

Clearly since this "foreign" investment was financed out of Canadian savings Michelin was not a "foreign" investment. The investors were ordinary Canadians, although the investment decisions were made for them by their governments and by the banks which handle their savings. Had the Michelin plants never opened, Canadians would have suffered the losses and Michelin might still have made a profit. Workers who installed the equipment noted that some of it was used, having been shipped in from other Michelin subsidiaries. Assuming that Michelin

---

* Reprinted with permission of the publisher and the author, from Michael Bradfield, "Michelin in Nova Scotia," *Canadian Forum*, December/January 1981, pp. 9-11.

made a profit from these intra-company sales, the company could have walked out before the plants opened and still have made a profit without putting up a franc of its own. So much for foreign investors taking risks in Canada!

In addition to financial assistance, Michelin obtained government assistance to keep its workforce in line. Michelin's first decade in Nova Scotia has clearly demonstrated how companies use the leverage of jobs to manipulate a government into selling out the workers — in order to get work, of course.

During construction of the Michelin plants there were threats of strikes. The Government of Nova Scotia acted quickly to pass an Act for the Stabilization of Labour-Management Relations Affecting Certain Construction Projects, to promote industrial peace and to prevent interruptions in the construction of the Michelin plants. The bill did nothing to correct the conditions creating the unrest; it simply put a lid on the pot. The bill could be proclaimed on a county by county basis, rather than for the entire province. It was not surprising, however, that the bill was proclaimed only for Pictou county, the site of the Granton plant.

Once the plants began production, there were several attempts to organize the workers. In 1973 it looked as if the International Union of Operating Engineers, despite company pressure, would be certified as the agent for the stationary engineers in the Granton plant; the Liberal government obligingly passed a retroactive order in council barring craft unions in industrial plants.

In 1977, the United Rubber Workers tried to organize the Granton Plant and were fought by the company, aided by government amendments to the Trade Union Act. The union was slowed down by the government's willingness to play "bash the unions" on behalf of Michelin, but it was not deterred. By 1979, having won three unfair labour practice charges against Michelin, the URW requested a certification vote for the Granton plant. Apparently afraid that the union would win the vote, new legislation was announced by the (now Conservative) government. The gist of this legislation was that a union must simultaneously organize all the plants of a multi-plant company. The legislation was quickly scuttled because it drew the ire of unions *and* management. The latter reflected the concern of multi-plant operations other than Michelin, for instance, fish processors. These companies often had both unionized and non-unionized plants, and they were afraid that the legislation would be a spur to unionization in their unorganized plants.

The legislation actually introduced met Michelin's needs, removed the concern of other multi-plant firms, and paid no attention to the workers' concerns. The new bill required the simultaneous organization only of "integrated" plants. Since the fish plants do not supply each other, they are not "integrated" and therefore not threatened by the "Michelin" bill. The bill met considerable opposition from the NDP and from the newly-sensitive Liberals. Despite extensive opposition, the bill was passed by the Conservative majority, without any attempt to respond to the criticism. The Government's rationale was totally open: Michelin would build a third plant in Nova Scotia to employ another 1800 workers. The government wished to guarantee "stability" in the labour market.

The bill was passed with unseemly haste. The Nova Scotia Labour Relations Board had set a date for counting the Granton certification vote, but since the bill became law before that date there was no need to count the vote. If the URW wished to become certified to represent Michelin's workers, it would have to have a vote in both plants. Since the bulk of the effort had gone into Granton, the union had no hope of quickly starting a membership drive in Bridgewater. The legislation stopped the union once again, without even giving it the satisfaction of knowing it had won in the Granton plant.

The "Michelin" bill of the Conservatives and prior Labour Act changes by the Liberals show how the interests of the companies take precedence over the rights of the workers. The price paid by labour has been high. The URW is reported to have spent over $1 million in organization drives frustrated largely by the willingness of the provincial government to condone and support Michelin's anti-union activities. The entire labour movement in Nova Scotia has paid a price in legislation which makes it more difficult to organize in all sectors of the province. The people of Nova Scotia will pay for the anti-labour legislation because it has led to a rupture in the relations between labour and government and labour and management — a rupture which will make it difficult to avoid confrontations in the future. Of such are the ties that bind economics and politics in Nova Scotia.

Many term the Michelin venture an unqualified success. There are 3600 jobs in the existing plants. The third plant will add another 1800. Michelin has been so successful that it is the province's largest private employer. Looking only at jobs and exports Michelin looks like a success story. However, we must also consider the costs which, whether in the form of direct financial assistance, tax concessions, or restrictions on the labour movement, have been large. These costs will increase with the coming of the third plant; in addition to the changes in labour legislation, another $54 million has been offered in government assistance. Furthermore, the loss of jobs in Ontario's tire industry may not be unrelated to the expansion of Michelin in Nova Scotia. Looking at only the grants and loans, ignoring the cost of the tax concessions, the first two Michelin plants received approximately $25,000 per job created. This could be compared to the limited experience of IEL with funding local, small firms, where the assistance has been less than $4,000 per job.

Michelin has certainly increased Nova Scotia's exports since almost all of the production from the two plants is sold in the United States. Despite their criticisms of Michelin on other accounts, McConnell and Pope note that Michelin's exports far exceed the loss of foreign exchange as profit flows out to the parent company and therefore "they help us pay our way in the world." However, Michelin is not quite the boon that McConnell and Pope believe. The increase in exports must be offset by two increases in imports — the original equipment for the plants and natural rubber. This means that the net benefit for Canada's foreign currency reserves may be quite small, at least relative to the millions Canadians have invested in Michelin.

The high level of imports, Michelin's penchant for corporate secrecy, and the research orientation of their technology probably mean that links between the plants and the rest of the economy are smaller than usual. The primary impact of the two Michelin plants on the rest of the economy of Nova Scotia is through workers' spending.

It is obvious that Michelin did not bring only benefits to Nova Scotia. The costs have been substantial, whether measured in government funds turned over to the company or in terms of government sell-out of the labour force. There may be other less obvious political costs. For instance the government's slowness to act on job safety and environmental issues may reflect its willingness to sacrifice health and the environment to obtain jobs. Since there has never been strong environmental protection legislation in Nova Scotia, we have not had the spectacle of the government changing it to suit the needs or demands of corporations, although industrialists say they like dealing with Nova Scotia because of its "reasonable" environmental standards. We have also seen safety standards go unenforced. How often has the provincial government gone out of its way to be "reasonable" for Michelin or other companies?

Can we really declare Michelin a success story? Only if the goals of Nova Scotians are measured in terms of jobs and it is assumed that there were *no other alternatives* to a development strategy which relied on investments like Michelin's. Consider examples of more efficient job creation — whether more careful, less desperate, such as the New Brunswick Development Corporation. Not as dramatic. Not as rapid. But also, not a giveaway and not a sell-out. Michelin costs too much both in terms of money and loss of political control.

Moreover, there are alternatives. Neither Nova Scotia nor Canada is really dependent on this kind of foreign investment to achieve reasonable success, to become truly "developed." We feel dependent on foreign investment because in the past it has turned control of our economy over to outsiders. It is not lack of technology or resources that makes us dependent, it is lack of imagination, lack of confidence; it is the "Canadian disease."

Michelin is typical of investment which comes from our traditional ways of thinking of ourselves and of the rest of the world. The costs of Michelin are the price of this kind of thinking. Companies controlling jobs even in prosperous areas can force exorbitant concessions from governments who see no other employment alternatives. Loss of jobs is too strong a threat for most governments to resist. Political independence is impossible if job leverage is successfully applied by private firms in private interests. Clearly, an industrial strategy which promotes long-term independence must mean that the most desirable large firms are those which cannot threaten job removal, worker or government-owned industries.

Another aspect of Michelin typical of past thinking is the illogical idea that we have no competitive advantage and therefore must subsidize. We must now emphasize those areas where we do have some competitive advantage, due to resources, geography, skills, or technology. We should look at stimulating (Canadian, where possible) industries which have no strong locational attachments. While these industries are more likely to come "unstuck" if conditions change, they are less likely to need incentives to develop in a particular region. *If they are worker owned, they will not move.* Finally, an industrial strategy must emphasize the development of industries in which we create our competitive advantage. Experience here and elsewhere indicates that ideas and new products can be developed in Canada. Products do not have to be "high" technology, but rather "appropriate" technology: appropriate to our needs, our resources, and our potential.

The policies which led to catering to Michelin can, at best, be said to reflect aspiration without analysis. There is in Nova Scotia a desire to be prosperous, to be like other parts of Canada, to be like Ontario. Since Nova Scotia has different resources, a different industrial base, and perhaps even different aspirations, it makes sense to start by defining what we want, what we are prepared to give up, and what our alternatives are. Only by such analysis can we hope to do what economics is supposed to tell us how to do — use our scarce resources to meet our unlimited wants.

References

Atlantic Provinces Economic Council, *Seventh Annual Review*, Halifax: APEC, 1973.

George, Roy E., *The Life and Times of Industrial Estates Limited*, Halifax: Institute of Public Affairs, Dalhousie University, 1974.

Kimber, Stephen, "Michelin Tire Rolls On," *Financial Post Magazine*, April 26, 1980, pp. 34-44.

Langille, Brian, "The Michelin Amendment in Context," paper presented to the Canadian Industrial Relations Association, Montreal, 1980.

McConnell, Campbell R. and Pope, William Henry, *Economics: First Canadian Edition*, Toronto: McGraw-Hill Ryerson, 1978.

30/Have Labor Unions Outlived Their Usefulness?[*]

John van der Feyst

Canada's industrial productivity this year will be sorely tested — and governmental efforts to combat inflation severely handicapped — by union bargaining activities on behalf of a workforce of an estimated one-and-a-quarter million people. With many collective labor agreements up for renewal, disturbing times can be expected since employees in many sectors of industry not only have set themselves high targets of wage increases, but also have become extremely militant in their demands.

In companies with more than 500 employees which are under federal or provincial jurisdiction, more than 400 agreements will be coming up for negotiation in 1975. This compares with 304 which had to be renewed in 1974, and which were concluded only after the loss of 7,254,300 man-days up to the end of August. And this does not include the construction industry or companies with fewer than 500 employees.

This increased tendency of labor to resort to strikes to achieve its aims, whether they are realistic or not, is a form of militancy which threatens to tear apart the fabric of an orderly society.

Time was when a trade union was an association, formed for the purpose of promoting the welfare of its members through bargaining for better conditions at the working place. It was motivated by the ideal to abolish abuse of the worker and to promote his dignity and living standard. This, so it appears, has gone by the board. Today unions have become groups which pressure society to obtain financial advantages through no matter what means, even if the community has to be held up for ransom. Thus, during the past year we have witnessed strikes accompanied by violence and wanton destruction of property (it looks as if "Luddism" is coming back), civil disobedience and disregard for the law, intimidation and threats against innocent bystanders and many other unsavoury acts.

One has only to remember the distasteful episode of the Lapalme postal drivers and the strike of policemen a few years ago, or more recently the $2 million destruction rampage at the James Bay site, the strike of firemen in Montreal and the violence in front of the United Aircraft plant in Longueuil, to see that unionism has degenerated to the level of underworld strongarm tactics and hooliganism.

Union executives appear to aim for goals which come close to blackmail and extortion, spurred as they are by a wave of "me-too-ism" to obtain for their mem-

[*] Reprinted with permission of the publisher from John van der Feyst, "Have Labor Unions Outlived their Usefulness?" *Canadian Business* 47, 12 (1974), pp. 49-50.

bers what other brotherhoods managed to squeeze out of government or management. The bargaining process has deteriorated into taking an entrenched position and threatening to take the place apart, irrespective of whether the community or the enterprise can afford their demands. And once one organization has managed to extract additional money at knifepoint, the other unions, like killer sharks, jump in to insist on equal treatment.

It is no coincidence that labor troubles always seem to break out at a propitious moment: the postal strike during the Christmas season, the air controllers during the holiday period, the grain handlers when there is an urgency to fulfill export commitments. It is a form of psychological warfare which aims for the soft under-belly of society to get the required results.

In the process, the word "inflation" is bandied about as the cause for all the misery in the world today, and responsibility for this unhealthy state of affairs is laid at the feet of big business which "rips off" the little man and is unmindful of his well-being. But it is high time that labor recognizes that — as Marvin Kosters of the Cost of Living Council has put it — "Labor costs are, of course, a large fraction of total costs in the economy. About two-thirds of the value of gross product for non-financial corporations is accounted for by employee compensation."

It is all right to discuss and bargain for legitimate wage increases and COLA (cost of living allowances) in an atmosphere of reason, but when these demands become excessive (and hikes of around 30% over a one-year contract definitely are) labor unions should realize that they fan the flames of inflation rather than extinguish them.

And what is most unfortunate is that the negotiations in the public sector set the example for the unions in industrial sectors such as steel, pulp and paper, textile mills, furniture and wood operations, construction, transportation and so on. Government largesse with tax dollars invariably leads to increasing the wage cost burden for private industry which, ultimately, has to pass part of these expenditures on to the consumer.

Are there Benefits?

But there is one question that is not asked often enough: do union members indeed benefit from the interventions of their brotherhood?

The answer can, perhaps, be found in a simple calculation. Assume that a worker in a plant has a take-home pay of $150 per week (basic wage, plus overtime, less deductions). His union organizes a strike which lasts, say, six months. Being a married man he will receive $35 per week from union coffers as strike pay, thus losing an income of $115 per week. This, multiplied by 24 weeks adds up to a loss of $2,760. Once the strike is over the man's gain as a union member may be a net 10% or $15 in his pay. To recuperate his loss of $2,760 at a rate of $15 per week would require him to work some 184 weeks before he is "even." But under today's labor relations climate, chances are that before that time another strike will be declared for even higher "gains," so the poor man never catches up, although the victories will be substantial in name only. (To counteract this, some settlements are retroactive to the original strike date.)

There is a danger that this situation may become even more serious now that there is a movement to internationalize unions to help their "brother" in other countries.

Multinationals a Problem

Postmaster-General Bryce Mackasey, himself a former shop steward in the International Brotherhood of Electrical Workers, recently told that union's convention in Kansas City, "We suffer from multinational corporations. We know what it is to have a plant close down in London, Ontario, and have its production transferred to Australia or to London, England, or to have Firestone and Goodyear close the plants in Canada and bring up the tires from the United States."

He advocated that unions should remain or become international so that they could form a united front. What this actually means is that, in future, work stoppages could be organized in Canadian plants in support of "comrades" in other countries. It remains to be seen whether Canadians, now earning $4 or $5 per hour, will voluntarily deprive themselves of thousands of dollars in income to help obtain wage increases for people in countries with rates of pay of say $2 per hour.

The question remains whether the unions, as they exist today, have not outlived their usefulness. Is there not a better way to cement relations between labor and management, without the economy of an entire nation being held at the mercy of a few unions' leaders whose income does not diminish during a strike.

Perhaps a first step towards a solution might be found in legislation obliging unions during a work stoppage either to pay their members the same wages they had before the strike started, or for union executives also to be deprived of income during a strike. They also should be held legally responsible for any material damages sustained by an enterprise as a result of unlawful activities.

Another remedy perhaps would be for management to make its employees shareholders in the enterprise. This might help to resuscitate pride and quality of workmanship, reduce absenteeism and reward loyalty with dividends at the end of the successful production year.

31/Ten Labour Myths*

Ed Finn

Mankind has always been plagued by myth and superstition.

There was a time when most people believed that the Earth was flat, and the Moon made of green cheese. There was a time when "witches" were burned at the stake, and "doctors" used leeches as a cure for every ailment.

We like to think we live in more enlightened times today. But myths still dominate the thinking of many people — and nowhere more pervasively than in the world of labour relations.

Most Canadians are labour illiterates. They accept as truth numerous lies and distortions about unions that have no more factual basis than those superstitions of the past that they now ridicule.

But a belief in labour "bogey-men" is no less ridiculous than a belief in witches or demons. A belief that unions are harmful to our economy is no less preposterous than a belief that the Earth is flat.

The truly intelligent and open-minded citizen will make an effort to find out the truth about unions. This brief examination of the 10 most widely accepted labour myths may serve as a learning tool in that re-education process.

1. Union-won wage increases are the chief cause of inflation, so controls on wage increases will keep down the cost of living.

If this myth hasn't been permanently punctured by our experience with wage controls (1975-1978), it never will be. During that period, average wage settlements were reduced to less than one-third their pre-controls level. If wages really are the chief factor in inflation, that should have produced a sharp drop in prices. But it didn't. Prices kept skyrocketing, forcing most workers to take cuts in their real income. The truth is that wage increases do not cause price increases.

Wages go up as a response to rising prices. That has been the finding of every objective, scientific study. Most economists would agree with economic columnist Dian Cohen's statement: "There has not been a shred of evidence . . . that wages have added anything to the Canadian rate of inflation." Over the past 50 years, total labour income, as a percentage of the Gross National Product, has fluctuated only a few percentage points — proving that rising wages and salaries have simply maintained their usual share of a growing GNP.

Wages are continually subject to restraint through the machinery of collective

---

* Reprinted with permission of the publisher and the author from Ed Finn, "10 Labour Myths," *Canadian Labour* 24, (October 12, 1979), pp. 13-16.

bargaining, compulsory conciliation, and legal restrictions on the right to strike. Unlike other forms of income — profits, stock dividends, rents, professional fees — wage levels must be set through negotiations with employers.

The only fair (and effective) form of wage control is price control. If limits were enforced on price increases, it would automatically lower workers' need and expectations, and they would gladly settle for correspondingly lower wage hikes.

2. Labour-management conflict can and should be replaced by labour-management co-operation.

As an ideal, this is quite acceptable. But unfortunately we live in a society that is based on competition, not co-operation: a society in which we are all supposed to compete with one another for our respective shares of the national income. That's the underlying principle of private enterprise.

No doubt the jungle, too, would be a much better place if the animals would stop hunting and killing one another. Given their nature, however, the suggestion that the lion and lamb lie down together is not very practical. Particularly not for the lamb.

The world of industry and employment is also a jungle, a world in which the strong prosper and the weak languish.

Many persons in both unions and companies wish it were otherwise. But they are trapped in the present system. They know that it will take a complete reversal of basic beliefs, and the abandonment of our entire economic philosophy, before a change to labour-management co-operation can take place.

Conflict is built into the present system, and strikes are simply one of its manifestations. As long as the relationship between management and labour is based on their respective power, the extent of that power will occasionally be tested — if only because so many employers refuse to take workers' requests for better pay and working conditions seriously unless they are willing to strike for them.

3. Unions don't need, and shouldn't be given the right to strike.

Although it's not generally realized, the right to strike is a fundamental right no less important than freedom of speech or freedom of the press. Why? Simply because it is a vital part of the collective bargaining process.

Free collective bargaining is the only instrument that workers have to protect and promote their interests in our economic system. Without that ultimate right to withdraw their labour, they would have no strength to bargain, and would have to accept whatever wage and working condition their employer decided to impose on them.

The only thing workers have to bargain with is their skill or their labour. Denied the right to withhold it as a last resort, they become powerless. The strike is therefore not a breakdown of collective bargaining — it is the indispensable cornerstone of that process.

4. The right to strike should be replaced by compulsory arbitration.

Compulsory arbitration has never worked in any democratic country where it has been tried. It has been a dismal failure in Australia, where the incidence of annual strikes is three to five times the Canadian average. It has flopped in both Britain and the United States as well.

When British Columbia introduced compulsory arbitration of labour disputes in 1968, the number of mandays lost through strikes and lockouts in that province quadrupled in the next two years. The B.C. experiment fizzled out shortly afterward.

The Federal Task Force on Labour Relations ruled out compulsory arbitration as an acceptable alternative to the right to strike. "The inconvenience caused by strikes," said the Commission in its historic report, "is a small price to pay for the maintenance of the present collective bargaining system and the basic human rights on which it is founded."

In any event, a ban on strikes is impossible to enforce in a free society. Only in a police state can workers be forced to work against their will. In a free society, compulsory arbitration doesn't eliminate strikes; it merely makes them illegal.

5. Unions are always making "unreasonable" wage demands.

What is a "reasonable" wage demand?

One that meets the workers' needs? One based on the employers' ability to pay? One that's tied to productivity?

The fact is that nobody has yet devised a workable formula for determining wage increases that would be considered reasonable by the workers, by their employer, by the public, the press and the government.

Besides, most employers — except occasionally when in genuine financial stress — still refuse to open their books to union negotiators.

Unions are thus denied access to the data on profits, productivity and labour costs that they must have in order to formulate "reasonable" demands. The only alternative in our private enterprise society is to go for as much as they think their members are entitled to get.

6. Strikes are the main cause of low productivity and do irreparable harm to the economy.

The costs of strikes are greatly exaggerated, amounting on average to the loss of only one-half worker-day a year for each employee.

As the Federal Task Force on Labour Relations pointed out, this is only a small fraction of the time lost through illness, accidents and unemployment.

An effective anti-flu vaccine would save far more working time than the most repressive anti-strike law.

Most companies can now completely offset the loss of production during a strike by stockpiling beforehand and using excess capacity and overtime afterwards. Most of the business allegedly lost during strikes is merely deferred. This is borne out by strike studies showing that most business firms affected by strikes have been able to maintain their annual production norms.

There is no reliable standard for assessing the effects of a strike or the damage (if any) it causes. There is a tendency to quote unverified estimates of the daily losses a strike is supposedly inflicting, without taking into account what a struck firm is saving in wages and other operating costs. Isolated cases of hardship are also widely publicized, giving the impression that they are numerous. In this way a strike can be made to appear much more harmful than it actually is.

7. *Workers in unions are pushed around and often forced to go on strike by power-mad "labour bosses."*

The term "labour boss" was coined to portray the typical union leader as the equivalent of the company vice-president he faces across the bargaining table. It implies that a union officer has the same authoritarian control over his members that the company boss exerts over his subordinates.

In fact, the union leader is elected by the union's rank-and-file members at a convention, and is answerable to them for his or her actions. The members dictate to the leader, rather than the other way around.

The Senate Report on Growth, Employment and Price Stability pointed out that "the Canadian labour movement is, for the most part, as far as any human organization can be from an obedient, boss-directed civilian army. . . . The typical union leader is much less a 'boss' than a replaceable politician with a difficult and turbulent constituency."

Unions always conduct membership votes before taking strike action, and a strike occurs only when approved by a clear majority.

It is inconceivable that workers would walk a picket line, in all kinds of weather, sometimes having confrontations with police and strike-breakers, existing on strike pay that is only a fraction of their normal income, if a majority of them were opposed to the strike. It simply couldn't happen.

Most union leaders measure their success by the extent to which they can avoid strikes, and they do manage to settle 95 out of 100 contract negotiations without a strike. But a .950 batting average evidently doesn't satisfy some of the public and the press. Though tolerant of most other imperfections in an imperfect world, they demand perfection from the collective bargaining process.

8. *Strikes could be eliminated by getting rid of unions.*

Sorry, that wouldn't do it. Workers have been going on strike since the dawn of recorded history, in every civilization, and under all kinds of political systems. Whenever workers' discontent rises to an intolerable level, they'll strike, whether they're building the great pyramids of Egypt, working as potters or goldsmiths in the Middle Ages, or sorting mail in the twentieth century. Canada's first recorded strike for better wages — by the fur trade voyageurs at Rainy Lake, in August, 1794, occurred long before the first union was formed in this country.

Modern unions, in fact, through collective bargaining, prevent many more strikes than they initiate. Do away with unions, and the ensuing economic chaos would make current strike disruptions seem trivial by comparison.

9. The public is not represented in — and is the innocent victim of — strikes by workers in the public sector.

Unions in the public sector have to bargain directly with government officials or their agents. Who are these officials representing if not the public?

The mandatory conciliation process, along with the other legal rituals that must be followed before a legal strike can begin, are all imposed by government in the name of the public.

Public employees are exactly what their label implies. They are the public's employees.

They are our employees, and when they go on strike they do so for the same reason employees in the private sector go on strike because they are dissatisfied with the way we — through our elected representatives — are treating them.

If the services provided by postal workers, by garbage collectors, by hospital workers, by workers in transportation and other key industries are truly essential, why are such workers so often among the lowest paid? If their jobs are so indispensable why are they not treated accordingly?

The public, as an employer, really has no more right to claim immunity from strikes than any other employer who doesn't make an honest effort to treat his workers fairly.

Unions representing public employees have no alternative when governments refuse to bargain in good faith than to exercise their right to strike, when their members vote for this action.

People who may be hurt by such strikes should make an effort to look at both sides of the dispute — to determine if their employees' demands are justified. If this is clearly the case, then public pressure should be directed at governments to offer a fair settlement, rather than to enact strike-breaking laws.

10. The strike weapon makes unions too big and powerful.

"Big" and "powerful" are relative terms. In actual fact, most Canadian unions are quite small, and together they represent less than 40% of the country's non-farm workers.

Because collective bargaining usually involves only one union local at a time, most strikes that take place are confined to one community or region.

Even the largest unions in terms of size and resources, pale by comparison with multinational corporations such as Inco, Imperial Oil, or Canadian Pacific.

If unions were even one-tenth as powerful as they are thought to be, they would be able to organize the five million Canadian workers still outside unions. They would be winning more of their strikes and increasing their members' wage rates a lot more than they actually are.

Besides, there's no relation between union size and power and the incidence of strikes. In Sweden and West Germany, for example, 80 to 90% of all workers belong to unions, yet these countries have few strikes — mainly because of the more enlightened policies of their governments and employers.

Granted, strikes sometimes hurt or inconvenience innocent people. But so does almost every form of economic activity. When prices go up, that hurts. When profits are taken out of the country and invested abroad, that hurts.

Anti-union spokesmen ignore the fact that workers are people, too. All they want is a fair payment for their labour — a fair share of the economic benefits which they help to produce. And why, when a strike occurs, blame only the workers and their unions, as if they were the only ones involved? It takes two parties to make a quarrel, and, more often than not in industrial disputes, it's management that is mostly to blame.

32/Why We Continue to Struggle*

Jean Claude Parrot

Why, with continuous attacks on our jobs and our rights, do we continue to struggle? Why do some unions have a more difficult time than others? Are the employers' allegations true — are we just a bunch of wild-eyed anarchists, hell-bent on destroying everything around us? *What's at stake?*

In 1947, during the Lachute woolen mill workers' strike, when Premier Duplessis changed the law to remove their right to strike, Brother Kent Rowley put it very well: "Slavery does not exist in the Province of Québec." Is there anything truer than that? A worker who does not have the right to withdraw his labour when the employer refuses to honour his right to negotiate is not a worker — he is a slave.

The law can recognize or not recognize our right to strike; the law can impose penalties on us for striking. But the law never gave us the right to strike and it cannot take it away. *The right to strike is simply part of being a worker — not a slave.*

But the right to strike is not the reason for our struggles. It is only a small part of what's at stake. What's at stake is our right, as workers, to some control over

* Abridged from Jean Claude Parrot, "Why We Continue to Struggle," *This Magazine* 13 (5 and 6) 1979, pp. 12-17. Reprinted with permission of the publisher and the author.

our lives, to decent living standards and working conditions and to the minimal protections, on and off the job, that workers have won over hundreds of years of struggle. What's at stake is our right to form democratic, militant unions, unions responsive to workers' needs, not to the employers' wish of higher productivity and higher profits at workers' expense.

Today, the challenge we are facing in the organized labour movement is as tough and critical as the challenges workers faced when they organized. We have some fundamental choices to make and these choices will have a dramatic impact, not just on our existing trade union rights, but on the shape of our whole society for decades to come.

Our right to strike, our right to negotiate, our right to decent employment, our right to indexed pensions, our right to unemployment insurance, our right to health care, our right to higher education, our right to privacy — all these rights, and many more, are under increasing attack from a business-government coalition dedicated to confrontation and determined to increase private profits at the expense of working people. Back-to-work legislation, right-to-work laws, the hiring of casual labour, contracting out, legislation making union certification more difficult, the exclusion of more and more workers from the right to unionize, the use of the courts and the police to break strikes and penalize workers — all these weapons and many more have been used against us with increasing frequency over the past few years. Meanwhile, employers continue to actively engage in union-busting activities without being prosecuted and at the bargaining table in both the public and private sectors, employers are increasingly offering nothing but rollbacks and reductions in real wages.

The Growing Strength of Employers

We should ask ourselves: Why is it that employers and governments are now much more confident in their attacks against workers? Is it because they have become more anti-worker in their views and are willing to take more chances? Or is it because the employers are realizing that during the last few years, developments have occurred which have served to shift the balance of power decisively in their favour? And that the labour movement has not been able to effectively respond to these developments?

The first thing that we must recognize is that, despite the economic crisis, the employers, as a class, have grown stronger and more organized.

Just look at the strength of the multi-national corporations when it comes to negotiating with their workers — corporations that are so large that they are able to withstand strikes because of their foreign subsidiaries which continue to operate and provide them with profits. And not only are these corporations becoming larger, but they are also becoming more diversified, crossing from industry to industry and country to country, thus making it much harder for even a major strike to affect their entire operation.

Just as workers organized during the 19th century to bring their collective strength to bear against employers, so too employers are organizing today, and *on every level*. Consider, for example, the emergence of province-wide "employers councils" in British Columbia, the enormous strengthening of such business-front groups as the National Citizens' Coalition, the open collusion of meat packaging companies throughout the industry during the meat packers' strike last year, or the private sector-public sector alliance of the Post Office Department and the Direct Mailers' Association during the CUPW [Canadian Union of Postal Workers] strike last fall. These are just a few examples and inter-employer co-operation doesn't even stop on these levels.

Employers are just as well, if not better, organized on the international level. At a recent meeting of the Organization for Economic Cooperation and Development — an international organization at which industrialized countries jointly develop economic strategies — government and business representatives from a number of countries decided on strategies to do away with collective bargaining. The measures they agreed upon included year-round media campaigns to break down public resistance to increasing profits; to isolate unionized workers and convince the public that the high unemployment, high inflation, and other economic problems are a result of their excessive demands; and to convince workers that collective bargaining is outdated and should be replaced with more informal, co-operative methods of dealing with labour-management problems. . . .

The main thrust of this high degree of organization, of this closer and more open co-operation between private and public sector employers is to attack the very basis of labour's strength — the rights to negotiate and to strike. And they are using a variety of tactics to achieve their objectives. The struggle of the postal workers illustrates many of these tactics.

CUPW's Fight

Is the postal worker's struggle a struggle for better wages and working conditions? Is it a struggle to eliminate the adverse effects arising from technological change? Is it a struggle for job security? Is it a struggle to ensure that postal workers share some of the benefits of automation? Is it a struggle to achieve protections against management's abuse of its disciplinary powers?

Yes, in a way, it is a struggle for all these things. But it is also a much more fundamental struggle.

The real battle is over the right to negotiate: the right to negotiate the demands put forward by the membership; the right to negotiate on the strength of the membership. This is a right the Government has continuously denied us for the past twelve years.

As you are aware, in 1967, the Federal Government passed the Public Service Staff Relations Act, the law which formally granted Federal Government workers the rights to unionize, to bargain collectively and to strike. The law was full of re-

strictions and exceptions, but despite them, postal workers took the right to negotiate very seriously.

The problem was that, right from the beginning, the Treasury Board refused
to accept the principle of negotiations. For the upper level bureaucrats in the
Treasury Board, it was unthinkable that they should share what they regarded as
their *right* to unilaterally determine our wages and working conditions.

They used a number of devices to prevent us from exercising our right to
negotiate. At the bargaining table, we soon learned that, according to the Treasury
Board, we have four types of demands. When we arrive at the bargaining table, the
Treasury Board looks at our demands and says, these ones are not negotiable,
these are management rights, these cannot be dealt with because they affect all
federal public service workers so they must go to a National Joint Council consultation committee. And all the others are too complex. We should deal with them
after negotiations, through consultation.

After going through a couple of rounds of so-called negotiations this way, we
realized that we had collective agreements full of committees and union- management consultation processes, but almost no solutions to the problems of the membership.

For the Treasury Board and the Post Office, this situation of consultation instead of negotiation was great. And this is the situation they want today.

Why? Because, like any other employer, they know that in consultation they
retain the arbitrary power to make decisions; discussions are on their terms; the
Union cannot use the strength of the membership; in time, the Union no longer
sees the need to motivate the membership on issues since the members never vote
on them; and the most important thing for the employer, in consultation the
Union eventually becomes a device to justify the employer's actions to its members rather than a vehicle to transmit the workers' demands to the employer. And
what more could an employer want?

Postal workers soon realized that, in order to be successful, negotiations
would have to be based on the strength of the membership. The best negotiators
in the world could not obtain concessions from our employer without the backing
of a militant membership ready to stand up for its demands. And this meant
adopting policies and changing the structure of the Union to make it possible for
the members to fight for their demands.

With these changes, the Govenment had two choices. It could begin to negotiate with us in good faith and thereby avoid strikes, or it could go all out to break
our Union.

The appointment of Bryce Stuart Mackasey as Postmaster General in 1975 was
a clear indication of what the Government had decided.

Mackasey likes to call himself "the friend of labour," and as we used to say,
"with friends like that, you don't need enemies." During the 1975 negotiations, he
did everything in his power to divide the Union and break the strength of the

members. . . .

At any rate, negotiations dragged on for nine months until finally, in October 1975, the postal workers struck. Mackasey's response was to say that we could strike "till hell freezes over" and to use the age-old tactic of name-calling and red-baiting. We were called muscle men, radicals, anarchists, communists and everything else he could think of — all because we insisted on our right to negotiate.

But none of it worked. We remained solid and after 42 days of strike, we signed a collective agreement with major breakthroughs in areas the employer had always refused to negotiate before.

But the struggle was far from over. Both Treasury Board and the Post Office Department refused to honour the collective agreement signed by B.S. Mackasey.

The result was 65,000 grievances, numerous wildcat strikes and an even further deterioration of relations between labour and management. Besides subverting the collective agreement, management subverted the grievance procedure, forcing us to file thousands of individual grievances to third party adjudication and then, when we had won them, forcing us to fight management's appeals to the Federal Court and even the Supreme Court. We still win, but sometimes it takes four or five years to resolve a case. For example, for the first two years of our collective agreement — that is for 1976 and 1977 — we succeeded in getting a decision from a third party adjudicator on only two hundred and forty-eight cases. Out of these, we won sixty-two, lost thirty-six — and guess what happened to the other one hundred and forty? The employer conceded them just before they were heard — this same employer who had turned them down throughout the grievance process.

The 1977-78 Negotiations

Despite the continuous attacks by management, postal workers entered the 1977 round of negotiations united and determined.

But once again, the employer was determined not to negotiate with the Union. To give you an indication of how hard-line their position was, they appointed as their chief Post Office negotiator a man who, when the 1975 collective agreement was signed, stated publicly that he objected to it and would never have signed it himself because it gave too much to the Union.

The negotiations dragged on for eighteen long months. The employer's only position after sixteen months at the bargaining table consisted of a negative wage offer and rollbacks in our rights: rollbacks on shop stewards' rights; rollbacks on casual labour; rollbacks on sick leave; rollbacks on seniority; rollbacks on overtime procedure; rollbacks on individual work measurement; rollbacks on our COLA clause; and many more. All rollbacks on gains made in 1975 with our forty-two-day strike.

Meanwhile, the employer tried to stop the Union from communicating with its members, stopped COLA payments to postal workers and started up a massive publicity campaign which cost hundreds of thousand of dollars and was carried in newspapers across the country to discredit postal workers and our Union in the eyes of the public. On the shop floor, members were fired, suspended and otherwise disciplined for imaginary offences. And the red-baiting and name-calling campaign was on again in full force.

At midnight on October 16, 1978, after eighteen months of this, postal workers from coast to coast — all those radicals working in one thousand postal installations across the country, those anarchists in Clarenville, Nfld., and Inuvik, N.W.T.; those muscle men in Sorel, Québec; those militants in Belleville, Ontario; those radicals in Prince Rupert, B.C. — struck for one reason and one reason only: to obtain a new collective agreement.

The government's response? Contrary to 1975, they did not respond with negotiations, but with back-to-work legislation 14 hours after we went out on our *legal* strike. They brought in this legislation despite the fact that they themselves admitted there was no national emergency; despite the fact that they did absolutely nothing to avert a strike and everything to provoke one; despite the fact that they admitted that banning our strike would do nothing to resolve the problems in the Post Office.

The legislation not only stripped us of our rights to strike and to negotiate, it also violated a number of our other human rights, including the principle that a law shall not apply retroactively. This was too much for postal workers. Solid across the country, we remained out on strike despite the legislation. The Government then replied with injunctions to stop picket lines. We maintained our picket lines. Then they sent the federal police to raid all our major Union offices and finally threatened to dismiss without right to appeal every postal worker. This last threat, the threat to the jobs of postal workers, leaving to Post Office management the arbitrary power to pick out and fire the ones they disliked coupled with the failure of any attempt to resolve the issues in our negotiations with the Government, led the Union to call off the strike.

Postal workers returned to work and shortly afterwards a new reign of disciplinary actions followed. All national officers of the Union were arrested and charged, under the Criminal Code, for not complying with the back-to-work order and more than eleven hundred postal workers were dismissed, suspended or had other penalties imposed upon them. And finally, by using the arbitration proceedings they had forced on us, the Government succeeded in removing some of the protections we had acquired in the past and in rejecting all our major demands.

A clear victory for the Government? Not quite.

As Deputy Postmaster General Corkery testified during my trial in May, the Government and Post Office Department fully expected that postal workers would abandon their Union in droves as soon as the back-to-work legislation was passed. And this was obviously the main point of their attack.

The Employer's Message

The point of their hard-line negotiating strategy, the point of their anti-CUPW media campaigns, the point of the legislation, the point of the regressive arbitration decision — all of this was to scare postal workers away from the Union and convince them that negotiations based on their demands and their strength would not work. The Government's message was, and still is, "consultation instead of negotiations." And is it not the same message employers are sending to other workers?

Whatever name it goes under — industrial democracy, worker participation schemes, worker self-management, quality of work life experiments, intergroup and so on — both private and public sector employers are pushing this concept of replacing collective bargaining by consultation schemes. And let's make no mistake. They are pushing this concept very hard.

But why? Is it because employers like ours who have refused to offer anything at the bargaining table unless they were confronted by the strength of the membership, is it because these employers have suddenly realized the injustice of their ways and are now interested in the welfare of their employees? Is it because these employers — employers who have fought bitterly to preserve the sanctity of management rights — have now suddenly "seen the light" and want desperately to share their power with workers? Can you see INCO sharing its power with its workers, or Noranda, or General Motors, or Ma Bell, or better still, IT&T? Or is it not because, through these industrial democracy schemes, all these employers know they can remove issues *away* from the collective bargaining process, *away* from the democratic control of the membership, *away* form the strength of the membership, *away* from any possibility of collective worker action or reprisals — and *into* the cozy atmosphere of back-room deals and bartered privileges which they call consultation? . . .

Why do companies push industrial democracy? Because it will increase profits, increase productivity, make it easier for companies to gain acceptance of their board decisions and, most of all, because union officials can then be used to impose the employers' order and exercise a "restraining influence" on members. . . .

Unfortunately here in Canada the employers' campaign to co-opt unions into consultation forums is far from being a failure. Too many people in the labour movement have bought the employers' line on industrial democracy without fully exploring or understanding its implications. But even where the employers' persuasion about "industrial democracy," "quality of work life" and all the other attempts to co-opt fails, *legalized union-bashing* to coerce workers into consultation schemes becomes the order of the day. The tactics may be a little different, but the object is exactly the same: to destroy the power of workers and reassert the unchecked arbitrary power of the corporate bosses, not just at the workplace, but throughout our society.

Part VI/Current Issues

Editors' Introduction

There are many work-related issues at the centre of current debates and discussions. In this part of the reader, we have chosen to focus on four of the most pressing of these: unemployment; the impact of microtechnology on work; occupational health and safety; and leisure and retirement. The breadth and complexity of these four topics could easily warrant separate volumes; our purpose is simply to alert students to prominent concerns in each of the areas.

In Chapter 33, Sunder Magun provides an analysis of what, in the minds of many, is the number one problem facing Canada today: unemployment. A careful examination of unemployment data for the 1975-1979 period reveals that the major burden of unemployment is concentrated among a relatively small number of individuals. This finding challenges the widely accepted view of unemployment as essentially a problem of labour turnover and therefore affecting a larger number of people but for shorter durations. Those most likely to experience long-term, chronic joblessness tend to be female, live in the Atlantic region and Quebec, work in primary industries or construction, and hold blue-collar rather than white-collar jobs. The fact that such workers experience recurring bouts of unemployment reflects, Magun argues, deep structural problems in our economy. In brief, opportunities to obtain rewarding and secure jobs are not evenly distributed across the labour force, something Clairmont and his colleagues demonstrated in an earlier chapter. Similarly, the hardships of unemployment are not equally shared.

The existence of pockets of chronic unemployment has, of course, been made much worse by the current recession. In many ways the recession has bred a sense of economic insecurity among Canadians. People in occupations and professions previously thought to be immune from the boom-bust cycles of the economy have been jarred by the stark possibilities of layoffs or firm shutdowns. In Chapter 34, J. Paul Grayson documents the impact on employees and their families of the sudden closure of SKF Canada Ltd.'s Scarborough, Ontario bearing manufacturing plant. From Grayson's account of the aftermath of the SKF closure, job loss is clearly one of the most traumatic life events a person can experience. Both former employees as well as their spouses suffered considerable anxiety over future job prospects. A good number saw losing their job as equivalent to a divorce or the death of a spouse, a graphic testimony to the upheaval it caused in their personal and family lives. Furthermore, unexpected unemployment took its toll on health, with former employees and their spouses exhibiting a range of medical problems. Looking beyond these employees and their families, one can imagine the detrimental impact of such plant closures on the larger community.

Some observers claim that the post-recession economy will be fundamentally different from what we knew in the boom period of the late 1970s. One of the major causes of this change is the microelectronics revolution that has been accelerating in recent years. Through the remarkable powers of the tiny silicon chip, microtechnology has advanced furthest in the office. Fully integrated electronic office systems now combine telecommunications, word processing, electronic mail and filing, and computerized data analysis. Clearly, the implications of this new technological revolution for office workers is staggering. Not only will jobs be transformed, but there is also mounting concern about the shrinking of the clerical labour force in the wake of automation. Heather Menzies has documented this gloomy scenario of clerical job loss in her books, *Computers on the Job* and *Women and the Chip*. In Chapter 35 she summarizes her argument that female clerical workers face massive unemployment because of the tremendous capacity of microelectronic equipment to perform routine clerical functions. Menzies also suggests that another negative consequence will be the deskilling of many remaining clerical jobs. At the same time, however, computer-related technical and administrative jobs will increase. Currently there are barriers to women entering these higher level positions. Thus, Menzies considers it a priority to devise recruitment, training and promotion programs which guarantee women a fair share of these more rewarding automation-related positions.

Recognizing the potential pitfalls of embracing microelectronic technology, the federal government commissioned a task force to study the general impact of this new trend on employment. In Chapter 36 we present selections from the report of the task force which highlight major areas of impact. One area of concern is the potential negative health effects such as radiation emissions from visual display terminals (VDTS), and the physiological and psychological problems that may arise from operating the new microelectronic equipment. A second issue, already mentioned by Heather Menzies, is the deskilling of job requirements and the fragmentation and routinization of task content. A third and more general problem is the deterioration of the quality of the work environment. For instance, workers will have their activities more highly controlled by the electronic monitoring of their output. And one likely outcome of reorganizing jobs around the new technology is an increase in shift work, part-time jobs and home-based work. All these arrangements undoubtedly pose problems for the female workers who are typically recruited into these kinds of jobs. Especially troublesome is the social isolation and lack of minimum employment standards, backed up by legislation, which will accompany electronic home work. The rise of this new kind of "cottage industry" is facilitated by linking remote terminals to an organization's central computer. In short, the microelectronic revolution does hold out obvious economic advantages, not the least of which are increased productivity and reduced labour costs. But there are also major costs, measured in terms of possible unemployment for clerical workers and a deterioration of the office work environment. Clearly, we must carefully examine these costs in order to ensure that technology will be applied in ways that maximize the benefits for as many people in society as possible.

Employees, unions, and management alike have grown increasingly concerned lately about occupational health and safety problems. Almost daily new health hazards are discovered in the workplace, raising our awareness that work indeed can endanger or seriously impair our health. The traditional view of health and safety in the workplace was confined largely to discussions of factories, mines or construction sites. Yet as Julianne Labreche indicates in Chapter 37, white-collar workers are now beginning to recognize the many health and safety hazards lurking in the office environment. Psychological stress induced by office machines, physical ailments due to stale air, and accidents resulting from unsafe equipment — these are some of the common complaints now heard in offices.

Any discussion of occupational health and safety must address what happens to those workers who are injured on the job or who contract an occupational disease. Presumably government legislation regulates health and safety matters, and workers' compensation schemes provide disability support. The Ontario government's 1979 Occupational Health and Safety Act was welcomed as a progressive move, facilitating a general clean-up of the workplace by setting minimum standards enforced by inspectors. The assumption underlying this and similar legislation elsewhere is that workers should not have to face conditions injurious to their health. In Chapter 38, Stan Gray's account of the tragic case of Terry Ryan, a young factory worker blinded in an industrial explosion, seriously challenges the effectiveness of existing legislation. Reluctantly, the government laid charges against Terry's employer, Westinghouse Canada in Hamilton, for unsafe work practices responsible for the explosion. Ultimately the firm got off the hook, according to Gray, paying only a small fine on a lesser charge.

The third chapter dealing with health and safety issues examines the role of the company doctor. One might expect that company physicians would act according to professional standards in order to protect employee health. Yet as Vivienne Walters argues in Chapter 39, her research shows that often these doctors place the interests of their employer first. The ambiguous position doctors occupy within the firm places constraints on their ability to act in a neutral, professional fashion. Walters identifies four areas of conflicting pressure: regulation of absenteeism; certification of workers' fitness to work; workers' compensation; and occupational health hazards. On all four counts, doctors are caught between the often opposing demands and interests of their two client groups: management and workers. Simply stated, managers place a priority on productivity and profits while workers put a premium on protecting their health, and company doctors are caught in the middle.

The final group of readings touches upon a fourth current issue: the links between work and the larger society, particularly leisure and retirement. The title of

Chapter 40, by Martin Meissner, captures the way work influences leisure. Meissner's thesis is that work, especially the nature of production technology and the degree of autonomy it allows workers, spills over into leisure. The long arm of the job shapes leisure pursuits by either restricting or enhancing workers' capacities to creatively use spare time and engage in meaningful social activities. Thus, even those employees who do not view their jobs as a "central life interest" may not be able to escape its influences outside working hours.

Equally important is the relationship between work and retirement, especially considering that Canada is an "aging society" with the average age of the population slowly increasing each year. In Chapter 41, Andrew Allentuck explores the implications of compulsory retirement at age sixty-five. As more and more workers approach retirement age, organizations may have to seriously reconsider the traditional practice of sending them on their way with a gold watch and a handshake. A living pension is a cornerstone of the modern social welfare system. But even so, many workers would prefer to continue working. Critics argue, however, that by not enforcing a mandatory retirement age young workers will have greater difficulty entering the labour market and, furthermore, firms will be under less pressure to provide adequate pensions. The desirable goal, it would seem, is to provide older workers both a decent pension and opportunities to engage in meaningful activity. In this way, we might avoid reproducing the problems faced by the "discarded workers" portrayed by Ustun Reinart in Chapter 42. After years of contributing to the economy, the workers at the bottom of the occupational hierarchy are often left with nothing but extreme poverty — and memories. Even worse off are the widows of low-wage workers, women who struggle to survive on meagre government pensions.

Suggested Readings

Ed Andrews, *Closing the Iron Cage: The Scientific Management of Work and Leisure* (Montreal: Black Rose Books, 1981).

Canada, *Canadian Governmental Report on Aging* (Ottawa: Supply and Services, 1982).

Labour Canada, *In the Chips: Opportunities, People, Partnerships: Report of the Labour Canada Task Force on Micro-electronics and Employment* (Ottawa: Labour Canada, 1982).

Barry D. McPherson, *Aging as a Social Process* (Toronto: Butterworths, 1983), Chapter 10, "Work, Retirement, Economic Status, and Coping."

Heather Menzies, *Woman and the Chip: Case Studies of the Effects of Informatics on Employment in Canada* (Montreal: Institute for Research on Public Policy, 1981).

_____, *Computers on the Job: Surviving Canada's Microelectronic Revolution* (Toronto: James Lorimer & Company, 1982).

K.L. Schlozman and S. Verba, *Injury to Insult: Unemployment, Class and Political Response* (Cambridge, Mass.: Harvard University Press, 1980).

A/Unemployment

33/Unemployment Experience in Canada: A Five-year Longitudinal Analysis[*]

Sunder Magun

This report presents a picture of Canadian joblessness over 5 years and reveals serious chronic unemployment. In a 1975-79 longitudinal analysis, we used three indicators: total amount of all unemployment across all spells over the period; the number of unemployment spells per person; and the average duration of such a spell. Also, we considered sex, age, province, industry, and occupation. Among our findings:

1. A few bear the greatest unemployment burden;

2. The people with histories of hardcore unemployment are at a relatively greater disadvantage in the labor market and risk further episodes of chronic unemployment;

3. Long-term spells are relatively few but account for much greater unemployment than would be expected on the basis of probability.

We find that the long-run structure of unemployment in Canada is not consistent with the "dynamic" or the "turnover" view of the labor market. According to this view, the characteristics of the unemployment problem are rapid job turnover and brief spells of unemployment, and the burden of unemployment is not concentrated, but is widely shared among workers. This "benevolent" viewpoint of unemployment contends that unemployment is mainly frictional and voluntary. The benign view, by rejecting the existence of chronic and persistent unemployment, de-emphasizes the social and economic costs of joblessness. Our results do not support the turnover view. As noted, there are, in fact, three aspects of the real problem of unemployment in the country.

We used the linked Longitudinal Labour Force Data Base, which is composed of several administrative data files of the Canada Unemployment Insurance Commission. This data base contains microdata on the labor market experience of a 10-per cent sample of all "insured" workers.[1] A sample of about 20,200 people who had at least one episode of unemployment from 1975 to 1979 was drawn from the data set. These individuals had filed regular unemployment insurance claims[2] for about 56,000 job separations over the 5-year span. The sample is a representation

* Reprinted, with permission of the publisher and the author, from Sunder Magun, "Unemployment experience in Canada: a 5-year longitudinal analysis," *Monthly Labour Review* 106(4) 1983, pp. 36-38.

of Canadian workers who have relatively more difficulties in the labor market and who are often clients of the Commission's manpower programs.

Who are the unemployed?

The bulk of the unemployment burden falls on a small proportion of workers. About 25 per cent of unemployed individuals accounted for almost half of the total time lost because of unemployment between 1975 and 1979. Each individual in this group experienced, on average, 2 years of unemployment, consisting of repeated and long spells of joblessness. This concentration of unemployment was not confined to a particular sex, age, or regional group but occurred among male, female, young, and adult workers in all regions.

There are, however, important regional differences in the distribution of the unemployment burden. In a region where the unemployment rate is high, unemployment is more equally shared. In the Atlantic region, the top one-quarter of workers accounted for 45 per cent of total unemployment, compared with 57 per cent in the Prairie region. Therefore, the unemployment burden is somewhat more equally shared in the Atlantic region than in the Prairie provinces. This is because unemployment is more widespread in the former region than in the latter.

We define the chronically unemployed as individuals with 27 weeks or more of unemployment during a given year without regard to the number of times they were out of work. Persons with less than 27 weeks of total unemployment we consider short-term unemployed, and those with no spells of unemployment during the given year we define as not unemployed.

The chronically unemployed as a proportion of the sample, ranged from 12.5 per cent in 1975 to 17.8 per cent in 1978, reflecting worsening economic conditions. Of great significance are the large movements of people among the three labor force categories. For example, a worker might be chronically unemployed in 1975, not unemployed in 1976, jobless for the short term in 1977, and then chronically unemployed again.

Despite these intergroup movements, a subgroup of individuals who remained over time in a given status had little likelihood of leaving the group. This aspect of unemployment experience can be expressed in terms of conditional probability. By creating a probability tree we can track the labor market experience of certain groups of individuals. We have constructed two probability trees — one relates to a cohort of the long-term unemployed and the other to a cohort of the short-term unemployed during the 4-year period, 1975-78. Both trees show the influence of hardcore unemployment.

A comparison of the two probability distributions reveals an important finding: those chronically unemployed in 1975 had a much greater likelihood of repeating their experience in the following 3 years than did the short-term unemployed in 1975. The probabilities of a period of prolonged joblessness (27 weeks or more) were 51 per cent compared with only 27 per cent for the 1975 short-term unemployed cohort. Moreover, the 1975 cohort of chronically unemployed had a five times greater probability of annual long-term unemployment than the 1975 cohort of short-term unemployed.

A sequence of chronic unemployment may have a cumulative effect by worsening job skills. If a person is chronically unemployed in 1976 as well as 1975, his or her chance of becoming so in 1978 is almost 50 per cent, compared with only 15 per cent for the short-term unemployed. Furthermore, if an individual is also chronically out of work in 1977, his or her risk in 1978 is 64 per cent, compared with 12 per cent for the short-term unemployed in 1975, 1976, and 1977.

Most of the spells of unemployment are less than 21 weeks. Longer spells are relatively fewer but account for much greater unemployment. Although this would be expected on theoretical grounds, the effect was substantially larger than would be expected on the basis of chance alone.

During 1975-79, the Canadian unemployment rate rose from 6.9 per cent in 1975 to 8.4 per cent in 1978. By quantifying the relationship between the unemployment rate and the unemployment experience over the 5-year period, we find that a 1-percentage-point increase in the unemployment rate reflected, on average, a rise in unemployment frequency by four-tenths of a spell, duration of a spell by 2.3 weeks, and length of total unemployment by almost 10 weeks.

A closer examination of unemployment spells shows that with increasing unemployment spell length, the probability of leaving unemployment and finding a job first decreases until the spell length reaches 26 weeks, but increases up to a length of 40 weeks, because of stricter benefit control activity of the Unemployment Insurance Program, and then drops off sharply. As noted, the majority of spells are 1 to 26 weeks. An important finding is the sharp decline in the probability of employment after 40 weeks. The individual with such a long spell of unemployment may have greater problems in finding a job, or may not be actively searching for employment in the labor market.

As mentioned, we investigated how unemployment experience — measured in total length of unemployment, spell incidence, and duration — is distributed among individuals by sex, age, province, industry, and occupation. The total duration of unemployment for men was lower than that for women; so were the number of unemployment spells per person and spell length. The main reason the male worker fared better than the female worker is that the spell length for the former is shorter, on average. This could be because men are subject to more layoffs and the length of those spells which start with layoffs is relatively shorter.

With regard to age, we find two fundamental tendencies in the labor market:

1. The spell *frequency* decreases with age, first slowly and then rapidly after age 44.

2. The spell *length* increases with age, first slowly and then sharply after age 40.

The offsetting influences of these two tendencies determine the variation in total duration of unemployment by age group. The duration first drops with age, then increases for the 35 to 44 age group and finally falls sharply for the older age groups (45 years and over). In general, spell frequency has a more pronounced influence than increasing spell length on total unemployment.

In keeping with the overall unemployment rates, people in the Atlantic provinces and Quebec suffered greater unemployment with more frequent and more prolonged spells. Those in Ontario and the Western provinces, however, incurred fewer and shorter spells of unemployment.

The disparity in unemployment experience by industry is not as great as the disparity by province. Greater unemployment occurred in primary industries, including farming, forestry, and fishery, mainly because of seasonal factors. Both the average number of spells and the length of each spell were substantially higher than the national averages. The workers in the construction industry had more unemployment, largely because of the frequency of joblessness, while those in finance, insurance, and real estate, and trade, experienced relatively less unemployment principally because of fewer episodes per person. In general, we found more and shorter spells of unemployment in the goods-producing industries than in the service sector. In the latter sector, the spells are longer because of relatively more quits by people who often search longer for a job in the labor market. By contrast, there are relatively more layoffs in the goods sector, and workers often find reemployment faster.

The analysis of unemployment experience by occupation indicates fairly large disparities. People working in managerial or professional positions; clerical, sales, machining, or product fabricating occupations, and other crafts experience less unemployment, whereas those whose work involves construction; processing; primary industries; transport equipment; or material handling experience more unemployment. These dissimilarities in unemployment experience by occupation come mainly from the differences in spell frequencies rather than from spell durations.

As we have suggested, most unemployment is not short term. On the contrary, the burden falls mainly on a small proportion of workers experiencing repeated and long spells of unemployment. For these workers, we would recommend intensive and carefully targeted employment and training programs.

Notes

1. Unemployment, as measured by weeks on regular unemployment insurance claim, constitutes the bulk of unemployment in Canada owing to the almost universal nature of the Unemployment Insurance Program.

2. Regular claims exclude sickness, maternity, retirement, fishing, and Adult Occupational Training Act claims.

34/Shutdown Canada[*]

J. Paul Grayson

In Canada, full and partial plant closures have been occurring at an alarming rate. By New Year's Day, 1983, 14,000 Sudbury miners were out of work because of curtailed operations by Inco and Falconbridge. Worse still, over the next five years these two companies will continue to reduce their numbers of "permanent" employees. In Port Alberni, B.C., because of cutbacks in forestry products, 6,000 of the 19,000 residents were on UIC and a further 2,000 were on welfare. In Windsor, Ontario, Canada's "Motown," Chrysler announced its decision to scrap plans for a diesel-engine plant and close another plant.[1] Overall, Statistics Canada estimated that in 1982 Canadian industry operated at only 66.9% capacity.[2] And the unemployment figures, growing from 8.2% in September 1981 to 12.7% in October 1982, reflected this sad situation.

The real state of the nation, however, may have been even worse than these figures indicate. David Dodge, Assistant Deputy Minister of the Department of Employment and Immigration, estimated that by October in the "recession" of 1982, as many as 250,000 jobs may have been eliminated permanently from the Canadian economy.[3] In addition, Frank Feather, President of Global Futures Network of Toronto, calculated that "if the jobless total [in January 1983] includes categories such as discouraged people who are no longer looking for work, underemployed people and the employable category among welfare recipients," the real Canadian jobless rate was more like 29%![4]

A growing body of evidence suggests that in part an explanation for high rates of unemployment can be found in the branch plant nature of our economy.[5] To make a long story short, in general, multinationals tend to transfer manufacturing jobs outside of the country. For example, R.C.A. Corp. of New York has three colour-TV tube plants in North America. Two are in the U.S. and one in Midland, Ontario. When they decided to consolidate production and shut one plant down, guess who got the axe. Right. The Midland plant.

In other instances multinationals have transferred jobs out of the country by purchasing the materials, etc., that go into their final products not from Canadian but from foreign sources. As Statistics Canada[6] points out, when foreign-based industrial firms were compared to all Canadian industrial firms, "The foreign manufacturing companies' rate of imports to sales (import propensity) of almost 30% was nearly four times larger than that of domestically controlled firms." It is ironic

---

[*] Reprinted, with permission of the publisher and the author, from J. Paul Grayson, "Shutdown Canada." *Atkinson Review of Canadian Studies* 1(1) 1983, pp. 21-24.

that many U.S. studies confirm the belief that the offshore activities of American corporations increase employment in the U.S.[7]

Although Statistics Canada reveals that in recent years there has been a slight decrease in the amount of foreign control of the Canadian economy, an International Labour Office publication released in 1981 made an important point. In terms of employment Canada has the highest proportion, 43.1%, of foreign control of industry of any country that is a member of the Organization for Economic Co-operation and Development (OECD).[8] However, we shouldn't lose sight of the fact that a number of domestic firms have also fully or partially closed their doors. The bad guys are not all foreign-based. Massey Ferguson, as any resident of Brantford Ontario knows, is a case in point. Unfortunately, the fact that Canada, unlike many European nations, does not have tough legislation governing the circumstances under which plants can close, does not help matters.

The consequence of shutdowns, unemployment, can have devastating effects on employees and their families. Apart from the economic consequences, loss of self-respect, insomnia, strained family relations, domestic violence, depression, alcohol abuse, and even suicide are well-documented reactions to job loss.[9] Although some would like to believe that "economic adversity brings us together," in general, this is not the case.

Job loss is also expensive for the community at large. For example, it puts a strain on welfare and medical facilities. In December of 1982, the situation in Sudbury, Ontario, was so bad that existing agencies were having a hard time dealing with the results of unemployment. As a consequence, Jim Grassby, a community activities consultant, got together a group to establish a local stress management centre. Mr. Grassby pointed out that "the stress being felt now is very different from the stress felt in past years when Inco and Falconbridge workers were laid off or on strike — this time workers are unsure whether they will ever return to work."[10]

The Closure of SKF Canada Limited

A closure in December 1981 at SKF Canada Limited, which put 310 men and women out of work, was the result of the transfer of production abroad by a giant multinational. The company in question, located in Scarborough, Ontario, was, and is, a wholly-owned subsidiary of the world's largest manufacturer of bearings, headquartered in Sweden. With global assets in 1981 of $2.9 billion, and sales of $2.7 billion, SKF was described in 1981 by *The Economist* as "one of the most resilient of Sweden's companies."[11] In 1981 it ranked 179 out of Fortune's largest industrials outside the U.S.A. In terms of total assets, SKF is roughly twice as large as MacMillan Bloedel, a third larger than Stelco, three times larger than Domtar and Husky Oil, and six times larger than Molson and John Labatt. SKF is the Exxon of the bearing industry.

As a consequence of world rationalization, the parent company, in 1980, decided to give Canadian workers a 14-month notice period and then to close its Canadian manufacturing operation. It would service its $80 million Canadian accounts with bearings made elsewhere. For this reason SKF still maintains a Canadian sales operation. In many ways what happened at SKF is a microcosm of the Canadian economy. Moreover, its closure provided the opportunity to examine in great detail some of the problems caused by plant shutdowns.

Anxiety and Stress

The revelation that the unemployment of men has negative consequences for both them and their wives is nothing new. For example, a major British study on women identified a husband's unemployment as one of the most important of a number of problems that can lead to depression.[12] Other studies have shown that a great deal of anxiety concerning future job prospects can be found among the wives of the unemployed.[13]

In general, a distinction can be made between the *specific* concern over getting a new job, or job anxiety, and the *general* stress caused by a shutdown. With regard to job anxiety, prior to the closure, 56% of male SKF employees were worried about their chances of finding re-employment. At the same time, 78% of their wives were concerned about their husbands' prospects. As one woman put it, "I'm not quite as optimistic as he [my husband] is. I don't think he will be able to find a job like this that pays as much." There is no doubt that workers and their wives feared for their futures. As one former employee recalled, "There are people who cried when they heard that SKF was closing. They cried and I can understand that."

Two months after the closure, among the unemployed, the number of worried husbands had increased from 56% to 65%. The change may result from the fact that many employees right up to the end were unwilling to accept the finality of the closure. As one woman said of her husband, "It didn't seem to affect him until the day it closed. The day it closed he was really beside himself. We had gone out for dinner and when he walked in the house he sat in the dark. He didn't seem to want anyone around. He didn't want to talk." In another instance, seven days after the closure, a former employee suffered a heart attack. As a consequence his wife revealed that "his doctor said he will have to retire because he has nightmares about SKF."

The number of spouses worried over husbands' job prospects remained roughly the same two months after the closure. In essence, for both former employees and their wives, anxiety over job prospects was high. For the former, not surprisingly, it had increased from its pre-closure level.

In terms of the general stress generated by the closure, 49% of unemployed former male employees thought that the closure was equal to divorce or death of a spouse. Slightly fewer, 39% of their wives felt that the stress of the closure was equal to that caused by divorce or death of a spouse. For both men and women, the general stress resulting from the closure was high.

Health

Researchers have established a clear link between unemployment in general, and plant closures in particular, and ill health.[14] While not all agree on the nature of the links between these factors, incidences of cardiac arrest, ulcers, and so on, have been related to job loss. The same was found among unemployed SKF employees and their spouses. For example, prior to the closure, a woman revealed that as a consequence of the closure notice, "I broke out in a rash and I went to the doctor about this rash and he said it was because of the stress. I had a hysterectomy a couple of years ago," she continues, and "I have a thyroid problem so I have to take thyroxin and this sort of worry has set it off . . . I have a feeling," she concludes, that "I am not being me." While comments similar to the above were made in interviews with both men and women, a more systematic picture of the impact of the closure was obtained by examining individuals' general health and the use of prescription drugs.

Prior to the closure, only 18% of employees reported that their health ranged from average to poor. The figure for their spouses was a far higher 33%. By the second month after the closure, the number of unemployed former employees indicating only average to poor health had doubled to 36%. The number for spouses remained more or less the same. Former employees, it seems, were feeling more than the economic costs of the shutdown.

Although there was a considerable increase after the closure in the ill health of former employees, there was little increase in the use of prescribed medication by the unemployed. The number of males using drugs increased only from 42% to 47%. The use of medication by spouses in the survey remained the same. The slight increase in drug use, despite a higher incidence of ill health, may be explained by the fact that with the shutdown employees lost their drug plans. As a result, some may not have been in a position to pay for needed medication.

Relation Among Job Anxiety, Stress, and Ill Health

In terms of job anxiety and general stress, men who were unemployed two months after the closure, and their wives, appear to have suffered considerably as a result of the shutdown. At the same time, it is possible to establish important and different links among the closure, job anxiety, stress, and ill health for the former employees and their spouses. To begin, many wives who were ill after the closure had not been suffering from ill health prior to the shutdown. In addition, for wives, the general stress generated by the closure did not usually lead to ill health. At the same time, two months after the closure, there was an important correlation between wives' *specific* anxiety over their husbands' chances of getting a job, and ill health.

On the other hand, for unemployed men, there was a clear connection between ill health prior to, and after, the closure. Despite general deterioration in the health of the unemployed, ill health after the closure was to a large degree a continuation of ill health prior to the closure. Not surprisingly, therefore, for unemployed men after the closure, there is virtually no relationship between ill health and general stress. At the same time, other evidence indicates little connection between *specific* job anxiety and ill health. In short, it can be argued that two months after termination the closure, via job anxiety, likely had some impact on the health of the wives of the unemployed, but not on the health of the unemployed themselves.

The explanation for this state of affairs can most likely be found in the family role of wives of the unemployed. In many cases it was revealed that the latter felt that they should try to maintain a brave front even though they feared the worst. In essence, they kept things bottled up inside so that they would not further alarm their husbands. As one woman put it, "I personally was more conscious of the things that were being said. I didn't want to upset him. For instance, I'd say: 'that bill from Texaco this month is very high.' Then I'd think: O dear!" These valiant attempts notwithstanding, wives' unspoken inner turmoil often led to illness.

Conclusion

The investigation of those who lost their jobs at SKF reveals that overall the closure had, in one way, a similar net impact on unemployed men and their spouses. Both agonized over job prospects and experienced general stress. Nonetheless, the closure also affected them in different ways. For some women, two months after termination the job anxiety associated with the shutdown was related to ill health. For their husbands, ill health does not appear to have been related to job anxiety. Rather, to a degree it was connected to the fact that many did not have good health prior to the shutdown.

As the closure, via job anxiety, appears to have affected the health — one of an individual's most important possessions — of wives negatively, its initial impact, in one sense, was more costly for wives than for their unemployed husbands. Should this effect stand the test of time it would have implications for the way in which we view unemployment in general and shutdowns in particular. It would, for example, have important implications for social workers involved in dealing with the effects of unemployment and family counselling. When all is said and done, however, the most effective way of dealing with the consequences of unemployment is to ensure that it never happens. This job falls not to social workers but to politicians. And in Canada it is about time that the efforts of the latter were directed toward the implementation of an effective industrial strategy and tough legislation governing plant shutdowns.

Notes

1. *Globe and Mail*, 1983, January 1.

2. *Globe and Mail*, 1982, December 23.

3. *Globe and Mail*, 1982, November 22.

4. *Globe and Mail*, 1983, January 5.

5. Britton, J. and James Gilmour, 1978, *The Weakest Link*. Ottawa: Science Council of Canada; Grayson, J. Paul et al., 1982, "SKF: Profile of a Shutdown -- Phase 1." Paper presented to the Annual Meetings of the Canadian Sociology and Anthropology Association, June, 1982; Laxer, James, 1973, "Canadian Manufacturing and U.S. Trade Policy," in R. Laxer, (ed.), Canada Ltd. Toronto: McClelland and Stewart.

6. Statistics Canada, 1981, *Canadian Imports in Domestic and Foreign Controlled Enterprises*, 1978. Ottawa, Statistics Canada, vii.

7. Bergsten, C. Fred et al., 1978, *American Multinationals and American Interests*. Washington: The Brookings Institute. (See for summary.)

8. International Labour Office (ILO) 1981, *Employment Effects of Multinational Enterprises in Industrial Countries*. Geneva: ILO.

9. Hayes, John and Peter Nutman, 1981, *Understanding the Unemployed*. London: Tavistock. (See for a recent summary.)

10. *The Sudbury Star*, 1982, February 12.

11. *The Economist*, 1981, April 4, p. 186.

12. Brown, George W. and Tirril Harris, 1978, *Social Orgins of Depression*. New York: The Free Press.

13. Maurer, Harry, 1979, *Not Working*. New York: New American Library; Slote, A., 1969, *Termination: The Closing at Baker Plant*. Indianapolis: Bobbs-Merrill.

14. Cobb, Sydney and Stanislav Kasl, 1977, *Termination: The Consequence of Job Loss*. Cincinnati: U.S. Department of Health, Education and Welfare.

B/The Impact of Microtechnology
35/Women and Microtechnology*

Heather Menzies

On the front cover of the book, *The Techno/Peasant Survival Manual*, the authors describe a "technopeasant" as someone who does not understand modern technology and is therefore in a position to be used or abused by someone who does. I suspect that we are all determined not to be technopeasants ourselves. We want to understand what computer technology can do to jobs and working. We *do not* want it to replace women workers or de-skill them. Rather, we want it to enhance women's employment opportunities and working environment.

Several studies, including an overview of OECD (Organization for Economic Cooperation and Development) reports compiled in 1979 by the Institute for Re-

* Reprinted with permission of the publisher from Heather Menzies, "Women and Microtechnology," *Canadian Women Studies* 3(4) 1982, pp. 13-17.

search on Public Policy (IRPP) of Montreal, have concluded that women are likely to bear the brunt of the negative employment effects of microtechnology. The *Siemens Report* (Republic of Germany) predicted that 40 per cent of office workers could become redundant through office automation. The *Nora Minc Report* (France) predicted a 30-per cent loss of employment in the tertiary sector in general and particularly among bank and other finance-industry workers. In the United Kingdom, the *Jenkins and Sherman Study* predicted that office and other computer-based forms of automation could boost Britain's unemployment rate to 25 per cent by 1990. Individual case studies there have revealed, for instance, a 33 per cent reduction in the number of secretaries and typists at the British Standards Institute after word processors were introduced. The reason lies in automated re-typing and printing of computer-stored stock paragraphs called "boilerplate."

In a series of studies I did last year (published by IRPP as *Woman and the Chip*, 1981) I traced the process and extent of this negative employment impact in some Canadian industries. Projecting from the trends I observed and comparing these with the continuing concentration of women in, and seeking, clerical work, the unemployment rate among female clerical workers could escalate to as much as 33 per cent by 1990.

We could see the pattern in 1981. In the banking industry, where women com-prise 70 per cent of employment (80 per cent of them in clerical positions), computerization has reached a fairly mature stage; banks can now offer automated teller machines and can finally enjoy major labour savings. Employment had been growing by about 10 per cent a year through the 1970s, well ahead of growth in the female labour force. In 1980, though, employment stagnated. It was a signifi-cant development.

In the insurance industry, where information handling has also been exten-sively automated and where 70 per cent of female employment is concentrated in clerical positions, clerical employment dropped by 11 per cent during the 1975-80 period.

Most significant of all, the cumulative negative employment effect of computerization seems to be a seriously reduced, overall clerical employment-growth rate at a time when women's labour-force participation rate is both con-tinuing to rise and expected to continue doing so.

Between 1961 and 1965, the female labour force grew by 20 per cent; clerical employment grew by the same amount. Between 1966 and 1970, the female labour force grew by 20 per cent again, while clerical employment grew by 23 per cent. Over the 1971-75 period, the female labour force grew by 24 per cent; clerical em-ployment grew by 33 per cent.

Female labour-force participation is expected to continue growing at about the same rate at least over the next decade. The economic pressures are still with us, the rising cost of living, single parenthood and so on. Sixty per cent of women work because they have to. They are either single, single parents, or married to men earning so little that, if their earnings were removed, the number of families living below the poverty line in Canada would increase by 50 per cent.

I think I have demonstrated that we might have a problem here. I also hope we will see it not only as an employment-adjustment problem but also as a women's issue, for two reasons: computer technology is increasing employment opportunities in the occupations where women are least represented; on the other hand, it is diminishing employment opportunities in clerical occupations and in the related administrative and supervisory positions which women were using as career ladders.

My second reason is that, if women are to gain rather than lose by computer technology, changing attitudes must be part of the approach: attitudes of employers (male) who still dismiss women as a secondary labour force and insist that they prove in a courtroom their right to equality in the workplace and attitudes among women themselves.

From women's entry into the Canadian labour force as domestic servants a century ago to currently being concentrated, to an over-whelming 66 per cent, in clerical, sales and service occupations, women have been socialized towards support-staff, assistant and other "helper" roles. Yet the computer is automating and de-skilling much of that work, everywhere from the factory to the office: clerical workers in insurance companies and banks; cashiers, telephone operators (reductions range from 30 to 40 per cent with semi-automated long-distance phoning). The automation includes administrative work traditionally associated with process and procedure, a promotion ground which women have gained only recently. It also takes in supervisory work since there are fewer people to oversee and computer monitoring automates a large measure of this familiar female stepping-stone to management.

At first people did everything by hand. Then mechanization removed manual work, leaving the worker with a craft. Within the confines of mechanization, craft itself was diminished to a series of procedures. Finally the procedures were standardized enough that they could be taken over by the machine as well.

Let me give an example of automation in the banking industry. First, a teller's daily records were manually recorded in ledgerbooks. Then keypunching and, later, data encoding were introduced. By that stage, work was done in central data centres. Now, bank branches are connected "on line" with the data centre's computer. The teller enters the transaction record herself, automatically, as she punches in the information on her keyboard for printing out onto a customer's pass book. Tomorrow (almost literally) as the automated teller-machines introduce us to self-serve banking, the customer will punch in her own transaction and everything else will be done automatically. We can see the decline and the final automation of clerical work.

It is also interesting to trace the shifting employment pattern. When computerization was introduced to the banks, employment grew at all occupational levels. At the clerical level, there was an overlap between the old paper-based information work and the new electronic form. At the more professional and technical levels, employment grew in response to the new services (such as on-line multi-branch banking and daily-interest savings accounts) which the advancing technology made possible.

With recent developments, clerical employment has relatively declined while professional and technical employment has continued to grow. For instance, the daily-interest savings service provided more work to professionals (accountants and computer specialists) but little extra work for clerical workers. The clerical employment decline would probably look more dramatic except that banks were sharing the diminishing workload by increasing part-time employment. Part-time hirings were double full-time hirings between 1968 and 1974.

As Automatic Teller Machines (ATM) become widespread over the next five years (shifting tellers into data centres where they will provide telephone back-up to the ATM terminals), the prospect of shift work raises questions about potential damage to family and social life and compounds the structural barriers to occupational mobility for women.

There is another, perhaps more insidious, distancing factor which *could eventually jeopardize all hope of occupational mobility*: the growing skills gap between clerical and professional information work. Work in planning, research and development, market and financial analysis and management decision-making (work in which women are seriously under-represented) is becoming more professional because of computer aids available in the computerized office.

In one company I studied, the composition of the Information Systems Department shifted from 80 per cent clerical in 1972 to 45 per cent clerical in 1980. Of the 140 workers removed from the clerical ranks, only two joined the 110 additions to the professional-managerial ranks. They were replaced by computer scientists and other highly trained specialists hired from outside the company and representing what one personnel official termed "a quantum leap" in skill difference from the former clerical workers. The other 138 clerical workers were given lateral transfers to as yet unautomated departments, some even accepting demotions.

Meanwhile, armed with their computer skills, the new professional-management workers will exacerbate occupational discontinuity by extending the range and sophistication of their work and thereby escalating standards of performance. "The ability to do (sophisticated computer modelling) generates the requirement that you do this," the personnel manager told me. The effect could be the institutionalization of a dual labour market within the company: a scenario featuring a group of low-skilled clerical workers feeding data into computer systems, a smaller group of increasingly sophisticated professional users of computers and computerized information systems and a huge, hostile and unbridgeable skills gap between the two groups.

And when the company no longer needs clerical staff, "They'll be sent off to wherever redundant clerks go," the personnel official told me matter-of-factly. "Unfortunately, that will be women. But it's a question of social responsibility versus running a company."

Affirmative-action programs, equal opportunities and, to a more subtle extent, equal-pay battles over the last 25 years have sought to break down job ghettos and integrate the male and female labour markets for equal occupational mobility. Such schemes, augmented with training opportunities both on the job and in institutions, are all the more required now as employment opportunities in the clerical, administrative and supervisory ranks decline, as the meagre mobility ladder which supervisory and administrative work represented for women collapses and as employment growth becomes increasingly concentrated in occupations traditionally dominated by men and increasingly enriched as computer technology advances.

It is critical that women gain access to the employment-growth areas *now* before the skills and performance-standards differences widen significantly. Now, it can rightfully be argued that a lot of the seeming "quantum leap" of difference is due to attitude. For instance, in the department where the clerical-to-professional ratio changed so dramatically as computerization was extended from data processing to a full range of automated information systems, the top 50 executives in the department now have their own desk-top computer terminals on which they type and receive up to 50 per cent of the memos, mini-reports and other correspondence which secretaries used to handle for them. The remaining two secretaries spend only about half their time on traditional secretarial work. One I spoke to spends the rest of her time on research and administrative work.

By another name, such a clerical worker would be considered a prime candidate for courses in computer programming or business administration and quickly move into some of the professional positions which will become increasingly available but ever harder to fill by outside hirings over the next five to fifteen years. But her boss still called her a secretary; nor could he conceive of her moving into a professional-management position: "You can't make a doctor out of a nurse," he said.

Such attitudes might return to mock industry in the years ahead. Women might indeed be on a collision course between their continuing concentration in clerical occupations and industry's diminishing clerical requirements. But industry could also be on a collision course between the computer-fired upward reprofiling of its skills needs and the relatively unchanging profile of the expected labour force over the next decade or so.

The bulk of labour-force growth anticipation for the 1980s will not come from young university graduates, but from the increased participation rates of women 25 years and older; in other words, women who have already completed their schooling, who are either returning to the workforce or will stay on through child-rearing years. In 1979, less than 10 per cent of the female labour force had a university education. Further, women's concentration in clerical occupations remained a fairly consistent 33 per cent of the female labour force during the 1970s. As well, the government's training programs for women are predominantly geared to teaching traditional clerical skills.

What would involve relatively little training if affirmative-action apprenticeship and training programs were initiated now could become a costly employment-adjustment program for government and industry in the years ahead, as industry strives to fill a crippling skills shortage.

Before summarizing what I consider to be the major areas on which policy action must be taken, there is one other theme I should like to touch on. It is that the *net* employment question in this period of technological change is not a subject for research but for policy action. As several research reports (including the *Nora Minc Report* to which I previously referred and one published last year from the International Labour Organization (ILO) in Geneva) have concluded that the final employment outcome of computer technology will depend on how it is applied and in whose interests.

We are part of that choice. Should computer technology be applied towards the three needs which employment has traditionally fulfilled: earning income, developing and expressing our abilities and achieving stature in our own and other people's eyes? Or should the technology be used primarily as a cost-cutting competitive tool, industry's main reason for technological change?

Recent experiments in Europe demonstrate that both sets of objectives can be achieved, and to the mutual advantage of management and workers. Some have resulted from technological-change clauses in union contracts, clauses requiring consultation, or from health-and-safety standards, which go beyond such minimums as employer-paid eye examination for persons using video-display terminals to include "quality-of-working-life" considerations. The Tavistock Institute in the United Kingdom has developed what it calls a socio-technical model for implementing technological change. It takes into account "quality of working life" as well as quantity of output as objectives of the corporate system to be enhanced by the new technology.

Utopian? Not really.

There are essentially two approaches to the automation process: one, with a master-plan implemented from the top down and featuring centralized computer power and related decision-making. The alternative is a decentralized approach with individual departments acquiring computer-based facilities and expanding outward in pace with their developing computer skills. In such an approach, a secretary in charge of customer-complaint letters in a consumer-products company might develop a filing system in her word-processing unit which later allowed her to have all letters scanned for references to say, legibility of package instructions. After some manipulation of the data, she might produce some interesting market research, worthy of promotion or at least a job reclassification. The advantage of this approach would be that the threat of a skills shortage in a bipolarized labour market could be avoided.

In my research however, I found a lot of the top-down, central-control pattern, in keeping with the personalities who spearheaded the office of future transformations. These were engineers and systems analysts who tended to view the office as a factory producing information rather than as a service and communications centre. They also focussed less on information as a resource in itself than on the process of compiling information and transmitting it to decision-makers. In other words they applied computer technology to reducing the cost of producing, distributing and storing information, not necessarily to enhancing what you can do with information.

In her report, *Drowning in the Pool*, Janice Manchee provides a vivid account of working conditions under such a factory approach to office work, with a pool of word-processor operators working on anonymous correspondence in isolation even from fellow workers but with every movement and every error monitored by the central computer. Some of the operators were on drugs from the strain. Some broke down and cried, regularly. Others developed the habit of chattering to their machines.

A 1980 report from the ILO in Geneva describes these symptoms as an increasingly prevalent psychopathology associated with office automation and one which is generating international concern. The report lists what the workers have lost: autonomy to vary work pace, diversity of work pattern, personal contact with the people who originate the work, communication and responsibility within the workplace.

The income objective of employment is being met; the other two are being *savaged*.

At this point, one could launch into a passionate prescription for humanism in the workplace. However, we seldom change the world by single strokes of passion, certainly not in Canada. Change comes from gradualism. The power of change comes from process.

There are obvious agendas for action; to summarize a few: a comprehensive employment-adjustment program for women to help them move out of assistant information work into professional computer-assisted information work. Such a program could integrate existing programs such as affirmative action and outreach. It could include educational leave, coupled perhaps with wage subsidies; training, with extra funds allocated from a special technology training tax; manpower centres for women, providing computer-skills training and counselling as well as job placement. Counselling will be needed not only among women conditioned to doubt their aptitude for computer science but among industry leaders as well. Finally, public information programs are needed to alert women to the diminishing employment prospects in clerical occupations and to the new career opportunities emerging with computer technology.

In addition, women's lack of union protection makes it urgent that the Labour

Act be amended to require, among other things, compulsory consultation, even collaboration, on the process of implementing technological change. Such a measure could help lay the ground-work for the decentralized scenario I spoke of earlier.

These changes will come about only with the utmost effort and commitment on the part of women. We must present briefs, draft policy papers, lobby, ask pointed questions at conferences. We must do whatever we can wherever we work, in government, business and labour, to ensure that women are not "technopeasants" in Canada's computerized society.

36/Microelectronics and Employment*

Labour Canada Task Force on Microelectronics and Employment

Quality of Working Environment and Work

In the last decade, increasing numbers of employers have attempted to develop management policies which integrate social and humanistic values with economic and efficiency imperatives. These policies are intended to create a working climate in which employees derive psychological satisfaction from their work, and hence motivate themselves to help their firm reach its productivity and profitability objectives. Quality of working life programmes in which workers participate in decision-making concerning their own activities, including ensuring a safe, healthy and secure workplace, design and organization of their work and the scheduling of their work time, are fundamental to these new management policies.

How does microelectronic technology affect the quality of work and of working life?

The information presented to the Task Force reflected sharply divergent views on the effects of chip technology on work and the quality of working life. According to CP Ltd., new office technology has had a positive impact on office employees; for example, machines' editing capabilities make it easier to learn new "keying jobs," reduce monotony, and thereby increase job satisfaction. Similarly, a study of the banking industry, commissioned by the Task Force, reported that as a direct result of automation, tellers' jobs have become more varied and interesting.

Other submissions presented a different view. For instance, the Canadian Federation of Communication Workers, whose members, predominantly women, operate Canada's telephone system, stated that in addition to threatening jobs,

* Abridged from Labour Canada, *In the Chips: Opportunities, People, Partnerships*. Report of the Labour Canada Task Force on Microelectronics and Employment. (Ottawa: Labour Canada, 1982), pp. 51-59. Reproduced by permission of the Minister of Supply and Services Canada.

computerization caused work speed-up, tighter supervision and hence a more oppressive working environment for the operators. The Canadian Air Line Employees' Association also felt that technological change has reduced the previously varied functions of passenger agents to simple information retrieval.

Public meetings, briefs and other sources revealed three main concerns related to the impact of chip technology on the quality of working life: health and safety issues; the downgrading of jobs through the alteration of job content, social isolation and electronic monitoring, and the organization of work time that may become detrimental to the workers and thereby defeat technology-driven productivity goals. . . .

Health and Safety

. . . . Questions and concerns about the occupational health and safety aspects of microelectronic technology were expressed in almost all submissions to the Task Force and examined in our own research report. During our public meetings these concerns were reinforced. Four interrelated questions quickly emerged:

1. Are visual display terminals (VDTs) a radiation hazard? Do they emit any kind of radiation — X-radiation, microwave radiation, ionizing radiation, very low frequency radiation — sufficient to endanger health?

2. Are there other symptoms of ill health that can be directly attributed to work with micro-electronic equipment, especially VDTs?

3. Are there special ergonomic considerations for microelectronic workplaces, especially VDT work-places, that could alleviate health concerns?

4. Are there quality of working life (QWL) considerations that could be promoted for microelectronic workplaces, especially VDT workplaces, and could further help promote health in the workplace?

In recent years, VDTs have come to be used increasingly in our workplaces and in society. Their manyfold increase has spawned a growing concern about the potential effects the use of VDTs has on the health and well-being of their operators.

Not surprisingly the area of greatest concern in the submissions to the Task Force focussed on the potential effects of low-level radiation emission from VDTs. It should be remembered that various types of radiation have the potential to cause problems including cataracts, cancer, genetic damage, blood disorders, premature aging, birth defects and miscarriages. This concern has also been expressed in sensational stories in the media, and repeated at countless conferences as fact. Currently the gravest worry is that radiation from VDTs is the cause of an unusually high incidence of miscarriages, and/or children with birth deformities born to women, who during pregnancy, worked with VDTs. To date, several such "clusters" of reproductive problems have been reported in North America.

Extensive research has attempted to measure radiation levels emitted by

VDTs. Reported results have mainly stated that measured radiation emissions from VDTs have been so low as to be negligible. Others have stated that there is more natural radiation in the environment in general than that emitted from VDTs. Health and Welfare Canada tested over 300 VDTs with their regulation instruments capable of measuring very low frequency radiation. It, too, concluded that there is no danger of radiation from VDTs.

If these results can be applied to models of VDTs not tested, this would seem to remove most of the basis for fears about any long-term genetic effects or cancer. Nevertheless, it seems that such arguments must still be given some weight in order to ascertain as to whether current standards are strict enough to preclude even such remotely possible negative effects.

Meanwhile, the fear is real, and so far neither the tests nor their results have managed to put the misapprehensions to rest. For example, the National Action Committee on the Status of Women brief reminded us that standards of what is "safe" can change, as is the case with asbestos. The argument goes that perhaps old VDTs or inadequately maintained VDTs emit more radiation. Or perhaps some sort of synergism occurs in a worksite comprised of several VDTs that could amount to a hazard?

The following excerpts from the many briefs we received show the quandary we found ourselves in. For instance, the Canadian Air Line Employees' Association stated that at Dorval Airport in February, 1981, seven out of thirteen pregnant VDT operators miscarried. The Hospital Employees' Union, Local 180, British Columbia, told us that out of six pregnant VDT operators, two miscarried; and of the four babies carried full term, only one was born normal. The B.C. Federation of Labour reminded that four out of seven pregnant VDT operators in the classified ad department of the Toronto Star gave birth to babies with congenital defects.

Other groups insisted that there is no health problem. For example, the Employers' Council of B.C. testified that, based on available medical evidence, VDTs pose no identifiable health or safety risk to pregnant operators or their unborn children; and The Federal Radiation Protection Bureau (Health and Welfare Canada) has stated that there is no reason for any person, male or female, young or old, pregnant or not, to be concerned about radiation health effects from VDTs. . . .

These conflicting views and perceptions are compounded by the fact that many symptoms may emanate not only from the equipment itself but also by the organization of work and the design of the workplace. In other words, psychological and stress-related problems of working with micro-electronic technology may manifest themselves physiologically.

Since we know very little about the potential long-term effects of exposure to low-level radiation, it would be best to reduce avoidable x-ray exposure to an absolute minimum, on the assumption that no level of exposure is absolutely safe.

The Task Force can only conclude that the research performed to date on the question of possible radiation hazard from VDTs is unlikely to find acceptance as the final answer to these concerns. Despite the views and assurances of experts who have conducted these studies, these have not been successful in allaying fear and apprehension. We urge, therefore, that other public health methodologies be applied to investigate this concern as quickly as possible. . . .

Numerous other health problems have been linked to microelectronics equipment, especially VDTs. Limited research exists on the possible health hazards caused by polychlorinated biphenyls (PCBs), used as insulating fluids in some VDTs. Concerns are only normal about the link between PCB concentration in offices where VDTs are used and spontaneous abortion, birth defects and skin disorders. In-depth research over time is also needed in this area. In addition, eye problems among VDT operators appear to be the most frequent, the most directly attributable to the demands of the job, and to have a physiological base. A typist looks primarily at the hard copy she is reproducing. In contrast, even the most experienced VDT operator must constantly shift the visual focus, from hard copy to screen to keyboard. Eyes constantly refocusing for distance and illumination can easily become over-strained, fatigued and blurred. Fortunately these symptoms disappear relatively quickly when the eyes are at rest. Additionally, vision that might have been adequate under other working conditions may be overstrained in a job using VDTs, and corrective lenses may be required.

Accordingly, the Task Force urges the appropriate authorities to establish health standards legislation to take into account the increased visual load imposed by such microelectronic equipment.

Some of the other physical complaints of VDT operators, such as head, shoulder, and neck problems, would also relate, in part, to the need to look frequently in different directions. Complaints touching on back and wrist seem to be more closely related to postural immobility throughout many hours on the equipment. The Task Force believes that the alleviation of eye problems will also, in part, help alleviate some of these other physical symptoms.

We also recognize that some of these physical problems might be caused by ergonomic considerations related to either the equipment itself or the worksite. Some of these ergonomic factors, for example, might be legibility of the display screen, glare from the screen, non-adjustable office furniture (especially seating), the general standard and lay-out of illumination, and such. We therefore believe that ergonomic standards relating to office automation equipment and worksites should be established to cover such factors as physical environment, and office equipment and furniture. . . .

Job Content

On the basis of the briefs we received and the case studies carried out for us, we are convinced that microelectronics may not only change the work content but also the organization of work. It is apparent that depending on the change in work content, the level of required skills would change correspondingly.

Evidence shows that, in order to get the maximum return from the investment made in expensive office equipment, secretaries or clerk-typists — mostly women — may be required to become fulltime word-processor operators. Their other tasks may be totally eliminated. Additionally, the pace of work is often accelerated to justify the purchase of the electronic machine — which was procured to increase productivity. Depending on the downgrading or upgrading of skills, this could lead to a decrease or an increase in financial compensation and benefits.

Some research suggests that an unguided introduction of microelectronic technology will polarize workers into two more distinct classes: knowledge-workers who are highly skilled, and unskilled workers. People who have the ability and opportunity to acquire higher skills would be able to plan for and ultimately rise to positions requiring higher skills, hence higher pay and benefits. Workers lacking these abilities and opportunities would be left behind in routine, monotonous, dead-end work. This scenario is predicated on the demise of a "thinking" role for middle management. Clearly, the last word on this debate has not yet been heard. Canadian research in this area is in its infancy and will require a great deal more work before any definite conclusion can be drawn. However, recognizing the perception of a problem is the first step to preventive action. As women make up now most of the currently low-paying, dead-end office jobs with very little opportunity to move out of these ghettos, systematic and pro-active corrective steps by employers are essential in this regard.

Electronic Monitoring

The most serious manifestation of the introduction of new electronic office equipment is its utilization to monitor the quantity of work performance. For example, we heard about the added stress on telephone operators — primarily women — who hardly ever have time to breathe, being caught in "endless loops" and being machine supervised to produce more. This type of electronic monitoring also attempts to place limits on workers' freedom to move around. They appear to be tied to their machines under the ever-watching and ever-recording devices.

The Task Force regards close monitoring of work as an employment practice based on mistrust and lack of respect for basic human dignity. It is an infringement on the rights of the individual, an undesirable precedent that might be extended to other environments unless restrictions are put in place now. We strongly recommend that this practice be prohibited by law.

Organization of Work Time

Other major concerns workers, mainly women, expressed about automation and the quality of working life tended to centre on shift work, part-time work, and home work (cottage industry). We repeatedly heard that often management wants to recoup its capital investment in the newly acquired technology by encouraging shift work. Many witnesses pointed out the deleterious effects on health of shift work, such as disturbed sleep patterns, digestive disorders, continual drowsiness and reduced family interaction. For single parents, many of whom are women, shift work poses a special problem — reconciling their needs for earning a livelihood and their obligation to find 24 hour quality child care.

The introduction of microelectronic technology is expected to result in an increase in part-time work. At present, most part-time workers are women. Many do not receive the wages and benefits pro-rated to the hours they spend on the job. In addition, most part-time workers do not have the benefits of unionization. Undeniably, part-time work has many advantages for women who must try to juggle and harmonize family and employment responsibilities. Moreover, women attempting to integrate themselves into a technological workplace require suitable opportunities for training, retraining, and promotions. However, most part-time work schedules do not provide such opportunities. (Part-time and other forms of work organization are now under study by Labour Canada's Inquiry Commission on Part-Time Work).

Isolation

Another theme that surfaced repeatedly in the briefs we received and at our meetings was apprehension about working from home ("cottage industry"). We were cautioned that while working out of the home could be an ideal setup for some workers including specialized professionals, disabled workers, people living in rural areas and women with young children, the potential problems are significant. Women pointed out that there is a serious danger of exploitation in a system of home work. They further emphasized that home work can lead to the re-isolation of women in the home, and in the case of women with young children, burdening them with two jobs instead of one. Isolation might mean little or no opportunity for advancement. The absence of effective labour standards for home workers, such as proper wages, good working conditions, sickness, accident and pension benefits were cited often.

No one is sure how many women are now working at home, and are connected to main computers located at an employer's headquarters. But isolated stories in the newspapers and sporadic comments by employers about future possibilities of decentralization of work make this issue a matter of serious concern. Images of piece work are resurfacing. We realize that some workers will always make a choice about the location of their work. We also recognize that in the present economic circumstances women may not have any choice but to accept any available work. For this reason, adequate labour standards must be developed to protect home workers, and employers must fully comply with those standards.

Research has proved that workers cannot contribute their best efforts if the working environment is intimidating and lacking in human sensitivity. Clearly, the new technology, intended to eliminate "dirty" routine work and drudgery, does not have to mean a more fragmented and boring work environment. The concerns about the introduction of microelectronic technology, more particularly de-skilling, the monotony of work, the social isolation of the worker, invasion of privacy, greater centralization of decision making and a more rigid and less human organization of work do not augur well for creating an environment that would lend itself to higher productivity.

It could be more beneficial to consider an alternative option. In this option, "stand-alone" machines might be considered rather than typing pools where terminals are connected to a central computer memory bank. Women can then use the new technology to free themselves from many of their routine and time-consuming tasks, and could profitably use the time gained to take on more administrative, research-related and decision-making duties. In this manner, many clerical and service jobs can be enriched with value, rather than diminished.

The Task Force recognizes that human choice in selecting the equipment and deciding on how it is to be used is the key factor determining whether microelectronic technology will enrich or impoverish jobs and workers. As we indicated in our considerations on industrial relations, we believe management and labour problem-solving together can help ensure that dehumanizing effects are minimal and job enrichment is maximized. . . .

Organizational improvements could result when workers who would be affected by technological change are consulted a) long before a decision concerning introduction of technology is made; b) at the time of selection of equipment (preferably ahead of time to influence its design and specifications); c) about work station design and final integration of the technological processes into the workplace.

C/Occupational Health and Safety
37/White-Collar Workers Beware[*]

Julianne Labreche

In Thunder Bay, Ont., provincial office clerk Darlene Weiss has cataracts. She blames her cloudy eyesight on a video display terminal at work. In Winnipeg, Man., Gershon Sucharov was president and general manager of his own insurance firm until his hypertension became so severe his doctor warned him not to work. He's convinced the tension, which caused him anxiety, high blood pressure and

* Reprinted, with permission of the publisher and the author from Julianne Labreche, "White-Collar Workers Beware," *Financial Post Magazine* (September 15) 1981, pp. 53-58.

depression, was aggravated by the stress of operating his own business. In Hull, Que., federal civil servant Vera Wall, who works in a government complex known as Les Terrasses de la Chaudiere, is plagued by headaches, a sore throat and exhaustion. She blames her trouble on the building's bad air.

Blue-collar workers move over. While white-collar workers haven't resorted to wearing safety helmets and steel boots yet, they're slowly starting to realize the occupational hazards inherent in their jobs, too.

"White-collar workers are coming out of the closet," says Colin Lambert, a special assignments officer mainly responsible for health and safety, with the Canadian Union of Public Employees (CUPE), whose union represents 275,000 people, one-quarter of them office workers. "Office workers used to be complacent about their health. Now, whenever we meet over occupational health and safety issues, the best response comes from office workers."

No wonder. Traditionally, office work has been considered safer than crossing a quiet street on Sunday. The notion is false. No reliable estimates are available in Canada, but in the U.S. the nation's 25 to 30 million office workers were reported in 1976 to suffer more than 40,000 disabling injuries and more than 200 deaths a year from job-related hazards. Overall, the direct cost to business and industry was figured, conservatively, at about $100 million a year in medical and indemnity expenses alone.

Hazards in the office environment aren't virgin research territory, but almost. Few office workers have been interviewed about the occupational danger of sitting behind a desk pushing paper all day. The only Canadian study of this sort was undertaken by a Quebec government health and social service clinic in 1978. The survey, entitled *A Report: Health Evaluation Of Office Workers*, involved 1,530 Montreal employees who worked in 10 offices in Complexe Desjardins on St. Catherine Street West, one of the city's largest office complexes, which then had 9,000 employees.

Many office workers interviewed complained about their offices, with 70 per cent saying they were bothered by noises and 22.5 per cent commenting that their office was too hot or cold for working comfortably.

More than 36 per cent said their job made them "anxious," 35 per cent said they had difficulty falling asleep at night because they couldn't forget work-related problems and 56 per cent felt tired when they started work in the morning.

Other health troubles related to the office showed up, too. Some 43.6 per cent of workers regularly complained of eye fatigue, 26.6 per cent had headaches, 25.6 per cent suffered from poor circulation and 12.6 per cent complained of stomach and intestinal problems.

Troublesome statistics. Especially when, according to Jean Ialongo, a Montreal psychologist, the findings apply to all employees who work in an office setting. Ialongo, along with seven others, spent more than a year conducting the survey. Of those 1,530 Montreal employees, most were typical of office workers throughout the country.

"It's true workers in factories and mines have more obvious physical health hazards," he concludes. "The problems of office workers are different, but just as important in their own way."

His words ring true. Just ask Darlene Weiss or Gershon Sucharov or Vera Wall.

Traditionally, office safety managers have been concerned with injuries and accidents that can be prevented simply by using a little common sense. An estimated 30,000 Canadians are injured in offices every year.

"There are lots of opportunities for accidents in the office," says Stan Fields, national safety manager for IBM Canada, Ltd., whose Toronto headquarters employs about 1,650 office workers. "Mostly, they're the same kinds of things that occur in the home, mainly minor things. We have not had anything we can consider a serious injury. Nor have I heard of any serious white-collar accidents."

Office safety manuals sometimes distributed to employees outline the everyday kinds of injuries. Slips and falls, according to the Canada Safety Council, are responsible for nearly one-half of all disabling injuries to office workers. Typically, these accidents are caused by tripping over waste paper baskets, open drawers or telephone and electrical cords. Or they're caused by walking through a coffee spill or using an unsteady chair to reach high shelves.

Back injuries affect office workers who try to lift heavy objects — a pile of books, a file cabinet, a desk, for instance, while those using worn or damaged electrical office equipment can get electrical shocks. Bleeding and bruised fingers are sometimes the consequence of leaving pointed instruments, such as compasses, scissors, pens and pencils, lying loose; painful wounds are caused by rubbing against furniture with metal burrs or wood splinters, and serious injuries occur when top file drawers are overloaded, causing the cabinet to tip when higher drawers are opened. All these accidents can easily be prevented by careful forethought.

Michael Hollett, formerly a spokesperson at the Ontario Workmen's Compensation Board, says that accidents occasionally happen that require more than just a few days of recovery. One Toronto employee missed 28 days of work after the wheels jammed on her office chair. She tipped over and struck her shoulder on the edge of her desk, suffering a contusion to her shoulder that temporarily limited her arm movements. Another employee missed 45 days of work when, after crouching to pick up some files, she stood up and struck her back on a drawer opened by a second employee. Yet another office worker broke his ankle when his crepe-soled shoes jammed as he stepped onto a carpet.

"The injury frequency in offices can be as high as in industrial areas. The difference is, the severity isn't the same," says Wayne Chambers, recently retired safety manager at Imperial Oil Ltd. in Toronto. The worst office accidents at Imperial, he recalls, involved an office worker who leaned back in his reclining chair and fell over, puncturing an eardrum, and a young woman who injured her back by tripping over a fiberglass pad laid under a desk. Not exactly comparable to mine cave-ins and broken necks from construction accidents, but serious all the same.

To guard against office accidents, health and safety committees, comprised of both office workers and management, have been set up at Imperial. Other companies, including IBM and Bell Canada, have safety audit groups that make regular inspections of offices to ensure their safety. Bell office managers even keep a prevention plan manual which contains an office safety quiz that is gone over individually with each employee.

While office accidents continue to concern safety managers, more recently, other aspects of white-collar occupational health and safety have caught the experts' attention. There are a number of low-level, longer-term risks associated with the physical design of the office environment, and an office's layout, air, noise and lighting all come into play. Because these risks are cumulative, they're hard to prove. Potentially, however, they're more hazardous than tripping over wastebaskets and telephone cords.

According to George Rand, a psychologist who teaches environmental design at the University of California in Los Angeles (UCLA), the typical enclosed office building has been designed to increase productivity by eliminating concern with external environmental conditions — dust, darkness, humidity and extremes of temperature.

Warns Rand, "In effect, the concept of environmental control may be backfiring." The artificial environment, he says, may be the cause of a wide range of pulmonary, digestive, ophthalmologic and dermatological diseases.

Take office air, for instance. With energy costs mounting, the trend is toward tighter insulation and more closely controlled ventilation systems. By sealing buildings tight, treated air can simply be recycled. But with recycling comes a buildup of chemical substances normally found in the office environment. There are chemicals released from indoor construction materials and furnishing, such as asbestos, formaldehyde and vinyl chloride, along with air fresheners, solvents, adhesives in building products, cleaning fluids, fire-retardant materials and cigarette smoke. The effect, says Rand, "may be turning the inside of sealed buildings into virtual gas chambers."

The effect on office workers is sometimes called "Office Building Syndrome" (OBS). At best, it means office workers experience a mid-afternoon slump, yawn a lot and are less productive. Often, it means colds, arthritis, allergies and eye irritations. Because serious toxicological studies are lacking, perhaps the worst effects remain unknown.

Shortly after Tamara Levine, a federal office worker, was transferred to Les Terrasses de la Chaudiere in Hull a couple of years ago, she began, for the first time, to feel fatigued and have headaches. Her eyes hurt and she suddenly had skin rashes, too. Although she didn't realize it, she had OBS. Like her co-workers, she complained, suspecting bad air, and was accused of being a hypochondriac. "It's all in your heads, they kept telling us," she says.

When an environmental working group consisting of Terrasses office workers decided to take a health survey, the results proved the symptoms real. Of the building's over 6,500 employees, nearly 2,000 employees had similar complaints. An uncommon number of pregnancy complications were reported in the survey and workers are worried there may be a link.

There have been other episodes involving bad air in the workplace. A couple of years ago, the trading floor of the Toronto Stock Exchange was cleared after traders complained of numbness in their chests and stomachs and incoherency in their speech. The suspected cause was lack of oxygen. In San Francisco, 250 employees in the Social Services Building, a tightly sealed government office building, were bothered by headaches and sinus conditions. OBS was suspected. In West Germany, several office buildings have been closed because of complaints among office workers that bad air quality was causing sickness.

Even less understood are airborne infections possibly carried in recirculated air. By minimizing the amount of fresh air, the likelihood exists that these infections will spread among office employees. There are documented cases in which pollutants in buildings have been suspected of causing disease, says Elia Sterling, of T.D. Sterling Ltd., an occupational and environmental health research and consulting firm in Vancouver, B.C. The so-called Legionnaire's Disease in Philadelphia, Pa., is a well-publicized example. The most accepted theory to explain the disease, which killed 29 people and affected 182 others back in July 1976, is that a breed of micro-organism, called *Legionella pneumophila*, somehow invaded the cooling system of the Bellevue Stratford Hotel in Philadelphia and spread among the guests. In another instance, also in the late '70s, a federal office building in Rockville, Md. was discovered to have a defective air-conditioning system that allowed micro-organisms to pass from the building's laboratory to its offices. No office workers died, although many suffered from nausea.

Recirculated air in offices can also carry spores and fungi, which sometimes breed in improperly maintained air-conditioning systems. This can lead to cold-like irritations and allergies.

When these infections strike an office building, trying to avoid catching them is akin to attempting to stay healthy in a submarine when the crew has a bad bout of flu. Unless everyone wears a gas mask, the sealed enclosure is bound to cause germs to spread.

With a trend away from natural daytime lighting and an increasing dependence on artificial lighting, office lighting may be a danger too.

Controversy rages about the safety of cool-white fluorescent lighting, found in virtually all Canadian offices. Carefully controlled studies have linked ordinary fluorescent lamps to hyperactivity in children. Plants grown in hot houses under fluorescent lights produce strange, mutagenic reactions — growing roots up instead of down, for instance. Office workers have complained of the lights causing them mental and physical stress. Fluorescent lighting has been linked with headaches, nausea, eye irritations and even tooth decay.

"Office lighting is a very understudied area," says Victor Rabinovitch, program officer for workplace health and safety at the Labour Education and Study Centre of the Canadian Labour Congress in Ottawa. Although not entirely convinced of the hazards of fluorescent lights (his own office has them), he has other concerns. Most offices tend to be underlit or overlit and glare is a problem, he says, causing headaches and nervous tension.

Noise is something that can't be controlled by office workers. Very infrequently will office workers suffer auditory loss from high noise levels, says Earle Slone, managing director of Hearing Conservation Consultants Inc. in Scarborough, Ont., a company that tests and analyzes the hearing of some 50,000 Canadian office and industrial workers annually. However, he does recall a couple of instances in which hearing loss occurred among office workers in computer rooms. Because of the loud noise of computer printers, workers became unable to hear high frequencies.

More often the effects of office noise are non-auditory and stress-related. Typewriters tapping, phones ringing, secretaries chatting, copying machines clacking, file cabinets slamming, are all, at times, nerve-wracking. "Our studies have shown that office noise causes things like elevation in the pulse rate and fatigue," says Slone. The rise in blood pressure means a greater likelihood of heart attack. Non-auditory effects of noise are more prone to happen with open-office landscaping, where large numbers of office workers are not even separated by cloth partitions.

To mask the sounds of conversation and office equipment in open offices, many architects and acoustical engineers are pushing "white noise." It's a slight hiss piped in through loud speakers, intended to create privacy by hiding other noise. This concept, too, may be backfiring.

When Robson Square, part of a $160-million courthouse complex in Vancouver opened a few years ago and white-noise makers were installed, office workers in the complex reacted immediately. They complained of nausea, headaches and fatigue. As usual with office-related illnesses, the case was difficult to prove.

As Elizabeth Wright of the British Columbia Workmen's Compensation Board says: "If somebody gushes blood, you know they have a problem. But when people say, 'Gee, I'm really fed up and don't know why, and I have headaches and nausea and irritation,' it's very hard to pinpoint."

Proving the dangers of office equipment is equally difficult. Like other parts of the office environment, office machines are not risk-free. Right now, the storm of debate centres on video display terminals (VDTs). Feminist groups nickname them Very Dangerous Technology. An estimated 250,000 VDTs are now in use in Canada.

A study prepared by Colin Lambert of CUPE explores the range of potential problems which exist with the terminals. One of the main complaints from VDT workers is that they suffer from eyestrain caused by flickering, reflection, glare and brightness. One survey cited by Lambert, conducted by the union representing Associated Press in the United States, showed that 33 per cent of workers polled complained that their eyesight had deteriorated since working with VDTs.

Eyestrain, in turn, can lead to a number of systemic symptoms: headaches, muscular aches in the neck and arms, fatigue, irritability, nausea and vomiting.

Physical hazards with VDTs, connected with muscle fatigue, are caused if the office worker's chair is too high or low, or if there is insufficient back support. There are physical stresses, too, because VDTs can create sufficient heat to make the office worker uncomfortable. There have also been reports of possible birth defects. Four pregnant women working on VDTs at the *Toronto Star* newspaper had birth abnormalities. Various studies have subsequently discounted this hazard, but uncertainty lingers on. Says Lambert, "The whole question of the mutagenic and carcinogenic potential of VDTs is still open and requires much greater investigation."

Like other unions representing white-collar workers, CUPE is also concerned with photocopying machines. In a health and safety alert issued by the union, CUPE warned that office workers exposed to photocopying machines in areas that lack adequate ventilation are complaining of a number of symptoms: skin rash, ringing in the ears, feeling light-headed, dizziness and coughing.

The machines release minute amounts of ozone (a highly toxic gas), heat, noise and light. Some of the chemicals used as toners — nitropyrene and trinitrofluorenone, for instance — have proven mutagenic properties. The best remedy, says the union, is to isolate the machine in a separate room and ensure it is well-ventilated.

In coming out of the closet, office workers are determined to reduce the odds of becoming just another statistic for Workmen's Compensation boards. For a start, they're taking better care of themselves — jogging, quitting smoking and reducing cholesterol, salt and refined sugar in their diets.

As well, they're pushing their unions to investigate the hazards connected with their work. The Canadian Labour Congress is currently involved in a survey of some 2,500 office employees in eight Canadian cities — the largest study of its kind. Workers are being questioned about a range of concerns — working hours, the nature of their work, light, air and chemicals. The survey will also attempt to determine the nature and extent of health problems involving VDTs.

At CUPE, Colin Lambert is cooperating with Jeanne Stellman of Columbia University in New York on a major study of office environments. They're examining a number of office buildings and interviewing employees about office stress related to lighting, noise, air and work itself.

Equally important, just like blue-collar workers, office workers are starting to stand up for their rights and demand that hazards in the work environment be eliminated. This won't be easy. Too often, office managers tend to ignore complaints of colds, arthritis, allergies and eyestrain, viewing them as minor irritations and easily treated by self-prescription. Besides, because so many office workers are women and women tend to be suspected of being hypochondriacs, many times their claims are considered exaggerated.

Even safety experts sometimes dismiss the dangers. Says Jim McLellan, director of occupational safety and health at Labour Canada in Ottawa, "It takes all of our resources to focus on blue-collar workers. I compare the hazards of office work to falling hair among men." In other words, minor compared with the lung diseases, cancers and physical disabilities which afflict workers in more dangerous occupations.

The claims by office workers will have to be fought case by case, before the courts, if necessary, when demands are made that financial compensation for office-related illness be awarded. For office worker Darlene Weiss, it meant taking her case to the Ontario Workmen's Compensation Board. Initially, her claim that a VDT caused her cataracts was rejected and she's now in the process of appealing the case. Should she win, the case will set a precedent for other provincial boards.

Last April, insurance president Gershon Sucharov was awarded disability insurance of about $70,000 in past benefits, with due opportunity to collect $230,000 over the next 16 years, providing he remains disabled. The amount is to be paid by Paul Revere Life Insurance Company where he had an executive disability insurance policy. Although an appeal date is set for October 26, the decision is significant because it recognizes that stress and strain in a managerial post can cause hypertension so severe it can prevent a person from working. And there are other hopeful signs as well.

Federal civil servant Vera Wall and her co-workers stood in the main lobbies of Les Terrasses de la Chaudiere asking for $1 donations to help their cause and handing out buttons marked "Terrases de la Shoddy Air." Eventually, after many months, they were successful in having a thorough study of the building's air and ventilation system launched by government authorities. Health and Welfare Canada came out with a report in July 1981 confirming that there are serious structural problems in the building.

The first hurrahs are finally happening. And not a moment too soon. As modern offices of the '80s turn increasingly into engineer-designed machines, the timing could not be better.

38/The Case of Terry Ryan[*]

Stan Gray

The battle of the uranium miners at Elliot Lake over cancer and silicosis claims, the revelation of the "cancer belt" next to the steel plants in Hamilton, the outrage over the mine accidents at Inco in Sudbury, the fight of steelworkers against toxic coke oven emissions . . . all these were part of the escalating struggle in the 1970s against workplace death and disease in Ontario.

The passage in October 1979 of Bill 70, or Ontario's *Occupational Health and Safety Act*, was greeted with enthusiasm by labour. It was the result of a long struggle by unions and the NDP. Even in its amended version, it had improved provisions for control of toxic substances, the right to refuse unsafe work, joint safety committees, employer obligations to give information on health hazards, and so forth. It gave workers and their unions a larger role to play and promised to be a big help in cleaning up the workplace.

The last three years, however, have seen most of these high expectations frustrated. The potentialities of the Act have not been realized and much of the law remains an unenforced piece of paper. Only five toxic substances have been regulated, safety committees are purely advisory to management, the Ministry of Labour is reluctant to enforce the regulations and much of the labour leadership has since downplayed the health and safety struggle.

The Act is enforced through the various branches of the Ministry of Labour. Their inspectors have the authority to issue compulsory orders and even close down operations for violations. But corporate muscle has been powerfully exerted in the health and safety arena from the moment the Act was passed. Due to pressure from the Conservative cabinet to go easy on the companies and the pro-management policies of a weak group of inspectors, violations are often not cited and the government walks away from its policing responsibilities. It often just encourages labour and management to work their problems out together, as if both had equal power to correct hazards, and as if unsafe conditions were just another negotiable bread and butter issue rather than a threat to human life or limb.

On toxic substances, unions have had trouble in getting even the existing standards enforced. The Ministry's health branch minimizes exposure levels in tests and reports that are often deliberately misleading. The Ministry rarely compels ventilation or engineering controls, as opposed to respirators or other personal protective equipment.

---

[*] Abridged from Stan Gray, "The Case of Terry Ryan," *Canadian Dimension* 16(7 & 8) 1983, pp. 18-26. Reprinted with permission of the publisher and the author.

A law is also enforced through the courts where violations should be prosecuted. But health and safety infractions are rarely the subject of charges. The few prosecutions have centered around critical or fatal injuries. Even here, not often does the Ministry do a *serious* prosecution, and rarely if ever have guilty companies had to pay substantial fines or otherwise face the consequences of their misdeeds.

All this has given the companies a clear message: they can continue to ignore health and safety regulations without suffering any major penalty as a result. Bill 70 will not interfere with business as usual. The price of maiming and killing their workers will still amount to a relatively minor "cost of doing business" in Ontario.

The State

One case with which I was involved sharply illustrates the many aspects of workers' experiences with Bill 70, the companies, the courts, the Ministry and the unions.

On Nov. 29, 1979, a barrel exploded on the shipping floor of Westinghouse Canada's Transformer Division, at its Beach Rd. plant in Hamilton. The explosion blinded Terry Ryan, a 22-year-old worker, hired 6 weeks earlier. Terry has lost his senses of smell and taste as well as sight from the accident, and has other continuing health problems as a result.

The 45-gallon barrel was only supposed to contain a water-detergent mixture to spray-clean assembled transformers prior to painting. After the explosion, it was found that toluol was in the drum and hoses and was the substance that combusted. Toluol is a flammable solvent, highly volatile, and was not officially to be used in the spray device.

I was the shop health and safety representative of the union, Local 504 of the United Electrical Workers. The local then represented about 1800 workers in 3 plants of Westinghouse in Hamilton. Bill 70 had a new provision that allowed the union's safety rep to do an investigation of a fatal or critical accident, and report his findings to a joint safety committee and the Ministry.

The Ministry officials came in to the plant to investigate. They did a snappy on-the-site inspection, took a few statements of witnesses the next day but did no follow-up investigation. They seemed over-eager to hear and see no evil and quickly clear the company of any fault.

The inspectors ignored indications I presented that pointed to company responsibility. They refused to probe or follow through with the leads on the unsafe practices with toluol that could be at the root of the explosion.

The Ministry did not even ask workers about the regular controls on flammables. They also papered over whatever violations they did observe. They even went further by blocking my own investigative efforts when these appeared to confirm company liability — for example, by interrupting and cutting off my questioning of a key management witness when he seemed to confirm the (unsafe) practice of spray-cleaning with toluol from the soap apparatus. They also obstructed my obtaining statements of witnesses and other information.

These Ministry officials uncritically accepted the company's say-so on a number of key points. In fact, they seemed to be colluding behind the scenes with Westinghouse to co-ordinate their stories, such as on witness statements and explanations of the accident. The Ministry inspector declared on Dec. 19 that his investigation at the plant was over, that he would issue no orders and was approving of the company's remedial measures. This was done *before* he interviewed the victim himself and before the Ministry had even received the report from their lab on the samples taken from the accident site!

(The Ryan family had to later repeatedly call the Ministry to get them to come and speak to Terry. Afterwards, Ministry officials were rude on the phone and told the family that the file was closed as far as they were concerned; they were also told to ignore Stan Gray who was only "fishing.")

The Ministry had other concerns which overrode a serious investigative effort, such as a public-relations one and an anti-union one. They misleadingly posted a report in the shop that said the union rep was "satisfied" with their investigation and had no further information. The inspector spent a lot of time browbeating and lecturing me on the problems and failures of trade unions, on "irresponsible workers," on what a fine company Westinghouse was, on why I should be more co-operative with management and sympathetic to their efforts on safety, etc. When I pointed to the company's failure to comply with the Act's provisions on reporting critical accidents, for example, the inspector gave me another scolding on my "hostile" attitude and how that must change. He spent considerably more time trying to extract from me a statement that I was "satisfied" with his efforts than he did on actually investigating the possible causes of the explosion.

I considered that the Ministry was covering for Westinghouse and had simply whitewashed the affair. I had therefore decided early on to use the Act's new accident investigation clause to do an independent inquiry of my own, separate from the Ministry's.

In the meantime the company was doing its own public relations job by spreading the rumor that a lighted cigarette caused the explosion, and that some mysterious prankster was behind the accident. Neither story had any factual backing or even relevance, but it helped to divert attention away from management responsibility.

I did my own investigation over a period of months. This was not a simple case with an obvious specific cause, like an unguarded punch press. I interviewed many workers and supervisors and examined various documents, photographs and other pieces of evidence. I compiled signed statements of many shop-floor workers. I finally issued a 40 page report in July 1980, 7 months after the accident.

Four weeks later, the Ministry laid charges against the company and two foremen.

My report stated that toluol was used in a very unsafe and irresponsible manner throughout the plant, as if it was water, not a dangerous and flammable chemical. Management not only knew about but encouraged its use in these ways. Few if any of the normal controls on flammables were in force, e.g. safety cans, isolation from sources of ignition, bonding and grounding of dispensers, protective equipment, etc. There was little if any safety instruction to employees.

Furthermore, I isolated some work practices closely linked to the precise circumstances of the explosion, such as the use of toluol in that barrel to spray clean transformers. I had some signed statements as well as a document on this. While no one ever did determine how that particular barrel was filled, I showed it could easily have happened from any number of regular and common practices in the plant.

The Act requires the employer to take "every precaution reasonable in the circumstances" to protect their workers. The report tried to show how the company officials here took precautions to protect *themselves* from the legal repercussions of unsafe practices that endangered the workers. Toluol was believed to speed up production times, but using it was dangerous in those conditions and it would be too costly to properly control. Management therefore arranged a method of making it freely available and used "unofficially" in production, in a system that would also give supervision "deniability."

Terry was the eventual victim of this system.

Charges were laid by the Ministry of Labour's Legal Services branch located in Toronto, based on "information" sworn by Hamilton officials. Brian Charlton, a Hamilton NDP member of the Ontario legislature, advised me at the time that the Ministry may lay charges, but may not go on to do a "serious prosecution." In other words, it may just lay the charges to cover itself, but somehow arrange for the case to be dropped or lost later on.

I checked this out and found that in fact the charges contained a number of major errors. These would have led to the case being thrown out of court at trial time. There was a mistake in the very listing of the date of the accident! Apart from that, some of the information in the charges was false or misleading, including the regulations allegedly violated. Also, the Ministry chose the weaker parts of the Act to base the charges on.

Furthermore, the company and Ministry agreed in September to remand the case to December 3, 1980, just a year after the accident. Bill 70 has a clause stating that no prosecution can be initiated more than a year after the event; so when the errors of fact would have been discovered and the case dismissed, it would have been too late to lay new charges and the company would have been off Scott-free!

There were then some unanswered phone calls and delays in seeing the prosecuting lawyer. I threatened to publicly demand the appointment of a special prosecutor, and after some further pressure the charges were revised. . . .

Once the charges were revised in November 1980, the Ministry was in a real spot. It had originally vindicated Westinghouse. Had the prosecution now been successful, it would also condemn the Ministry for the original whitewash. A conviction of Westinghouse would have disturbing implications for Ministry officials.

It appeared that the Ministry was not going to allow its own prosecutor to do a proper job. At our first meeting, he told me he had never been given my report, which was sent to the Ministry months earlier and which had the bulk of the evidence for the case. He asked me to give him a copy.

The prosecutor seemed very unfamiliar with the details and reluctant to take the steps to do a serious prosecution. This would include requiring the production of company records, interviewing witnesses beforehand, examining evidence and so forth. There were delays in seeing him and aborted meetings.

Even had the Ministry taken a serious interest in pushing the case, it hardly had the resources to do the job. Health and safety violations are treated at a very low level of the court system in Ontario — Provincial Court, often before Justices of the Peace. Trials are normally expected to be quick affairs of a few hours, with few complications. The agency that prosecutes is not the Attorney General's office but employees of the Legal Services branch of the Ministry. They are few in number and have limited resources. (The Government's directory lists 5 Ministry solicitors for all of Ontario.) They can't come close to matching the resources of the big legal firms hired by multinationals like Westinghouse. This is especially true if the company chooses to make a fight out of it.

In Terry's case, Westinghouse was determined to use all its powers to get itself off the hook. Westinghouse is known as one of the harder-line employers and has traditionally had a confrontationist approach to labour relations. Within Westinghouse, Transformer Division is on the hawkish wing — safety conditions are worse there and the safety struggle has been more polarized as have labour-management relations generally. The company treated the court case as part of its continuing battle with labour. It would fight the prosecution tooth and nail.

It filed a procedural challenge, for example, demanding the case be thrown out for "lack of particularity" in the charges. Later, at the trial itself, the Westinghouse legal team used every form of obstruction and delay. After 2 days of hearings we were nowhere into the main body of evidence.

The company also played the delay and remand game, getting the trial postponed from the first September 1980 trial date to December, and then to March 1981, and then to June, where after two days of hearings it was adjourned to August, whereupon the company got a postponement to the end of September. By then it was close to 2 years after the accident.

Such delays generally help the companies, for the original events become more distant to witnesses. And the passage of time only continually builds up the fears and insecurities of shop floor witnesses, scared by the prospects of company retaliation, direct or indirect. Also, the trial takes place after much of the publicity and community pressure has died down.

At the time the charges were revised, the case attracted a lot of attention. The

Ontario Federation of Labour safety centre used it as an example of the Ministry not enforcing the Act, and the union doing its job. Then the NDP group in the provincial legislature followed up by asking some pointed questions of the Minister of Labour in the House and in the Estimates Committee, all of which attracted publicity in the media.

At a public meeting in December 1980 sponsored by the Hamilton and District Labour Council's safety committee, I and some other Hamilton unionists spoke strongly against the Ministry's mishandling of safety precautions. The Westinghouse case was cited along with others in the steel industry. All this was related as part and parcel of the Ministry's refusal to enforce the Act and regulations, whether in the plants or courts.

The public pressure was now on and the Ministry became more careful with us. The prosecutor met often with me, and did actually spend some time interviewing witnesses and preparing questions and arguments. Reluctant at first, he later agreed to try to expand the area of evidence beyond the simple prosecution routine in safety cases — introducing "confessions" of the accused, "similar fact evidence" showing a general pattern of unsafe handling of flammables by the company, testimony of expert witnesses and so forth. With the help of some legal friends, I developed these and was able to muster a strong array of evidence on company negligence.

Over time it became quite evident that the higher-ups of the Ministry were being pressured to scuttle the prosecution. While I and other union people could talk to inspectors and prosecutors, the big corporations deal at an entirely different level, with Cabinet people, Deputy Ministers, top influence makers and so on.

Also, from what I could see, the Hamilton Ministry officials were unco-operative with the prosecutor. They were eager to see Westinghouse acquitted, for that was the only way to justify their earlier exoneration and save their own skins.

The prosecutor himself behaved in a curious and often contradictory manner, perhaps as a result of the different pressures he was being subjected to. He performed at times quite competently. However, he worked for the Ministry of Labour, the top echelons of which had an interest in losing the case, and they made all the major decisions.

Although the company's procedural challenge was lost, for example, the prosecutor handed the company lawyer a precedent at the special hearing that he thought proved the company's case; he told me he assumed the challenge would succeed. When he interviewed our witnesses, whom I had gone to great pains to re-assure and conceal from the company, he joked to them about giving the company their names. He made a point of telling one key witness that he had no protection against company reprisal for his testimony.

The first day of trial, June 3, 1981, was a farce. The Ministry paraded a group of its witnesses, half of whom did nothing but testify about the paperwork and routines involved in filing reports and tests. The other witnesses made out a fine case for Westinghouse, the defendant they were supposed to be prosecuting. The inspectors who did the investigation did not tell of the violations they found and they minimized any hazards that could be associated with flammables like toluol. The Ministry's own scientific "experts" could hardly state that some of the basic safety precautions with flammables, as required by the law, were necessary. The prosecution even called up one of the accused supervisors who proceeded to give the company's version of events, unchallenged.

The second day of trial, June 9, was a bit of a turnaround. Terry himself testified, and went through many of the unsafe practices with toluol, such as its being squirted about right next to a welding operation. He also showed the lack of proper instruction and supervision on the use of flammables. The company lawyer then went at him for several hours and tried to confuse him and twist his words.

Terry's father and wife then took the stand and related that one of the foremen had come to them after the accident and said it was negligence on the company's part. The judge accepted this as evidence of a confession, though the Westinghouse lawyer challenged its accuracy and then harrassed Terry's father on the stand, implying he was a stooge of the "union functionary" Stan Gray.

For the Sept. 21 continuation we had many witnesses prepared for the bulk of our evidence. I was to take the stand and present the results of my investigation, along with some testimony on the general safety problems in the plant, including the lack of controls on flammables. I would also give some background material on toluol and solvents since the Ministry's "experts" had minimized its dangers. We had a lot of shop floor people coming to testify and document the case with first-hand knowledge. They would tell the court what the Ministry's officers wouldn't.

We also had safety reps from Inco in Sudbury, Local 6500 of the Steelworkers, and from another UE plant in the area. They were to testify on the kind of safety policy on flammables at their workplaces, as evidence on what are reasonable steps for an employer to take in the circumstances.

All that evidence never saw the light of day. Before the start of the trial, the Ministry prosecutor suddenly told me that he and the Westinghouse counsel had made an arrangement. They would agree on a minimum statement of facts, have the company foreman testify and then conclude the case that day!

A deal had been made, no doubt at the higher levels, and they were determined to see it through. Our witnesses would not be allowed to testify, the statement of facts was neutral and implied no company responsibility for the explosion. We made some strong protests. We were then told that the company would plead guilty to reduced charges; 6 of the 7 were dropped, one was amended.

The company pleaded guilty to minor infractions. It loudly made the point that these were not related to the explosion, and that the company was not accepting any responsibility for the accident. The prosecutor did not challenge that, and then went on to ask the court not to be too hard on Westinghouse. He stated falsely that the company had no previous safety convictions.

The company got off with a fine of a mere $5,000 and 14 charges against the two foremen were dropped. (The Judge couldn't quite buy the story the company and Ministry were giving him, he stated that he could tell from the limited evidence he had heard that proper safeguards were not enforced in the plant and the company did have some degree of responsibility.)

The whole exercise smelled of a fix. Terry and I screamed blue murder to the press, as did the rest of Hamilton labour.

Two days later, a Hamilton company faced safety charges because a worker was killed at Lake Erie because of unsafe scaffolding. The court was told that the Ministry inspectors had cited the company for unsafe scaffolding a month before the accident and nothing had been done to correct it.

The company pleaded guilty. It was fined $2,500. The Ministry dropped 16 charges against the company and 7 against the foreman.

Money doesn't talk, it swears. . . .

As for Terry, he is making out as best he can. He has further medical problems and has to fight the Workmans' Compensation Board's attempts to chisel on his entitlements. He and his family are still pursuing every avenue in their search for justice.

39/Company Doctors' Perceptions of and Responses to Conflicting Pressures from Labor and Management[*]

Vivienne Walters

A number of writers have argued that the interests and ideology of professionals coincide with those of the dominant class, and that professional expertise and authority legitimize existing power structures and operate as a form of social control (Brown, 1979; Daniels, 1972; Esland, 1980; Friedson, 1970; Johnson, 1977; Navarro, 1980). Most discussions of occupational medicine have fallen within this tradition. The literature on the politics of occupational health and safety (Berman, 1978; Epstein, 1978; Navarro, 1980; Reasons et al., 1981; Tataryn, 1979) is highly critical of company doctors who, it is argued, have served the interests of employers to

[*] Abridged from Vivienne Walters, "Company Doctors' Perceptions of and Responses to Conflicting Pressures from Labour and Management," *Social Problems* 30,1 (1982), pp. 1-12. Published with the permission of The Society for the Study of Social Problems and the author.

the detriment of workers' health and safety, and helped to legitimize relations of domination in the workplace. This image is very close to common stereotypes of the incompetent, unsympathetic company doctor who has "retired" to a sinecure. However, these analyses have not been based on systematic empirical research, but have relied largely on workers' views of company doctors. Other studies (Daniels, 1975; Field, 1966) drawing on doctors' accounts of their work in other settings have shown how the structural context of medical practice can shape the content of practice, so that doctors are called upon to make decisions which have little to do with medicine per se. This paper explores the constraints which shape the practice of occupational medicine and examines how company doctors perceive and respond to their two sets of clients: managers, who represent the interests of those who own and control the organization, and workers, for whom doctors have medical responsibility.[1]

Profile on the Sample

I interviewed 23 doctors employed by 10 companies in the province of Ontario, Canada.[2] The companies included the following: unionized and non-unionized workers; capital- and labor-intensive industries; large and small companies; predominantly male and predominantly female employees; a company town; industries in which there has been considerable public debate over health hazards; and those which have less frequently been the focus of such attention. They included steel, chemical, clothing, photographic processing and supplies, oil, electrical, and mining industries.

Ten doctors were medical directors of major companies and were involved largely in administration and policy formulation. Six others were employed full time as practicing physicians in a company. Two were involved in occupational medicine full time but contracted their services to many different companies. Five combined occupational medicine with general practice. Over half had earlier practiced occupational medicine in a different setting from that in which they were presently employed. They ranged from doctors in their first five years of practice to those who were close to retirement or had recently retired. Two of the doctors were women. Most interviews lasted for a little over two hours and all were tape recorded.

Conflicting Pressures

The doctors faced contradictory pressures in four main areas: (1) regulation of absenteeism; (2) certification of workers' fitness to work; (3) workers' compensation; and (4) occupational health hazards. They were concerned about the health of their patients and with achieving improvements in the workplace, and several were critical of lower levels of management for their failure to give health and safety issues higher priority. Nevertheless, the doctors were constrained by pressures from labor and management. Such constraints encouraged the reconstruction of medical definitions; caution in classifying workers as fit to work; watchfulness for workers who might be "cheating" the company through unnecessary absences or compensation claims; a frustration that workers overestimated hazards in the workplace; and an emphasis on "realistic" budgets and less costly strategies for improving occupational health and safety. One doctor highlighted the contradiction between productivity and health when he described the constraints and compromises in industrial practice:

. . . physicians accept production as a priority too; we do work in that situation, and that priority to a lesser or greater degree takes priority over health. You just have to bargain to sort of push health a bit, they push production, and you bargain. . . . You push a little, but you also tolerate a lot of unhealthy conditions as well.

Absenteeism

Management expects company doctors to prevent unnecessary absence from work and to return the worker, at least to light duties, as soon as possible. This pressure reflects the interests of employers in maintaining or increasing production levels and avoiding lost time for which workers will be compensated and which can lead to higher assessments by the provincial Workmen's Compensation Board (which decides whether illnesses and injuries are eligible for compensation). Workers, on the other hand, do not necessarily wish to return to work speedily, and may be reluctant to be placed on light duties. Such conflicts raised a number of problems for doctors.

You cannot please union, supervisor, and the patient. . . . Something as simple as a sprained ankle — what you would like that worker to do is put some ice on that ankle, rest it for a couple of days, and by that time maybe he could do some light work. . . . But that couple of days of rest would make him a lost-time accident. So the supervisor will want him back and will go to the extent that they will sit him in the welfare room reading a comic for a couple of days. This is purely politics, it's purely keeping your numbers down. Now, some employees don't mind that . . . but 20 to 30 per cent of workers would want some time off, no matter what. If you give them what they want, you lose with the supervisor. If you try to say, "Well, you really could do something in there," they go to their family doctor who puts them off anyway. And that affects your relationship with the union because that will get back to them.

In response to these pressures, company doctors try to counteract the power workers derive from the support of their family doctors and resist pressures to become a disciplinary tool of management. They must define what is an acceptable reason for absence and, in so doing, they emphasize the therapeutic value of work to justify keeping absence to a minimum. They claim that they are better able than family doctors to recognize when a worker could go back to work because they have superior knowledge of the type of work an employee would be required to do. And they point out that family doctors have no feeling of responsibility toward the employer:

The family doctor is really not terribly interested in the welfare of the company. They're interested in their patient and so they're inclined to say, "well, take a few more days off." But we sit here paying the shot when we'd like this fellow back to work.

. . . .Fitness For Work

Company doctors certify workers' fitness to work through pre-employment or pre-placement examinations. They examine workers before or soon after they are hired to screen out the unemployable. These initial examinations have traditionally been a central component of the work of company doctors and all the doctors in this study were involved either in performing such examinations or in establishing policies and criteria for them. Since unions have shown almost no interest in protecting workers in this initial selection process, management has been relatively unconstrained in the implementation of policies. Thus, company doctors usually err on the side of safety by certifying doubtful cases as unfit to work; they identify with their companies and try to protect them from "bad risks." They do not recommend employment of workers who might incur occupational illnesses or injuries and for whom the company would "unfairly" bear the compensation costs. One doctor described pre-employment examinations as "worth gold to a company. They don't want to be handing out compensation for these guys." His sympathy for workers who "would come in sweating to get jobs, they'd been out of work so long" did not alter his primary emphasis on the company's need to screen out potential problems. But not only do pre-employment examinations exclude bad risks; they also provide companies with baseline data on new employees. Medical data, as well as other information on life styles, are available for assessing the validity of future compensation claims. In this way also, these initial examinations can help to reduce the costs to companies of occupational illness and injury.

Doctors claimed that they protect individuals from hazards in the workplace by denying them employment. They recognized the discriminatory effects of pre-employment and pre-placement examinations but argued that the tests protected the best interests of either the individuals concerned or those with whom they would otherwise be working. The examples interviewees gave of such cases were often extreme — the problems of employing epileptics as crane drivers or legless workers as truck drivers. Should disabled workers be given the chance to demonstrate their ability to perform the work in question? Should women be allowed to work in jobs with potential reproductive hazards? Most doctors did not favor exclusion and preferred an advisory role in which they would warn workers of potential hazards. But a few had already placed firm limits on employment. For example, one medical director, assuming that all women of childbearing age are at risk of becoming pregnant, had established a policy of exclusion in certain areas of the plant because "there are some situations where I don't have enough evidence and the prudent thing would be to avoid exposure of the fetus to certain agents." . . .

In addition to these initial medical examinations, company doctors evaluate workers' continued fitness for their jobs. A number of dilemmas can arise here. A worker might develop health problems in the course of, though not necessarily as a result of, working. Or, the conditions of work might change in such a way as to create health problems for a person. Here, the doctor plays a part in recommending that the worker be "let go" or transferred to other work. The latter option often involves a loss of pay as well as a break from what may be a tightly-knit work group. For these reasons, workers may be reluctant to be labeled as unfit for their normal work. It is in the interests of workers to remain in their job and to have the hazardous conditions removed wherever possible. Insofar as this might be costly or disrupt normal work processes, management is more likely to favor job transfers or firing workers. . . .

Workers' Compensation

Workers' compensation has been a contentious issue since its inception, and the involvement of company doctors in compensation cases has played a major role in creating worker mistrust of them.[3] In the past, workers have placed greater emphasis on securing compensation for work-related injuries and illnesses than on improving conditions of work (Navarro, 1980); organized labor has pressed for an extension of the range of illnesses subject to compensation and for more adequate remuneration for workers. Clearly, it is in the interests of workers to have work-related illness and injury recognized as eligible for compensation. For employers, workers' compensation represents the internalization of some of the costs of occupational disease and disability (Ashford, 1976). It is in companies' immediate interests to keep assessments as low as possible, to resist an extension of the range of illnesses subject to compensation, and to oppose any case where the occupational basis of a worker's illness or disability is open to doubt. In consequence, this has been an area of bitter and lengthy disputes between workers and management.

Almost all the doctors I interviewed noted the conflicting interests surrounding compensation. None exhibited willingness to become involved in appeals; they were reluctant both to contest workers' appeals of decisions by the Workmen's Compensation Board not to grant compensation, and to act on behalf of companies in appealing decisions favorable to workers. One doctor recalled his last appearance at an appeal: "Well, they thought I was just Frankenstein, trying to deprive that poor crying widow of so much money a month." He decided this was an inappropriate role for a doctor and one not likely to help establish good rapport with employees. Many others echoed these sentiments and indicated that they no longer involved themselves in compensation decisions other than to provide the basic information required by the Workmen's Compensation Board. In this way they hoped to play a neutral role.

. . . it's nebulous, it's a difficult decision, and I think it should be done by specialists at the board level. It's a nice cop-out, too, because I see myself as a buffer, as a guy who's here trying to portray that we are concerned about the worker. If I have at the same time to make decisions that really affect the outcome of this guy's life in the sense of when he retires, if he's going to get an award from the board . . . that would put me in a position where I wouldn't be a very good buffer. I would be seen as the guy who makes or breaks things and not as a guy you can go and talk to. And the more of that you're involved in, the worse your position is.

Professionals do not like to acknowledge their control over patients or clients and the unpleasant or "dirty work" that they do (Daniels, 1975; Hughes, 1962). This may explain the reluctance of company doctors to discuss this contentious aspect of their work and to limit their formal involvement in compensation issues. But though most doctors claimed that they were content to "leave it to the board," this posture may be misleading. Several doctors noted informal channels for influencing compensation decisions. One doctor claimed that he would arrange agreement between specialists if he felt that a worker was "committing a real crime" by claiming compensation. Several others noted that they would informally advise the company which compensation decisons were worth appealing and which specialists could be relied upon to give supportive opinions. And another doctor pointed out that it was easy to imply doubts about the validity of a claim in the formal report to the Workmen's Compensation Board. . . .

Health Hazards in the Workplace
Since the early seventies, there has been increased public concern with occupational and environmental health hazards, and unions have accorded higher priority to occupational health and safety (Walters, in press). Moreover, provincial legislation in the late 1970s has further encouraged companies to reduce health hazards in the workplace. These changes have helped to create an expansion of occupational medical services, yet they have also increased the potential for conflict. The impact of these changes on smaller companies has been relatively small; doctors working on a contract basis for such companies showed little concern for, or knowledge of, occupational health hazards. Their primary responsibilities were pre-employment examinations and the certification of workers as fit to return to work. In the big corporations, where medical departments often employed two or more doctors and a medical director responsible for corporate policy, occupational health hazards have become a major concern. All had introduced extensive medical monitoring programmes for the early detection of health problems and all monitored either the worker or the workplace for hazardous exposures. . . .

The doctors I interviewed exhibited a certain lack of sympathy with or intolerance of workers' attitudes towards health and safety in the workplace. One doctor noted that there were "fashions in these things": pesticides in the 1960s; air pollution in the 1970s; occupational health, particularly cancer and reproductive hazards, in the 1980s. Another doctor argued that workers were overly fearful of hazards: "They're frightened of things it would never enter my head to be frightened of." He claimed that concerns over the slightest leak of radiation were inappropriate and he argued that many pesticides are so harmless "you could eat them." In his opinion, public outcry and fears for pregnant women were not realistic. Other doctors minimized hazards in the workplace by pointing out that "any substance can be toxic, including water, if you handle it the wrong way.". . .

Doctors' responses to workers' concerns about occupational health hazards reflected the dual and contradictory character of occupational health and safety. On one hand, companies seek to maintain or increase profits by minimizing production costs and resisting investment in health and safety. Yet it is also in the interests of companies to avoid the losses in productivity and other costs associated with work related illness and injury. The cost of creating a safer and healthier work environment is both a drain on profits and a necessary part of the expenditure involved in increasing productivity and profits (Schatzkin, 1978). While the bulk of the costs of occupational disease and disability have not been borne by industry (Ashford, 1976; Reasons et al., 1981) increasing pressures from labor, together with increased legislative controls, have heightened these contradictions. Doctors mirrored this duality. They did not knowingly wish to kill, injure, or maim workers, and many spoke of the fear that "another vinyl chloride" might exist.[4] They were sensitive to the need to minimize companies' compensation costs, and several recognized that, in the long term, this could best be achieved by reducing health hazards in the workplace. But they also recognized the costs associated with reducing or eliminating occupational hazards: many argued that these had to be taken into account in establishing "reasonable risks" and the most appropriate strategies for coping with hazards. This appreciation of cost limitations has led doctors to emphasize the exclusion of supposedly "hyper-susceptible" workers, the use of protective equipment rather than engineering controls, and careful monitoring of workers to determine whether their health problems might be related to non-work factors. Yet pressures from labor have challenged such strategies and accentuated these contradictions, and doctors have often reacted with cynicism and a sense of frustration that workers cannot be more realistic about the nature of occupational hazards and appropriate measures for reducing them. . . .

Conclusion

Company doctors are faced with constraints arising from often contradictory pressures to safeguard health and, at the same time, promote productivity and profits. Such contradictions are embodied in the different positions which management and labor frequently assume over absenteeism, certification of workers' fitness to work, workers' compensation, and strategies to reduce health hazards in the workplace. It is not that management ignores the health of workers, but rather that it balances health issues against costs. As Schatzkin (1978) has argued, health related costs are both a drain on profits and an essential expenditure in order to increase productivity and profits. Workers do not simply strive for health; their reactions to health issues are shaped by broader struggles with management and, in part, represent strategies for asserting control over their lives and conditions of work.

Company doctors are constrained by these conflicts. Their reliance on management approval of budgets and research projects, pressures from management to minimize lost time, and, in some cases, restrictions on their contacts with union personnel, indicate limits to doctors' autonomy and ways in which occupational medicine can be shaped by organizational priorities. Doctors who cannot adjust to such constraints, or who are employed in companies where they are particularly strong, may resign, for these pressures are obviously easier to accept if they agree with the tenets of their employers. In consequence, the decisions of doctors I interviewed were often biased toward management priorities. Pressures from workers were often considered problematic; doctors were cynical and frustrated that workers tried to "get away with" too much and were unrealistic. Yet such pressures had a dual effect, for, in addition to increasing the constraints in industrial practice, they also benefitted doctors: several doctors noted how labor's increasing concern with occupational health had helped to generate legislation, thus increasing budget allocations and the size of medical departments.

Doctors' bias toward the companies which employ them has resulted in a negative image of company doctors. In an effort to improve this image, they are seeking to limit their formal involvement in some contentious issues and to establish better channels of communication with workers. This often involves explaining issues and encouraging workers to accept a different definition of reality. In so doing, doctors rely on an ideology of medical objectivity which, because of its claim to impartiality, can strengthen medical authority and inhibit the consideration of alternate definitions of reality. Occupational medicine can thus reinforce management's control over labor. In this respect, of course, company doctors are not distinctive. A number of writers have indicated how medicine operates as a form of social control and constructs definitions of illness and appropriate therapies which are often congruent with the interests of the dominant class and reinforce existing inequalities (Ehrenreich and Ehrenreich, 1978; Freidson, 1970; Navarro, 1976).

Notes

1. This research was funded by a grant from the Social Sciences and Humanities Research Council (410-81-0014). The author thanks Jack Haas, Ted Haines, Joseph Smucker, Barrie Thorne, and two anonymous *Social Problems* reviewers for their comments.

2. I also attended four conferences on occupational medicine at which company doctors were well represented. These confirmed that the issues raised in the interviews were also broad concerns within the profession.

3. The Ontario Workmen's Compensation Board was introduced in 1915. It is financed by companies which are rated on the basis of their past illness and injury records. Such compensation schemes have been criticized because they do not accurately reflect the real costs of occupational health. For example, the stringent criteria established by the boards do not recognize and provide compensation for a range of diseases which are occupationally related. For a discussion of the origins and operation of boards in Canada see Reasons et al. (1981); in the U.S. see Ashford (1976).

4. Vinyl chloride workers have a high probability of developing angiosarcoma of the liver, a rare cancer. Epstein (1978) documents the debates surrounding the recognition of the carcinogenicity of vinyl chloride.

References

Ashford, Nicholas A.
1976   Crisis in the Workplace: Occupational Disease and Injury. Cambridge, Mass.: MIT Press.

Berman, Daniel M.
1978   Death on the Job: Occupational Health and Safety Struggles in the United States. New York: Monthly Review Press.

Brown, Richard E.
1979   Rockefeller Medicine Man: Medicine and Capitalism in America. Berkeley: University of California Press.

Daniels, Arlene Kaplan
1972   "Military psychiatry: The emergence of a subspecialty." Pp. 145-162 in Eliot Freidson and Judith Lorber (eds.), Medical Men and Their Work. Chicago: Aldine Atherton.
1975   "Advisory and coercive functions in psychiatry." Sociology of Work and Occupations 2(1):55-78.

Ehrenreich, Barbara, and John Ehrenreich
1978   "Medicine and Social Control." Pp. 39-79 in John Ehrenreich (ed.), The Cultural Crisis of Modern Medicine. New York: Monthly Review Press.

Epstein, Samuel S.
1978   The Politics of Cancer. San Francisco: Sierra Club Books.

Esland, Geoff
1980   "Professions and professionalism." Pp. 213-250 in Geoff Esland and Graeme Salaman (eds.), The Politics of Work and Occupations. Toronto: University of Toronto Press.

Field, Mark G.
1966   "Structured strain and the Soviet physician." Pp. 194-208 in W. Richard Scott and Edmund H. Volkart (eds.), Medical Care: Readings in the Sociology of Medical Institutions. New York: John Wiley and Sons.

Freidson, Eliot
1970   Profession of Medicine. New York: Harper and Row.

Hughes, Everett C.
1962   "Good people and dirty work." Social Problems 10(1):3-11.

Johnson, Terence
1977   "The professions in the class structure." Pp. 93-110 in Richard Scase (ed.), Industrial Society: Class, Cleavage and Control. New York: St. Martin's Press.

Navarro, Vincente
1976   Medicine Under Capitalism. New York: Prodist.
1980   "Work, ideology, and science: The case of medicine." International Journal of Health Services 10(4):523-550.

Reasons, Charles E., Lois L. Ross, and Craig Paterson
1981   Assault on the Worker: Occupational Health and Safety in Canada. Toronto: Butterworths.

Schatzkin, Arthur
1978   "Health and labour power: A theoretical investigation." International Journal of Health Services 8:213-234.

Tataryn, Lloyd
1979   Dying for a Living: The Politics of Industrial Death. Toronto: Deneau and Greenberg.

Walters, Vivienne
In press   "Occupational health and safety legislation in Ontario: An analysis of its origins and content." Canadian Review of Sociology and Anthropology.

D/Work, Leisure and Retirement

40/The Long Arm of the Job: A Study of Work and Leisure[*]

Martin Meissner

Does work affect leisure?[1] In particular, what effect does work in a factory have on the employee's life away from work? There is a long history of debate on this question.

Wilensky,[2] in one of the more recent statements on work and leisure, neatly phrases the main contending positions in the debate. Reviewing arguments starting with Engels, who flailed the working class of England for too much sex and liquor, Wilensky draws out a "compensatory leisure hypothesis" and its alternative, a "spillover leisure hypothesis." These hypotheses, and others related to them, have been discussed and analyzed in a number of recent writings and researches. Unfortunately, many of the arguments have not been accompanied by supporting data, and the data which have been examined have not been suited to a thorough test of the hypotheses. A brief examination of the literature is illustrative.

Wilensky examined his hypotheses in the context of a study in Detroit and proposed that:

> Where the technical and social organization of work offer much freedom — e.g., discretion in methods, pace or schedule, and opportunity for frequent interaction with fellow workers ... then work attachments will be strong, work integrated with the rest of life, and ties to community and society solid. Conversely, if the task offers little workplace freedom ... then work attachments will be weak, work sharply split from leisure, and ties to community and society uncertain.[3]

However, while Wilensky did study the influence of occupational histories on social participation, there were *no data* on the technical and social organization of the work place.

Larrue, in her report of the leisure of metal workers in Toulouse,[4] offers a proposition similar to that of Wilensky:

> Le travailleur heureux à l'usine aurait des chances de l'être aussi dans ses loisirs, de même que l'ennui et la passivité se retrouveraient dans l'un l'autre domaine; ou bien, au contraire, l'attachment au travail risquerait de s'accompagner, au niveau des loisirs, d'un certain désintérêt, tandis que l'insatisfaction professionelle y trouverait sa revanche.

Larrue's data, however, showed *no relationship* between work satisfaction and leisure activities (lecture, bricolage, spectacle sportifs, cinéma, sorties à la campagne). There was also no relation between reported fatigue from work and leisure activities, except for going to the movies and out into the country.

---

[*] Abridged from Martin Meissner, "The Long Arm of the Job: A Study of Work and Leisure." *Industrial Relations* 10(3) 1971, pp. 239-260. Reprinted with permission of the publisher and the author.

A variant of the "compensatory" hypothesis was examined by Hanhart[5] in a study of workers in Zürich. Hanhart argued that workers "who designated their work as not so strenuous would turn more to free-time pursuits which presuppose a certain degree of independent action," and that "with strong physical exertion at work, the requirements for recuperation would be greater during free time." Although Hanhart's report contained *no data* concerning the predicted relationship, it does suggest, however, that work satisfaction does not appear to be related to visiting, club membership, participation in active sports, attendance at sports events, and listening to the radio. The only exception was that less satisfied workers go more often to the movies.

Dubin[6] found only few workers with a "central life interest" in work and assumed that this lack of interest would find compensation in greater interest elsewhere, away from work. There were *no data* to support that assumption.

Seeman[7] predicted from a scale of work alienation (with questions such as "Is your job too simple to bring out your best abilities?" and "Does your job make you work too fast?") that the more alienated would more often display feelings of general powerlessness, prejudice against ethnic minorities, and little political knowledge. Data gathered showed *no relationship*.

In sum, the available writings and reports have suggested that work places vary in the discretion which workers can exercise and in the constraints which factory technology imposes upon their actions. Also, work places differ in opportunities for social interaction or degree of social isolation on the job. These conditions of work are taken to have a profound influence on the workers' lives off work.

The available data, however, describe only the workers' attitudes and evaluations and fail to demonstrate the expected effect on activities away from work. Despite a long history of concern, apparently no research has identified dimensions of constraint and discretion in industrial work and dealt with the effects of such work constraint on social participation and leisure.[8] The present study was designed to provide detailed data on the employee's conditions of work and the nature of his leisure activities. These data allow close analyses of the hypothesized relationships between work and leisure which, in the main, suggest that employees choose leisure activities whose characteristics are similar to those of their jobs — the long arm of the job reaches out into life away from work.

Three Propositions

Throughout most of the debate on the topic, the specification of the relations between work and leisure has remained unclear. Superficially, there are three possible relations, and processes will be described later which may lend themselves to an explanation of each of these. The options are as follows: (1) Workers *compensate* for the constraints (or lack of discretion) and social isolation of the job in their free time. (2) The experience of constraint and isolation *carries over* into free time. (3) Life away from work is unaffected by the job.

The form of these hypotheses still begs the question of what the relevant dimensions are of both work and leisure, and how the dimensions in each of the two spheres are meant to correspond. In the following section, three such dimensions will be suggested — discretion, an expressive-instrumental dimension, and social interaction — each of which is applicable to both the compensatory and the carry-over hypothesis.

Discretion in work and leisure
Leisure activities and work can both be ordered on the dimension of discretion so that discretion at work corresponds to discretion away from work. Jobs with little technical constraint require more discretion of a worker. Alternatively, when a worker is confined to a fixed work place or small area, when his work activity is paced by machine or production line, and when his job is part of a production system of interdependent tasks, his choice of actions is reduced, that is, it is less discretionary.

Free-time activities also vary according to the amount of discretionary action they demand. For example, one might assume that active participation in voluntary organizations, the construction of a house, or certain hobbies require more deliberate decisions regarding one's choice of action (according to time, space, and function) than driving around in the car or watching television. If one expects a *compensatory* relation between work and leisure, one would find confirmation when people with little choice over their work activities engage more in discretionary free-time activities. If one expects work to *carry over* into leisure, people with little choice over their work activities would participate less in discretionary leisure activities. If one expects *no effect* of work on other activities, then freedom of choice at work is unrelated to the rate of discretionary nonwork activity.

The instrumental-expressive dimension
Relationships between work and leisure may lie in an instrumental-expressive dimension. Instrumental activities are performed for the purpose of an extended output, and expressive activities are an end in themselves. Work is more instrumental in character when the activities required for getting work done are constrained (in time, space, and function) in order to fit them into a mechanized organization of production. The less technically constrained jobs contain a greater opportunity for doing work for its own sake.

Spare-time activities may be ordered on the same dimension, according to the extent to which they have, or are part of, a purpose-directed structure or are primarily carried out for their own sake. Religious activities have often been seen as expressive behavior par excellence, and talking over a glass of beer is clearly not purposive activity. Other pursuits may as a whole be expressive but take place in a structure through which activities are given purposive direction — an example would be organized sports.

Using this dimension, compensation between work and leisure would then consist of making up for the instrumental constraints of the job by engaging more actively in expressive free-time activities. However, if work is expected to *carry over* into free-time, one would expect people in jobs with little expressive opportunities (i.e., the technically more constrained jobs) to participate more in activities with an instrumental structure. If there is *no relation* between work and leisure, participation in expressive free-time activities is not influenced by the degree to which workers are fitted into the work process merely as instruments of production.

Social interaction dimension

A third type of correspondence between the properties of work and leisure can be located on the dimension of social interaction. There are jobs with greater opportunity for talking with one's workmates than others, and free-time activities vary by amount of social interaction. Workers may then *compensate* for social isolation on the job by greater social interaction off the job. More talking on the job may *carry over* into more talking away from work, and isolation on and off the job would go together. Social isolation at work would make *no difference* for free-time social participation if the spheres of work and leisure are, in fact, unrelated or insulated from each other. . . .

Without developing the idea in detail, it is suggested that the dimensions of discretion, expression, and social interaction are of varying importance both on and off the job, and that the process which links work and leisure may differ according to the level of experience on the job. Particularly, the exercise of discretion is crucial for the coordinative problems of complex organizations; it is perhaps valued more than expression and interaction; and it involves a skill which is necessary for the more visible community activities. It may well be that workers in the more constrained jobs do not have the skills for discretionary activity off the job, and do not receive the potential rewards of discretion in either sphere. One may expect them to compensate, however, for the instrumental constraints of their jobs by greater involvement in expressive activities off the job.

So far we have dealt only with the possibility of compensating separately on each of the three dimensions (discretion, expression, and interaction) toward a balance at a preferred level of each. Alternatively, we have pointed to the possibility of carrying discretionary and social skills into free-time activities at the level at which these skills are being reinforced on the job. A combination of the two processes would postulate that workers will maximize on any of these dimensions *where they can*, that is, they will optimize within and across dimensions. It can also be suggested that discretion has greater value than social interaction, and that both are more valued than expression. Thus, workers with high job discretion will do more of a good thing: they will also participate more in discretionary activities off the job. Workers with little discretion will go for nondiscretionary social interaction off the job and for expressive alternatives. Finally, we can expect that workers with little experience in job-based social interaction will participate less in off-the-job social contacts but compensate through an increase in expressive leisure activities which are comparatively less demanding in discretionary and social skills. . . .

Study Site and Subjects

The data for the following analysis deal with a subsample of 206 industrial workers from an interview survey of presently working adults in an industrial community of about 20,000 population on Vancouver Island. The subsample is restricted to employees of a large wood-products manufacturing company with a number of integrated operations in the community, including two logging areas, two sawmills, a shingle mill, a ply-wood mill, and a pulp and paper plant, as well as large-scale transportation and loading operations. The company employs about half of the labor force of the area. The subsample is further restricted to men, wage earners, union members, below the level of foreman. These restrictions eliminate or reduce the potential effects of industry characteristics, sex, occupational prestige, and formal authority. The subsample gives access to a full range of variation in the technical organization of modern industrial work. . . .

Job Constraints and Social Participation

Let us now turn to the effects of technical constraints on participation in voluntary organizations. Technical constraints describe the degree of discretion over the time, space, function, and coordination of work. Active participation in organizations implies discretionary activity. By a simple and direct compensatory hypothesis we would expect a positive relation of work constraints with various indicators of participation in voluntary associations except, perhaps, in churches. If we expect that work carries over into corresponding levels of participation, the relation should be generally negative, that is, men working under more pronounced technical constraints would participate less. . . .

As shown in Table 1, excluding church attendance for the moment, one can see that 15 of the 16 possible relations between indicators of work constraint and measures of organizational involvement are negative, and the effect tends to be strongest for the average number of offices held, the most demanding indicator. This finding clearly favours a "carry-over" hypothesis.

If one were to argue that religious activity is expressive behavior (while the structure of activities in the other organizations is more instrumental, one would predict that church attendance would be greater for the technically more constrained workers who are church members. The results shown in Table 1 are mixed, however, with only two of the four possible relations suggesting a compensatory process.

Table 1. Technical Constraints and Social Participation

Technical constraints at work		(N)	Number of Memberships[a] Mean	Offices held[b] Mean	All clubs Mean	Trade union Mean	Church (members only) Mean	(N)
Machine pacing								
	Low	(114)	2.22	1.51	7.45	3.16	18.52	(46)
	High	(92)	2.11	.88	7.91	2.13	17.49	(45)
	Difference		- .11	- .63	+ .46	-1.03	-1.03	
Spatial confinement								
	Low	(101)	2.28	1.50	8.90	3.41	16.21	(42)
	High	(105)	2.07	.97	6.46	2.02	19.55	(49)
	Difference		- .21	- .53	-2.44	-1.39	+ 3.34	
Task dependence								
	Low	(108)	2.27	1.69	8.01	3.15	19.32	(44)
	High	(98)	2.06	.72	7.27	2.20	16.79	(47)
	Difference		- .21	- .97	- .74	- .95	- 2.53	
Constraints of work type								
	Low	(86)	2.21	1.34	8.55	3.19	17.57	(37)
	High	(120)	2.14	1.15	7.02	2.35	18.31	(54)
	Difference		- .07	- .19	-1.53	- .84	+ .74	

The header spans: **Participation in voluntary associations** over all value columns; **Number of** over Memberships and Offices held; **Meetings attended in six months** over All clubs, Trade union, and Church.

a. Number of memberships in all associations, including church and union.
b. Number of official positions of committee memberships held now or in the past, in all associations.

Job interaction and participation

Participation in organizations is also a matter of social interaction in a relatively more formal order of things. In Table 2 we see the relationship between the extent of social contacts at work and the degree of participation in voluntary organizations. A positive difference indicates that workers participate more in voluntary associations if they have a chance for social interaction on the job. Of the 16 possible differences of participation rates in associations other than church, 14 are positive and two are zero or close to zero. These findings suggest that social skills maintained at work help meet the demands of voluntary organizational activity, and that the compensatory hypothesis should be rejected. The effects of on-the-job social contact on church participation are inconsistent, but show perhaps a slight balance in favor of a compensatory relation.

Table 2. Interaction at Work and Social Participation.

			Participation in voluntary associations					
			Number of			Meetings attended in six months		
			Member- ships	Offices held	All clubs	Trade union	Church (members only)	
Social interaction at work		(N)	Mean	Mean	Mean	Mean	Mean	(N)
While actually working:								
With nonworkmates								
	No	(71)	2.01	.79	4.52	1.58	19.44	(32)
	Yes	(135)	2.25	1.46	9.30	3.29	17.24	(59)
	Difference		+ .24	+ .67	+4.78	+1.71	- 2.20	
By number of others								
	No	(42)	1.90	.74	3.13	2.07	15.93	(14)
	Yes	(164)	2.24	1.35	8.77	2.86	18.39	(77)
	Difference		+ .34	+ .61	+5.64	+ .79	+ 2.46	
By content								
	No	(36)	1.81	.47	2.44	1.69	23.00	(9)
	Yes	(170)	2.25	1.39	8.76	2.91	17.46	(82)
	Difference		+ .44	+ .92	+6.32	+1.22	- 5.54	
During Breaks:								
	No	(22)	2.18	1.23	4.05	1.36	16.27	(11)
	Yes	(184)	2.17	1.23	8.09	2.86	18.25	(80)
	Difference		- .01	.00	+4.04	+1.50	+ 1.98	

Summary: Job Characteristics and Participation in Voluntary Associations

The purpose of the preceding data analysis was to choose from among three apparently incompatible propositions by which to account for differences of involvement in voluntary associations. The first proposition specified a compensatory relation between the socio-technical features of work and organizational participation. The second proposition predicted that the experience of work would carry over into social participation. Finally, according to the third proposition, work would have no effect on participation.

Workers' jobs with relatively high degrees of technical constraint were distinguished from those which permitted discretion over the temporal, spatial, and functional arrangements of work activity. Men at work were also classified by the extent to which their work inhibited social interaction with fellow workers. Finally, it was argued that participation in voluntary associations makes demands on discretion and organized social interaction, and these were the dimensions on which jobs had also been classified.

The results of the preceding analysis indicate strongly that neither the proposition of "compensation" nor the proposition of "no effect" are viable for participation in voluntary organizations other than church attendance. Instead, experience with work of little discretionary potential carries over into reduced participation in formally organized activities. Similarly, the experience of social interaction opportunities on the job carries over into greater participation in voluntary associations. Tables 1 and 2 constitute a test of many operational hypotheses related to the three propositions. They show the direction and amount of difference in several indicators of organizational participation associated with several indicators of job constraint and social interaction at work. Excluding church attendance, 15 of the 16 possible relations between constraints and participation are negative, and 14 out of 16 relations of job interaction with participation are positive. In both cases, they correspond with the "carry-over" proposition.

The main exceptions to these findings involve church attendance. Religious activity is potentially expressive behavior, but also takes place in an organized context. The relative weight of these two dimensions varies for different religious groups and might explain the inconsistent results for church attendance. . . .

The Long Arm of the Job

Workers are instruments of production on their jobs. The extent to which they are merely instruments depends on the technical design of the work operation and the freedom of action it permits and demands. The ecology of modern communities tends to make industrial work quite invisible. Work and community may well be so effectively insulated that whatever happens on the job could be shaken off on the way home. The results of this paper suggest that the extent to which a man is used, as a resource in the organization of work, is a burden — light or heavy — not easily dropped at the mill gates. Not only are 40 hours of work over one-third of the waking hours of a week, but work is also important because most men actually work for a living, whether they like it or not.

The design of industrial work creates or prevents opportunities for the development or maintenance of discretionary and social skills. When choice of action is suppressed by the spatial, temporal, and functional constraints of the work process, worker capacity for meeting the demands of spare-time activities which require discretion is reduced. They engage less in those activities which necessitate planning, coordination, and purposeful action, but increase the time spent in sociable and expressive activities.

When work is socially isolating, workers reduce their exposure to situations in which they have to talk, and also spend less time in organized and purpose-directed activities. They make up for it and spend a lot of time fishing on the weekend, and pushing the shopping cart through the supermarket on workdays. Lack of opportunity to talk on the job is associated with dramatically reduced rates of participation in associations, that is, in activity commonly believed to help integrate individuals into the community.

Previous research did not succeed in showing that work makes a difference for life away from work. By attempting to elicit preferences, evaluations, and attitudes, it did not get at the question of how activities may be influenced by the most obvious features of the environment in which men work. In my view the findings here indicate that, when questions are put which are designed to find out what people actually do with their time and if they have control over the space, time, and function of their work, the job has a long arm indeed.

Notes

1. Revision of a paper presented at the annual meeting of the Canadian Sociology and Anthropology Association, Winnipeg, 1970. I would like to thank Neil Bull, Gerald Merner, and Peter Wiebe for their contributions to the work on this paper. I also want to acknowledge the help of the Vancouver Foundation, the Institute of Industrial Relations of the University of British Columbia, the Canada Department of Labour, and the International Institute for Labour Studies in Geneva.

2. Harold Wilensky, "Work, and Social Integration," *International Social Science Journal* XII (Fall, 1960), 543-560.

3. Harold Wilensky, "Orderly Careers and Social Participation," *American Sociological Review*, XXIV (August, 1961), p. 522.

4. Janine Larrue, *Loisirs ouvriers chez les métallurgistes Toulousains* (Paris: Mouton, 1965), pp. 122-128.

5. Dieter Hanhart, *Arbeiter in der Freizeit: Eine Sozial-psychologische Untersuchung* (Bern: Huber, 1964), pp. 199-216.

6. Robert Dubin, "Industrial Workers' Worlds: A Study of the Central Life Interests of Industrial Workers," *Social Problems* III (January, 1956), 131-142; and Robert Dubin, "Industrial Research and the Discipline of Sociology," *Proceedings of the 11th Annual Meeting, Industrial Relations Research Association*, 1958, pp. 152-172.

7. Melvin Seeman, "On the Personal Consequences of Alienation in Work," *American Sociological Review*, XXXII (April, 1967), 272-285.

8. One possible exception was an aggregate analysis of occupational groups in a research organization and in schools, and has dealt with a partly similar theoretical problem concerning professionals. See Robert Hagedorn and Sanford Labovitz, "Participation in Community Associations by Occupation: A Test of Three Theories," *American Sociological Review*, XXXIII (April, 1968), 272-283.

41/The Gold Watch Syndrome*

Andrew Allentuck

Sixty-five-year-old newspaper editor Bill Jasper will retire in May from the major daily newspaper where he's worked for the past 40 years. He's leaving not by choice but in compliance with company policy: although he's a leader in his field and more physically fit than the majority of men half his age, Jasper is regarded by senior management as ready for the geriatric pasture. Paradoxically, another newspaper in the same city has agreed to hire him the week he retires to fill duties similar to the ones he's leaving. His new employer is confident that Jasper will help to make his new newspaper the best in the community.

Bill Jasper's dilemma — and its solution — is just one example of a growing trend in the Canadian marketplace. Executives, professionals and even blue collar workers approaching 65, the customary age of retirement, are reassessing if they really want to quit working. After weighing their options, many are deciding to continue. And they're receiving support for their decision from government, business and management.

Surprisingly, there is no Canadian law stating that workers must retire at age 65. Instead, compulsory retirement evolved as a business practice after World War I when the growth of private, employer-sponsored pension plans and the federal government's 1919 change in tax laws permitting tax deductions for pension contributions, made retirement a financially feasible option for employees.

Three provinces have recently moved, however, to limit the legality of compulsory retirement. In June, 1977, the Manitoba Human Rights Commission ruled that terminating employment because a person has reached the age of 65 contravenes the province's Human Rights Act. In July, 1977 the Ontario Human Rights Commission proposed that the province's Human Rights Code be revised to prohibit discrimination by age against persons over 65 (this recommendation has yet to be acted on by the legislature). And in May, 1978, Vancouver lawyer Leo McGrady, appearing before the British Columbia Supreme Court, successfully argued that the B.C. Human Rights Code outlaws discrimination on the basis of age. This precedent, followed by an arbitration decision last August means that, in theory, employees in British Columbia have a basic right to continue to be employed after age 65.

The trend to eradicate the gold watch syndrome has also infiltrated the offices of federal cabinet ministers and senators. In December, 1978, federal Health and

---

* Reprinted, with permission of the author, from Andrew Allentuck, "The Gold Watch Syndrome," *The Financial Post Magazine* (May) 1979, pp. 51-58.

Welfare Minister Monique Bégin told the Senate Committee on Retirement Age Policies (formed in December, 1977, the committee is an ongoing inquiry into the issue of retirement) that "greater flexibility must be provided to Canadians in choosing their retirement ages, whether before or after age 65." While the Senate committee has yet to make any final recommendations, its inquiry adds status and urgency to the need to re-evaluate Canada's retirement system.

At the same time that legislators have been taking a look at the country's retirement customs, there are signs that business opposition to compulsory retirement has also been waning. Leading companies such as Boeing of Canada in Winnipeg, for instance, now allow employees to retire when they — and the company — think best. "Age should not be a factor in retaining or retiring an individual," says Boeing's director of personnel, Russ May.

Boeing employees are also warming to the idea of non-compulsory retirement. "I may want to continue to work in 10 years when I'm 65," says Ken Emberley, a 55-year-old production line worker at Boeing. "But if inflation keeps eroding my insurance and pension, then I'll have to work. What I really want is the choice."

If statistics are accurate, there are growing indications that many Canadians may have no choice but *to work* past the age of 65 before the century is out. While 8.73 per cent of Canada's population is now over age 65, according to Statistics Canada, 11.36 per cent of Canada's population will be 65 or older in 2001 and 19.36 per cent will be over 65 in 2031. This means that a large proportion of the population will be elderly — and in need of pension income and other costly social and health services in future. As the population over 65 rises, payouts from Canada's pension systems will rise and become progressively more difficult to finance by a young — but shrinking — population. What's more, the Canada Pension Plan, an inflation-indexed system that is supposed to pay contributors money they put into the fund, must now depend on current contributions to pay current benefits. Only one-third of Canadians 65 years of age or older are now entitled to draw CPP benefits.

The strain on the CPP kitty is expected to become even more severe in coming years. And the cause of this strain can be firmly pegged to Canada's declining birth-rate in the '60s and '70s. While this phenomenon has had social repercussions for many Canadians, it is also having an effect on the CPP. Because the pension system is indexed to the inflation level, it supposedly pays ever-increasing benefits to retired Canadians. But what has economists and other social scientists concerned is that at the turn of the century there will be fewer and fewer young Canadians to finance such a costly pension scheme. The only alternative, it would seem, is to raise contribution rates to finance these benefits.

Canada's auditor-general, J.J. MacDonnell, reports that payouts could exceed income by 1983 and that by 2000 everyone born after 1958 will find himself without a pension. The only alternative, says MacDonnell, is to raise CPP premiums drastically. Charles J. Stafford, vice-president and senior actuary at Monarch Life in

Winnipeg, estimates that "CPP contribution rates will have to double if the present pay-as-you-go system is maintained." Thus an employer plus employee maximum CPP contribution of $1000 per year in the year 2000, based on current contribution calculations, would have to be raised to $2,000 a year to keep the system in operation on a pay-as-you-go basis.

Faced with this impending situation, Canadian employers and employees may have little choice but to allow workers to stay on past age 65. There are already indications that many in the work-force would be wanting to stay at their jobs rather than at home. A 1975 survey by Health and Welfare Canada of broad areas of the labour force indicates that 50 per cent of Canadians would like to work at least part-time after age 65.

"There are several types of workers who are not forced to retire at any specific age" says Tom Clark, Winnipeg's Civic Pension Board chairman. They are "people at the bottom of the pile who have no pension funds and who must work or go on welfare, and professionals and self-employed people, including farmers and top officers and directors of corporations who are above the retirement rules system. In every case it seems that some combination of money to earn and a sense of contributing to society keeps the person at work."

Some of the highest corporate officials stay on the job well past age 65. Armand Hammer, 80, chairman of the board of California's giant Occidental Petroleum Corp., is actively in charge of the firm he took over when he was 59. The late Samuel Bronfman is another case in point. He remained head of Seagram's until his death in 1971 at the of 80.

There are substantial benefits to be gained from an end to compulsory retirement. Dr. David Skelton, head of the department of geriatric medicine at Winnipeg's St. Boniface General Hospital, says that "people over 65 are an enormous resource that has not been adequately tapped. People are productive in spite of age. Physical changes, except in times of stress, do not affect the work performance of the elderly. Allowing for such treatable illnesses as thyroid disease, depression and anemia, which can occur at any age, it is true to say that the post-65 worker can make a great contribution to the economy."

Other geriatric specialists are also confident that the elderly can play a useful role in the economy. "People working in offices can continue quite satisfactorily after age 65," maintains Dr. John Brocklehurst, head of the division of geriatric medicine at the University of Saskatchewan in Saskatoon. "I think it's nonsense to say that the person over 65 is addled. Of course there may be a gradual diminution of mental ability but the person is not disqualified by age alone. Chronological and biological aging do not go hand in hand.

"Retirement, ideally, should be flexible and people should be able to retire at the age which best suits them. If people retire with regret and if the person has nothing else to which to turn, he can become depressed."

Depression may be just one effect of premature retirement. And unlike Bill

Jasper, most Canadian retirees are unable to find new jobs, much less careers, at age 65. "If the individual loses the main identity he gained from work, he suffers a loss of prestige," says Ed Schludermann, professor of psychology at the University of Manitoba in Winnipeg. "He gets little prestige as a retired person. Indeed, a survey made in Canada in 1968 of different types of occupations showed that the retired person had only slightly more prestige than a person who is unemployed or on welfare."

Schludermann also emphasizes that compulsory retirement can harm the retiree's health and emotions. "His family suffers and, of course, the family's standard of living declines. If husband and wife have not had a good relationship for many years, the sudden presence of both spouses in the house all day long can provoke difficulties that eventually lead to divorce. So destroying a man's job can lead to destruction of his home, his self-confidence, even his health. And in spite of the many problems of measuring the health of populations, retirement appears to increase the likelihood of death in the first two years following retirement by as much as five per cent."

Dr. Skelton admits that there are situations in which the older worker may not be the best person for the job. "Where a person has to perform against a clock or needs fast reaction time — airline pilots are an example — there may be a need to give preference to the younger worker. The elderly though, can learn as well as younger people and can most certainly keep up with new and changing tasks. The important thing is to keep skills up through constant use and practice. And this means staying on the job."

The trend to keep older workers on the job is not unanimously accepted by all groups, of course. From the point of view of the 2.3 million-member Canadian Labour Congress, the loss of compulsory retirement will effectively place a tourniquet on the flow of new blood into the labor force. And CLC president Dennis McDermott has let it be known that he is "emphatically opposed" to any law eliminating the custom of compulsory retirement.

On this point, the Canadian Life Insurance Association notes that the alternative to ending compulsory retirement is firing the elderly when they can no longer do their jobs. Furthermore, babies born in the early '50s are now entering middle management. They face intense job competition simply because of the large size of their generation in the workforce. If promotion ladders are jammed at the top by people reluctant to leave, the careers of young employees could be stunted. An analysis done by the U.S. retailer Sears, Roebuck in 1977, for instance, indicates that if one-third of its 433,000 employees continue to work after age 65, 20,000 job changes would be torpedoed during a sample five-year period and hiring would have to be reduced by seven per cent.

How will this schism between the needs of the elderly worker and the needs of his younger counterparts be resolved? "In the balance of the interests of young and older workers," says Tom Clark, "governments will be forced to side with the elderly; after all, the young can take care of themselves but the elderly cannot be left to face inflation without help. So pension benefits will have to be increased." It will also be necessary to end compulsory retirement or to push it up to the age of 70, as was done effective January 1, 1979 in the United States by the Age Discrimination in Employment Act.

If people work longer, they won't need to draw pensions; they may be able to contribute to their own pensions and support as long as they continue to be employed. As productive employees, the elderly will be able to finance their generation's retirement as well as social welfare costs such as hospital and medical services (of which those over 65 make particularly heavy use). Thus, Ottawa and the provinces will probably opt to allow those who wish to work to do so until they are no longer able to continue.

Ending the dilemma of the involuntarily retired worker won't happen overnight and it won't happen without a struggle. The important goal which legislators — and business — will have to achieve is greater democracy in the workforce to end discrimination against the elderly. Though the younger worker may have to pay a price in terms of slightly reduced work and promotion opportunities and may even have to pay higher taxes to finance public pensions, there is no doubt that Canada's present retirement system will have to adapt to meet the needs not only of the elderly, but of younger workers following in their foot-steps.

42/Discarded Workers*

Ustun Reinart

On summer evenings, old men stand behind the windows of the Roblin Hotel. Across treeless Adelaide street they stare at a dusty concrete landscape of locked-up warehouses and half-empty parking lots.

Rooms cost $35 per month at the Roblin. Companionless men move here after retirement, when they can no longer afford to pay for rooms elsewhere.

Inside the Roblin Hotel, the "lounge" feels like a forgotten waiting room where men who've grown shabby during a long wait, sit and smoke silently on chairs lined up against the walls. There is nothing else in the lounge, only five chairs. It smells of stale tobacco.

Toothless Maurice grins:

---

* Abridged from Ustun Reinart, "Discarded Workers," *Canadian Dimension* 16(7) 1981, pp. 20-27. Reprinted with permission of the publisher and the author.

"Waiting for a nice woman," he says with a Quebecois accent, "I always look for a nice woman." The other three men burst into laughter that sounds like coughing.

Maurice once had a wife but she died back in 1947. He had been a farm worker in Quebec in those days. He moved to Manitoba, "Oh, about 15 years ago." He worked for Dominion Catering "cleaning, making beds, washing the sinks you know," at construction camps.

At the camps, drinking was the main recreational activity.

"Oh, we sometimes had a show." When Maurice retired in 1979, at age 65, he hadn't worked for Dominion Catering long enough to qualify for a pension. He found he couldn't afford to drink or to go to a show.

Throughout years of work, Maurice had earned only enough to sustain a hand-to-mouth existence. After retirement, he continued to do so with his Canada Pension and Old Age Pension.

"My Canada Pension is $250 and $100 Old Age Pension. That's enough," Maurice says "if you don't go no place, if you don't drink, if you just wait."

So he waits his days out at the Roblin Hotel Lounge.

"Ooh, in summer, all day I do nothing. Just wait for a nice woman," he winks.

"And in winter?"

"Stay in bed. What else is there to do?"

Another "old" man in the lounge, Fred, turns out to be only 55.

"I worked in mines across Canada for 25 years." He chews on an unlit cigarette, then lights it with shaky hands. "I drilled underneath the ocean to rip a rock before they blew it up. But the Workers Compensation Board wouldn't cover me anymore after 50." So now Fred works "now and then, when there's work around." What kind of work? "Oh, drive a truck, move furniture, anything. I'm used to working in the mines."

Fred isn't old enough to receive CPP or Old-Age Pension. He is visiting the Roblin Hotel lounge. "I used to live here. I live at Sally Ann now. I eat there too, once a day." It is the present he doesn't know what to do with.

"Nothing to do," he fidgets with his cigarette, "the days are too long."

The lives of Maurice and Fred and of thousands of other aging unskilled workers have become vacant.

Men like Maurice and Fred grew up in the Depression. They worked at heavy jobs for minimal wages, with no job security and no medical attention. Worn out early by physical work — the only meaningful activity they know — they now spend empty days waiting for the end. It is often not a very long wait.

Sheila Crawford, director of the senior citizen's job bureau in Winnipeg confirms that unskilled workers deteriorate rapidly after retirement.

"These seniors are not recreation-oriented. They didn't have a great deal of time to spend with recreation. Frugal living was their pattern. At 65, they have Old-Age Pension, Canada Pension and guaranteed income supplement. These are absolute securities. So at 65, the unskilled worker has income security which he never had before."

The irony is that the old worker who has income security for the first time in his life is in no shape to enjoy freedom from work, either because his health deteriorates, or because his life becomes useless if he doesn't know how to fill his days.

"Even if he is in any shape to continue to work," Sheila Crawford says, "he doesn't want to. Because if he earns anything, he'll lose some benefits. He has never had security before, he doesn't want to lose it. These people weren't social all their lives, their work was physical. So now they do nothing."

The residents of the Roblin Hotel are the starkly visible scraps from a marketplace community. They were of little value in their youth; and are totally inconsequential now since they are no longer efficient instruments of cheap labour.

The majority of old people, however, live with a poverty that isn't as visible, a loneliness that isn't as conspicuous and a purposelessness that isn't as simply expressed.

A different scenario awaits the aging skilled worker who has been able to attain a "middle-class" lifestyle during his working years. Along with unaccustomed "leisure," retirement brings him a sharp drop in income. It is not uncommon for these workers' wives to look for work for the first time in their lives.

"When I retired," says 72-year-old Norman, "my wife said: 'What have we got to live on now?' And I told her: Old-Age Pension, Canada Pension. She says 'Oh I'm going to work, that isn't enough for me.' So she's working at VIA Rail now. She is a lot younger than me. About 15 years younger. I'm paying only for the minor expenses of the house. . . ."

Norman was assistant night supervisor at the Swift Canadian Co. plant. Now he cleans up around the house, makes beds, washes dishes and vacuums. "I never seem to do enough, of course," he says with a good-natured shrug. "When the lady comes, she always finds something not done well enough for her."

Norman was used to working from 4 p.m. to midnight. "Now I don't know what to do with an evening. So many years my wife and I haven't been out together, we aren't used to being together in the evening."

The only thing Norman ever worries about is "whether we've got enough money to hold out — that's all."

Other retired skilled workers are forced either to change their lifestyles, or to look for lower-paying casual work. "My legs aren't strong enough to climb those poles anymore," complains Alfred as he pours whitener into his styrofoam coffee-cup.

"I was an electrical construction worker. I pulled cables, installed switch gear, climbed 30, 40, 60 feet. The work was seasonal. Summers, I left the family in Winnipeg and went north. The pay was good then."

Alfred had to retire at 59. Today he's only 62.

"I don't feel any older now than I did a long time ago. Age doesn't seem to make any difference — you don't think about it. Other than getting cramps in my hands and in my foot I don't notice it."

But lately, the going has been tough for Alfred and his wife. He would rather not discuss how his wife feels about having him home much of the time. He pauses, hesitates and asks to change the subject.

Any pension?

"No, you can't build up a pension when you work for numerous companies."

"My income since then? It depends on what's available. I go out on calls, I do casual repairs, remodelling. To get six hours of wages, I have to be out for 14 hours. I can't make up for those hours on the road."

He chuckles without humor, "You can say we don't eat steak." Then he adds more quietly, "When things are worn out, we can't replace them anymore. . . . I wish there was steadier work."

At 59, Alfred had embarked on the complex process by which this society discards old people and by which 67 year-old Maurice and 55-year-old Fred at the Roblin Hotel have already been dumped. But for the majority of people, the aging process is longer. And the majority of old people are women.

Widowhood and Poverty

"Sometime I see myself in the mirror. I cry."

The bingo game is over for the afternoon. Lina, 73, is having coffee and cookies with the other old women who regularly come for the game.

"You leave room empty. You go back, empty. Daytime people here. But nighttime I feel very very bad. Too lonely."

Lina belongs to a loneliness and poverty-stricken minority group that's gradually growing: she is a widow.

For more than twenty years, she cooked and kept house in the bush for her husband, a CNR section trackman.

She was 56 when he got very sick.

"We come to Winnipeg to my daughter in Transcona. My husband had disability pension then. He died a year after. There was nothing. No pension, no nothing.

"I apply welfare, they don't wanna give. I go to work — Marlborough Hotel as kitchen lady, you know. Then I got heart attack. Have to stay home, I can't work. So I apply welfare again. Had hard time. They say 'you have daughter, look after you'."

Some months, after Lina moved to her daughter's house in Calgary, her welfare application was accepted. She returned to Winnipeg and took a room in a rooming house.

It was not until age 65, that Old-Age Pension and guaranteed income supplement brought Lina some relief. Her income is still below the poverty line but she has a room at the North Point Douglas Manor, a building that houses an Age and

Opportunity drop-in centre.

Lina describes with bitter matter-of-factness, how at age 59, she used to walk all the way from downtown government offices to the cemetery in Transcona, to her husband's grave. "I walk crying to the grave and I lie on ground and I cry."

She considers herself "better off" now than she was some years ago.

"But it's late now" she shrugs with a matter-of-fact tone of defeat. "It's too late.". . .

The "golden ager" of middle-class myths appears in Ex-Lax commercials; well-to-do, self-reliant, responsible for her own well-being, busy with hobby-like recreational and community activities, gracefully self-effacing, undemanding and unneedy. In real life, the picture is different.

Loss of Dignity

At first glance, Rosa McKenzie is a "golden ager" who bustles with cheerful but quiet energy. Her conservative navy dress is attached with a brooch at the neck, her gray hair is in a modest bun.

It's 20 years since Rosa's husband Burt passed away.

Burt worked for Keewatin Lumber Co. in Winnipeg while Rosa looked after their three children, worked in the garden, sewed, knit and made the family's clothes. "It was hard work," she recalls. "I didn't have sewer and water available. I had a quarter of a mile to carry the water. Then we lost our home in the 1950 flood and we were never back on our feet again. We had to take out every penny that we could scrape up."

When Burt died, their children were all married and Rosa was left alone with no income. She went to work as a bookkeeper and continued to work until she was 70.

Since retirement, Rosa has lived below the poverty line.

Now, I'm really hurting," she says. "Right now, I need a new pair of shoes in the worst way and I cannot afford to take out of my present income that amount of money for a pair of shoes. You look at me, and I need a haircut badly. And ooh, do I wish I could go this afternoon and get a haircut and a permanent. It would cost me $25 and I can't."

"I belong to some groups but I'm beginning to feel a loss of dignity when I meet these people . . . I just can't dress properly anymore. There's no way."

Rosa's situation is typical of healthy and vigorous elderly widows. If she attempts to keep working, the aging widow will discover that only the lowest-paying service jobs are open to her: housekeeping, babysitting and kitchen cleaning. If she took such a job, since even small earnings will result in reduced pension benefits, the net increase in her monthly income may not exceed $20.

"I keep busy without paid work," Rosa says, congratulating herself. "I'm so busy, I sometimes wish they would forget my phone number."

Keep Busy...

"Keep busy, get involved," is the dictum of the Golden Age Myth. "Busyness" is assumed to be an antidote for feelings of loneliness and purposelessness as if it were entirely a matter of the old person's choice. The obvious fact that purposeful activity enhances well-being at any age blurs the direct connection between income and the choice of activity after retirement.

A YWCA brief presented to the Manitoba council on aging states that even the degree of volunteer involvement among the elderly directly corresponds to their income level. A suitable image has to be purchased with clothes and cosmetics. Entertainment has to be purchased: restaurants, movies, club and spa memberships, tickets and means of transportation are all costly. At that, interviews with 30 aging people reveal that random busyness replaces neither a genuine sense of purpose, nor the meaningful intimacy of close relationships.

Clichés like "I should be busy," or "Oh, I'm so busy," bring with them restlessness and an anxiety about not doing enough. The afternoons of bingo, the trips to Woolco, the coffee and doughnuts with other ladies or the volunteer answering of office phones all fill some hours. But a 65-year-old widow may have another 20 years during which her income falls and some of her old friends move away or die. Meanwhile, she feels and needs the same things she always has.

University of Manitoba sociologist Emily Nett reported to the Canadian pension conference on equality in October, 1980, that 82 per cent of the widowed persons in Canada are women and that the proportion is increasing both because women live longer than men, and because men may marry women younger than themselves.

"About one-third of widows have no personal income. Even where husbands collected pensions prior to death, about half of their widows are left with no provisions since the pension plan covers only the worker, not the woman who has been doing his homemaking without pay for whatever long number of years of their married life," Nett said.

The Canadian Council on Social Development's fact book on poverty states that to be old and female is the best combination to ensure being poor in Canada. Louise Dulude adds in her report on women and aging that to be old and a widow is an even better one. . . .

Part VII/Comparative Perspectives

Editors' Introduction

Throughout this reader we have been gazing inward, examining central problems and issues in the Canadian workplace. Canada in many important ways is a unique country: our colonial past, our northern frontier, the historical reliance on resource exports, close connections with the United States, the existence of separate French and English cultural-linguistic groups, and our relatively sparse population spread over a vast area all attest to this uniqueness. Yet at the same time we share basic commonalities with other advanced, capitalist industrial nations of the world. We might be able to learn from the experiences of others.

Donald Nightingale leads off our comparative discussion, in Chapter 43, by citing strike statistics and asking whether or not such conflicts reflect Canadians' deep dissatisfaction with their jobs. He reports the highlights of a major study of worker attitudes and beliefs in a dozen industrial societies. It is noteworthy, especially in light of our earlier discussions of participative management, that a major goal of the study was to determine the effects on workers' attitudes and behaviour of various forms of worker ownership and control. The results seem to indicate that the amount of worker control in the enterprise does in fact influence the levels of employee morale, satisfaction, and motivation. The most positive worker attitudes were found in Israeli kibbutz organizations while the least positive existed in Italian firms. Surprisingly, however, the Canadian employees surveyed were nearly as satisfied, seemed just as committed and loyal, and showed less alienation than did employees in Israel or Yugoslavia where formal systems of workers' control exist. This unexpected discovery, Nightingale argues, is largely a result of Canadian employees having considerable informal influence over supervisors regarding immediate job issues. Still, while informal mechanisms are sometimes effective, the best way of ensuring that workers have a say and are satisfied is to build their participation into the formal structure of the organization.

Nightingale ultimately concludes that labour unrest in Canada does not appear to be related to underlying dissatisfaction with working conditions or to a lack of participation. But perhaps what the cross-national study really measured was the degree to which workers had adjusted to their work situations. Recalling Rinehart's line of argument in Chapter 3, the "happy worker" may simply be expressing resigned acceptance to his or her present job in the face of limited opportunities elsewhere. According to this view, strikes are but one device available for expressing the discontent beneath the superficial happiness detected by attitude surveys.

We once again encounter the recurrent theme of industrial conflict in Chapter

44. Roy Adams begins from the premise that major surgery is necessary to achieve peace in the Canadian industrial relations system. His reflections on this topic, and the accompanying proposals for change, were prompted by first-hand observations of the Swedish system of industrial relations. Far from urging a wholesale importation of the Swedish model — rooted as it is in distinctive historical circumstances and socio-political factors — Adams uses a comparative approach to obtain a better understanding of the problems underlying Canada's adversarial system. A key difference between the two countries is that Swedish unions are accepted as a legitimate and necessary part of society. Management and labour operate on the basis of mutual respect. From our previous readings on Canadian labour history, we know that Canadian employers have doggedly resisted unionization efforts. This barrier to union growth is virtually unknown in Sweden, where a great majority of employees are union members. Because of the different labour-relations climate, Swedish unions have been able to engage in collaborative efforts with employer associations and government to devise national social and economic programs aimed at improving the overall quality of working life.

Because of its long social-democratic tradition, Sweden has achieved a far more egalitarian distribution of wealth and power than has Canada. Recognizing that such fundamental inequalities underpin many labour disputes, Adams goes well beyond usual collective bargaining considerations in calling for a more equitable distribution of income. Perhaps then, unions could work with employers and the state to improve other areas of the work environment. But despite this note of optimism, one is left with the nagging question of just how far reforms can be pushed in the direction of achieving greater social and economic equality. According to one perspective found in several previous chapters, the fundamental conflict of interests between management and workers in Canada makes a Swedish-inspired solution to workplace problems rather like an impossible dream.

In Chapter 45, the focus of our attention shifts to Japan. Written by J.E. Struthers, an official of the Canada-Japan Trade Council, the chapter offers some interesting comments on Japan's amazing economic success. North American businessmen have become keen Japan-watchers, awed by the remarkable industrial apparatus that floods world markets with quality products. In searching for the secrets of this success, observers have focussed on the Japanese system of production with its novel style of employee relations. Earlier chapters by Frazee and Baskin confirmed that Canada's lagging productivity is not due to worker laziness. Now in the case of Japan, the opposite logic is often applied: soaring output is seen as a result of high levels of employeee motivation and dedication. However, when examined more closely one can largely account for the apparent enthusiastic loyalty of Japanese workers in terms of the nature of their work organizations and the larger socio-cultural context. Organizationally speaking, the paternalistic, long-term view of employment provides life-long job security which in turn encourages loyalty. And socially, factors such as austerity and respect for authority underlie Japan's late-nineteenth-century industrial revolution. Much like the case of Sweden, we can derive useful insights from studying Japan. It is prudent, though, to stop well short of transplanting what we find in Japanese organizations into the Canadian workplace.

When examining Japan or any other society, there is a natural tendency to be captivated by the good points while ignoring the bad. This calls for a more critical perspective on the Japanese auto industry, which is exactly what Martin Glaberman provides in Chapter 46. Glaberman's article is a good antidote to the excessive praise one so often hears from businessmen about the Japanese style of management. The Japanese auto workers with whom he spoke, far from being blindly obedient to management and toiling with robot-like efficiency, did exhibit signs of discontent. However, their dissatisfactions were expressed only in sporadic and muted forms because of the tight control which management exercises over workers' entire lives, and the close integration of auto unions with management. Dissent of any sort is therefore discouraged among Japanese workers, and a premium is placed on loyalty at all costs.

Our final selection takes us to Spain, where in Chapter 47 Tom Webb documents the fascinating successes of the Mondragon worker cooperative network. Like Canada, Spain is a capitalist economy built on individual property ownership. Yet operating within this system is an island of collective ownership and self-management involving over 22,000 individuals. In short, while worker co-ops are clearly compatible with capitalism, they also offer a major alternative for future social and economic organization. Canadians, Webb asserts, have little say in their economic affairs and often suffer the negative consequences of unbridled pursuit of profits. Mondragon thus provides a contrasting example of political and economic democracy in action. Such a system may at first appear to be overly cumbersome, yet Mondragon co-ops have been able to make major advances in new production technologies, educational programs, and social services. Co-ops do exist in Canada, but mainly in the form of wheat pools, credit unions, housing co-ops, and co-op food stores. These co-ops are solidly established, but whether they can serve as a springboard for a major program of industrial co-ops is another matter. The implication of Webb's discussion of Mondragon is that we may very well be short-changing our economic future by not seriously considering this option.

It is now evident that there are many pressing issues Canadians must address if the workplace of the future is to be any better than what exists today. The role of unions in society, equality for women in the work world, more challenging and rewarding jobs, reduced worker alienation and increased satisfaction, full employment, healthier and safer work environments, more democratic organizational structures — these are only some of the challenges facing us in the 1980s and beyond. In searching for answers and solutions it is important to derive lessons from the successes and failures of other nations. But it should be clear that no instant cure can be imported from elsewhere. The utmost in collective creativity will be required to develop uniquely Canadian strategies for achieving a better workplace.

Suggested Readings

John Crispo, *Industrial Democracy in Western Europe: A North American Perspective* (Toronto: McGraw-Hill Ryerson, 1978).

David Jenkins, *Job Power: Blue and White Power Democracy* (Baltimore, MD: Penguin Books, 1973).

Satoshi Kamata, *Japan in the Passing Lane: An Insider's Account of Life in a Japanese Factory* (London: George Allen & Unwin, 1983).

Charles King and Mark van de Vall, *Models of Industrial Democracy: Consultation, Co-determination and Workers' Management* (The Hague: Mouton, 1978).

Walter Korpi, *The Working Class in Welfare Capitalism: Work, Unions and Politics in Sweden* (London: Routledge & Kegan Paul, 1978).

William Ouchi, *Theory Z: How American Business Can Meet the Japanese Challenge* (Don Mills, Ont.: Addison-Wesley, 1981).

Henk Thomas and Chris Logan, *Mondragon: An Economic Analysis* (London: George Allen & Unwin, 1982).

43/Canadian Working People And Their Counterparts Abroad*

Donald V. Nightingale

In recent years, Canadians have found themselves confronted with widening labor unrest and with increasingly bitter and prolonged work stoppages of different kinds. Between 1968 and 1972, 1,724 days per 1,000 workers each year were lost because of work stoppages in Canada. This figure compares unfavourably with those of almost every other Western industrialized nation (Sweden, 62; West Germany, 74; Great Britain, 968; and the United States, 1,534). Only Italy with 1,912 days lost has a worse record of labor peace than Canada.

Do these work stoppages signal a widespread and continuing disenchantment with the workplace among Canadian employees? Do the commitments, motivations and attitudes of Canadian working people compare unfavourably with those of working people in other countries?

Surprisingly little is known about the attitudes and feelings of Canadian working people and even less is known about how these attitudes and beliefs compare to those of working people in other countries. But the preliminary results of an international study of working people provide some answers to these questions. The

---

* Reprinted, with permission of the publisher and the author from Donald V. Nightingale, "Canadian Working People and Their Counterparts Abroad," *Canadian Personnel and Industrial Relations Journal* 22(6) 1975, 17-19.

purpose of the study is to provide a controlled and systematic comparison of the attitudes and beliefs of working people in twelve industrialized nations (including Canada, the United States, West Germany, Japan, Sweden, Yugoslavia) and to explore the effects of major experiments in participative management in each of the above countries.

The results from nearly 3,000 employees in six of the countries — Canada, the United States, Austria, Italy, Yugoslavia and Kibbutz organizations in Israel — offer some interesting glimpses of how Canadian working people compare to their counterparts in other countries.

Worker Participation

With the countries surveyed to date, we can examine the effects of worker ownership and control (industrial democracy) on employee loyalty, commitment and satisfaction with the workplace. Experiments in worker participation are becoming more commonplace in Europe and are intended by their designers to overcome some of the debilitating conditions that characterize organizations of more conventional operation.

The Yugoslav organizations in our sample operate under the Worker Council system of self-management in which workers elect the chief executive officer and participate in decisions about products, wages, prices and the disposal of profits. This arrangement which is formally codified in law was designed to give workers ultimate control of the enterprise.

Kibbutz organizations in Israel are among the most egalitarian and participative industrial enterprises in the world. All leaders are elected by workers and hold office for a period of two to five years; there are no wages, Kibbutz members draw from the profits of the enterprise in proportion to their needs and not according to criteria employed in this country such as contribution, skills or ownership.

Does it Work?

Do the results support the notion that worker ownership and control reduce the frustrations and dissatisfactions of workers and lead to greater employee involvement and commitment? It is difficult to respond with a simple yes or no to this question because the attitudes of employees in each of the countries cannot be rank ordered in the same way for each of the issues we examined. In general, however, the attitudes of workers in the six countries can be ordered from most to least favourable in this way: Kibbutzim, Yugoslavia, Canada, the United States, Austria and Italy. The differences between the first four countries are rather small, Austria follows the United States by a longer margin and Italy follows Austria by an even larger margin.

The overall ranking of the countries confirms the belief that the amount of worker control over the enterprise influences the levels of morale, motivation and satisfaction of workers. The rigid and authoritarian manner in which Italian employers deal with their employees contrast sharply with the style of Kibbutz managers, who must use persuasion to get work done.

There are some surprises, however. Satisfaction with pay, work and fellow employees among Canadians in our sample is nearly as high as that found in Kibbutzim and Yugoslavia, roughly the same as that found in the United States and higher than that found in Austria and Italy.

Attitudes toward the company, commitment and loyalty to the firm in our Canadian sample are as positive as those found elsewhere. Also, Canadians experience far less alienation than working people in other countries.

Not So Necessary Here?

Why are the attitudes and feelings of Canadian and American workers nearly as positive as those of workers in countries where they have a good deal of influence over the company? The answer seems to be that Canadian and American employees, although they have no formal voice in the management of the company, nevertheless exercise a good deal of informal influence over their foremen concerning matters on the shop floor. Yugoslav workers, despite the workers' council do not have this same sense of control.

It appears then, that worker attitudes in organizations where employees have a formal say in the affairs of the organization tend to be more positive than those found in organizations where they do not. (As pointed out in an earlier article, French-Canadian workers are more committed, loyal and satisfied with the workplace than their English-Canadian counterparts despite the fact that they have less influence over their superiors. Beliefs about how much worker control is legitimate affect how satisfied employees are with the influence they have).

What About Managers?

But what about managers? Are they more satisfied with the workplace in those countries with formally participative systems? We find that in Kibbutzim and Yugoslav organizations senior level managers tend to be less satisfied, committed and loyal to the firm than their counterparts in capitalist countries. There is noticeably lower morale among senior executives in Kibbutzim and Yugoslav companies than in Canadian and American companies.

This finding is not surprising because managers in Yugoslavia and Kibbutzim tend to have less freedom of action and are subject to many competing and conflicting demands that their counterparts in North America are not. The curious result is that differences between employees at the highest and lowest hierarchical levels in the company are less in Kibbutzim and Yugoslav organizations than in organizations in the other countries in the sample. However, the *overall* level of satisfaction, morale, and motivation is the same in Canadian organizations as in American, Yugoslav and Kibbutz organizations.

North American management publications frequently report on European experiments in worker participation (such as co-determination and workers councils), yet there is little evidence that Canadian and American managers are anxious to experiment with European-style industrial democracy. The reaction of Canadian labor has been cool and even among some European workers, support for industrial democracy is by no means unanimous. Chrysler's British subsidiary, driven to the wall by strikes, recently offered the workers a seat on the board. The proposal was met with divided opinion. Many workers believe that the worker representative on the board could not adequately represent their interests and the interests of the company at the same time. Nevertheless, over the long term, participative plans of different kinds are likely to become more popular in North America.

Our data suggest that labor unrest in this country does not result from or reflect negative reactions or lack of adjustment to the workplace. Canadian working people (and especially French-Canadians) on the whole are quite satisfied with their companies and most aspects of their working lives.

It seems then (as many have pointed out) that work stoppages in Canada are the result of other factors such as escalating expectations about salaries and working conditions, and the scramble to maintain equality with other wage earners in a system which has become unfrozen. The basic motivation and commitment among employees is there — and more stable economic conditions might well significantly improve the state of labor relations in Canada.

44/Conflict and the Nature of the Industrial Relations System*

Roy J. Adams

The right to strike has long been a keystone of the labour policy of most advanced industrial nations. Implicit in the right, however, is the understanding that conflict should not result in significant losses to "innocent" third parties. In recent years this criterion has often not been met. Instead, in many disputes the public has emerged as the greatest loser. This situation has given rise to an increasing public outcry for change.

The most widely heralded proposal has been to outlaw the strike for certain employees — those performing "essential services" — and to replace the strike with some formula composed of conciliation, mediation and arbitration. Arguments for

* Reproduced by permission of the Minister of Supply and Services Canada from Roy J. Adams, "Conflict and the Nature of the Industrial Relations System," *Labour Gazette* (April) 1975, pp. 220-224.

and against various combinations of these procedures have been presented in a recent series of articles in this journal. Little is to be achieved by reviewing the arguments here. That task has already been ably accomplished by John Crispo (Labour Gazette, Sept. 1974, p. 619). One of the most interesting aspects of the series was the fact that, either implicitly or explicitly, all of the authors basically reaffirmed the essential soundness of the system of industrial relations. There were no proposals for radical change. Instead, all of the authors seemed to be saying that our system is either fine the way it is, or that a significant reduction in conflict can be achieved by modifying our industrial relations practices in certain minor ways. This presumption is, I believe, absolutely false. Commenting on indexing as a response to inflation, Jean Poulin states that it is "not a remedy: it is the Aspirin tablet that prevents us from feeling the pain but doesn't attack the disease itself" (Labour Gazette, Oct. 1974, p. 718). In my estimation, minor modifications suggested as remedies for conflict are neither likely to cure the disease nor substantially reduce the pain. Indeed, such suggestions are dangerous because they create expectations that will almost certainly be disappointed.

The conflict problem in Canada is not just one of essential industries. Conflict is inherent in the logic of the system of industrial relations. Over the past two decades, conflict has been the subject of more public debate and research than any other aspect of industrial relations. The pay-off has, however, been negligible. Instead, the level of overt conflict in the United States and Canada has consistently been among the highest in the industrialized world.

Recently I spent the better part of a year in Sweden studying the Swedish industrial system. For many years Swedish industrial relations have caught the eye of the international community because of the relatively high level of industrial peace in that country. Many foreign observers who have visited Sweden have returned home with the conclusion that the system works for the Swedes primarily because of historical, political and social factors peculiar to Sweden. I do not wish to take up that debate here. However, regardless of the accuracy or inaccuracy of the belief that Sweden is a special case, it is still useful to compare Canadian industrial relations practices with those of Sweden in order to illustrate the fundamentally conflictive nature of the "adversary" system we have created.

In Sweden there is a genuine respect and acceptance between management and labour. It is generally accepted that trade unions play an essential and positive role in society, and consequently the position of trade union officials is one of considerable status and prestige. In Canada, as John Porter has pointed out, "trade unions are intruders whose presence is only grudgingly accepted by other institutional elites and by the rest of society. They are accepted for their power rather than any contribution they are thought to make to social life." P.M. Marcus has made the following observations about American unions, which are equally applicable to Canada:

Unions . . . seldom receive publicity except during strikes, violence, or when under investigation. They are depicted primarily as "taking" something or making demands. (Unions always *demand* in the press, while management always *offers*.) Unions are seen as disrupting an on-going, constructive process.

Furthermore:

Because little is known about the operations of unions, and because of their low prestige, immoral acts discovered receive heightened importance and generality.

Management, on the other hand, is portrayed quite differently:

Management supplies goods and services to the general public and has higher prestige. Newspaper and other mass media consistently report their operations and contributions to community and national welfare.

One might take issue with the universality of this statement but the thrust of Marcus's argument is, I believe, sound. Business is generally thought of as constructive while organized labour is generally considered to be disruptive. In short, Canadian society has granted only marginal legitimacy to unions. As a result, Canadian unions often perceive themselves as being under attack and they feel that they must be constantly on guard to protect the shaky rights they have had to struggle so hard to establish. Employers, especially unorganized employers, reinforce this attitude by fighting every effort of the unions to expand their influence. The Swedes would be shocked by the publication of a book entitled, *Labour Unions: How to Avert Them, Beat Them, Out-Negotiate Them, Live With Them, Unload Them*; but such titles are common in North America.

Hostile Environment

This milieu is hardly one in which the public can or should expect the unions to behave in a manner calculated to maximize public interest. Indeed, it is incredible how responsible the majority of unions have acted, given the hostility and animosity of the environment in which they must operate.

Employers in Sweden are forbidden by law to oppose unionization and many assist unions in their recruitment efforts. In Canada, employers are accorded the right, within certain legal guidelines, to fight unionization and most exercise this right to the limit. Where unions have not been able to survive the rigors of a certification campaign, they are entirely excluded from the employment relationship.

The main argument put forth for the perpetuation of this situation is that employees have the right to freely choose union or no union and further, that employees should have the benefit of the views of both management and labour unions in order to make an intelligent choice. Although this logic has considerable appeal, it obscures the reality of the situation.

First, management has a long-standing relationship with employees in any union recruitment situation, and many employees do not wish to anger or upset their employer. Management typically attempts, however, to convince employees that by joining a trade union they are being disloyal to the firm. Second, employers have far greater access to employees during recruitment campaigns and thus have a somewhat unfair advantage over the unions in presenting their case. Third, if the union should win certification, negotiations are very difficult because of the inflammatory situation that existed just prior to certification. These realities add to the instability of the system.

Finally, to many non-union employers, "keeping the union out" is a criterion of the success of their personnel administration policies. Most employers argue that if they do a good job of personnel management, unions are unnecessary. This argument should, I believe, be totally discredited. Due process of law is a basic right in a democratic society. If this right is to have meaning it should extend to the employment situation, because one's job in modern society is by far the most important determinant of his standing in society. Where unions are recognized, this right is protected. Although the grievance process has come in for substantial criticism in recent years, its existence is an immense improvement over the procedural void existing in non-union situations. Where employees are not represented by unions, whatever rights they have are granted, for the most part, as the result of management benevolence and may easily be taken away or abused.

Most Important Union Function

In my opinion, the guaranteeing of due process is the most important function of trade unions in our society. The great majority of laymen and far too many "experts" fail to appreciate this. Instead, the goal of unions to acquire "more, more, more" through collective bargaining is continually stressed to the point where the due process function becomes obscure and hidden. Management may have a case when it argues that it can provide terms and conditions of employment equal to or better than those of unionized employees. It cannot, however, adequately provide industrial justice. Where there is no union, management is both judge and jury of employee conduct. By this statement, I do not mean to impugn the motives of management. In my experience, the majority of managers sincerely attempt to be fair in their dealings with employees. Differences in interpretation and perception do occur, however, and in such situations, where unions are absent, employees have no recourse from unilateral management decisions.

Neither do I mean to suggest that in every union-management situation workers are ideally represented. Some unions are corrupt, others are undemocratic and still others are run by irresponsible or complacent officials. But these are not inherent characteristics of trade unionism, as so many people seem to assume. They are a blight upon a fundamentally sound social institution. Few people despise and condemn such dysfunctions more than responsible trade unionists.

Unions represent only about 35 per cent of the non-agricultural labour force. The 65 per cent of employees who are not represented by a union are subject to what is, in effect, industrial autocracy. For decades, critics have delighted in trumpeting the inadequacies of union democracy. But with the exception of a handful of intellectuals the total absence of democratic rule-making and interpretation in most of industry has been either ignored or fully accepted. In a society that takes pride in its democratic political process and often ridicules "foreign dictatorships," this situation is an anachronism.

In Sweden both unions and employers are highly organized into strong industrial and national organizations. The large majority of blue-collar, white-collar and professional employees have joined or formed organizations which negotiate with employers, and the preponderance of employers have, likewise, constituted organizations to deal with labour issues. These organizations each have fashioned unified national wages policies designed to achieve an equitable and just distribution of income. In Canada, in most industries, employer policy has been intensely individualistic.

Conflict All But Inevitable

Canada is one of the few industrial nations where there is no national employer organization capable of representing the employers to the government, the unions and the public. Although the unions have moulded national organizations, their bargaining policies are, in most instances, separate and unco-ordinated. This excessive individualism and competition has given rise to an income determination system in which a high level of conflict is all but inevitable. Each time one union makes a gain, pressure is exerted upon another union to win equal or greater increases. The spiral has a limit, but conflict is usually necessary to bring it to a halt. Because of varying bargaining power, some unions do consistently well while others do poorly. Traditional wage differentials are stretched and feelings of perceived inequity lead to desperate outcrys of injustice. Conflict is the usual result.

Because of co-ordinated national wages policies, conflicts for the above reasons are kept to a minimum in Sweden. They do, however, occasionally occur. For example, in recent years the Swedes have encountered problems because of the differing policies of blue-collar, white-collar, and professional federations.

In Sweden, the quality of labour negotiations is very high. Both unions and employer associations do a great deal of research and labour negotiators on both sides of the bargaining table are well trained and highly competent. Large scale educational efforts extend deep down to the shop floor. Professionals employed by organized labour and organized management have the highest prestige in society.

In Canada, the quality of labour negotiations in many instances is as high as anywhere in the world. Many unions, however, are too small to do adequate research or to train their negotiators properly. Those who negotiate for small and medium-sized employers are also less competent, in the main, than might be expected. Union members, often poorly informed about the realities of the economic situation, are distrustful of their leadership and this leads to contract rejection problems. Many strikes occur as a result of these inefficiencies.

In order to adequately represent the interests of their members, trade unions and employer associations might be expected to do a substantial amount of research into basic employment issues. In Sweden, for example, the concept of "active manpower policy" was pioneered by trade union economists. Subsequently, this concept has been widely adopted not only in Sweden but throughout the western world. At present, trade unions and employer organizations are carrying out research of the highest quality into new forms of work organization, new wage payment systems, education policy, immigration policy and numerous other issues of critical importance to Swedish workers. Such research by labour market organizations in Canada is rudimentary or non-existent. Most often, the research that is done is contrived to support pre-conceived positions. The sensibilities of the concerned public have been dulled by these incessant polemics and the credibility and potential influence of the labour market organizations suffer as a result.

Employer Associations Weak

Employer associations in Canada, where they do exist, are generally weak and whatever efforts they make to provide information and expertise to small and medium-sized organizations are insufficient to insure competent labour relations policy. For the most part, associations have abdicated to labour lawyers and management consultants the responsibility of providing expert assistance. This is quite unfortunate. In many European countries, employer associations have taken on the task of easing the tensions between individual managements and unions. The associations have generally been more committed to positive and constructive labour relations policies than have their individual constituents. Association officials usually bring a high level of professionalism to their tasks.

Many employers in Canada complain of what they believe to be excessive union power. They apparently fail to realize that by pooling their resources they could achieve a level of power far in excess of that of most employee organizations. This basic fact was clearly realized early in the century in Sweden. One of the major findings from my Swedish study was that employers played a critical role in the development of the Swedish industrial relations system. They were unwilling to be buffeted about by the varying and often contrary objectives and tactics of different factions of the labour movement or by the political expediency of government. Instead, they took the initiative in building a viable and stable system of job regulation. In Canada, however, employers have been either unable or unwilling to meet the challenge. They are, instead, fond of portraying themselves as pawns of forces beyond their control.

The Canadian system does have certain clear advantages. It recognizes a wide variability in occupations and employment situations and provides machinery for small groups of employees with uniquely common interests to jointly regulate their employment relationship with their employer, who may feel that his situation is equally unique. Furthermore, where collective bargaining has been established, employees in Canada receive a degree of procedural protection that is, in most cases, probably as high as anywhere.

In contrast to Sweden, Canadian priorities have been placed on individual freedom, diversity and decentralization. In practice, this choice has produced intensive competitiveness, high levels of animosity, widespread inefficiency and narrow self-interested behaviour. Whether or not this trade-off is "good" or "bad" requires the making of a value judgment by each concerned person individually. Some may feel that the benefits of the system outweigh the costs. Others may disagree. It is essential, however, that the existence of the trade-off be clearly understood because it implies that the timid and conservative proposals currently in vogue are unlikely to significantly reduce the level of overt conflict.

Three Critical Questions
If a major reduction in conflict is considered to be a serious priority, answers to three critical questions must be sought:

1. What can be done to enhance the status, prestige and legitimacy of organized labour?
2. What can be done to ensure a more equitable system of income distribution rather than one that is based primarily upon power and circumstances?
3. What can be done to improve the efficiency and responsibility of the labour market organizations in providing useful services to their members?

There are no easy or pat answers to these questions. They imply fundamental change for which there is likely to be difficulty in winning acceptance, hazards in implementation, and uncertainty as to the outcome. To denote the problems without suggesting a solution, however, would be little more than intellectual gamesmanship. Therefore, the following proposals are suggested for discussion. Each could be highly qualified. However, black and white is more likely to produce a meaningful debate than the tedious gray of most intellectual discourse.

Proposals for Discussion
1. Federal and provincial governments should support the philosophy that trade unions are a necessary and positive force in Canadian society. Organized labour should be recognized as the legitimate representative and spokesman of working people in general, and working people should be strongly urged to join or form an appropriate employee organization.
2. Employers should be denied the "right" to oppose unionization. It should be government policy that all employed people have the right to due process and that the unions are the appropriate vehicle through which this right is to be guaranteed.
3. Unions should explore the possibilities of providing service to employees even in situations where they have not attained a majority representation. This pro-

cess should be facilitated by the government through legislation requiring employers to at least meet and confer with unions acting on behalf of their members who are not represented by a certified bargaining agent. Present certification procedures would, however, remain and unions would continue to be forbidden to strike for recognition.

4. Employers should seriously consider the benefits of unified action on the industrial, provincial and national level. Strong employer organizations could form a bulwark against extreme union demands and through research and service could enhance the quality of labour negotiations. To facilitate this development governments should consider the use of legislated inducements.

5. Trade unions should speed up the merger process so that unions of a viable size may exist in all sectors. Governmental incentives might be considered to aid the process.

6. In our complex modern society the position of labour negotiator requires a level of skill and knowledge similar to that of other professionals. Both the public and the membership of the relevant organizations have a right to expect professional competence from those involved in the bargaining process. Therefore, federal and provincial governments should explore ways and means of ensuring such competence. The self-governing procedures of the established professions might be given consideration as relevant models.

7. Academics should be encouraged to pursue research into the efficient administration of trade unions and employer organizations. There has been a vast amount of research concerning the administrative efficiency of business and government but practically none concerning trade unions or employer associations. Governments could facilitate such research by providing substantial research funds.

8. The proposal put forth several years ago by Harry Waisglass that all incomes and prices be made public should be required by law. This would put massive pressure on employers and trade unions to rationalize and justify their wage policies and would more clearly illuminate income problems than do currently available statistics.

9. Trade unions should give pay inequity the highest priority and a concerted attempt should be made to produce a national co-ordinated effort to achieve an equitable distribution of income. Federal and provincial governments should make it known that their support is contingent upon union efforts in this regard.

The effect of these proposals would be to radically change Canadian industrial relations. Therefore, I have no idealistic illusions about their immediate widespread acceptance. I realize that it would be very difficult to implement some of them. Nor can one be absolutely certain that they would have the desired effect even if they were adopted. It is, however, important to realize that alternatives to our current practices do exist. Our system was not created by God but by men and, given the will, it can be changed. To achieve industrial peace, fundamental change is essential. Anything short of radical change would leave the root causes of the conflict problem untouched.

45/Why Can't We Do What Japan Does?*

J.E. Struthers

Japan's production and exporting successes seem almost unbeatable. The world looks with admiration and envy on the industrial achievements of that country, and many key planners in North American and European industries are studying the elements of Success Japan with a view to transplanting, buying, borrowing or recreating those elements.

Along with remarkable production and exporting achievements, Japan also now enjoys the PR "image" of success. The Japan image, like a coin, has two sides. Opposite the glittering success side is a picture that hints from time to time of technical bankruptcy. Japan fell into deep economic trouble, for example, as a result of the world's oil crisis of 1973-74 and recovered. Again, due to the Iranian situation, which started two years ago, expensive oil has put Japan's balance of payments into deficit.

Having almost no indigenous raw materials, Japan needs to import 90 per cent of its energy, three quarters of which is oil, and therefore it pays an enormous price for its successes. Its trade deficit in 1979 was almost $2.5 billion, and the deficit continued into 1980.

The grimmer side of the coin is pictured here merely to put the success side into perspective, so that minds this side of the Pacific, filled with the excess of wonderment about the production and exporting "magic" of Japan, will not be overcome by feelings of envy, awe, jealousy or resentment. (Can it be imagined what would happen to the lot of Canadians if Japan instantly fell off the face of the earth — if our $2 billion trade surplus with Japan instantly disappeared?)

Meanwhile, in both the private and public sectors of Canadian life, business minds have been concentrating on the Japan success story. In recent months there has been a starburst of conferences, symposia, panel discussions, public pronouncements and media comment on the success side of Japan and what at times seems like a scavenger hunt for the secrets of the success.

* Reprinted with permission of the publisher from J.E. Struthers, "Why Can't We Do What Japan Does?" *Canadian Business Review* 8 (Summer) 1981, pp. 24-26.

Basic Statistics — 1980

	Canada	Japan
Area	3,851,809 sq. mi.	143,750 sq. mi.
Population	23.9 million	115.9 million
GNP	$288.1 billion	$1.3 trillion
GNP per capita	$12,409	$11,217
Total imports	$92.4 billion	$174.5 billion
Total exports	$89.6 billion	$160.2 billion
Merchandise imports from Japan	$2.8 billion	
Merchandise exports to Japan	$4.4 billion	

Note: Japanese figures are for the 1980 fiscal year and were converted into Canadian dollars by The Conference Board of Canada at the rate of $1 = 183.4 yen.

Sources: for Canada, *Canadian Statistical Review*, February 1981. Reproduced by permission of the Minister of Supply and Services Canada; for Japan, Japan Trade Centre, Toronto.

Interpretations of ruminations by business and industry, which do at times border on petulance, are expressed occasionally. For example, one news report paraphrased parts of an address by the president of General Motors of Canada Ltd. and headlined him as being "critical of Japan trade policies." The president was said to have been critical of the Japanese automotive industries for concentrating production at home. "By simply exporting and exporting, Japanese manufacturers do not contribute to the industrial development of other countries, only to the service industry that sells and services their products," the news report of his address stated.[1] This generalization, of course, is not supportable. The Japanese are contributing to the development of industries in many countries.

Besides the direct input of Japanese plant capital investment to other countries and the purchase of products from other countries, there is yet an indirect contribution being made by the Japanese, most noticeable in the United States recently and now in Canada. It is the introduction of their so-called secrets of success into the North American manufacturing process.

We on this side of the Pacific are just beginning to do what the Japanese have been doing for some time, and we will be hearing more about intelligent robots, numerical control equipment, quality control circles among employees and computer-controlled production. This sounds like new industrial initiative motivated by the example of Japan's success. The Japanese, however, are consistent in acknowledging that they learned much, especially about productivity and quality control, from American experts who visited their country in the 1950s. They took the knowledge and technological developments of the world's industrial leader and applied them to the needs of Japan. In other words, they took U.S. industrial know-how and improved on it at a time when people began to build "a pile of rubble into a nation with the second-largest gross national product in the free world," as a leading Japanese banker has expressed it. Some North Americans today say that "Yankee" ingenuity crossed the Pacific 35 years ago and has now come back again with quite a bit of Japanese content added.

While Japan's economy was growing, the North American "plant" and a lot of other elements of its industrial capacity were allowed to fall into obsolescence, and the results are well known — loss of markets for North American products and unemployment being among them.

There are, of course, many elements that make up the production and exporting success story of Japan. They are bound up in a system of industrial policy-setting not familiar to many Westerners. The system binds Japanese labour, management and government leaders more closely than in most developed countries.

A viewpoint that has been expressed by leaders in the labour union sector of Japanese society may sound impressively responsible to Japan's North American critics, including the president of G.M. Canada Ltd. An example of the kind of public statement by labour that also makes some North Americans and Europeans scratch their heads a bit was demonstrated not long ago by Ichiro Shioji, president of the 570,000-member Confederation of Japan Automobile Workers.

Shioji had proposed creation of a tripartite committee of labour, industry and government leaders in Japan to take steps to counter a rising protectionist mood in the U.S., Britain, West Germany and other countries where domestic auto sales have slumped. It was not the content of his proposal that made the example noteworthy so much as the words he used in association with it.

In an interview, Shioji did blame low sales and high unemployment in the U.S. auto industry on "the failure of the American auto industry in its long-term policy-making," but added, "This does not justify the prevailing attitude of Japanese auto makers to exploit this opportunity to sell more cars. I believe this attitude has to be changed."[2]

Asked if he believed Japan's auto makers should manufacture overseas even if it meant a loss of Japanese jobs, Shioji replied, "That's right. I do not go along with the idea that as long as Japan enjoys prosperity and no unemployment we should tolerate unemployment in other countries. If Japan continues to export and unemployment results in the other country, Japan is obliged to consider that unemployment as its own problem."

Today it would seem we have much to learn from Japan. In North America quality control campaigns within industry seem to have been one-shot events, as pointed out by Joji Arai, who heads the Japan Productivity Center in Washington, when he spoke at a quality seminar in Toronto early last November. Quality control (QC) must be a continuing process, but it won't work unless the chief executive officer of the company is part of it, he told the seminar jointly sponsored by the Ontario Ministry of Industry and Tourism, the Metro Toronto Board of Trade and the Japan Trade Centre. Unfortunately, few, if any, chief executive officers of manufacturing companies were present. An employee of a large Canadian manufacturing company in attendance commented after the seminar, "I am responsible for quality control at our plant, but I'm really not the one to be here; I report to the personnel manager."

There is a colloquial saying in Japan that seems to have a North American slang to it: "Don't work harder; work smarter." This philosophy pervades blue-collar workers as much as any other group, and in their circles they accept the idea that if they increase productivity and quality control "tomorrow will be better" for them and everybody in Japan. Compensation for this extra effort is not their motivation. Aria cautions that this kind of blue-collar worker philosophy cannot be transplanted easily to North America. He points to an important qualifying factor: a Japanese worker, generally speaking, is guaranteed employment in his company for life.

Arai is also frank about Japan's extra capacity to invest in new plant and equipment, which he explains, is partly because it does not pour as much money into defence as the U.S. finds it is obligated to do. The widespread introduction of exotic tools of production, such as industrial robots and numerical control equipment, further advances Japan's rate of quality output.

Other Japanese business experts elaborate further on the unique factors leading to Japan's economic success. "The key element in our economic growth is the Japanese society itself," says Kyonosuke Ibe, chairman of one of Japan's largest banks, Sumitomo.

Japan has been shaped by history and geography to be austere and adaptable. In a country where only 15 per cent of the land area is arable and a large population must be supplied, austerity developed long ago from an economic necessity into a way of life and a form of art. Our paintings and sculpture, our architecture and our gardens have been designed on the premise that 'less is more' because less is all there is.

When Japan's industrial revolution, the Meiji Restoration, took place in 1868 the austere character of the society was already well-defined within the feudal system. Change came so quickly that the feudal ties of loyalty were not eroded but were transferred . . . the newly industrialized worker gave his loyalty to the employing corporation. In return, the corporation gave the worker the assurance of lifetime employment.[3]

Ibe credits two national characteristics of Japan, namely austerity and total loyalty to the company, as having been the basis of the spectacular rise in the economy. They have provided a highly motivated, team-spirited work force that identifies with the fortunes of the company.

Ibe challenges a Western perception of the Japanese as being obedient "workaholics" by saying, "I would be happier if I could also say that we don't have any bumbling bureaucrats, mediocre managers, or inept workers, as other countries do." But a co-operative labour-management relationship there is:

Memories are still fresh from the years following 1945 when management and labour together picked up the pieces of what had been industrial Japan and a dedicated work force kept production moving every minute to earn enough income for the burden of interest payments and high depreciation costs. The work force came through and developed a tradition of participation as thinking human beings rather than as cogs in production machinery.[4]

Can Canada learn much from Japan to achieve our own economic successes? Yes, but the foregoing indicates that not all elements of Japan's accomplishments are transplantable to Western industrial societies and few can be adopted easily.

One example of a fairly successful transplant is found in Wales, where a Sony television manufacturing plant has an impressive production line and a quality control system functioning along Japanese lines. The general manager, Tetsuo Tokita, who earlier worked on the development of the famous Trinitron television picture tube, is responsible for transforming in seven years an empty piece of property in economically depressed South Wales into a $250 million business employing 900 people. For this Tokita was made an honourary Officer of the British Empire, the first Japanese to ever have been so decorated.

Certain deep-rooted Western perceptions of the Japanese take a long time to fade, however. The uninformed hold onto the notion of a low-paid, subservient work force in that country which competes with our industries. It doesn't take much study, however, to learn that the opposite is true. The well-trained, thoughtful, well-educated management-worker teams of Japanese industry today are moving rapidly into an era of industrial automation. They have a view of technology that has two positive premises: that automation makes their industries more competitive, and that humans should not be expected to be cogs. "Work smarter, not harder" is the operative phrase, and there is agreement that the new products of research and development, such as robots, can assume more of the "cog" role.

While Canada lacks a robot industry as such, several firms have developed robot components and related remote-control equipment. Diffracto Ltd., in Windsor, Ontario, is producing a vision system that enables automotive robots to spot the difference between various car models, thus enabling the robots to select which programmed routine to perform. Jarvis Clark Co., a North Bay mining equipment manufacturer, worked with Falconbridge Mines to develop the Farco Scoop, a remote-control ore-loading machine. The new Windsor transmission plant of GM of Canada Ltd. is to install 22 miles of new assembly lines that will use many elements of automation, including major transfer equipment manned by robots.

Productivity, quality control and new automation technology are key elements needed to aid economic recovery of sick industries, but they certainly do not create instant cures for unemployment and accompanying social ills; in the interim, they may actually make them worse.

Look across the other ocean to the United Kingdom's gigantic British Steel Corporation. It is undergoing massive surgery, in the hope that it can be made efficient and productive again. British Steel's new chairman and "surgeon," Ian MacGregor, makes wistful references from time to time about a Japanese steel mill where "you could fire a gun through the middle of their steelworks and the chances of hitting anyone would be virtually nil; but they still produce a lot of steel."[5] The implication is clear but, unfortunately, MacGregor says, the work force of British Steel must be cut by 22,000 in the next year in order to first reduce its inefficient productive capacity, introduce efficiency and start trying to regain lost markets.

The socio-economic dilemma exemplified by the British Steel situation could be part of an answer to the broad, general question, "Why can't we do what Japan does?" The truth is we simply cannot do, in short-term programs, what Japan has done during the long evolutionary recovery from its "pile of rubble" condition of 1945. We also cannot make Western society Japanese. Nonetheless, we can look to the Japan example as a guide to the resetting of some standards for our own future achievements.

Notes

1. "GM president is critical of Japan trade policies," *The Globe and Mail*, December 5, 1980.

2. "Automobile union head suggests Japan curb vehicle exports," *St. Catherines Standard*, September 15, 1980.

3. "It took the Japanese to build Japan," *Business Week*, October 6, 1980, p. 17.

4. Ibid.

5. "MacGregor takes the scalpel to British Steel," *World Business Weekly*, January 12, 1981, p. 10.

46/Building the Japanese Car[*]

Martin Glaberman

The view of Japanese auto workers as mindless robots who love nothing better than to work long hours for low wages has been repeated so often it has become dogma. It has also become very useful in the attempt to pressure U.S. and Canadian auto workers into paying for the problems and mistakes of management. It did not come as too great a surprise, after two weeks of discussion and observation in Japan last year, to learn that the dogma was false.

What emerged, after visits to Japanese auto workers, and talks with Japanese

---

* Reprinted, with permission of the publisher and the author from Martin Glaberman, "Building the Japanese Car," *Canadian Dimension* 17(1) 1983, pp. 17-19.

academics doing research on labor relations in the auto industry, was a complex pattern of social controls which limit the ability of workers to resist management pressures on the shop floor. These controls appear in three basic areas: the structure of the wages, the organization of work and supervision, and the union.

Unequal Pay

Japan is no longer a low wage country. Japanese auto workers make wages comparable to the wages of North American industrial workers (although lower in the case of auto workers). The wage structure, however, does make a difference. Here, the fundamental principle of auto union contracts is equal pay for equal work. Everyone working the same job gets the same pay for equal work. Everyone working the same job gets the same pay whether they have been with the company one year or thirty years. This tends to encourage workers' solidarity, since no one can get a raise unless everyone gets a raise. In Japan there is a rather small basic wage and, then, a whole series of allowances — family allowances, longevity allowances, job allowances (for more dangerous or uncomfortable work), commuting allowances, and most important of all, merit allowances.

There are two important consequences of this structure. First, there is a rapidly rising wage curve based on longevity which tends to tie workers to their employer and reduce labor turnover. A worker who changes employers after a few years must start again near the bottom and pays a considerable penalty. He must pay an additional penalty: Japanese employers make a point of encouraging loyalty to the firm and look askance at any employee, at no matter what level, who wants to change employers.

The second consequence is even more significant. The merit factor is based on regular evaluations of each employee by group leaders and junior foremen. It is generally acknowledged that "merit" has little to do with these evaluations. On production jobs which can be learned in hours or, at most, days, and on which everyone makes production quotas, merit has no significance. What does have significance is loyalty and discipline. So that lateness, uncooperativeness, unwillingness to attend meetings on unpaid time, not to mention more overt forms of shop floor resistance, can readily show up in your paycheck in ways that can reduce your income for years. Canadian employers can punish lateness or absenteeism and workers can resist that through the grievance procedure. But there is no long term penalty that affects your income.

Housing Subsidies

In addition to the wage there is a fringe benefit which is important both economically and socially. Japanese auto firms, unless they are very small, provide company housing and housing subsidies. For the larger firms there are huge blocks of dormitories for single workers and flats for married workers. The living quarters are small, but no smaller than would be generally available in Japan at this income level. In a country in which housing is extremely tight and expensive, subsidized housing is a real financial benefit. There is generally a 10 year limit on how long workers can live in company flats. But after that companies, such as Toyota, provide mortgages for their employees to buy their own homes at interest rates that are below the level of the market.

One obvious result of this is that it contributes to tying the worker to his employer. But in addition, it provides employers with an additional level of social control. These huge blocks of company housing resemble company towns and provide management with many eyes and ears through which they can learn of dissident behavior. I visited some workers' apartments in Toyota City (the name itself is indicative) and took photos of the interiors. I noticed that one worker who had a framed family portrait sitting on a cabinet stopped me until he could turn the photo around so that he could not be identified.

The wage structure ties in with the structure of work. The use of the small group of from six to ten workers including a group leader is common throughout Japanese industry. There is a foreman for each two or three groups. The group leader works alongside the other workers and is, technically, not management. However, he has the authority to evaluate the workers as the first step in that process. That gives him management authority which is not available to a foreman in a Canadian auto plant.

In addition, junior foreman can work. Here, auto contracts foremen are not permitted to work. The adversary relationship, which is quite visible on the shop floor in a Canadian plant, may exist in Japan. But it is made invisible by foremen and group leaders working alongside the other workers. And, of course, management is provided with contacts and sources of information (and control) on the shop floor. The cumulative effect of work organization and wage structure tends to inhibit the kind of shop floor resistance for which Canadian (and American) auto workers are noted — absenteeism, wildcat strikes, sabotage, etc. There is no indication, however, that the causes for resistance are not present.

Company Unions

The usual place that resistance to management will first be made evident is through the union. In Japan this is virtually impossible. The auto unions, by an acceptable definition are company unions. At Toyota the union is so weak that it has no significant impact in the shop, although it formally negotiates wages and the like. At Nissan (makers of Datsun cars) there was once a militant union. The company broke the union after a 100 day strike in 1953 by splitting the union. A company union was created which has bargaining rights with the company. Lower management and even higher management can belong to the union.

A Tokyo University professor showed a pattern of employment of graduates of Tokyo University by Nissan. The new employee spends several years working in management. He then spends two or three years as a union official. He then moves up in the Industrial Relations Department of the firm. Apparently union office is a necessary step for promotion in management. These Tokyo U. graduates form a kind of old boy network. Until 1975 the annual wage negotiations required exactly two meetings between union and management negotiators. At the first meeting the union presented its demands. At the second meeting the company accepted 100% of these demands. Obviously the real negotiations took place over glasses of sake and beer at which time the union negotiators learned from their colleagues on the management side what the management was willing to accept. After 1975 this became a bit too crude to continue.

One Slate

The union elections at Nissan permit only one slate. A worker cannot run for union office without permission from the union leadership. In spite of having no opposition candidates, the workers are not permitted to abstain. Voter turnouts vary from 99.5% to 99.9%. Winning candidates get from 99.7 to 100% of the vote. Professor K. Yamamoto of Tokyo University notes that "if the voter turnout is low or if votes critical of union leadership are cast, the shop steward in charge of the district is forced to submit a written apology called a 'summary statement of resolution' to the union, and is criticized for neglect of duty." He also reported that the requirement of a secret ballot in the union constitution is regularly violated.

There have been cases of workers being fired. Although this is rare, it does happen. I talked to workers who were fired from Toyota and from Mitsubishi. The union, naturally, was of no help. They turned to the labor commissions and to the courts and won their cases against management. The courts ruled that management was in violation of Japanese labour laws. (The cases were appealed and are still continuing.) What was fascinating was that the companies returned these fired workers to the payroll but refused to let them back into the plants.

Loyalty Built on Fear

We hear, often enough, of the natural loyalty of Japanese workers to their employers. The behaviour of management and unions in the auto industry would seem to cast doubt on that loyalty. Instead one sees a fear that borders on paranoia of any kind of dissident voice on the shop floor. Toyota workers told me of workers being roughed up in the plant for being dissidents. Others told me of the difficulty of distributing leaflets and shop papers outside the plant or at train stations near the plants because management people would surround and impede the distributors. In most cases, opposition groups in the union will get the assistance of others who do not work for the same company to help with such distributions. Disagreeing with union or management publicly is like [homosexuals] coming out of the closet. Several workers told me of the isolation they felt after they took a public stand. But they also said that other workers would express their support when they were not being observed. This does not mean that shop floor resistance does not take place. One Nissan worker who was told by his foreman that he was to be transferred to another plant got into a major argument which stopped all work by his group for 15 minutes. The foreman finally apologized to him and agreed that the transfer was arranged improperly — although the transfer had to stand.

The apparent lack of confidence in their workers' loyalty of Japanese auto management seems justified by an overall view of Japanese labor. About one-third of Japanese workers are unionized. There are three union federations. The largest, Sohyo, has 4.5 million members and is the most militant. Most of the unions in Sohyo are in the public sector — railroad workers, municipal workers, teachers, etc.

The second largest is Domei with over 2 million members, mostly in private industry such as steel, auto, ship-building, etc. It is extremely conservative and nationalistic. The third federation is Sorengo with about 1.5 million members. The Japan Auto Workers Union belongs to Domei. Its head, Shioji, regularly supports Asian dictatorships, as in South Korea and the Philippines. The auto union is a loose federation of company based unions.

At the very least, this does not indicate that there is any traditional docility on the part of Japanese workers. If auto workers in Japan are less militant than auto workers in Canada it is largely because of circumstances which they cannot easily overcome.

I asked Japanese auto workers what they thought of the problems of the North American auto industry. It is featured regularly in the Japanese press. The workers' attitude, however, was that they would face the same situation within the next five or ten years. Given the cyclical nature of the Japanese economy since World War II, their prediction seems justified. Sooner or later (and sooner, more likely than later) the lack of confidence of the Japanese auto corporations in their workers' loyalty will be tested. It will be interesting to see how the coming contest will work out.

In the early fifties the United States adopted a policy of reindustrializing Japan as a barrier to Chinese Communist expansion. The same policy was applied to West Germany in Europe. An American Productivity Institute was established with American funds to make the Japanese more efficient. In addition, there were two American supplied spurts of expansion for Japanese industry. The Korean and Vietnamese wars, for which Japan was major supplier of war materials, helped lay the basis for the current auto boom. The end to each war led to a major economic slump in Japan.

Japanese efficiency and relative labour peace do not come naturally out of Japanese culture, although certain elements from Japan's past are used as forms of social control in the present. It is not likely, therefore, that the militancy which has already appeared in the Japanese working class can be sealed off indefinitely from the auto industry. The Japanese auto corporations will have considerably less flexibility in dealing with that militancy when it appears.

47/Workers' Industry*

Tom Webb

One reason that co-operatives are attractive is that they provide a form in which groups of people share their individual talents and pool them. They pool their ideas as free individuals. For three weeks recently, a group of Canadians saluted the memory of Alex Laidlaw and his generous contribution to the co-operative movement in Canada and the world by travelling to Europe to learn what they could from those involved in the worker co-operative movement in England, France and Spain. The group was made up of people who had some connection with the co-operative housing movement in Canada and had been brought together by Glenn Haddrell from the Co-operative Housing Foundation of Canada. . . .

For the uninitiated, worker co-operatives are businesses which are owned by the workers. Each worker is a member and has one vote. The workers elect the Board of Directors and control the management of the company. There are variations, but that is the basic form of organization. What the group of Canadians went to see in Europe was worker co-operatives on the ground and functioning. They found a wide variety. Some were strong and some were weak, some were new and some were very old. Some were "greenfield" co-operatives, started where no workplace had existed before. Others were "rescue" co-operatives, the result of workers taking over a failing company from the private sector.

The group found that where co-operatives were supported by a strong institutional framework, in some cases with government support, they thrived and were healthy. Indeed, they were healthiest under an institutional umbrella provided by the co-operative movement itself. The best example of such a network was the Mondragon worker co-operative network in Spain. The following facts attest to its health, strength and size:

1. There are over 22,000 worker-owners involved in the Mondragon co-operative system.

2. The foundation of the network rests on some 100 industrial co-operatives pro-

* Abridged from Tom Webb, "Workers' Industry," *Policy Options* 4, 3, The Institute for Research on Public Policy, 1983, pp. 48-52. Reprinted with permission of the publisher and the author.

ducing a wide range of heavy industrial products, consumer durables and high-technology products.

3. The co-ops range in size from 50 to 3,500, but most are in the 100-700 range.

4. This worker co-operative network owns its own bank (the Caja Laboral Popular), its own research and development institute (Ikerlan), and its own social security co-operative (Lagun Aro).

5. The network operates a substantial school system, including 31 primary and secondary schools as well as 6 post-secondary institutions, including a polytechnical institute which gives degrees in engineering.

6. The system includes agricultural co-operatives, housing co-operatives, and consumer co-operatives.

7. In the network of over 100 industrial firms which has grown since 1956, there have been no business failures.

8. The network includes Spain's largest manufacturer of household appliances and largest machine tool manufacturer.

9. The social security co-op, Lagun Aro, provides a full range of benefits at levels of compensation higher than those of the state.

10. The research and development institute employs over 65 engineers and scientists.

Looked at in any way, the Mondragon co-operative system provides an impressive list of accomplishments. When we look at the problems which bedevil our economy, they seem to be handling them in a more productive, more competent fashion. That the Mondragon system is not perfect was underlined in response to our questions about environmental pollution. The head of the social security co-operative, a doctor, who had answered excitedly and enthusiastically all of our other questions concerning social security and occupational health, expressed his disappointment and chagrin that the system has not done more to reduce and curtail environmental degradation. An absence of government concern has led to little or no environmental regulation for either the private or co-operative sector. He did indicate, however, that this was one of their priorities for the future and this at a time when many industries in the West are seeking ways to avoid their responsibilities for the environment and passing short-run costs on to government for long-term payment.

It is time for Canadians to think seriously about co-operatives. The problems which face the Canadian economy are not short-term. . . . The mistrust which exists in Canada exists because some people eat caviar and others eat macaroni. Some wear mink while others struggle to buy any clothes for their children. It exists because our economy is based upon the assumption that in the final analysis, only greed will make the economy function. It exists because management is pitted against labour. Distrust exists because fewer and fewer people control the

Canadian economy.

A growing number of Canadians feel that they have little or no control over their economic lives. They feel that they are pawns having little real role in their own country. They live in other people's houses, work in other people's industries and buy in other people's stores. They feel, and they know, that economic decisions are taken by fewer and fewer people and that those decisions affect their lives. We do need to begin to foster trust but the question is how. Unfortunately, the answer won't just come from beating inflation; there are other serious problems which face us. These problems are long-term and rooted in the very nature of our economy. They can be grouped under several broad headings:

Labour Relations

We have an inherently adversarial system which pits management against labour in almost every major workplace across the nation. I remember a number of years ago, the characterization given to labour-management relationships in the coal mines of Cape Breton prior to the creation of the Cape Breton Development Corporation. I was told that "management had but one goal, and that was to make as much profit as possible by removing as much coal from the ground and paying the workers as little as possible. If arms and legs and lives were lost in the process, that was an act of God." "On the other hand," I was told, "the view of the miners was to take as little coal as possible out of the ground for as much salary as they could squeeze out of the agreements and if you could steal two shovels, that was considered a reasonable part of the collective agreement."

That description may not do complete justice to either side, but it does characterize, in general terms, the basic attitudes that labour and management have towards each other. Certainly, if they don't see themselves the way they were described, each often tends to see the other in those terms. Much of the energy of both labour and management is spent fighting each other rather than producing the goods and services necessary to our lives.

Productivity

In private or even public-sector enterprises, the workers have little or no stake in the enterprise. It's not their company so why should they care about it? After all, if they're really productive, all it will do is line the pockets of management and shareholders. Many Canadian firms have lacked the proper levels of investment and re-investment. Little research and development have been done by companies in Canada and many Canadian plants are hopelessly out of date. Productivity, often only talked about in terms of output per manhour, is not only a question of how hard the workforce works. It is also a result of labour management relations and the quality of investment and management. When investors refuse to invest, they go on strike because they feel they are not getting a fair return on their investment. When investors go on strike, productivity suffers. Finally, in the area of productivity, management often sees new equipment and increases in productivity as an opportunity to shrink the labour force and eliminate as many as possible of those perverse, unpredictable elements of the production line called human beings. Why should we be surprised if the workers react negatively to that kind of thinking?

Stability

The poor regions have long noted the instability of Canadian industry. It is now being noticed in Ontario and even in Western Canada. Multi-national corporations, be they Canadian or foreign, have little or no commitment to the communities in which they exist. Decisions to close plants can be made even though a plant is relatively profitable. It can be made because the plant no longer fits the corporate plan decided upon, some thousand miles away. It can be made because the plant is the least well-known to management. It can be made because the profit margins are a per cent or two below what the remote corporate managers feel they should be. This has contributed to industrial instability in the poorer areas of Canada and increasingly in the richer areas also. This instability has long been a major source of need for government spending.

Social Costs

Those involved in public policy over the last twenty years must indeed feel extremely frustrated to hear the captains of industry say, "It's time to cut back on government spending." So much of government spending has resulted from social costs, very efficiently handed on by the private sector to government. Alcan walked away from St. Lawrence, Newfoundland and Reed Paper from Northern Ontario to name just two of many cases. They left behind environmental, health and social costs of staggering proportions. In Northern Ontario, whole native communities have been devastated. Many other communities, large and small, could be mentioned.

Those are obvious social costs. The construction industry walks away from the unemployment insurance and welfare collected by labourers during seasonal and cyclical layoffs. Many occupational health problems are years in developing, yet they cost billions of dollars in health bills to governments and tax-payers every year. When an industry decides to shut down, the cost to government is often greater in social terms than the cost of keeping the industry open. The cost of labour mobility, in terms of its impact on neighbourhoods, communities and families, has been very expensive for governments at all levels. We have organized our workplaces with little thought or regard to the social impact and the social cost. Social costs are often hidden and delayed. That is why, in the ubiquitous cost-benefit analysis, they seldom play much of a role. They are externalities. That they are difficult to count makes them no less real and, for governments, no less expensive. What percentage of our present deficit has obscure and not so obscure roots in passed-on industrial social costs?

Alienation

A politician who had just been asked by three different groups for funds under a federal program so that they could build outdoor rinks in their communities once wondered out loud to me what was happening to his people. "Fifty years ago," he mused, "they would have come and asked me to open the rinks they themselves had built. Today they can't build them without some help from Ottawa." A few years later, at a development conference in Cape Breton, I heard an economist describe the Cape Breton economy of fifty years ago and the Cape Breton economy of 1975. "Fifty years ago," he said, "we produced 95% of our own shelter, 90% of our own food and 60% of our own clothing." "Today," he noted, "we produce less than 2% of our own clothing, less than 5% of our own food, and about 30% of our own shelter, but most of that is the labour involved in putting together the materials that come from somewhere else."

This type of analysis could be applied elsewhere with similar results. It struck me that the economic thumb-nail sketch answered the politician's musings. His people were more dependent because they had become pawns in a dependent economy. Decisions as to what they ate, what they wore, whether they had work, the kind of houses they lived in, and the quality of these houses depended upon decisions taken thousands of miles away. Was it any wonder that they would look thousands of miles for the money for an outdoor rink?

Political and Economic Democracy

Whether we like it or not, our political democracy is linked inextricably with the state of our economic democracy and there are many signs that both are in trouble. A survey done in the fall of 1981 by a group at York University showed that Canadians had less and less faith in the governments that are supposed to serve them. People believe more and more that politicians do not care what they think. People feel government to be remote and uncaring, bureaucratic and clogged with red tape.

Studies also show that people feel the same way about large corporations. As Canada moves farther and farther from being a nation of shop-keepers and small businesses to being a nation of multi-national department stores and multi-national industrial workplaces, Canadians seem to have less and less faith that anyone cares what they think. They have less and less feeling that their contribution is important.

At our current point in history it is not much consolation to know we have arrived at this sorry state of affairs in the company of other Western countries. A look around the world will give one serious doubts about liberal capitalism and state capitalism. The problems outlined above, and the list is by no means exhaustive, exist not only in the so-called "free world," but in the countries under Soviet domination as well. Most of these problems are equally evident in state-run industry, or in industry run by a private sector. Hope, if we are to find it, lies in another alternative, in abandoning rigid ideology. . . .

In terms of ideology, co-operatives are strange birds indeed. There are those on the right who consider them to be left-wing and those on the left who consider them to be right-wing. There are also many in the left, right, and middle, who think they're an interesting alternative; that they offer hope for a more stable, more just, more productive, more democratic economy.

While an exhaustive analysis is beyond the scope of the article we can look at what happens if we take the list of problems referred to above and compare the experience in the Mondragon co-operative system to see how it has fared in meeting these problems faced by industry in both the capitalist and communist countries.

Labour Relations

The Mondragon co-operative system has had one strike since 1956. The flavour of that lonely work stoppage was captured by Thomas and Logan in their book, *The Mondragon System*:

Rather than use the normal channels for the discussion of their problems, the dissidents then called for a strike, which lasted eight days and involved 414 co-operators. Ulgor's supervisory board exercised its authority, ordering the dismissal of 17 workers and disciplinary measures against 397 others who had been involved in the dispute and the subsequent action. This decision was challenged at an extraordinary general assembly held in an acrimonious atmosphere replete with mutual accusations. But the board's decision was endorsed by a majority vote of 60%. . . .

But that was not the only response of the co-op network. It raised questions about whether Ulgor had become too big and steps were taken to deal with the size of co-ops. There were also institutional innovations started to ensure all co-ops were more responsive to their worker-owners and that traditional worker-management concerns would be dealt with more effectively by the co-operatives. With over 20,000 workers and more than 100 workplaces, there have been no further strikes and the relationship between the co-operatives and the Spanish union movement is one of close co-operation.

Productivity

Each of the workers in the Mondragon system has a capital stake in the enterprise. It is his or her enterprise. Each has a say in how it's run and if it does well, his or her capital stake increases. Needless to say, co-operators are anxious to keep the productivity of their industry high, not only in terms of their own productivity on the job, but in terms of the productivity of capital as well. In Spain, we toured Matrici, which manufactures dies or molds to make parts for the car industry in Europe. At present, the dies are made much in the way we make a key; they use a plastic mold and a machine follows the plastic mold while cutting an identical shape in a steel slab. The factory is changing to a technology which will use laser photography to develop a mathematical model of a car part. The mathematical model will be fed into computer-guided machinery.

There was a great deal of enthusiasm about the modernization in the plant. As one worker expressed it, "When the new machine comes in, it will need only three to look after it instead of eight and it will produce 20% more." He was delighted. Perhaps it was because the workers set the ground rules for modernization. No one in the plant will lose their jobs as a result and most of the modernization team was taken off the plant floor and trained. The co-operators at Matrici had nothing to lose and everything to gain by being as modern and as productive as possible. At Matrici, the workers are not just a factor of production but the reason for production.

Stability

The Mondragon co-operative system has a solid record of growth and stability. Not one of the more than 100 co-operatives, which have been started by the system, has failed. The only case of defeat which they have had was a joint government-co-op endeavor in the fishery. This was the only co-op that was allowed to vary basically from the tried and true formula for success that the movement has developed. Without exception, the industrial and commercial co-operatives affiliated to the Mondragon system have prospered. As a measure of this, the worst month of unemployment from the current recession has seen 153 persons in receipt of unemployment insurance from the social security co-op. With a workforce of over 20,000 and in Spain, surrounded by 19-20% unemployment levels, that is stability.

How has the recession in Spain, with unemployment levels pushing near to 20%, affected the co-operative network? Instead of expanding at a rate of four new enterprises per year, the movement has had to cut back to two new enterprises. They have also responded to requests from unions in failing private sector companies to convert them into co-operatives. These new rescue co-operatives are part of the record of success. A similar co-operative development network might have rescued such Canadian companies as Enterprise Foundries in Sackville, New Brunswick.

Social Costs

Because the Spanish government under Franco regarded co-operators as being self-employed, it would not pay social security benefits. The co-operatives responded by setting up their own social security system. It includes pensions, workmen's compensation, medicare, unemployment insurance, maternity leave, family allowances, and other forms of insurance. These benefits are paid at a rate higher than that of state benefits. In addition, the social security system provides preventive and occupational health care. To this end, a complex and effective system of incentives has been created for the co-operatives to create as healthy as possible a workplace. Standards for hazardous substances were based on the toughest

American standards of several years ago; since then, they have been made twice as stringent.

The approach to social security problems is typical of the Mondragon system. Their occupational health program is representative of the approach. The social security co-operative, Lagun Aro, did not impose standards. They set the standards and then told the co-operatives that if they did not wish to meet those standards, they would have to pay their workers more for working in substandard workplaces. They also asked for higher medical premiums for their medicare system because co-operatives with substandard workplaces would generate higher health costs. In addition, they set up a low-interest loan account in co-operation with the co-operative bank, the Caja Laboral Popular, which co-operatives could use to improve their workplaces. Finally, they established a system to collect health information and to do occupational health audits. The audits must be done when a group of co-operators ask and all health information is available to all members through the social committee of each co-operative's Board of Directors.

The program is highly effective and has generated a high level of interest and action on occupational health problems within the network and beyond it. This kind of multi-faceted incentive approach is in contrast to the kind of coercive single-solution method which governments often have to use and it was developed by a co-operative enterprise which is owned and controlled by the whole co-operative network. The unemployment insurance scheme is similarly complex and effective, in so far as it is needed.

Alienation

The strike referred to above at Ulgor, Spain's leading manufacturer of household appliances, has led to a policy of decentralization within the Mondragon co-operative system. Ulgor, with its 3,200 workers, was considered too large. Yet the co-operative system did not want to lose the advantages of scale. The result has been groupings of co-operatives, federated with each other, where the size of individual plants has been restricted but economies of scale maintained through the co-ordination of their efforts.

The reseach arm of the network purposefully seeks technological innovation which combines high productivity and small size. This commitment to smaller size, combined with organizational innovations, has ensured that workers really do have a voice in the running of their companies. Alienation is minimized because decisions are made at the closest level to the people affected.

During our visit to Mondragon, we were able to talk to workers on a number of occasions because a few in our group spoke Spanish and some of the workers spoke French. We also spoke to the people outside of the co-operative movement. Workers were positive beyond the perfunctory necessity and those who worked outside the network were very interested in getting into it. Even managers were enthusiastic about the system: "I would accept lower pay to work here," said one, "because it is so free of tension and no one climbs over others. It is a good climate in which to be creative, but of course, if you need to yell at people, it's not for you."

Economic Democracy

The Mondragon system is a good example of political and economic democracy. Within each co-operative, an annual general assembly elects a supervisory board. The supervisory board acts in much the same way as the board of directors of a private sector Canadian corporation. It chooses management and closely follows the progress of the co-operative. The general assembly also elects a social council which makes binding decisions in such matters as accident prevention, work safety, work hygiene, social security, wage levels and the administration of social funds. The ultimate safeguard for the system is the watchdog council, also elected directly by the general assembly. Its purpose is to oversee the management, the supervisory board, the social council and the management council to ensure that they all work in an effective manner together. The result is a complex system of democratic control, which ensures that the workers have a say, not only in the day-to-day running of their plant, but in its long-term direction as well.

The European tour revealed a very clear message for the development of healthy worker co-operatives. The stronger and more integrated the development support system, the better the success rate of the individual co-operatives. In the United Kingdom, support systems are just now starting to emerge. They are fragmented and uneven in quality and none of them pull together all of the necessary inputs to ensure success in business development. Individual co-operative development agencies are each busy re-inventing the wheel. Each is small and lacking in expertise and financial muscle. The co-operatives themselves often display weak management. Most have little or no working capital and few have access to necessary fields of expertise. Technological problems abound. There are not yet enough strong workers' co-operatives to support strong development institutions. . . .

In France, the co-operative movement, with the participation of a good number of strong, large worker co-ops, has set up a development agency which has some promise. The Society of Co-operatives (SCOP), with its headquarters in Paris and regional offices across the country, is able to provide advice and support to the co-operatives which is of a reasonably good quality and quite sophisticated. Regional offices are, however, not yet well developed and support services, while improving, are still far from fully developed. The base of strong working co-ops and an encouraging success rate in developing new "rescue" co-ops will provide an increasingly strong base from which to grow. It will also provide experience and resources from which SCOP can draw.

It is, however, the integrated, sophisticated and geographically concentrated Mondragon system which provides the best example of what can be done. The key elements of development include expertise in management, planning, marketing, finance, law and the organizing of co-operatives; access to technology; training capability; and venture capital.

While the English development associations have few of these elements, and SCOP in France has a moderate capacity to deliver, the Mondragon system has every element in abundance and has integrated them into a complex and sophisticated delivery system. Thus, an integrated network, the bank, social security co-op, research institute and post-secondary educational institutions, all owned and controlled by the worker co-operatives, combine the necessary development inputs with an aggressive development philosophy. It works.

In Canada, we have strong co-operative business organizations. For the most part, they are consumer and producer owned. They include credit unions and caisse populaires, garages and department stores, food processing plants and even an oil company. What is lacking is a set of development-oriented support institutions designed to foster new enterprises which are worker-owned.

In the British tradition, following the dictums of Beatrice and Sydney Webb, we have shied away from industrial worker-owned co-operatives because they would not work in theory. What the Mondragon system proves beyond doubt is that they work in practice and that they provide obvious economic benefits. What we need to learn is how to develop them. How can our strong co-op institutions create development-oriented institutions which perform the functions of the Mondragon network?

Canadian co-operatives, in part because of their primarily consumer-producer orientation, do not provide in the same way for industrial expansion, growth and development as does the private sector. Consumer co-operators are not, by nature, oriented toward industrial production. Producer co-operatives, owned by farmers and fishermen, historically have not included plant workers as members, but rather have hired them as employees. Consumer co-ops have followed the employee model also. While there is a great deal of interest in Canadian co-operative circles in the potential of worker co-operatives, no major impetus is yet underway to create strong agencies for developing them.

Government can help create such development agencies. At all levels, it has to ensure that the climate exists for co-operative institutions to provide the same kind of support system in Canada as exists in Spain. It won't be the same system. We can learn from the Spanish model but we cannot re-create it. We must build our own. The government of Canada needs to begin seriously to re-think its relationship with the co-operative sector and to encourage it to develop worker co-operatives in a stable and yet aggressive way in this country.

Worker co-operatives will not be a panacea. They will not instantly solve the problems discussed above, nor will they instantly solve the problems of unemployment. Nevertheless, they could provide our children with a healthier economy. An economy based more on co-operation and less on greed.

134

DATE DUE
DATE DE RETOUR

NOV 2 6 1991			
DEC 1 0 1993			
DEC 1 0 1993			
DEC 1 1 1995			
NOV 2 3 1996			
NOV 2 3 1997			
DEC 1 4 1997			
DEC 0 1 1997			
NOV 0 6 1998			
NOV 0 9 1998			
DEC 1 7 1998			
NOV 2 6 1998			
MAR 1 8 1999			
MAR 0 6 1999			